Mastering Flow

Mastering Flow

*Perform Better, Experience More Joy,
and Live a Happier Life*

Nils Salzgeber

First paperback published 2024.

FIRST EDITION.

ISBNs:
978-3-9525069-4-3 - Ebook
978-3-9525069-5-0 - Paperback
978-3-9525069-7-4 - Hardcover
978-3-9525069-6-7 - Audiobook

www.njlifehacks.com

Contents

. . . They concentrate their attention on a limited stimulus field, forget personal problems, lose their sense of time and of themselves, feel competent and in control, and have a sense of harmony and union with their surroundings. . . . They cease to worry about whether the activity will be productive or whether it will be rewarded. . . . They have entered a state of flow.[1]

—MIHALY CSIKSZENTMIHALYI

Introduction

Have you ever been so immersed in an activity that you completely forgot about everything else? Perhaps you lost track of time and failed to notice that you were hungry, thirsty, or in need of a bathroom break? Did it feel easy and effortless? Did you feel strong, confident, and in total control? Did you "wake up" from the experience feeling excited, energized, refreshed, capable, and on a high?

This type of experience goes by many names. Psychologists sometimes call it "optimal experience." Athletes may speak of "being in the zone," musicians of "being in the groove," runners of "runner's high," and writers of "writer's high." We will call it "flow." It's what this book is all about.

My first in-depth encounter with flow was when I read Steven Kotler's *The Rise of Superman*. The book depicts some of the world's best action and adventure sports athletes and how they use flow to "push human performance farther and faster than at any other point in the 150,000-year history of our species."[1]

I was hooked instantly. I thought to myself: *WOW. Flow is incredible. I want that for myself. No, I need that for myself. How can I make it happen?*

This initial spark led me down a four-year journey of researching and writing about flow. The result? The book you're holding in your hands.

What is Flow, and Why Does it Matter?

Flow is the experience of total involvement in an activity. You're so absorbed in what you're doing that everything else falls away. You're so laser-focused on the task at hand there is no attention left for daydreaming, worrying, second-guessing, or doubting yourself. You forget your troubles and stop worrying about what other people think of you. In flow, you're relieved from the nagging inner voice that is so prevalent in everyday life. You are temporarily freed from the "burden of selfhood."[2]

When people describe their flow experiences, they report feeling strong, capable, optimistic, and in control. They report being switched on and tuned in. In flow, there's a letting go of conscious control. You get out of your own way and allow your unconscious to take over.[3] You're not *making* things happen; you're *letting* them happen.[4] In flow, everything feels smooth, fluent, easy, light, effortless, and spontaneous. Everything seems to be moving of its own accord, seamlessly, automatically, without friction. It feels like you're floating or being carried by a current or gentle wind. Everything just flows—hence, the term flow.

Flow experiences are deeply enjoyable and are described by many as the best moments in their lives. These experiences are so rewarding that we want to repeat whichever activity provided it.

A couple of years ago, I went sledding with my father and my three brothers. I still remember where we parked the car, purchased the tickets, what the ski lift looked like, the photo we took afterward, and many other details from the event. Most vividly, however, I remember the feeling I had after one of our descents—I felt fully alive, strong, excited, energized, euphoric, and on a high. It felt like my system had just been flooded with a bunch of feel-good hormones. I recall thinking to myself, *whoah, that felt gooood! That was fun! Let's do it again.*

But flow is more than a feel-good experience. What makes it special is that it's highly enjoyable and beneficial at the same time. Flow feels fantastic *and* allows you to perform at your best *and* helps you build an overall better quality of life.

Whatever you do in flow, you're doing it to the best of your ability. If you think about the best performances of your life, you'll find that you've been in flow. If you think about the worst performances of your life, you'll find that flow was absent—you probably thought too much, doubted yourself, felt overly anxious, or got distracted somehow. You got in your own way. The "dreaded choke" is an anti-flow experience par excellence.

By allowing you to be at your best, flow helps you build skills, accomplish goals, and grow your character. You become more capable and confident. You grow to like yourself better. Decades of research have shown that flow holds the key to performance, skill development, health, success, and happiness.

Let me put it bluntly: Creating your best life depends on your ability to experience flow. You can't be at your best, and you can't become your best, without flow. It's not a nice-to-have; it's a necessity. The better you become at accessing flow, the better equipped you are to create the life you desire.

The good news is, regardless of your current ability to experience flow, you can learn to experience it more often. You can become more *flow-prone*—you can improve your ability to move in and out of flow. That's what *Mastering Flow* is all about. My goal with this book is twofold: teach you about flow and help you experience it more often.

What You'll Learn in This Book

This book is organized into three parts. Part 1 is all about what flow is and what we know about it. Think of it like a Tour de Flow. I'll share the foundational as well as the most intriguing and helpful findings from over 50 years of research on flow. The Tour begins with a broad overview that puts flow in context. Next up are the origin story of flow, its definition, and a brief discussion of the different types of flow. You'll then learn about the circumstances under which flow occurs and the components that come together to create the holistic sensation of being in flow.

Other highlights of the Tour include: the personality traits that support or hinder your ability to experience flow; the various methods researchers have used to uncover the many findings I share in this book; the activities and contexts in which flow is experienced most frequently; and finally, the fascinating world of your brain and body in flow.

Part 2 covers the benefits and dangers of flow. I've stated that flow holds the key to happiness and success and that creating your best life depends on your ability to experience flow. In chapters 10 and 11, I'll back up these claims. I'll provide examples of athletes, musicians, writers, entrepreneurs, and businesses that credit flow with their gold medals, world records, bestsellers, scientific breakthroughs, and other achievements. I'll also share the scientific studies that have vigorously tested the many anecdotal benefits of flow. Finally, in chapter 12, I'll discuss the dangers and downsides of flow. Flow is powerful; that much is certain. But flow isn't good or bad in an absolute sense. It can build or destroy. It can make you or break you. While flow is always fun, its consequences can be everything but.

Part 3 is all about making it happen. Think of it as your toolkit. You'll discover a smorgasbord of tips and strategies for experiencing more flow. You'll learn about activities, jobs, environments, skills, mindsets, routines, and habits that facilitate flow. You'll learn how to structure your life, tweak your surroundings, and manage your thoughts and emotions to make flow more likely. Most importantly, you'll learn how to become more flow-prone—how to become better at moving in and out of flow at all times in all areas of life.

Flow can transform your life. Are you ready? Let's make it happen.

Part 1

The Basics of Flow

To feel completely at one with what you are doing, to know you are strong and able to control your destiny at least for the moment, and to gain a sense of pleasure independent of results is to experience flow. [1]

—SUSAN A. JACKSON, FLOW RESEARCHER

Chapter 1

The 10,000-Foot View

Flow is defined as an optimal state of consciousness, a state where you feel your best and perform your best. More specifically, the term refers to those moments of rapt attention and total absorption, when you get so focused on the task at hand that everything else disappears. Action and awareness merge. Your sense of self vanishes. Your sense of time distorts (either, typically, speeds up; or, occasionally, slows down). And throughout, all aspects of performance, both mental and physical, go through the roof.[1]

—STEVEN KOTLER

We begin our investigation into flow with the 10,000 foot view—a broad overview of the topic. The goal of this chapter is to set flow in context and to give you a basic understanding from which we'll be able to build in the coming chapters. Each point mentioned here will be discussed in greater detail throughout the book.

So, what is flow? Flow is a state of consciousness. Many such states exist, including everyday states like anger, anxiety, or boredom, dream and sleep states, and more exotic ones like hypnotic, trance, or meditative states.

Like other states, flow is transient and exists on a continuum ranging from mild to more intense. Mild experiences are sometimes referred to as *micro* or *shallow* flow, while more intense experiences can be referred to as *macro* or *deep* flow. As we go about our lives, flow comes and flow goes. We experience it intensely in some moments and only mildly or not at all in others. A comparison to anger illustrates the point: We enter and exit the state of anger throughout our everyday lives, feeling angry sometimes but not other times. And we experience anger in varying degrees, ranging from mild frustration to full-blown rage.

Flow tends to happen under certain conditions. In the case of anger, this might be when a hair-trigger temper is paired with perceived injustice. In the case of flow, it's when the right attitudes and abilities meet an activity and environment conducive to flow. While everyone can experience flow, some of us do so more easily and frequently than others. And while flow can be experienced in almost any activity and environment, some are more likely to bring forth the state than others.

Flow has certain experiential qualities that define and differentiate it. These six characteristics are: (1) intense and focused concentration, (2) merging of action and awareness, (3) loss of reflective self-consciousness, (4) a sense of control over one's action, (5) distortion of time, and (6) a feeling that the activity is deeply rewarding. No component on its own produces the holistic feeling of being in flow. It's only when the six show up together, in their interplay, that the sensation of being in flow—the feeling that everything is moving of its own accord, seamlessly, effortlessly, and without friction—is experienced. This is the case for all states of consciousness. For example, the experience of anger may arise when a number of the following characteristics show up together: hostile thoughts, muscle tension, an increased and rapid heartbeat, feelings of heat, a churning feeling in the stomach, sweaty palms, and feelings of resentment, humiliation, or disrespect.

Flow has a specific signature in our brain and body. Among other things, this includes heightened but not excessive arousal, moderate levels of cortisol, and increases and decreases in activity in certain brain areas.

Flow is universal to the human experience. It's experienced by men and women, young and old alike, all over the world, regardless of cultural differences.

Flow has its advantages and disadvantages. Anger provides plenty of energy but often results in behavior we later regret. Flow enhances mental and physical performance, creates lasting motivation, and typically leads to greater long-term health and happiness. On the flip side, flow also comes with risks, including addiction and neglect.

So there you have it, that's a broad overview of flow. In short, flow is a universal state of consciousness with certain peculiar and fascinating characteristics. Human beings enter the state given the right circumstances—and that's where things get exciting: We can investigate and learn more about these circumstances. And by then structuring our lives, acquiring skills, adopting attitudes, and implementing habits accordingly, we can experience more flow and reap the rewards.

Now that we've covered the bird's eye view of flow, it's time to dig deeper and fill in the details.

Chapter 2

Flow's Origins

[W]hen people enjoy most what they are doing—from playing music to playing chess, from reading good books to having a good conversation, from working their best to trying to beat their own record in sport—they report a state of effortless concentration so deep that they lose their sense of time, of themselves, of their problems. We have called this the 'flow experience,' because so many of the persons describing it used the analogy of being effortlessly carried by a current—of being in a flow.[1]

—MIHALY CSIKSZENTMIHALYI

Human beings have probably been experiencing flow for tens of thousands of years. When our ancestors hunted megafauna, danced around the fire, sang songs, or engaged in ceremonies—I strongly suspect they were in flow. However, while the experience has existed for a long time, the scientific investigation into it is relatively new. The term flow has only been around for approximately 50 years. In this chapter, we'll discuss the origin story of flow. We'll see who came up with the term, and why.

So, where did flow originate? The term was coined in the 1970s by Hungarian-American researcher Mihaly Csikszentmihalyi. It made its first appearance in the literature in Csikszentmihalyi's book *Beyond Boredom and Anxiety: Experiencing Flow in Work and Play.*[2] The 1975 book details the beginnings of flow research and presents the first version of flow theory.

The concept of flow is very much the brain child of Csikszentmihalyi. He did all of the initial research, coined the term, came up with the original theory, and then continued to study the concept and update the theory for more than 40 years until his death in 2021. He published hundreds of scientific papers and multiple books on the subject, including his 1990 bestseller *Flow: The Psychology of Optimal Experience.*[3] For all these reasons, he's rightfully known as the "father of flow."

Csikszentmihalyi started his research career in the 1960s by studying creativity. He made two observations when studying the creative process of painters. First, he noticed that the painters sometimes entered a "trancelike state" when the work was going well: "Once the painting started to take shape, the artist became completely enthralled. The motivation to go on painting was so intense that fatigue, hunger, or discomfort ceased to matter."[4]

Second, he noticed that the painters weren't very interested in the end result or potential rewards of their paintings. Instead, they were much more interested in the process of painting itself: "[I] noticed that the artists I was observing almost immediately lost interest in the canvas they had just painted. Typically they turned the finished canvas around and stacked it against a wall. Nor were they particularly eager to show it off, or very hopeful about selling it. They could hardly wait to start on a new one."[5] At first, the behavior seemed strange to Csikszentmihalyi. However, upon reflection, he realized it wasn't unusual at all: "After all, there were hundreds of activities that people did simply for the sake of doing the activity, without expecting any external rewards for it."[6]

Csikszentmihalyi realized that the painters were primarily intrinsically, rather than extrinsically motivated. They pursued painting primarily for the sake of it rather than for extrinsic rewards like money, prestige, power, or admiration. When an activity is primarily pursued for the sake of it, it's said to be intrinsically motivated. When an activity is primarily pursued for money, prestige, power, or admiration, it's said to be extrinsically motivated. Flow research originated in Csikszentmihalyi's desire to understand the former.

To investigate the nature of intrinsically motivated activity, Csikszentmihalyi and his research team interviewed rock climbers, chess and basketball players, dancers, and composers of music. The interviewees had in common that they seemed to be doing what they were doing for the sake of it rather than for extrinsic rewards—they were intrinsically motivated. In the words of Csikszentmihalyi: "All groups studied had one thing in common: they consisted of people who devote much energy to some activity which yields minimal rewards of a conventional sort."[7]

Csikszentmihalyi started with a simple question: Why do you spend so much of your life doing something for which you don't expect either fame or fortune? In hindsight, the answers were rather obvious. The interviewees devoted time to climbing rocks, playing chess, or dancing—even when no external rewards could be gained—because the activities were rewarding in themselves. The activities provided highly enjoyable and deeply satisfying experiences. It was the quality of these experiences that made up for the lack of external rewards. The doing was reward enough. The act justified itself; composing music was not a means to an end but an end in itself.

Not exactly a groundbreaking insight, is it? We are probably all familiar with pursuing certain activities just because they are fun or meaningful.

The truly fascinating finding came about when Csikszentmihalyi asked his interviewees to describe the enjoyable experiences they had in their activities. Here's what he found: His interviewees described what they experienced in the same manner, regardless of the activity pursued. The way the climber felt moving up the mountain was identical to how the chess player felt during a close game or the musician composing a new masterpiece. They all described being intensely focused, feeling confident and in control, forgetting about themselves and their problems, losing touch of time, and immensely enjoying themselves—they described the hallmarks of the flow experience. What they *did* varied; what they *experienced* was the same.

And what they experienced, many described with the word flow and through the metaphor of a water current carrying them along. "It was like floating," one might have said. "I was being carried by the flow," another. A young poet and rock climber put it as such: "The mystique of rock climbing is climbing; you get to the top of a rock glad it's over but really wish it would go forever. The justification of climbing is climbing, like the justification of poetry is writing; you don't conquer anything except things in yourself. . . . The act of writing justifies poetry. Climbing is the same: recognizing that you are a flow. The purpose of the flow is to keep on flowing, not looking for a peak or utopia but staying in the flow. It is not moving up but a continuous flowing; you move up only to keep the flow going. There is no possible reason for climbing except the climbing itself; it is a self-communication."[8]

The word flow recurred spontaneously in many interviewees' descriptions of what they experienced when they greatly enjoyed themselves during intrinsically motivated activities. And so, Csikszentmihalyi and colleagues used the term flow to name the universal experience they had discovered.[9] That's the origin story of flow. To put it in a single sentence: The term was coined by Csikszentmihalyi to name the universal state people enter when they enjoy themselves during activities they engage in for their own sake.

As mentioned earlier, Csikszentmihalyi then continued to investigate the flow experience for 40+ years. He quickly learned that the experience was indeed universal—people experience flow all over the world and in all kinds of different activities. He also quickly learned that flow doesn't just occur in intrinsically motivated activities, but also in extrinsically motivated ones. You can experience flow during a game of chess even if you're playing primarily to win money or become a world champion. Likewise, you can experience flow on the job even if you're primarily motivated by money or prestige.

Since its conception in the 1970s, flow has steadily risen in popularity. Thousands of studies and countless books have been and continue to be published on the subject. Flow is sought after by elite athletes, musicians, artists, peak performers, and large corporations all over the world.

But precisely how is flow defined? How does it come about? What does it feel like? That's what we'll explore next.

Chapter 3

Flow Defined

Flow is an optimal state of consciousness, a peak state where we both feel our best and perform our best. It is a transformation available to anyone, anywhere, provided that certain initial conditions are met.[1]

—STEVEN KOTLER

Now that we've covered the bird's eye view and the origin story of flow, it's time to dig deeper into what flow is and what we know about it. In the current chapter, we'll first tackle the "official" definition of flow—the definition most researchers use when investigating flow scientifically. We'll then consider other perspectives on flow and briefly touch on the different types of flow. We continue to build the foundation that will help you better understand the rest of the book. Think of it this way: The more fully you understand flow, the easier it'll be for you to experience it more often.

The "Official" Definition

In the research literature, flow is typically defined as a multifaceted experience consisting of nine elements. The holistic sensation of being in flow is comprised of, or results from the interplay of, the nine components.

Three of them can be viewed as conditions or antecedents of flow. They describe under what circumstances flow occurs. They are: (1) *clear goals*, (2) *immediate feedback*, and (3) *challenge-skills balance*.

The remaining six elements can be considered experiential or phenomenological characteristics of the state. They describe what's experienced during flow. They are: (4) *intense concentration*, (5) *merging of action and awareness*, (6) *loss of self-consciousness*, (7) a *sense of control*, (8) *distortion of time*, and (9) the feeling that the *experience is deeply rewarding*.

We'll discuss the three conditions and six experiential characteristics in greater detail in chapters 4 and 5 respectively.

The Flow Experience

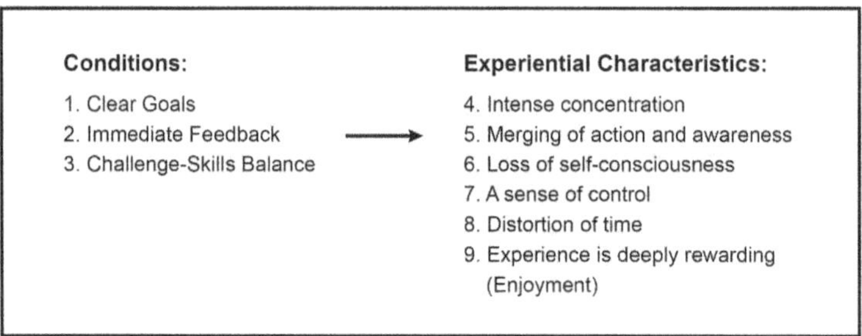

FIGURE 1: Conditions (antecedents) and experiential characteristics of flow.

As mentioned, no single one of these elements is flow. It's only when they show up together that the holistic sensation of being carried along by a water current occurs. The more strongly each component shows up, the more intense the flow experience becomes. As you've learnt, flow exists on a spectrum ranging from micro or shallow flow to macro or deep flow. Losing yourself in a good book is a relatively mild flow state. Playing a close game of chess or tennis is likely more intense. Skydiving down a canyon, I assume, is even more intense. Flow thus covers a huge range of experiences, going from the relatively mundane to the ecstatic and blissful.

On the mild end of the spectrum, there's no clear boundary between what "counts" or "qualifies" as flow and what doesn't. The definition doesn't clarify how strongly each of the components has to show up (e.g., just how focused attention has to be or how in control you have to feel). There are no official borders that mark the transition between non-flow and flow. Of course, depending on how the researchers measure flow, they do sometimes make arbitrary cut-offs, but that's something we'll discuss in chapter 7.

People sometimes ask if what they experience in a certain activity is flow. That usually means that the experience hovers somewhere around the border between non-flow and flow, and therefore, there's no right or wrong answer.

If the activity is enjoyable, there's an argument to be made that it involves at least a mild flow state. That being said, it doesn't really matter if we regard it as flow or not. If the activity is enjoyable, that's good either way.

It should be noted that while there is general agreement on the multidimensionality of flow, the details are still the subject of lively debate. Among other things, researchers disagree on the exact number of facets, their terminology, and their classification into conditions and characteristics. For example, some researchers argue that there are only three rather than nine defining components. Other researchers suggest that the components "focused attention," "a sense of control," and "enjoyment" should be viewed as both antecedents and characteristics.[2] That said, the nine-component view that I've presented here is currently the closest thing to an agreed-upon definition we have.

Other Perspectives on Flow

A tree can be described as a woody plant with an elaborate root system, a trunk, branches, and leaves. It can also be described as an evolutionarily successful species, a provider of shade, a home, ecosystem, or target for hugging. Each perspective can be true, and each can tell us something unique and interesting about trees.

The same goes for flow. It can be described as a multifaceted experience. But it can also be described in other ways. In the coming pages, we'll look at five additional perspectives on flow. Each perspective broadens our understanding of the phenomenon of flow.

Flow as the State Between Boredom and Anxiety

We are most likely to experience flow when we engage in activities that provide a so-called *challenge-skills balance*. This is one of the three conditions of flow we'll discuss in greater detail in chapter 4. When the challenge is too great for our skills, anxiety ensues. When the challenge is too minor for our skills, boredom ensues. To enter flow, we must thus engage in an activity that provides the right balance between the challenge and our skills.

Let me give you an example. If I was to play tennis against Roger Federer, whose skills far exceed my own, I would be so inferior and overwhelmed that it would make me anxious. If I was to play against my father, who's far less skilled than me, I would probably get bored. Flow only happens when I play against an evenly matched counterpart, such as my younger brother Yanis, in a scenario where the challenge matches my skills. Hence, flow can be viewed as the state between boredom and anxiety. We're neither under-challenged nor over-challenged. Neither bored nor anxious. Neither disengaged nor over-aroused. Csikszentmihalyi illustrated this idea in his very first model of flow, which is now known as the *Flow Channel Model* (Figure 2).

The Flow Channel Model

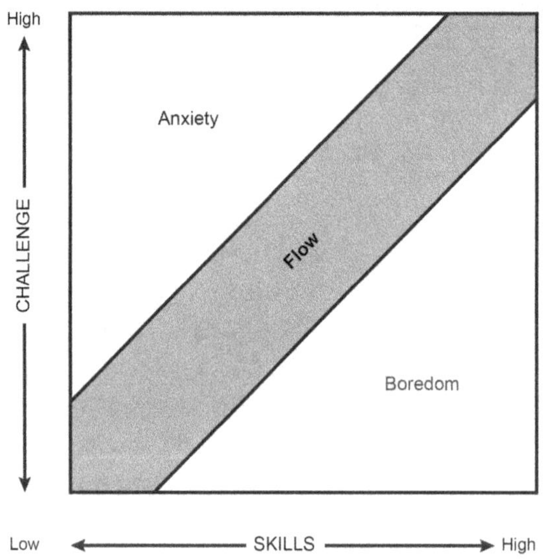

FIGURE 2: Csikszentmihalyi's first model of flow. Flow is described as the state between boredom and anxiety. It occurs when challenges and skills are balanced. Later models clarified that flow only occurs in the top right corner of the graphic when challenges and skills are both high (see chapter 7). Adapted from Csikszentmihalyi (1975).[3]

You may recall that flow made its first appearance in the literature in Csikszentmihalyi's book, *Beyond Boredom and Anxiety*. You now understand where that title came from.

This perspective obviously isn't perfect. You don't necessarily feel anxious when challenges exceed skills, or bored when skills exceed challenges. But the perspective is nonetheless valuable and insightful. It also gives you some first cues on how to create more flow in your life. For example, if you don't experience much flow at work, it could be because your skills exceed the challenges. If that was the case, you could consider ways to make work more challenging. You could ask for more challenging tasks or look for a new job.

Flow as Optimal Experience or an Optimal State of Consciousness
Csikszentmihalyi often used the term *optimal experience* as a synonym for flow. The subtitle of his bestseller *Flow* literally reads *The Psychology of Optimal Experience*. Steven Kotler, meanwhile, defines flow as "an optimal state of consciousness, a peak state where we both feel our best and perform our best."[4] Kotler is an American author and the cofounder and executive director of the Flow Research Collective.[5] He's one of the world's leading experts on flow and has done a lot to bring flow into the mainstream.

Flow can be viewed as optimal in the sense that it's simultaneously a highly enjoyable and highly functional state. During flow, you feel confident, strong, and sometimes even ecstatic. At the same time, you are able to perform to the best of your ability. During flow, creativity, problem-solving, concentration, physical strength and endurance, and other performance attributes are heightened. Flow is characterized by both high enjoyment and high performance. For this reason, flow can be described as optimal.

That being said, flow also has its downsides and can have *sub*-optimal consequences. Flow can lead to addiction and neglect. For extreme sports athletes, the pursuit of flow can result in injury or even death. In times of war, flow can aid soldiers in committing war crimes. We'll discuss these dangers in greater detail in chapter 12.

As you can see, describing flow as optimal requires nuance. The quality of being optimal may apply to some aspects of the experience but not others. Still, the perspective adds another intriguing element to the phenomenon of flow and illustrates well the beneficial and highly functional nature of the state.

Flow as a Non-Ordinary State of Consciousness
In their book *Stealing Fire*, Steven Kotler and Jamie Wheal describe flow as a *non-ordinary state of consciousness* (NOSC).[6] They use the word *ecstasis*, borrowed from the ancient Greeks, as a synonym for such states: "Plato described ecstasis as an altered state where our normal waking consciousness

vanishes completely, replaced by an intense euphoria and a powerful connection to a greater intelligence."

"When we say ecstasis," they explain, "we're talking about a very specific range of non-ordinary states of consciousness (NOSC)—what Johns Hopkins psychiatrist Stanislav Grof defined as those experiences 'characterized by dramatic perceptual changes, intense and often unusual emotions, profound alterations in the thought processes and behavior, [brought about] by a variety of psychosomatic manifestations, rang[ing] from profound terror to ecstatic rapture. . . . There exist many different forms of NOSC; they can be induced by a variety of different techniques or occur spontaneously, in the middle of everyday life.'"

Ecstasis officially translates as "stepping beyond oneself" or "to be or stand outside oneself." It's the antecedent to *ecstasy*, which is both the street name for MDMA and a term used to describe a profoundly unusual state of consciousness defined as "a trance or trance-like state in which a person transcends normal consciousness."[7]

Kotler and Wheal describe three types of NOSC in the book: (1) *contemplative and mystical states*, which they say can be experienced with techniques like chanting, meditation, prayer, or with wearable technologies; (2) *psychedelic states*, which can be experienced by ingesting substances like MDMA, LSD, or magic mushrooms; and (3) *flow states*, which can be experienced in all kinds of different activities.

The characterization of flow as a NOSC adds a fascinating element to our understanding of the state: According to Kotler and Wheal, flow is remarkably similar to the other non-ordinary states. While these states may appear different on the surface, our experiences of them and their biological underpinnings in the brain are said to be nearly identical. It's an intriguing idea, isn't it?

Personally, I haven't had enough experience with contemplative and psychedelic states to say how similar they are to flow. I imagine that the similarities mostly apply to flow experiences at the deep end of the spectrum. We know that intense flow states can far transcend normal waking consciousness and are frequently described as ecstatic. The mild flow experiences, on the other hand, probably aren't comparable to the other non-ordinary states. Either way, I'm intrigued by the connection and the potential similarities between these different experiences. Just how similar they are to each other, only more research, or personal experimentation, will tell.

Flow as Inner Harmony or Order in Consciousness

Csikszentmihalyi had another way of describing flow, namely as the experience of *inner harmony* or of *order in consciousness*. For example, he once wrote that "'flow' is the way people describe their state of mind when consciousness is harmoniously ordered."[8]

Imagine floating down a river. As you move along the shore, various thoughts and emotions come into your awareness. If the thoughts are positive—*you're doing well, this is awesome, everything is going smoothly, keep going*—you feel encouraged and content. You're able to be fully present on your trip, your attention wholly used up by the experience of paddling. You're engaged with life. It's a harmonious, frictionless experience. You are in flow.

If, on the other hand, the thoughts and emotions coming into your awareness are negative—*this isn't working, I'm no good at this, this sucks, I'd rather be doing something else*—suddenly you're feeling discouraged, frustrated, angry, or otherwise dissatisfied. Your experience ceases to flow. There's now an inner conflict. There's friction, disorder, and disharmony. Chaos ensues.

Csikszentmihalyi explained it as such: "In ordinary life, people typically experience conflict in consciousness. For example, an office worker might be sitting at his desk and adding up numbers, with part of his attention focused on the job and part of it focused on his wish to be out with his girlfriend. He resents having to sit, to be indoors, to work on his task. By contrast, in the flow state a person's subjective states are in harmony; the body and mind are working together without internal conflict. This state of ordered consciousness is one of the main rewards of the flow experience."[9]

Again, I find this to be an interesting and valuable perspective. It not only expands our concept of flow but can also help us understand why flow may be present or absent in our lives. If you're in a disharmonious relationship or work in a disharmonious environment, the outer turmoil may result in inner turmoil, and, as such, may get in the way of flow. Outer conflict can result in inner conflict; outer harmony can result in inner harmony and can therefore help you experience more flow. If you want more flow in your life, find ways to make your life more harmonious.

Flow as Enjoyment

Think about the most enjoyable experiences of your life. What you'll probably find is that you're in flow during these experiences. Regardless of the activity, when people describe their most enjoyable experiences, they usually describe the flow experience, or at least elements of it. They describe being intensely focused, feeling in total control, forgetting themselves, and so on.

For this reason, Csikszentmihalyi used the terms enjoyment and flow interchangeably.[10] He referred to flow as "the experience of enjoyment" and to the components of flow as "the elements of enjoyment."[11] He said that to the extent the components of flow are present, "a person enjoys what he or she is doing."[12] According to this view, an enjoyable experience always entails flow. And being in flow is always enjoyable.

In everyday language, this is different. We can speak of enjoying an experience even if it doesn't provide flow. We can enjoy watching television, taking a hot bath, or watching the sunset, even though these are not typically flow experiences. While flow is always enjoyable, enjoyment in the conventional use of the word doesn't require flow.

Csikszentmihalyi used the word pleasure to describe satisfying experiences that don't involve flow. So in his lingo, flow activities are enjoyable. Meanwhile, activities like watching Netflix, drinking wine, or eating doughnuts are pleasurable. We'll come back to this differentiation and its implications in chapter 10.

Types of Flow

As we've established, flow experiences are remarkably similar, regardless of the circumstances in which they are experienced. The experience you have during a close game of chess is similar to the experiences you have during your favorite work activities or your favorite hobbies. Still, there have been attempts to distinguish between different types of flow. In fact, I've already mentioned one such distinction: micro or shallow flow and macro or deep flow.

Another distinction that's been made is between *individual flow* and *group flow*. The former refers to a single person being in flow. It's the type of flow I've been writing about so far. The "thing" that experiences flow is the individual. In group flow, the "thing" that experiences flow is the group as a whole. It's the group that either is or isn't in flow. Keith Sawyer, the man who coined the term, defines group flow as "a collective state that occurs when a group is performing at the peak of its abilities."[13] Sawyer suggests that the group can be in flow even when its members are not. Likewise, members can be in flow even when the group is not. Most things that can be said about individual flow can also be said about group flow. First and foremost: Group flow is a highly enjoyable and functional state.

Another distinction that's been suggested is between *solitary flow* and *social flow*.[14] The former describes instances when an individual experiences flow with nobody else present. Examples include me being alone in my office working on this book or a solo kayaker paddling by themselves on a secluded river. The latter refers to an individual experiencing flow in the presence of others. There are two kinds of social flow: (1)

- *Co-active flow* happens when an individual experiences flow while others are present. It doesn't require any communication or interaction. Examples include me being in a writing flow while my girlfriend is reading a book in the same room or students listening to an engaging lecture in the presence of other students.

- *Interactive social flow*, in contrast, involves communication and interaction among group or team members. Examples are when I'm experiencing flow during football or when you're conversing and laughing with friends.

Solitary, co-active, and interactive flow arise under slightly different circumstances, are said to feel slightly different, and are said to have slightly different consequences. That being said, little research exists on these proposed differences.

Over the years, other distinctions have been suggested.[15] I won't mention them here and won't expand on the concepts of group flow and social flow in any greater detail. The reason I wanted to briefly touch on them is to clarify something: When I'm writing about flow in this book I'm referring to an individual being in flow, regardless of whether that's in a solitary or social context. When I mean group flow, I will explicitly state that I mean group flow.

As you can see, flow can be described in many different ways. Next up, we're spending some more time on the official definition of flow. In chapter 4, we'll discuss the three conditions. In chapter 5, we'll discuss the six experiential characteristics.

Chapter 4

The Three Conditions of Flow

When goals are clear, feedback relevant, and challenges and skills are in balance, attention becomes ordered and fully invested. [1]

—*MIHALY CSIKSZENTMIHALYI*

As discussed in the last chapter, flow is commonly defined as a multifaceted experience consisting of nine elements. Three of them refer to conditions, while the other six refer to experiential characteristics. The latter tell us something about what flow feels like, while the former tell us something about when flow happens—flow happens when the conditions are fulfilled: when there are (1) clear goals, (2) immediate feedback, and (3) a challenge-skills balance.

But what exactly are clear goals? Why does feedback have to be immediate? How does the challenge-skills balance work? That's what we'll discuss in the coming pages.

1. Clear Goals

Flow tends to happen when an activity provides *clear goals* that keep you interested, focused, and engaged. One of the defining characteristics of flow is intense concentration on the task at hand. Clear goals facilitate that kind of intense concentration.

We're not talking about long-term goals here, but rather about proximal, moment-by-moment goals that emerge out of your interaction with the activity. When I play tennis, I have to hit the ball over the net, then move into a good position, then watch where my opponent's next shot is going to land, run to that place, hit the ball, run back into a good position, and so on. New goals are continuously emerging. These goals keep my attention locked in the here and now. They keep me focused on the task in front of me. Abstract and distal goals such as "beating my opponent," "winning the tennis match," or "winning the tournament" do very little to keep me zoned in throughout the game.

Csikszentmihalyi clarifies: "What counts is not that the overall goal of the activity be clear but rather that the activity present a clear goal for the next step in the action sequence, and then the next, on and on, until the final goal is reached. What focuses a mountain climber's mind is not the intention of reaching the top of the climb but the problem of which outcrop of rock to use for the next handhold and where to place next the toe of the boot. It is not winning the game that keeps the chess player's attention —that is too distant a goal—but the next move, and a few after that. What focuses the pianist's mind is not the goal of finishing the piece, but the chord, the next cluster of notes to be played just right."[2]

In summary, clear goals facilitate the kind of task-focused attention that is characteristic of flow. Without clear moment-by-moment goals, attention is likely to wander away from the task. Instead of focusing on what's in front of us, we start thinking about the future or worrying about the past. Clear goals keep us focused. Without them, we're unlikely to experience flow. That's why they're a condition or antecedent of the experience.

2. Immediate Feedback

The next condition is called *immediate feedback*. "Clear goals do not sustain attention unless the activity also provides immediate feedback," explains Csikszentmihalyi.[3] "If, for instance, I cannot hear myself playing the piano, my attention is likely to wander. Why pay attention if I can't tell what difference my actions make? . . . [If] we get information about how well we are doing, attention will focus spontaneously on the ongoing action. The feedback to the climber is seeing that every move brings him or her higher up the rock face; the feedback to the chess player is seeing the strategic position on the board change as a result of the last move. Surgeons say that one reason operations are so enjoyable is that they provide immediate information—if there is blood in the cavity, the scalpel must have slipped."

Every time I hit the ball during a game of tennis, I receive new information about how well I've struck it, where it lands, and whether my opponent is able to return it. My actions are coupled with immediate feedback; I always know how well I'm doing and can adjust accordingly. That feedback keeps me engaged, interested, and focused.

Imagine if I never received information about where the ball went that I just hit. Every time I hit it, the ball just disappears into a black hole. I would get bored instantly. As Csikszentmihalyi put it: Why pay attention if I can't tell what difference my actions make? Or imagine I played an alternative version of tennis in which I hit the ball but had to wait for 60 seconds to see where it went. I would get impatient and frustrated and would lose interest in the game. Feedback would not be timely enough.

Without immediate feedback, attention is likely to wander away from the task at hand. Instead of being zoned in, we start to zone out. Without immediate feedback, we have a hard time sustaining the task-focused attention that is characteristic of flow.

3. Challenge-Skills Balance

The first two conditions are generally not sufficient for flow to happen. There may be clear goals and immediate feedback when washing the dishes, yet we rarely experience flow during that activity. What's missing is the third condition: *challenge-skills balance.*

Challenge refers to the demands or difficulty of the activity, which must be in balance with your skill level. We've already discussed this in the previous chapter. If the challenge exceeds your skills, you're likely to get anxious. If your skills outmatch the challenge, you're likely to get bored. In both cases, it's hard to achieve the complete task-focused attention necessary for flow. When you're under-challenged, you have too much free capacity and likely start thinking about task-irrelevant topics. When you're over-challenged, you're likely to start worrying, become overly self-conscious, and get stuck in your head.

For flow to occur, challenge and skills must be in balance. In fact, they must not just be in balance but they must also both be reasonably high. If both skills and challenge are low, as is the case in washing dishes, you're more likely to experience apathy than flow. This principle is illustrated in the *Octant Model of Flow*, which divides everyday experiences into eight distinct states as a function of the balance between challenges and skills (Figure 3).

Though clearly oversimplified, the model illustrates well the fact that flow depends on a fit between challenges and skills. It also neatly highlights how flow fits into everyday life: Like other states, flow comes and goes as the result of situational characteristics. We move in and out of flow throughout our waking lives. Sometimes we're in flow, other times we're bored, apathetic, or anxious, depending on the balance between challenges and skills in whatever we're doing.

The Octant Model of Flow

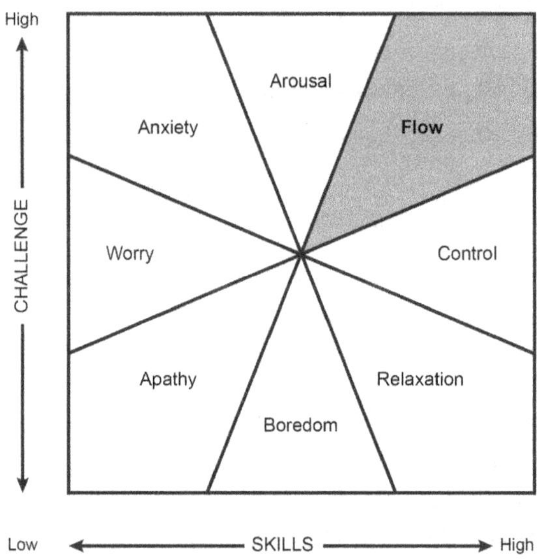

FIGURE 3: The Octant Model of Flow divides everyday experiences into eight distinct states as a function of the balance between challenges and skills. Flow occurs when both variables are high. Adapted from Massimini, Csikszentmihalyi, and Carli (1987).[4]

Obviously, the model isn't perfect. We experience more than just eight different states and there are more factors than just challenges and skills that influence us. Still, the model is useful and points out well how the challenge-skills balance influences our experience.

Now that we've covered the three conditions, I would like to point out one last detail: The conditions refer both to objective features and subjective experience. Let me explain. When I play tennis against my younger brother (an evenly matched opponent), the activity provides clear goals, immediate feedback, and a challenge-skills balance. From an objective standpoint, the three conditions are fulfilled. However, whether I experience flow or not, ultimately depends on my subjective experience of the conditions. In order to experience flow, I must perceive clear goals, immediate feedback, and a challenge-skills balance. If I play tennis but am thinking about my taxes, I'm not likely to perceive the relevant goals and feedback, and I'm thus not experiencing flow.

Activities provide stimuli, and some stimuli are more conducive to flow than others. Generally speaking, an activity that (1) continuously tells you what to do (clear goals), (2) tells you how well you're doing (immediate feedback), and (3) provides a level of challenge that matches your skills is highly conducive to flow. Generally speaking, tennis provides stimuli that are more conducive to flow than washing the dishes. Ultimately, however, it's your response to the stimuli that determines whether flow occurs or not.

Flow Triggers

There's another popular framework that explains under what circumstances flow happens: Steven Kotler's concept of triggers. Kotler coined the term *flow trigger* in his 2014 book *The Rise of Superman*.[5] The term conveys the idea that certain factors can help to activate or initiate the state of flow. Kotler refers to the triggers as "preconditions that lead to more flow."[6] He suggests that the triggers promote flow by driving attention into the present moment.

At the time of this writing, Kotler has identified 22 triggers, which he separates into internal, external, creative, and social triggers.[7] You can find a complete list of the triggers below. For a more detailed description of each trigger, and for ideas on how to translate the triggers into practical strategies for experiencing more flow, check out Kotler's 2021 book *The Art of Impossible*.[8]

Internal triggers: (1) *Autonomy* (a sense of feeling in control), (2) *Curiosity-passion-purpose* (three sources of intrinsic motivation), (3) *Complete concentration* (attention focused on the task at hand), (4) *Clear goals* (perceiving clear proximal goals on a moment-by-moment basis), (5) *Immediate feedback* (receiving real-time information about how one is doing), and (6) *Challenge-skills balance* (challenge and skills both high and balanced). If the last three sound familiar, that's because they refer to the three official conditions.

External triggers: (7) *High consequences* (some kind of risk: physical, social, emotional, etc.), (8) *Novelty* (shiny new objects in the environment that one hasn't encountered before), (9) *Unpredictability* (not knowing what happens next), (10) *Complexity* (expansion of the brain's perceptual capacity), and (11) *Deep embodiment* (engagement of multiple senses at once). The middle three are sometimes taken together and referred to as the *rich environment* trigger.

Creative triggers: (12) *Creativity* (pattern recognition and risk-taking). At the time of this writing, there's just one creative trigger.

Group or social triggers: (13) *Complete concentration* (like individual flow, group flow requires focused attention), (14) *Shared goals* (everyone is heading in the same direction), (15) *Shared risk* (everyone has skin in the game), (16) *Close listening* (everyone's attention is fully engaged in the here and now), (17) *Good communication* (constant dialogue and information sharing; the group version of immediate feedback), (18) *Blending egos* (everyone is thoroughly involved, and no one's hogging the spotlight; a collective version of humility), (19) *Equal participation* (everyone has a part to play, and everyone plays their part), (20) *Familiarity* (the group has a shared knowledge base; everyone's on the same page), (21) *A sense of control* (the combination of autonomy and competence), and (22) *Always say yes* (interactions are additive more than argumentative).

Beyond Official Conditions

The three conditions tell us *something*—but not *everything*—about when flow happens. Before we move to the next chapter, I want to clarify that there are many factors beyond the three conditions (and beyond the 22 flow triggers) that influence whether flow occurs or not.

Broadly speaking, there are factors pertaining to the person, the activity, and the environment. Some people are more likely to experience flow than others. Some activities are more conducive to flow than others. And some environments are more conducive to flow than others. A general way of answering under what circumstances flow happens would thus be: Flow happens when a flow-conducive person engages in a flow-conducive activity in a flow-conducive environment.

We'll learn a lot more about the various factors that influence flow throughout the book. But first, it's time to learn precisely what we experience when we're in a state of flow. In the next chapter, we'll discuss the six experiential characteristics of the flow experience.

Chapter 5

The Six Experiential Characteristics of Flow

I was totally absorbed, 110 percent; that was all that mattered in the whole existence. It just amazed me how I could maintain such high concentration for three hours. . . . Nothing, you feel like just nothing can go wrong and there's nothing that will be able to stop you or get in your way. And you're ready to tackle anything, and you don't fear any possibility happening, and it's just exhilarating. Afterward, I couldn't come down, I was on a high. I felt like I wanted to go ride, ride up that hill again.[1]

—ELITE CYCLIST INTERVIEWED IN JACKSON AND CSIKSZENTMIHALYI, FLOW IN SPORTS

When we're in flow, everything feels smooth and effortless. We're zoned in and fully engaged in what we're doing. We feel strong, capable, and in control. The cyclist from the above quote describes a state of total absorption and supreme confidence. People frequently use words like "ecstatic," "exhilarating," or "blissful" to describe the experience. In short, flow feels fantastic.

But what exactly are we experiencing when we're in flow? What makes up the experience? What are its different components? That's what we're about to discover. Over the next couple of pages, we'll pick apart the subjective experience of flow. We'll discuss the six underlying components that, in their interplay, create the sensation of being in flow.

As you're about to see, I've included a lot of quotes from people describing their flow experiences and the various proponents of it. I've done my best to place the quotes right where they best support the text. Most of the examples are from the relatively deep end of the flow spectrum.

The Holistic Sensation of Flow

Before we discuss each of the six components individually, let's recap what the complete experience feels like. So, what does flow feel like? In short, it feels... flowy. When we're in flow, it feels like we move effortlessly from one moment to the next—every action, every decision seems to flow perfectly and seamlessly from the last. Hence the descriptions: "I was being carried by the flow." "It was like floating." During the experience, action follows upon action according to an automatic, internal logic, seemingly without any conscious intervention by the actor.

> "I feel as if I'm very involved in the event, but my involvement is without a huge input on my part. It's almost as if I'm floating from one place to another . . . purely through instinct more than anything else. . . . You don't feel like you're going too hard or too softly; you just flow."[2] —Athlete interviewed in Jackson and Csikszentmihalyi, *Flow in Sports*

In flow, everything feels smooth and fluent, easy and light, effortless and spontaneous. There are no interruptions, no bumps, and no second guesses. The mind is still, yet highly focused. Things seem to just happen automatically, as if remote-controlled. And all the while, everything clicks. Everything comes together. People describe "being in the groove," "in the zone," "totally involved," "tuned in," "switched on," or "on auto."[3]

The Six Experiential Components of Flow

Flow theory suggests that this holistic sensation results from the interplay of six components. When all of them show up with full force, you experience macro or deep flow. When they show up less strongly, then you have micro or shallow flow. Let's now look at each component separately.

1. Intense Concentration

Flow is a state of intense focus. During flow, you are fully concentrated on the task in front of you. According to Csikszentmihalyi, intense concentration is perhaps *the* defining quality of flow.[4]

"Your concentration is very complete. Your mind isn't wandering, you are not thinking of something else; you are totally involved in what you are doing . . ."[5] —Dancer interviewed in Csikszentmihalyi, *Flow*

Activities that bring about deep flow states tend to have in common that they challenge you to the utmost of your capabilities. Because of that, you simply cannot afford to waste even the tiniest bit of attention on anything other than the activity itself. If the skier shooting down a slope thinks of their taxes, they'll find themselves head first in the fresh snow. If the wrestler's mind wanders, they'll find themselves on the mat. If the surgeon gets distracted during an operation, they put the life of their patient at risk.

If concentration wanes and your attention wanders away from the task, technically, you're out of flow, at least for that very instant. Thoughts or other task-irrelevant stimuli have intruded. The experience has been interrupted and has ceased to flow.

As you'll learn in chapter 9, task-focused attention and mind wandering are mutually exclusive phenomena. You're either focused on the task, or you're thinking about something unrelated to it. It's an either-or relationship; the corresponding brain regions work like a seesaw. If the focus circuitry goes up, the mind wandering circuitry goes down. And vice-versa. During the deep, intense focus of a flow experience, attention is completely on the activity. Mind wandering has stopped. Task-irrelevant thinking has come to a halt. The mental chatter has ceased. This is one of the reasons why the experience is so enjoyable. If all of your attention is used up by the task at hand, you are free from the nagging voice in your head. You forget about your problems, worries, self-doubts, and insecurities.

"I am less aware of myself and my problems. . . . [A]t times, I see only the positions."[6] —Chess player interviewed in Csikszentmihalyi, *Beyond Boredom and Anxiety*

This is also one of the reasons why flow is facilitative of high performance. The intense focus keeps performance anxiety, negative self-talk, doubts, and second-guesses at bay. Without intruding thoughts, you are free to perform to the best of your abilities.

An interesting aspect of focused attention during flow is that it's effort*less* rather than effort*ful* attention. You're intensely focused on the task in front of you, but not in a teeth-gritting way. You're not straining. You're not tense. You're not working hard to stay focused. Attention during flow is relaxed and non-forced. Flow is defined by *high concentration* and *high ease of concentration*.

2. Merging of Action and Awareness

In everyday life, it often happens that our minds are disconnected from our actions. What we do and what we pay attention to are separated. We're doing one thing but thinking of another. We're engaged in an activity, but our mind is somewhere else. We eat lunch but think about our afternoon schedule. We sit in class but daydream about dinner. We cook dinner but worry about tomorrow's presentation. Action and awareness are split.

In flow, there's no such split. All of our attention is focused on and absorbed by the activity itself. It's not action here and awareness there. It's a union of the two, a merging together. Because we are so fully involved with the activity, we become one with it.

> "You are so involved in what you are doing [that] you aren't thinking of yourself as separate from the immediate activity. . . . You don't see yourself as separate from what you are doing."[7] —Rock climber interviewed in Csikszentmihalyi, *Flow*

In extreme cases, awareness is so completely used up by the activity that people mention becoming almost oblivious to what happens around them.

> "The roof could fall in and, if it missed you, you would be unaware of it."[8] —Chess player interviewed in Csikszentmihalyi, *Flow*

Aspects of the environment sometimes merge into the experience as well. Athletes may describe how the noises and movements of the crowd have meshed into the totality of the experience. Rowers may describe the oar as becoming an extension of their arms. Basketball players may feel merged with or part of the team as a whole. Musicians mention "unique suspended moments" of becoming "the emotional or sensory quality of the music—the colors, the water, the love."[9] The poet William B. Yeats once wrote: "O body swayed to music, o brightening glance, how can we know the dancer from the dance?"[10]

3. Loss of Self-Consciousness

During normal waking consciousness, we have a non-stop, backgroundish awareness of our sense of self. We're conscious of our *selves*: of who we are, who we should be, and who we could be; of our past, present, and future. We're constantly monitoring and evaluating our behavior and the world around us and relating it back to ourselves and our story. "How do *I* look?" "Should *I* not have said that?" "What should *I* have said instead?" "What do they think of *me*?"

In flow, with all of our attention used up by the task at hand, this awareness of and preoccupation with the self drops away. In flow, we're temporarily freed from the "burden of selfhood."[11]

"So one forgets oneself, one forgets everything, seeing only the play of the boat with the sea, the play of the sea around the boat, leaving aside everything not essential to that game."[12] —Long-distance ocean cruiser interviewed in Csikszentmihalyi, *Flow*

Our sense of self is sometimes replaced during flow by a feeling of oneness and union with the world. "When not preoccupied with our selves, we actually have a chance to expand the concept of who we are," explains Csikszentmihalyi.[13] "Loss of self-consciousness can lead to self-transcendence, to a feeling that the boundaries of our being have been pushed forward."

A sailor may feel that the boat is an extension of himself. A climber may feel a sense of kinship develop between fingers and rock. A surgeon may have the sensation that the entire operating team is a single organism, moved by the same goal. Franciscan nuns report experiencing oneness with God's love, what they call unia mystica. Tibetan Buddhists report absolute unitary being, the feeling of oneness with everything.[14] Members of motorcycle gangs may speak of becoming one with the entire gang.[15]

Once the flow experience is over, we tend to emerge from it, oddly enough, with a stronger self-concept. We feel more capable, able, efficacious, and confident than before.[16] This is one of the benefits of flow we'll discuss in Part 2.

4. A Sense of Control

As we've seen in chapter 4, flow typically occurs when three conditions are met: When we perceive clear goals, immediate feedback, and a balance between challenge and skills. Put differently, you tend to experience flow when you know what to do, feel like it's difficult but possible to do, and while you're doing it, are feeling like you're doing well and are on the right track. The result: You feel a sense of control. You feel in control of the situation. You feel like you have control over what happens. After all, you know what to do, and you know you're capable of doing it. You've got this. You feel strong, efficacious, and confident. The feedback streaming into your awareness is confirmative—yes, you're indeed in control. Trust and self-belief go way up in flow.

> "A strong relaxation and calmness comes over me. I have no worries of failure. What a powerful and warm feeling it is! I want to expand, hug the world. I feel enormous power to effect something of grace and beauty."[17] —Dancer interviewed in Jackson and Csikszentmihalyi, *Flow in Sports*

In flow, you feel like you're in charge. You feel like you've got the resources to cope with what's coming your way. In extreme cases, this sense of control may make you feel like you can take on anything. Like nothing can go wrong. Like you can do everything. You feel a sense of empowerment, conviction, and self-esteem. Perhaps even a feeling of invincibility and of being unbeatable.

Compare this to the sensations conferred when you feel things are beyond your control, when you feel like you can't enact your own will and control your destiny. You may feel anxious, worried, nervous, and powerless. These feelings, which are so prevalent during everyday life, are absent during flow. You have no worries, no fear of failure, no doubts, and no second guesses. You feel instead a sense of power, strength, and confidence. It's an exhilarating experience. No wonder people describe those moments as the best of their lives.

That being said, these positive feelings aren't necessarily only a good thing. The feel-good nature of flow carries the potential for addiction, and the sense of control is a subjective, not objective, experience. Just because someone perceives themselves to be in control doesn't mean they are. The dancer may slip and ruin their performance. The mountain climber may fall and break a leg. As Steven Kotler puts it, "Flow makes you feel invincible, right up to the moment you're not."[18] We'll discuss the risks of flow in chapter 12.

5. Distortion of Time

In flow, time generally seems to pass faster than normal. Hours feel like minutes or minutes like seconds. "Time flies," we might say.

> "For sixteen and a half hours I was in it [flow] basically. If you ask me, did that feel like sixteen and a half hours? I'd say it felt like about three hours."[19] —Ultramarathon runner interviewed in Jackson and Csikszentmihalyi, *Flow in Sports*

Oddly enough, time can also slow down. Sometimes, there can even be both a speeding up and a slowing down of time.

> "Two things happen. One is that it seems to pass really fast in one sense. After it's passed, it seems to have passed really fast. I see that it's 1:00 in the morning, and I say: 'Aha, just a few minutes ago it was 8:00.' But then while I'm dancing…it seems like it's been much longer than maybe it really was."[20] —Ballet dancer interviewed in Csikszentmihalyi, *Flow*

Not everyone experiences this distortion of time, either. If timing is an important element of the activity, such as in surgery or during certain races, this dimension of flow typically doesn't show up, or certainly not in an extreme way. The transformation of time thus depends on the activity and its specific requirements.

6. The Activity Becomes Deeply Rewarding

Consider the experience we've described so far. You're totally absorbed in what you're doing. You're deeply and intensely focused. The "me," with its fears, worries, and doubts, is absent and replaced by a sense of union. You feel at one with the world, and you feel strong, powerful, capable, and in control.

When these elements show up together, you have the recipe for a deeply rewarding and highly enjoyable experience. Any activity that provides such an exquisite experience becomes an end in itself. The intrinsic rewards of the experience overshadow the extrinsic rewards. Even if initially undertaken for other reasons, an activity that produces flow becomes intrinsically rewarding.

"There's nothing, there's no experience in sport that is as exhilarating or rewarding as being in flow. That's what it is. That's what makes me keep riding, knowing that I might get it again."[21] —Cyclist interviewed in Jackson and Csikszentmihalyi, *Flow in Sports*

Flow is a feel-good experience par excellence. In chapter 10, we'll see that flow can provide such profound, ecstatic, blissful experiences that some people are willing to die to experience these highs.

Before we get there, though, we have a few more stops to get to on our Tour de Flow. In the next chapter, we'll discuss the factors that make certain people more likely to experience flow than others. It's time to meet the autotelic personality.

Chapter 6

The Autotelic Personality

Autotelic personalities tend to position themselves in situations which enable frequent experiences of flow states. They have a greater capacity to initiate, sustain, and enjoy such optimal experiences.[1]

—*NICOLA BAUMANN, FLOW RESEARCHER*

In chapter 4, we learned that flow shows up when certain conditions are met. When you perceive clear goals, immediate feedback, and a balance between challenge and skills, then you're likely to enter flow. While this is true, it's also not the complete picture.

When researchers artificially induce flow in the lab, such as by having participants play flow-conducive games, some participants report lots of flow while others report little flow. Participants differ in the amount and intensity of flow they experience, even under the same conditions. Such studies showcase the importance of personality traits—attitudes, skills, behaviors, and patterns of thoughts and feelings that influence a person's ability to experience flow. As I've mentioned, some people are more likely to experience flow than others.

A person who possesses many favorable attributes and therefore tends to experience lots of flow can be described as *flow-prone*—such a person has a high tendency to experience flow.[2] Alternatively, a person with favorable attributes may also be referred to as, or said to possess, an *autotelic personality*.[3] The word "autotelic" comes from the Greek autotelḗs (auto = self; telos = goal) and refers to "someone or something that has a purpose in, and not apart from, itself."[4] (See the Notes section for a more detailed discussion of the term.) I use the terms autotelic and flow-prone as synonyms in this chapter. When I write about autotelic or flow-prone individuals, I mean individuals who experience flow relatively easily and frequently.

Well, then, what are the common attributes of flow-prone people? Which personality traits influence whether you are more or less able to experience flow? That's what we're going to find out in this chapter.

The "Official" Seven

In 2018, a group of researchers suggested seven personality traits said to make up the core of the autotelic personality: (1) curiosity, (2) persistence, (3) low self-centeredness, (4) intrinsic motivation, (5) enjoyment and transformation of boredom, (6) enjoyment and transformation of challenges, and (7) attentional control.[5] These are believed to be the most important traits influencing a person's ability to experience flow. A person who possesses many or all of these attributes is expected to experience flow easily.

To test this assumption, the researchers created a self-report questionnaire with 26 items designed to measure the seven attributes. The questionnaire is called the *Autotelic Personality Questionnaire*, or *APQ*. Initial studies have shown that scores on the APQ do a good job of predicting both flow proneness and satisfaction in life: Individuals who score high on the APQ tend to report more flow and greater life satisfaction than individuals who score low.[6]

Imagine giving two people the APQ and then asking them to perform a task. With the results of the APQ, you can predict who will experience the most flow. Those who score high on the seven autotelic personality variables will experience more flow than those who score low. The former will also typically report higher well-being and life satisfaction than the latter.

In the coming pages, we'll have a closer look at the seven attributes. If you feel like you don't possess these personality traits, don't despair. Personality is malleable, and we'll learn plenty of ways to become more flow-prone in Part 3 of the book.

1. Curiosity and Interest in Life

Autotelic individuals are curious. They tend to possess a natural interest in solving problems and are often driven to understand how the world works. They generally enjoy learning and exploring.

How does this relate to flow? If you're curious, you are easily fascinated, which helps you get involved and absorbed in activities quickly. With your attention locked on the respective object of interest, you forget about yourself and your problems. You lose touch of time. And with relatively little effort on your part, you find yourself in flow. If, on the other hand, you lack curiosity and find nothing particularly interesting or fascinating, you often find yourself bored and left with self-conscious concerns. All things being equal, the highly curious are more likely to experience flow than the less curious.

2. Persistence

Flow-prone individuals are persistent. They endure when the going gets tough. Instead of throwing in the towel, they roll up their sleeves and persevere.

Flow is sometimes preceded by a period of frustration. As a long-distance runner, you may go through pain and exhaustion before experiencing runner's high. As a writer, you may go through agony and irritation—I'm speaking from experience here—before experiencing writer's high. Persistence facilitates flow by allowing you to push through the discomfort that sometimes shows up right before flow. If you lack that persistence, you will give up too early and thus forfeit your chances of experiencing flow.

A 2008 study illustrates the point.[7] Upon arriving at the lab, participants filled out a questionnaire measuring their so-called *task-related action orientation*, a personality variable that "reflects the ability to stay in an action-oriented mode when engaged in a task, to effectively maintain focus on an activity, and to persevere until the task is complete."[8] After filling out the questionnaire, participants were randomly assigned to one of three game conditions and asked to play Tetris for eight minutes. After playing, subjects completed a questionnaire to assess how much flow they experienced.

The three game conditions were:

- A boredom condition (low task demands; skills > demands)
- An adaptive condition (task demands automatically and continuously adapted to participants' level of skill; skill = demands)
- An overload condition (very high task demands; skill < demands)

The researchers expected those playing the game under the adaptive condition—the one that always provided an optimal challenge-skills balance—to experience more flow. This is exactly what they found. None of the participants in the boredom or overload groups got into flow. The game was either too easy or too hard. Participants in the adaptive condition, however, consistently got into flow, and those who scored highest on persistence reported the most flow. All things being equal, the persistent are more likely to experience flow than the less persistent.

3. Low Self-Centeredness

Autotelic individuals score low on self-centeredness, which is defined here as "occupation with thoughts of one's image." They are not overly aware of and sensitive to the attention and opinion of others. They are not preoccupied with how others might perceive their appearance or behaviors.

Self-centeredness gets in the way of flow because it interferes with the loss of self-consciousness that is characteristic of flow. If you're unable to turn off the "me" centers in your brain (see chapter 9), you can't let it rip. You have a hard time getting out of your own way. Instead of fully engaging with the task in front of you and getting absorbed in the doing, you find yourself stuck in your head. Your attention is used up by worries and self-centered concerns. Attention is focused inwardly instead of outwardly; it's self-focused instead of task-focused attention. If, on the other hand, you are free from excessive concerns about the opinions of others, you can put your attention on the outside world, can fully engage with life, and can get absorbed in whatever you're doing with relative ease. All things being equal, those who are less self-centered are better positioned to experience flow than those who are more self-centered.

4. Intrinsic Motivation

Intrinsic motivation is the tendency to engage in activities because you find them interesting, challenging, and enjoyable, whereas extrinsic motivation is the tendency to engage in activities because of activity-unrelated factors such as anticipation of rewards (e.g., money, prestige, power, or admiration), surveillance, pressure, or competition.

Flow-prone individuals tend to be highly intrinsically motivated. They are attracted by the innate qualities of activities themselves rather than the extrinsic rewards they provide down the line. They play chess primarily to enjoy the game rather than to win money, attain a competitive ranking in the chess world, or achieve some other outside goal. They are interested in things for their own sake, not in order to gain something or enhance the self. They tend to engage in activities because they genuinely want to, not because they feel pressured or otherwise feel like they should or have to.

The two forms of motivation have different effects on our attention, thoughts, and emotions, and that's why they have a different influence on flow. When you're intrinsically motivated, you are naturally fascinated by and drawn to activities. Your attention easily and effortlessly fuses with the task, and, with relatively little effort required on your part, you achieve the total involvement and absorption of flow. Because you are genuinely motivated to engage in the respective activity and find it deeply rewarding and enjoyable, you experience few conflicting thoughts and desires. You experience inner harmony, excitement, enthusiasm, and curiosity—all aspects supportive of flow. When you're extrinsically motivated, you must put your attention on the task more forcefully, requiring greater effort and leading to more strain. You experience more flow-disrupting thoughts concerning the utility and results of your time investment. You also suffer from greater stress and negativity due to conflicting desires—deep inside, you may wish to be doing something else.

Intrinsic motivation is much more conducive to flow than extrinsic motivation.[9] All things being equal, those who are more intrinsically motivated are more likely to experience flow than those who are more extrinsically motivated.

Clarifications:

- Nobody is purely intrinsically or extrinsically motivated. Even a person who is usually primarily intrinsically motivated can sometimes be extrinsically motivated, depending on the activity and situational characteristics. Your level of both forms of motivation vary across situations and time.

- Intrinsic and extrinsic motivation are states that can change quickly. For example, feeling pressured, evaluated, micro-managed, surveilled, or controlled can turn off intrinsic motivation and promote extrinsic motivation. As I've mentioned, some environments are more conducive to flow than others. In this case, environments that promote intrinsic motivation are more conducive to flow than those who promote extrinsic motivation.

- It's entirely possible to begin an activity with primarily extrinsic motivation but to then find the experience so satisfying that one continues for and experiences the activity as deeply intrinsically rewarding. In fact, that's precisely what happens when we experience flow: The activity becomes a reward in itself.

- Interesting fact: According to Csikszentmihalyi and others, having frequent flow experiences is the very thing that creates intrinsic motivation in the long run. You may start off playing the guitar with the idea of impressing others. As you keep practicing month after month, however, you find yourself enjoying the actual playing more and more until you reach a point where you will play just for the sake of it. You will reach the point where you are no longer primarily interested in the extrinsic rewards (impressing others) but the intrinsic ones (the sheer joy of playing the instrument).

5. Enjoyment and Transformation of Boredom

Autotelic individuals are good at enjoying and transforming boredom. This ability is sometimes called *boredom coping*, which can be defined as "a disposition to relate to and perform potentially boring tasks in such a way as to make them more intrinsically rewarding."[10]

Let me give you a personal example to illustrate the point. A while ago, I participated in a lab experiment at the University of Bern, Switzerland. For three hours, I sat in front of a computer and indicated on hundreds of trials whether a line appearing in my peripheral vision was straight, bent to the left, or bent to the right. It was a tedious and repetitive task. My experience was marked by feelings of boredom and watching the clock. My girlfriend participated in the same study; she sat on the same chair, in front of the same computer, doing the same task. Only her experience was decidedly different. She wasn't nearly as bored. In fact, she reported enjoying the task. And this isn't an isolated finding. When faced with mundane tasks, I tend to get bored much more quickly and easily than her. She is able to enjoy and get absorbed in activities that induce boredom in me. Considering only this aspect of personality, it's clear that she's more flow-prone than me. All things being equal, those who are better at coping with boredom are more likely to experience flow than those who are worse at it.

6. Enjoyment and Transformation of Challenges

Flow-prone individuals enjoy difficulty. They relish a proper challenge. They get a kick out of being stretched to the limits of their abilities and tend to perform well under adverse circumstances. Situations that overwhelm others and that make them tense up in anxiety and falter under pressure, are the kind of situations autotelic persons are able to transform into flow.

If you're able to concentrate and get involved in an activity despite difficulties, and you tend to interpret stressful situations as challenging rather than threatening, you're clearly more likely to experience flow than if you have a tendency to get easily overwhelmed and anxious. All things being equal, those who are better at enjoying and transforming challenges are more likely to experience flow than their peers.

Csikszentmihalyi once said: "The traits that mark an autotelic personality are most clearly revealed by people who seem to enjoy situations that ordinary persons would find unbearable."[11] Flow-prone individuals are able to enjoy and transform both boring and challenging situations.

7. Attentional Control

Autotelic individuals are good at controlling their attention. They can shield their attention from distractions and stay focused for extended periods. They are able to direct their attention away from self-conscious, anxiety-provoking, and other distracting thoughts and stimuli. They are able to concentrate so fully that they lose track of time and get absorbed in the action. And they are able to wield this kind of control over their attention with relative ease, efficiency, and little effort.

Given that focused attention is one of the hallmarks of flow, it's obvious why this ability matters. If you find it difficult to concentrate on the task at hand, you either can't enter flow at all, or you can't stay in flow for a meaningful amount of time. Csikszentmihalyi went as far as to say that attentional disorders "effectively rule out the possibility of experiencing flow."[12] He gave the example of a schizophrenic unable to keep things either in or out of consciousness. The person attends indiscriminately to everything and, as a result, can't ever stay focused on just one thing. In this person's own words: "Things are coming in too fast. I lose my grip of it and get lost. I am attending to everything at once and as a result I do not really attend to anything." All things being equal, the person who is able to control their attention easily and efficiently is far more likely to experience flow than the person who struggles to control their attention.

Additional Aspects of the Autotelic Personality

I've referred to the seven traits discussed so far as "official" because they're measured with the APQ. However, they are not the only traits that have been shown to influence a person's ability to experience flow. At the time of this writing, more than 30 traits have been identified, and the list is growing rapidly.[13] In the following section, I'll share nine additional traits with you.

Before we discuss these traits, I would like to point out that most of the research on flow and personality is correlational at this point. When things are correlated (i.e., related or associated), this simply means they tend to go together. For example, as we're about to see, optimism and flow proneness are positively correlated. This means that people who score high on optimism tend to score high on flow proneness. We can also say it the other way around: People who score high on flow proneness, on average, score high on optimism. But it's just a correlation, and a correlation doesn't say anything about the directionality of the relationship. We can't say for sure if optimism causes more frequent flow or if frequent flow makes people more optimistic. Either one could be true, or both. In the coming pages, I'll argue that the traits make flow more likely; just know that from a strictly scientific perspective, this is speculative. With that caveat out of the way, let's dive deeper into the autotelic personality.

Neuroticism

Neuroticism can be defined as the tendency to experience anxiety, worry, self-doubt, and other negative states. People with high levels of neuroticism are usually highly self-conscious, respond poorly to stressors, interpret ordinary situations as threatening, and can experience even minor frustrations as hopelessly overwhelming.

The trait is negatively correlated with flow proneness.[14] People who score high on neuroticism tend to experience relatively infrequent flow. That's because anxiety, worries, self-doubts, high levels of self-consciousness, and poor stress tolerance all get in the way of flow. All things being equal, low neurotics are more likely to experience flow than high neurotics.

Conscientiousness

Conscientiousness can be defined as the tendency to be organized, responsible, hard-working, goal-directed, and to follow rules and norms.[15] Conscientious individuals are generally self-disciplined, motivated, and driven. They score high on intrinsic motivation, life satisfaction, and overall well-being.

Unlike neuroticism, conscientiousness is consistently positively correlated with flow proneness.[16] People who score high on conscientiousness tend to experience flow frequently. Why is that? It's because they possess the motivation, work ethic, discipline, and positivity to pursue the kind of challenging activities that potentially lead to flow. They're also able to continually work hard and increase their skills; because flow happens more readily and intensely in activities characterized by both high challenge and high skill, this confers an advantage. All things being equal, the highly conscientious have an edge over their less conscientious peers.

Anxiety and its Interpretation

Anxiety refers to both a transient state and a relatively stable trait. The *state* of anxiety is characterized by feelings of tension, apprehension, nervousness, and worry, and by activation and arousal of the body. The *trait* refers to individual differences in how easily and frequently states of anxiety are experienced. People with high trait anxiety tend to experience the state of anxiety more frequently and intensely than those with low trait anxiety; the more trait-anxious an individual is, the more likely they are to experience intense states of anxiety in stressful situations.

Flow-prone individuals tend to score low on trait anxiety.[17] Put differently, anxious people tend to experience less flow than their more relaxed and calm peers. I see two main reasons for this. First, the highly anxious are less likely to enter certain potential flow situations. That's because anxiety leads to avoidance. The socially anxious, for example, may decline public speaking opportunities or interview requests—two activities that generate flow for some people—and thus forfeit their chances of experiencing flow in those situations. More importantly, though, once the highly anxious do find themselves in potential flow situations, they find it harder than others to enter and sustain a flow state. Why? Because they struggle to get out of their way. They can't let it rip. The constant worrying prevents the involvement, engagement, absorption, and complete focus necessary for flow. The highly anxious have a hard time making the switch from self-focused to task-focused attention. They struggle to turn off the worry and self-consciousness centers in their brains. All things being equal, those who experience less anxiety are more likely to experience flow than those who experience more anxiety.

That being said, there's another variable at play here. Researchers have found that, yes, autotelic individuals experience less frequent and intense anxiety. However, they have also found that when autotelic individuals *do* experience anxiety, they are able to interpret their symptoms as facilitative rather than debilitative to their performance.[18] For less autotelic individuals, they have found the opposite pattern. Typical anxiety symptoms include bodily sensations like sweaty palms, a racing heart, jitters, butterflies in the stomach, the body feeling tight and tense, but also anxious thoughts and concerns about what might or might not happen. A facilitative interpretation of such symptoms could be: "My body is getting ready to perform. The adrenaline is flowing. This is good. I'm excited. I'm pumped. This will help me rise to the occasion." A debilitative interpretation could be: "Uh oh, I'm getting nervous. This isn't good. I'm too aroused. I'm thinking too much. I can't perform like this. I need to calm down." The first type of interpretation is more conducive to flow than the second.

Self-Confidence

The word confidence comes from the Latin word "fidere," which means "to trust." Self-confidence means trusting yourself. It entails self-assurance in your ability and judgment and a positive belief that you can generally accomplish what you wish to do. It's both a trait and a state. Self-confidence is inversely related to anxiety. While the two aren't mutually exclusive—it's theoretically possible to have high confidence and high anxiety or low confidence and low anxiety—their relationship is typically characterized like a seesaw: Those who are highly anxious tend to be low on confidence; those who are highly confident tend to be low on anxiety.

We would therefore expect confident people to experience more flow, which is exactly what researchers find.[19] Those with greater self-confidence consistently experience more flow than their less confident peers. It's a very robust finding. Confidence is one of the most important personality variables when it comes to flow.

This can be explained via the two mechanisms mentioned earlier. First, confidence makes you more likely to enter potential flow situations. While a demanding situation creates a sense of threat and apprehension if you're anxious, it triggers a sense of challenge and excitement if you're confident. So, if you're self-confident, you'll put yourself in more potential flow situations. Second, confidence makes it more likely that you'll rise to the occasion. Feeling calm, collected, at ease, and full of self-trust, you're able to turn off the worry centers in your brain and "let it rip." You feel optimistic, excited, strong, and in control. If you're anxious, on the other hand, you'll feel intimidated, overwhelmed, and nervous. Flooded with negative thoughts, you'll have a hard time experiencing the necessary engagement, focus, and absorption so characteristic of flow.

Anxiety makes you choke; self-confidence makes you flow. All things being equal, the confident are more likely to experience flow than the less confident.

Consider the following statement by an elite golfer about the kind of confidence that facilitates flow for him: "The confidence that I had in my own game . . . and the belief that I could play any shot when required, brings you to a point where you walk on the first tee and I shake your hand and look you in the eye and say 'play well today,' in the full knowledge that . . . I know that you know that I'm going to beat you. . . . That's exactly what the zone is."[20]

Optimism

Optimists expect good things to happen; pessimists expect bad things to happen. It's a simple difference that matters big time. People who score high on optimism report higher overall quality of life and well-being, experience less depression and anxiety, cope better with stress, take more action in the face of adversity, and exert more effort toward their goals.[21] Optimistic sports teams and athletes perform at higher levels, optimistic salespeople generate more sales, and optimistic politicians win more elections.

Given these differences, it comes as no surprise that optimists experience more flow than pessimists.[22] Put differently, flow-prone individuals tend to score high on optimism.

How does optimism relate to flow? The mechanisms should sound familiar. If you're optimistic, you expect positive outcomes and are thus more likely to put yourself in challenging situations. If you're pessimistic, you're less likely to put yourself in the same situations. If you doubt you'll succeed, you may never give something a try in the first place. Once in the situation, having positive expectations translates into confidence and positive thoughts. If you expect to do well, you'll be in a positive mind state. You'll feel excited, strong, and capable and experience an absence of doubts, second-guesses, worries, and other processes known to interfere with flow. If, on the other hand, you expect to do poorly, you'll feel nervous and worried, will second-guess and doubt yourself, and will have a litany of negative thoughts running through your mind. You'll find it hard to concentrate and will have difficulties entering the state of flow.

Furthermore, when confronted with a challenge or setback, optimism will help you respond with confidence and persistence. You'll feel capable of overcoming the difficulty and reaching your goal in spite of it. Pessimism will make you react with doubts and hesitation and may make you withdraw effort. All things being equal, optimists are therefore more likely to experience flow than pessimists.

Mental Toughness

Mental toughness is about thriving under pressure. It can be defined as the ability to effectively deal with challenges, stressors, and pressure.[23] A longer definition reads: "It's the ability to handle situations. It's somebody who doesn't choke, doesn't go into shock, and who can stand up for what he believes. It's what someone has who handles pressures, distractions, and people trying to break their concentration. It involves focusing, discipline, self-confidence, patience, persistence, accepting responsibility without whining or excuses, visualizing, tolerating pain, and a positive approach."[24]

Mental toughness overlaps with several traits we've already discussed, including persistence, enjoyment and transformation of challenge, self-confidence, and optimism. It is, therefore, unsurprising that mental toughness is strongly positively related to flow.[25] All things being equal, the mentally tough are more likely to experience flow than the mentally sensitive.

A few things to note: Mental toughness has nothing to do with being uncaring, self-centered, or macho. The mentally tough can be just as supportive, caring, and compassionate and can function just as well in teams as others. While they are often competitive, they are often simply competitive with themselves. Women can be equally as tough as men. The opposite of mental toughness isn't mental weakness; it's mental sensitivity.

Perfectionism

When it comes to perfectionism, the devil is in the details. That's because different forms of perfectionism exist. *Positive striving perfectionism* refers to having high personal standards and a drive for excellence. *Self-critical perfectionism*, on the other hand, involves negative self-evaluations, constant concern over mistakes, and being overly self-critical when expectations aren't met. People can be high on both facets of perfectionism, or they can be high on one and low on the other, or they can be low on both.

For flow, it seems that the ideal combination is to be high on positive striving perfectionism and low on self-critical perfectionism.[26] Why would that be? The former is associated with intrinsic motivation, high effort, positive affect, and high levels of skills—these are aspects that are likely to benefit flow. The latter is associated with extrinsic motivation, negative affect, anxiety, fear of failure, and harsh self-judgment—these are aspects that are likely to get in the way of flow. For these reasons, positive striving perfectionism confers an advantage, while self-critical perfectionism confers a disadvantage when it comes to flow.

Locus of Control

Locus of control (LOC) is the degree to which people believe that they, as opposed to external forces beyond their influence, have control over the outcomes in their lives. "Locus" is Latin for *place* and refers here to the place where control over outcomes resides. This place can be believed to be either internal (believing you can control your own life) or external (believing life is controlled by outside factors, such as other people, fate, luck, or chance).

Most people possess a dominant orientation: They either believe that outcomes in their life derive primarily from their own actions (internal LOC), or they believe that outcomes derive primarily from outside influences (external LOC).[27] Individuals with a strong internal LOC tend to praise or blame themselves for success or failure, while individuals with a strong external LOC tend to assign responsibility to factors outside their influence. For those with an internal LOC, receiving a good grade is the result of hard work; for those with an external LOC, it's the result of luck or natural talent.

People with an internal LOC tend to experience more flow than those with an external LOC.[28] Why might this be? One possible explanation is that people who believe in personal control are more likely to experience the feeling of being in control, which could make flow more likely. Another explanation is that internal LOC has a positive effect on intrinsic motivation, which could indirectly lead to more flow. Either way, those who believe outcomes derive from their own actions are more likely to experience flow than those who believe outcomes derive from outside influences.

Emotional Intelligence

Emotional intelligence refers to the ability to recognize, understand, manage, and influence one's own emotions, as well as the emotions of others.[29] Emotionally intelligent individuals are good at regulating their emotions and impulses, withstanding pressure, dealing with stress, and motivating themselves. They are socially aware and possess good social skills. They are capable of taking someone else's perspective, understanding others' feelings, and communicating their feelings to others. Emotional intelligence encompasses a great number of important life skills and has been shown to be an absolute key to human flourishing. [30]

When it comes to flow, research consistently shows that flow-prone individuals score high on emotional intelligence. [31] Being emotionally intelligent helps you reduce the frequency, intensity, and duration of negative thoughts and emotions that can interfere with flow. It helps you recover from emotional upsets and helps you stay in control rather than at the mercy of your emotions. In social settings, emotional intelligence supports the kind of positive and harmonious interactions that are conducive to flow. All things being equal, the emotionally intelligent are therefore more likely to experience flow than the less emotionally intelligent. We'll return to this topic in chapter 21.

What Else?

The personality traits we've discussed so far are the ones that have most consistently been linked with flow in the research. However, still more variables have been investigated.

For example, researchers have looked at flow proneness and general intelligence (IQ), expecting to find a positive relationship between the two. But that's not what has been found so far; several studies failed to find an association between IQ and flow proneness.[32] One possible explanation is that while IQ plays a role in effortful attention, it may not be involved in the kind of effortless attention that is so characteristic of flow.

Researchers have also looked at self-esteem (a healthy sense of overall personal worth or value), grit (perseverance and passion for long-term goals), self-compassion (a compassionate relationship with oneself), mindfulness (a predisposition toward acceptance and present-moment awareness in everyday life), and self-control (the ability to control and override impulses), and have found that all of these traits are positively related to flow proneness. [33] Three other relatively well-known traits—openness to experience, agreeableness, and extraversion—have been investigated and found to be slightly positively correlated with flow.[34]

As I've mentioned, the list of personality traits related to flow is growing rapidly. It's a fascinating and rapidly expanding area of research.

Good News

If you feel that your personality is not very conducive to flow, please don't let that discourage you. You can experience plenty of flow even if you're relatively neurotic, anxious, or lacking in confidence. The picture of the autotelic personality I have portrayed here is an ideal to strive toward, not a requirement to experience flow. My own personality falls way short of what would be deemed optimal, but I still experience plenty of flow.

We now know that many aspects of personality are malleable. It's possible for us to become more persistent, conscientious, confident, optimistic, mentally tough, or emotionally intelligent. In Part 3, we'll encounter many studies that show changes in attitudes, skills, and behaviors related to flow. And we'll see that these changes lead to subsequent changes in flow proneness. Consider, for example, a 2022 study that split senior music students and active musicians into two groups: an intervention group that received online self-regulation skills training over a period of 12 weeks and a control group that received no such training.[35] At the end of the 12 weeks, the intervention group showed decreases in performance anxiety and self-consciousness and an increase in flow.

If I compare my current self with my self from ten years ago, I see definite improvements in some of the personality traits we've discussed. I'm more conscientious, emotionally intelligent, gritty, self-compassionate, mindful, and possess greater self-control. Some of these changes are simply the result of growing older, learning from experiences, and maturing. Other changes are the result of dedicated effort. Either way, change is possible. If you apply the strategies discussed in this book, I have no doubt that you'll become more flow-prone.

A Brief Summary of the Autotelic Personality

Let me sum up the personality of a highly autotelic, flow-prone individual. Such an individual is curious, persistent, low in self-centeredness, intrinsically motivated, capable of enjoying both challenging and boring situations, and good at controlling their attention.

They tend to be conscientious, self-confident, optimistic, mentally tough, emotionally intelligent, self-disciplined, mindful, self-compassionate, gritty, open to experience, agreeable, and extraverted. They score low on neuroticism and anxiety, possess healthy self-esteem and an internal locus of control, and tend to positively but not self-critically strive for perfection.

An individual with these personality traits experiences flow easily and frequently.

The Autotelic Personality

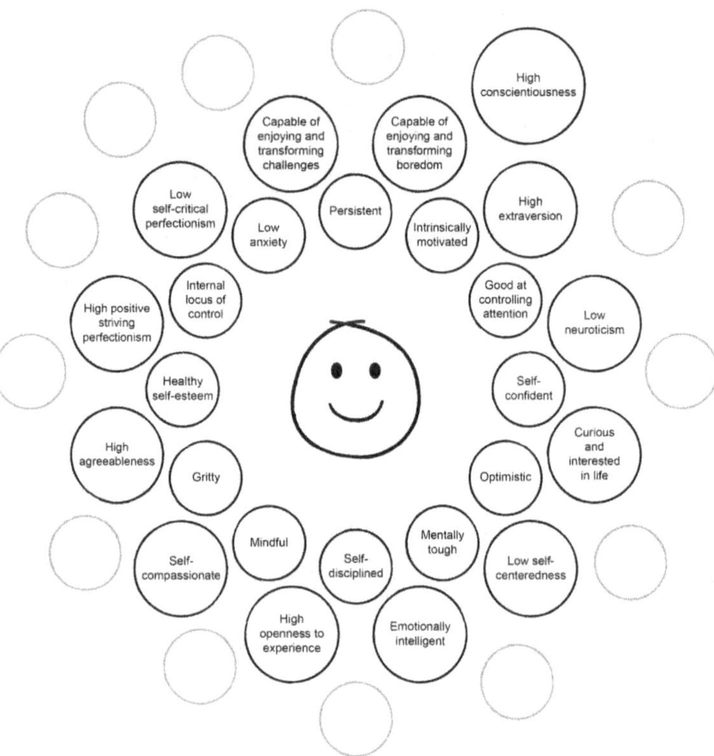

FIGURE 4: Personality variables of an autotelic, flow-prone individual.

Chapter 7

Measuring and Researching Flow

By now, you've probably realized that flow is the subject of ample and rigorous scientific research. As mentioned previously, Csikszentmihalyi himself researched flow for more than 40 years after coining the term in the mid-1970s. Nowadays, in the mid-2020s, hundreds or perhaps even thousands of researchers worldwide study the concept of flow.

Have you wondered how exactly they do this? How do they know if you're in flow or not? How do they assess your flow proneness? How do they know that confident individuals experience more flow than their less confident peers? Is there some kind of flow monitor they can put on participants' wrists to measure their level of flow? What tools and methods do they use? That's what we're about to find out. While this may perhaps sound like a dull and dry topic, it's actually quite fascinating, and it can help you understand flow even more deeply. It can also help you better interpret the many research findings presented in this book.

As of this writing, flow has been researched with four main tools: (1) interviews, (2) the Flow Questionnaire, (3) the Experience Sampling Method, and (4) modern questionnaires.[1] In this chapter, we'll discuss these methods in the chronological order that researchers developed them. Let's begin with interviews.

1. Interviews

The concept of flow emerged from Csikszentmihalyi's initial interviews described in chapter 2.[2] He learned that when people most enjoyed themselves during intrinsically motivated activities—whether during rock climbing, playing chess, dancing, or writing poetry—they all experienced a state characterized by focused concentration, intense absorption, loss of self-consciousness, a strong sense of control, distortion of time, and so on. That universal state Csikszentmihalyi then coined flow because that was the analogy many of his interviewees used to describe the experience. It was these first interviews that led to the definition and description of flow.

Interviews have always been and continue to be a crucial part of flow research. In 1995, Susan A. Jackson used interviews with elite athletes to learn about various aspects of flow in sports, including factors that help or hinder entry into the state, factors that disrupt it, degree of control over it, and more.[3] In 1999, Susan K. Perry interviewed writers regarding the most recent occasion when they were in flow while writing, asking them to describe what led up to the experience, how they dealt with blocks, and what kept them out of flow.[4] Most recently, since 2016, Christian Swann and colleagues continue to interview world-class athletes and recreational exercisers following recent flow experiences in sports or exercise.[5]

Though time-consuming, interviews are excellent for exploring new aspects of flow, such as antecedents, consequences, or experiential characteristics.

2. The Flow Questionnaire (FQ)

Once Csikszentmihalyi had come up with the definition and dimensions of flow, he and his colleagues went about designing the first questionnaire to measure the construct more rigorously. The so-called *Flow Questionnaire* (FQ) was born.[6]

The original FQ begins with three quotes describing the flow experience:

"My mind isn't wandering. I am not thinking of something else. I am totally involved in what I am doing. My body feels good. I don't seem to hear anything. The world seems to be cut off from me. I am less aware of myself and my problems."

"My concentration is like breathing, I never think of it. When I start, I really do shut out the world. I am really quite oblivious to my surroundings after I really get going. I think that the phone could ring, and the doorbell could ring or the house burn down or something like that. When I start I really do shut out the world. Once I stop I can let it back in again."

"I am so involved in what I am doing. I don't see myself as separate from what I am doing."

Participants are asked to read these quotes and indicate via a yes-or-no answer if they have ever experienced something similar. This allows classifying respondents into flow-ers (people who experience flow in their lives) and non-flow-ers (people who do not experience flow in their lives). Results consistently showed that the vast majority of people are familiar with the state of flow and experience it in their lives.

If the answer to the question, "Have you ever felt similar experiences?" is yes, the participants are then asked to indicate what activity or activities provide such experiences for them—they are asked to list their flow activities. Researchers learned that people experience flow in countless different activities across many diverse contexts.

From their list, participants are then requested to choose the activity associated with the most intense and pervasive flow experiences, referred to as their primary or predominant flow activity. They are then asked to indicate the levels of challenges and skills perceived in the activity, as well as to rate various aspects of experience on scales from 0–8 (ranging from "very little" to "very much"). Sample items include: "I am involved," "I enjoy doing this and using my skills," "I wish I could do something else."

Through the same scales, respondents are then invited to rate their average experiences associated with other activities, such as when being at work, with their family, alone, or during religious activities. Using this part of the questionnaire, researchers were able to confirm that people enjoyed themselves more, were more involved and concentrated, felt less self-conscious, and just generally had a better time during flow activities compared to other activities.

At the end of the questionnaire, a number of open-ended questions are asked, such as: How does the experience get started? What keeps it going? How does it feel? Answers to these questions provided researchers with a plethora of information regarding the antecedents and experiential characteristics of flow.

The FQ was crucial in confirming many of the findings obtained in Csikszentmihalyi's original interviews. The questionnaire also yielded excellent data on the frequency of flow across distinct contexts and activities. By administering the FQ to different cultures and demographics, researchers were also able to gauge differences in the flow experience across groups of people.

Due to its time-consuming nature in coding and analyzing the responses, the FQ is no longer widely used today. That said, a newer version of the questionnaire was, for example, administered in 2010 to 393 workers from a wide range of occupations in the United Kingdom.[7] The updated version provided participants with quotes describing deep flow as well as quotes describing shallow flow experiences (see Notes section for the quotes).[8] It was found, among other things, that a third of people reported experiencing shallow flow but not deep flow. This was expected because most of us experience low to medium levels of flow regularly throughout our everyday lives, while more intense experiences tend to be rare.

3. The Experience Sampling Method (ESM)

In-depth interviews and the FQ both had their advantages, and each played a crucial role in the initial clarification and conceptualization of the flow experience. Both, however, were also limited in that they relied on retrospective reconstruction of past experiences.

The study of flow has been so rich and popular in part because Csikszentmihalyi and colleagues came up with the *Experience Sampling Method* (ESM) that allowed them to overcome these limitations and measure flow on the spot in everyday life.[9]

Participants are equipped with paging devices (pagers, handheld computers, programmable watches, or their smartphones) that signal them, at preprogrammed times, to fill in a so-called *experience sampling form* (ESF)— a questionnaire asking them to describe various aspects of their experience at the moment they are beeped. Typically, participants are beeped eight times a day for a week, resulting in a total of 56 in-depth snapshots of everyday experience.

Each ESF contains open-ended questions as well as numerical scales. It typically starts by asking participants to indicate the date, the time they were beeped, and the time they filled in the form (which could be immediately upon beeping or a few minutes afterward). Then come questions designed to reconstruct the activity, context, and aspects of motivation and interest. Sample open-ended questions are: "What were you thinking about?" "Where were you?" "What was the main thing you were doing?"

This is complemented with questions where participants can choose from a number of available answers. For example, for the question, "Why were you doing the activity?" the options might include: (1) Because you wanted to, (2) Because you had to, (3) Because there was nothing else to do. For the question, "Who were you with?" the options might include: (1) Alone, (2) With family, (3) With friends, (4) With strangers.

The remainder of the form contains scaled items. Typically, sixteen of these are ten-point scales ranging from zero ("not at all" or "low") to nine ("very" or "high") designed to measure various elements related to the experience. Questions may include: "How challenging was the activity for you?" "How skilled would you consider yourself in this activity?" "How well were you concentrating?" "Was it hard to concentrate?"

The remaining thirteen items ask participants to rate on scales from one ("not at all") to seven ("very") how intensely they experienced various subjective feelings. These may include: "alert," "happy," "strong," "lonely," "anxious," "involved," "creative," or "relaxed."

The exact format of the ESF can vary from study to study. Questions can be removed or added. Wordings and scales can be tweaked (e.g., scale going from 0–12 instead of 0–9). In general, though, the outline and content remain similar to what I just described.

The ESM yields a huge amount of data on people's experiences in everyday life. Each data point can be connected to flow, allowing researchers to create an incredibly detailed picture of how and when flow occurs, what it feels like, what effects it has, and much more. It can be seen, for example, whether people are more likely to experience flow when alone or with people, at work or during leisure, while watching television or playing sports. It can be seen how frequently people experience flow, which activities produce the state most consistently and intensely, or what thoughts people think prior to or during flow. When discussing the contexts of flow in chapter 8, we will rely heavily on findings obtained via ESM studies.

First, however, we need to clarify how flow is defined in these studies. Which of the ~30 data points obtained in each ESF is used as the measure of flow? Is it the intensity of positive feelings (how happy, alert, and cheerful a participant felt)? Or the amount and effortlessness of concentration? Or the degree of control experienced? Or the lack of self-consciousness? Or a combination of all these? Let me explain.

In the original ESM studies, the metric used to measure flow was the challenge-skills balance (each ESF asks participants to indicate how challenging the respective activity is and how skilled the person is in this activity). According to the theoretical model at the time, flow was thought to occur whenever challenges and skills were in balance (Figure 2 in chapter 3). In the studies, therefore, participants were defined as having been in flow during an activity when both items were given the same numerical value; for example, when both challenges and skills were rated as zero, when both were rated as nine, and so on.

Because it was expected that this balance would coincide with the flow experience, it was also expected that it would correlate with other positive aspects of experience measured in the ESF, such as how happy, strong, motivated, and concentrated one felt. However, when Csikszentmihalyi and co. analyzed the first thousands of self-reports generated through the ESM, their prediction was not confirmed. People did not feel more alert, more motivated, more strong, more in control, and less self-conscious when challenges and skills were in balance.

These findings puzzled and frustrated Csikszentmihalyi and co. for years until a breakthrough occurred in 1985. Italian flow researchers Fausto Massimi and Massimo Carli proposed that flow happens only when challenges and skills are in balance and are above a certain level. If both are low, they postulated, the experience would be one of apathy, as illustrated in their revised model of flow, the so-called *Quadrant Model of Flow* (Figure 5).

With the reformulation of the model in this way, flow was defined as a state in which a participant reported challenges and skills greater than the weekly average and in relative balance with each other.

When flow was defined in this way, the ESM data fell beautifully in line with the theoretical predictions.[10] People reported the most positive states when challenges and skills were balanced and above their average levels for the week. Participants felt happier, stronger, more in control, involved, creative, free, active, open, clear, motivated, excited, and satisfied when both challenges and skills were in balance and above average.

The Quadrant Model was later updated to the Octant Model (see chapter 4) in an attempt to provide a more accurate and realistic picture of everyday experience. The updated model provides a narrower definition of flow and a more detailed characterization of non-flow states.

Studies using the ESM with either the Quadrant or Octant Model yielded rich and robust findings and contributed greatly to our understanding of flow. It should be noted, however, that these models are not without critics.[11]

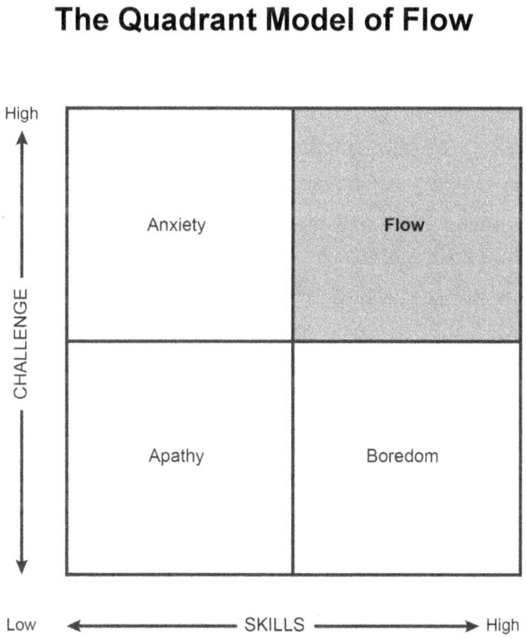

The Quadrant Model of Flow

FIGURE 5: The Quadrant Model of Flow. It splits everyday experience into four quadrants depending on the level of challenge and skill involved in an activity. When researchers updated to this model, the ESM data fell in line with expectations from flow theory. The model was later updated to the Octant Model (see Figure 3 in chapter 4). Adapted from Csikszentmihalyi and LeFevre (1989).[12]

While the ESM method was the primary research paradigm in the 1980s, it has since largely been replaced by more modern and far less resource-intensive questionnaires. That said, researchers still occasionally conduct ESM studies. Depending on the research goal, they vary the paging schedule, length of study, experience sampling form, and even the way flow is measured.

To give an example, a 2016 study used the ESM to collect data from 100 employees in different professions.[13] They beeped participants seven times a day for a week, resulting in a total of 4,504 measurements. Instead of measuring flow as an above-average challenge-skill balance, they measured it in all its components with scaled items (see next section for an explanation). Their findings confirmed the so-called *paradox of work*, which we'll discuss in chapter 8: Participants experienced more flow at work than at leisure but at the same time indicated a preference for leisure rather than work activities.

4. Modern Questionnaires

The next addition to flow research were the more typical questionnaires consisting solely of numerical scales. They differ from the previous two methods (FQ and ESM) in that they are far less time-consuming for researchers and participants. They also measure flow differently and are primarily used to gauge intensity rather than frequency or prevalence of flow.

While several scales exist, the two most prominent and frequently used are the *Flow State Scale-2* (FFS-2), which measures the intensity of flow as a state, and the *Dispositional Flow Scale-2* (DFS-2), which measures the intensity of flow as either a broad or a domain-specific trait (how frequently and intensely a person tends to experience flow across a wide range of situations or in specific contexts).[14]

Both scales consist of 36 5-point items ranging from "strongly disagree" to "strongly agree," designed to measure each of the nine components of flow (each component is tapped by four items). The main difference between the two lies in the instructions given to participants. The state questionnaire asks respondents to answer the questions in regard to a specific activity they just completed. The trait questionnaire asks respondents to answer the questions in regard to their general experience across situations and times or in regard to their average experience when engaged in a context of activity (e.g., at work or during leisure).

Sample items of the state questionnaire include: "It is really clear to me how my performance is going," "My attention was focused entirely on what I was doing," "I found the experience extremely rewarding."

Sample items of the trait questionnaire include: "I am not concerned with how others may be evaluating me," "I lose my normal awareness of time," "I have a sense of control over what I am doing."

By measuring all nine components of the experience (the three conditions and six experiential characteristics), these and similar questionnaires reveal something about the intensity of a participant's flow experience. If someone scores high on all the nine components of flow on the state questionnaire, that person experienced a very intense, deep, or macro flow state. If the person scores high on some aspects but medium or low on others, his or her state will have been less intense, describing a shallow or micro flow experience.

By measuring the intensity of flow during a single episode (e.g., during a competition or an important exam), researchers can gauge the effects of flow on performance. They might find that those who scored high on the nine components of flow, on average, also scored higher in the competition or on the exam. By administering other questionnaires alongside, they can see how flow correlates with other metrics. For example, they might see that those who scored high on flow also scored high on confidence and self-belief.

Similar insights can be gained with the trait questionnaire. Researchers might learn, for example, that those who tend to generally experience a high level of flow during studying also tend to score higher on exams, on average.

Using such correlational approaches is how flow is most prominently studied these days. Researchers correlate questionnaires of flow with questionnaires of other constructs of interest. This way, flow can be related to various personality traits, attitudes, behaviors, or performance measures.

The correlational nature means that these findings should be taken with a grain of salt. Just because there is a positive correlation between flow and performance doesn't mean flow causes performance improvements. Just because there is a correlation between flow and confidence doesn't mean flow causes people to be more confident or that confidence causes people to experience more flow.

Newest Developments

All measurement methods discussed so far are limited in that they rely solely on asking people about their experiences. The trouble is that such self-report measures are always flawed to some degree. Human perception is biased. Our memories of the past (near and distant) are half-truths rather than accurate recollections of what happened. Our explanations for what happened and why are inaccurate and biased as well.

Thanks to technological advances, new measures of flow are able to add objective markers to the subjective reports given by participants. This allows us to create a fuller and more accurate picture of the flow experience. Studies using such technology have been conducted for a while and will only become more prevalent.

In lab studies in 2008 and 2010, for example, researchers investigated physiological markers of flow during music performance.[15] They found unique patterns of heart rate, blood pressure, heart rate variability, depth of breathing, and facial muscle activation when professional musicians experienced flow. Similar studies using brain scan techniques found unique brain region activation patterns during flow.

In general, such studies find that the physiological and neurological markers line up nicely with people's subjective experiences. Brain regions related to effortless concentration become more active; those related to time processing and self-consciousness become less active. Facial muscles related to smiling and enjoyment become more active; those related to frowning become less active. We'll return to some of these findings in chapter 9, in which we'll discuss the brain and body in flow.

I hope you've enjoyed this brief look at the different methods through which flow is investigated. In the next chapter, we'll continue to discuss the many findings these methods have generated. We'll turn specifically to the contexts of flow. We'll see when and where people most frequently and intensely experience flow.

Chapter 8

Activities and Contexts of Flow

Old Korean women enter the flow state when reading the Bible, when knitting, or when cooking an elaborate dinner; the Australian sailors when their boat loses sight of the shore; the young Japanese when their motorcycles begin to rumble in unison. The old Walse mountaineers seem to find it in almost every detail of their daily lives, whereas their children need special leisure activities and entertainments to experience it. . . . [E]very activity including work, child care, and study can produce the focused well-being that is characteristic of flow.[1]

—*MIHALY CSIKSZENTMIHALYI*

At this point, we know how flow is defined, its conditions and experiential characteristics, how it's measured and researched, and much more. In this chapter, we address the following question: Where does flow show up in our lives? In what activities and contexts do we experience flow?

The main tool for tackling this question is the experience sampling method (ESM) discussed in the previous chapter. ESM studies often generate thousands of self-reports containing information about where a person was, what they were doing, and if they were in flow or not. This allows researchers to compare the frequency of flow in different activities and contexts.

To get an idea of how ESM data are analyzed and interpreted, we'll first look at two sample studies that used this method. We'll then look at general findings derived from many such studies and make conclusions regarding the frequency of flow across various activities and contexts.

We begin with a study from the mid-1980s that used the ESM to examine flow in the everyday life of 47 Italian students aged 16 to 19.[2] The study collected a total of 1,682 self-reports and used the challenge-skills balance as the measure of flow: When participants indicated high skills and high challenges, the researchers counted that data point as an instance of flow. When participants indicated high skills but low challenges, then the researchers counted that data point as an instance of boredom, and so on.[3]

	Flow	Boredom	Anxiety	Apathy
Art and hobbies	**47.2**	20.8	28.3	3.8
Socializing	**32.2**	24.5	31.5	11.7
Sport and games	**26.3**	36.8	31.6	5.3
Reading	**24.6**	34.8	24.6	15.9
Classwork	**23.8**	20.1	37.2	18.8
Studying	**23.7**	22.2	37.4	16.7
Transportation	**19.2**	41.1	17.8	21.9
Thinking	**18.2**	21.4	36.5	23.9
Chore and errands	**16.1**	54.0	10.3	19.5
Listening music	**11.8**	17.6	52.9	17.6
Other leisure	**10.8**	41.5	20.0	27.7
Rest and napping	**10.5**	44.7	13.2	31.6
Eating	**9.9**	56.0	7.7	26.4
Personal care	**3.5**	69.4	7.1	20.0
TV watching	**2.8**	45.8	12.1	39.3

TABLE 1: Distribution of activities in four buckets (flow, boredom, anxiety, and apathy) defined by the challenge/skills ratio. The data show how consistently an activity is associated with flow. The data also show how conducive to flow the different activities are in relation to one another.

Table 1 shows the average quality of experience associated with the 15 main activities reported by the teenagers. By looking at the flow column, we immediately see that some activities are more conducive to flow than others. The activities most reliably associated with flow are "art and hobbies" (47.2%), "socializing" (32.2%), "sport and games" (26.3%), "reading" (24.6%), "classwork" (23.8%), and "studying" (23.7%). Students experience flow quite frequently when engaged in these activities. In contrast, students rarely experience flow while "TV watching" (2.8%), during "personal care" (3.5%), or when "eating" (9.9%). These activities are not conducive to flow. Instead, they mostly result in boredom or apathy.

We also see that activities don't always produce the same experience. Each activity can be experienced as flowy, boring, anxiety-producing, or apathy-producing. Even "TV watching" and "personal care" can occasionally bring forth flow-like experiences, and even "art and hobbies" and "sport and games" can occasionally result in apathy.

Let's move on to the second study.[4] The study was published in 2016 and collected data from 100 German employees with different professions (including staffers, research assistants, scientists, secretaries, technical staff, students, and others). The average age was 39. Participants were beeped seven times per day, between 8:30 a.m. and 9 p.m., for an entire week. In this case, flow was measured with a scale similar to the Flow State Scale-2 described in the previous chapter. Flow values ranged from 1 to 7, with low scores indicating zero or mild experience of flow and high scores indicating intense experience of flow. The experience sampling forms also measured *positive* and *negative activation.* The former refers to how energetic, wide awake, elated, and highly motivated you feel; the latter refers to how stressed, annoyed, nervous, and worried you feel.

The researchers coded all activities into four main categories (Table 2) and various subcategories (Table 3, discussed later). As far as the main categories are concerned, participants spent 35% of their time on work activities, 20% on active leisure activities, 10% on passive leisure, and 36% on obligations. (I'm aware that these percentages add up to more than 101%; I'm simply reporting the numbers provided in the study.) The average flow score was highest when working (5.28), followed by active leisure (5.20), obligations (4.71), and passive leisure (4.33). This is a pattern observed across many studies, regardless of how flow is measured: People tend to experience the most flow when working or in active leisure activities and the least flow in passive leisure. I'll give possible reasons for this pattern in a bit.

That's it for the two sample studies. I hope they have given you a better understanding of how ESM data can be analyzed and interpreted and what the results can look like. Next up, we discuss the major findings this research has produced in regard to activities and contexts. Where do people most reliably find flow?

	N	%	Flow	Positive activation	Negative activation
Working	1,577	35	**5.28**	4.97	3.01
Active leisure	888	20	**5.20**	4.88	2.45
Passive leisure	455	10	**4.33**	3.66	2.34
Obligations	1,556	36	**4.71**	4.40	2.91

TABLE 2: Frequency of activities/categories and average flow scores. (N indicates the total number of data points in a category. % is the percentage of that—35% means that in 35% of cases when participants were beeped, they were engaged in that activity/category. Positive activation is a measure of how energetic, wide awake, elated, and highly motivated someone feels. Negative activation is a measure of how stressed, annoyed, nervous, and worried someone feels.)

Flow at Work

ESM studies consistently reveal two major findings concerning people's experiences on the job.[5] First, people experience plenty of flow at work. In fact, most studies show that people experience more flow at work than at leisure.

Second, despite experiencing a lot of flow, people at work frequently express the wish to be doing something else. (Remember that experience sampling forms ask people, *Do you wish you had been doing something else?* Possible answers range from "not at all" to "very much" on a Likert scale.) This is true not only when they are beeped during routine, mundane, objectively boring, low-challenge, and low-skill activities but even when beeped during their core work activities—even when participants are working on their favorite task, when challenges and skills are both high, when they are feeling confident, in control, alert, and focused, they still frequently indicate that they would rather be doing something else.

This phenomenon has been labeled the *work paradox*: Despite having some of their best experiences on the job, people still indicate that they would rather be somewhere else, doing something else. This has been found across a wide range of professions, including assembly-line workers, white-collar workers, professional rescuers, managers, and high school teachers.

What's going on here? How can we make sense of this paradox?

One possible explanation by Csikszentmihalyi is that people judge their experiences by social conventions rather than by their feelings.[6] Work is generally associated with duty, constraint, and boredom. We *have to* work to earn a living; fun, freedom, and self-actualization happen elsewhere. Even though work provides plenty of enjoyment and meaning, our mind overrides the positive experience by pointing out its obligatory nature.

Another explanation is that the question itself—*Do you wish you had been doing something else?*—makes people think of an even more enjoyable activity. Sure, they may enjoy their current work activity, but they might enjoy their favorite leisure activities even more. The experience sampling form itself could thus be misleading and contribute to the paradox.

One final explanation is that while work provides flow and is indeed enjoyable, it is also frequently accompanied by negative elements, such as stress, time pressure, performance anxiety, fear of failure, lack of freedom, worry, or fatigue. It might be these negative factors that overshadow the otherwise so often positive experience. The 2016 German study confirmed this last hypothesis. The researchers found that both flow and positive activation were highest at work. But they also found that negative activation was highest at work (Table 2). When participants indicate wanting to do something else, they may think of active leisure activities that provide flow without the negative elements present at work.

What about the finding that flow is higher at work than at leisure? Two main explanations stand out. First, many jobs offer excellent conditions for flow to occur: structured activities, clear goals, feedback, social interactions, and challenges that match the employee's skills. Concentration is often relatively high at work. Autonomy, feelings of being in control, and a sense of pride and accomplishment are also readily accessible in many professional environments. Second, work may provide more flow because many of us are unable to structure our leisure time in flow-conducive ways. We may rely too heavily on passive activities like watching television, listening to music, or otherwise consuming media. As we're about to see, such activities don't usually bring forth flow.

To sum up, flow is generally a frequent occurrence at work. Of course, some jobs (and some tasks) are more conducive to flow than others. For example, one study showed that managers and engineers experience more flow at work than assembly-line or clerical workers.[7] But still, even less popular jobs provide plenty of opportunities for flow.

Flow at Leisure

In comparison to work, leisure comes with both more opportunities and more risks.[8] On the one hand, leisure is when many of us have our most intense flow experiences. These happen in activities like dancing, singing, playing musical instruments, exercising, playing computer games, doing crafts, or long-distance running. Think hobbies, sports, games, creative and artistic endeavors; activities we are skilled in, that challenge us, and that we pursue voluntarily.

On the other hand, leisure is also when many of us succumb to boredom, apathy, anxiety, depression, addiction, and other mental disturbances. Being alone with nothing to do can be hard. As we'll see in chapter 9, the mind, in such cases, defaults to mind wandering, and the places it wanders to are often bleak and dark. We may find ourselves grappling with feelings of inadequacy, guilt, remorse, or sadness. To escape from these uncomfortable feelings, we may then resort to binge-watching Netflix, frantically checking social media, gambling, getting drunk, taking drugs, or anything else of that nature. Free time is a double-edged sword.

When examining leisure and flow, researchers often make the distinction between active and passive leisure. In study after study, across age groups and demographics, the finding is always the same: Active leisure is far more exciting, enjoyable, and flow-promoting than its passive counterpart. In the study with Italian teenagers, "TV watching" was associated with flow only 2.3% of the time and "listening music" only 11.8% of the time. "Art and hobbies," in stark contrast, were associated with flow almost 50% of the time, "socializing" 32.3%, "sport and games" 26.3%, and "reading" 24.6% of the time.

The passive activities simply don't provide the conditions for flow to happen. They involve almost no skills. They don't challenge or stretch us. They don't require effort or concentration. And they certainly don't make us feel strong and alert, confident, and fully alive. That doesn't mean these activities have no right to exist. They do. But when it comes to flow, they don't do the trick.

Within the subcategory of active leisure, the most flow-conducive activities tend to fall into the realm of games, sports, artistic and creative activities, and just generally hobbies of all kinds. In the 2016 German study, flow was highest in the subcategories "creative active" (5.72), "sport/exercise" (5.52), and "mental active" (5.29; Table 3). While the subcategories "walking" (5.09) and "affiliation and intimacy" (4.95) were less conducive to flow than their active leisure alternatives, they were still far more conducive than each of the passive leisure subcategories, "consuming" (4.35), "resting" (4.25), and "break" (4.38).

	N	%	Flow	Positive activation	Negative activation
Working					
Core work	716	16	**5.4**	5	2.97
Cooperation and communication	470	11	**5.19**	5.07	3.14
Routine	268	6	**5.01**	4.61	2.96
Planning and organizing	123	3	**5.53**	5.2	2.79
Active leisure					
Affiliation and intimacy	379	8	**4.95**	4.82	2.49
Mental active	228	5	**5.29**	4.52	2.44
Sport/exercise	107	2	**5.52**	5.52	2.66
Creative active	87	2	**5.72**	4.52	2.25
Walking	87	2	**5.09**	4.97	2.19
Passive leisure					
Consuming	272	6	**4.35**	3.75	2.38
Resting	131	3	**4.25**	3.26	2.26
Break	52	1	**4.38**	4.19	2.37
Obligations					
Housekeeping	484	11	**4.93**	4.38	3.04
Basic needs	475	11	**4.73**	4.45	2.5
Transportation	363	8	**4.44**	4.29	3.04
Routines others	125	3	**4.83**	4.74	3.18
Duties (social)	72	2	**4.76**	4.6	3.4
Waiting	37	1	**3.61**	3.65	3.36

TABLE 3: Frequency of activities and average flow scores. (N indicates the total number of data points in a category. % is the percentage of that—35% means that in 35% of cases when participants were beeped, they were engaged in that activity/category. Positive activation is a measure of how energetic, wide awake, elated, and highly motivated someone feels. Negative activation is a measure of how stressed, annoyed, nervous, and worried someone feels.)

Explanations for subcategories in Table 3:

Working

Core work – "activities that represent the main task of the respective work (e.g., data management for a technical staff)."

Cooperation and communication – "includes activities to share information with others (e.g., talking to colleagues, emails)."

Routine – "all highly repetitive work, which could be managed with basic skills only (e.g., sorting incoming post)."

Planning and organizing – "(e.g., making schedules)."

Active leisure

Affiliation and intimacy – "includes all instances of being with friends and loved ones."

Mental active – "includes activities like reading, learning a language, visiting an exhibition, and surfing in the internet."

Sport/exercise – "includes all kinds of physical activities ranging from playing golf to weight training."

Creative active – "activities like gardening, making music, or painting."

Walking – "all instances w[h]ere individuals report going for a walk alone or in the company of others or with a dog."

Passive leisure

Consuming – "includes watching television, watching a movie in the cinema, and listening to music."

Resting – "includes lying on bed/couch, taking a bath, and lounging around."

Break – "includes coffee or lunch breaks that did not have an explicit affiliative quality."

Obligations

Housekeeping – "includes activities like cleaning, cooking, and shopping for food or other daily products."

Basic needs – "eating and drinking (not explicitly affiliative in nature) and showering/bathing or otherwise preparing for the day (e.g., shaving, putting on makeup)."

Transportation – "includes car driving or riding in a car, public transportation or getting around on bike or by foot (not explicitly taking a walk or riding a bike for fun)."

Routines others – "private desk work like home banking, repairing the car, visiting the doctor's office, and preparing for travel."

Duties (social) – "taking care for children and doing work for others."

Waiting – "coded whenever the participants mentioned waiting for an upcoming event."

Affiliation and intimacy (aka socializing) deserves special attention. According to Csikszentmihalyi, it is the least predictable of all the things we do, "At one moment it is flow, the next apathy, anxiety, relaxation, or boredom."[9] On average, interacting with others is a surprisingly high-flow activity. For example, "socializing" was second in flow only to "art and hobbies" for the Italian teenagers (Table 1).

Socializing involves many elements conducive to flow. It certainly requires its fair share of skill, effort, and concentration. We have to be aware of the other person's feelings, emotions, goals, desires, and fears and cognizant of their feedback in the form of facial expressions and gestures. We have to express our own emotions and viewpoints and find the right words and phrases to do so. We have to gauge when to speak and when to listen and be cautious not to take over the conversation or rub our vis-à-vis the wrong way. We must listen carefully, attentively, and with the intention to understand. It helps if we can be vulnerable, open-minded, tolerant, confident, and relaxed rather than shy and reserved.

We don't usually think of the skills involved in interacting with others, but they are certainly there. And the more advanced these social and interpersonal skills are, the more likely we are to experience flow when interacting with others. Granted, socializing rarely produces the deep flow states experienced in some hobbies. But the frequent mild level of flow it produces is crucial in keeping our minds from descending into chronic overthinking.

What about other activities that fill our days? What about eating, cooking, cleaning, showering, shopping, driving to work, or paying the bills? These tend to produce less flow than work or active leisure but more flow than passive leisure. If you check our two sample studies, you'll find this to be true for all of them.

To sum up, leisure tends to be highly variable, much more so than work. In leisure, we experience the highest of highs, lowest of lows, and everything in between. As it relates to flow, we tend to experience high levels of flow in hobbies and other active leisure activities, low levels of flow in passive leisure activities, and mild to moderate levels of flow in most other activities that fill up our days.

The Easiest Way to Get More Flow

The goal of this book is to help you experience more flow in your life. The easiest way to make this happen is to spend more time on your hobbies. A hobby is, by definition, something you do voluntarily and for enjoyment's sake; when you pursue a hobby, you're intrinsically motivated. As we've discussed, being intrinsically motivated is highly conducive to flow, much more so than being extrinsically motivated. We've seen it in this chapter as well: Hobbies allow people to have frequent and deep flow experiences.

Unfortunately, many of us neglect our hobbies (and our well-being) in the pursuit of material and professional achievement. Modern society pushes us toward working more and more; hobbies take a backseat and are often regarded as an indulgence and a waste of time. Nothing could be further from the truth. Hobbies are good for you. They have been shown to reduce stress, improve mental and physical health, boost confidence, and even improve performance on the job.[10] By helping you experience flow, they provide you with a temporary hiatus from your worries and can leave you feeling stronger and more optimistic. If you've been neglecting your hobbies, consider making more time for them. Reconnect with old hobbies or pursue new ones.

For me, my favorite hobbies include playing tennis and football, playing board and card games, reading, and hiking. These hobbies not only allow me to experience flow, they also help me recharge and return to work feeling refreshed, energized, and motivated. Hobbies allow me to experience more flow at leisure and more flow at work.

Bottom line: Hobbies are worth cultivating. They're good for you. As the American poet Phyllis McGinley once wrote, "A hobby a day keeps the doldrums away."

Caveats and Conclusion

I would like to end this chapter with some caveats and a short summary. The main caveat is that the generalizations I've made in this chapter are just that—generalizations. Just because flow is generally higher at work than at leisure doesn't mean this is always the case. Whether it's true for you or not will depend on your motivation, job, boss, co-workers, work environment, and how you spend your leisure time.

Just because sports are associated with high levels of flow, on average, doesn't mean this is true for all people. Think back to sports class in school, and you'll realize that sports can be everything but flow-promoting for some people.

Just because an activity is low in flow, on average, doesn't mean it can't produce frequent and intense flow for some people. Just because a category is associated with a certain average level of flow doesn't mean all of its activities are the same. Some chores or sports are no doubt more conducive to flow than others. Some individuals surely experience lots of flow during cooking, while others experience the same activity as mostly boring.

I should also mention that there are huge individual differences in how frequently and in which contexts flow is experienced. When researchers compare ESM data between individuals, they see that some experience flow very frequently in their lives, while others do so almost never. Some people—the most autotelic among us—can enter flow even in mundane activities. Others can only do so in their favorite hobby, or perhaps not at all. Speaking of hobbies, these can be as diverse as hiking, playing board games, learning new languages, drawing, painting, baking, gardening, sewing, knitting, fishing, skiing, roller skating, and reading—all of them can bring forth flow.

Individuals also differ in how intensely they experience flow. Most of us will probably never know the deep flow states experienced by world-class mountain bikers, kayakers, boxers, musicians, or athletes of all kinds.

Lastly, I should note that all the numbers and percentages presented in this chapter are somewhat arbitrary and should be taken with a grain of salt. Why? Because they depend on how flow is measured. If we count even mild instances of the state, the frequency will be far higher than if we only count the most intense experiences. "ESM will give a different reading on the frequency of flow depending on whether flow is defined broadly or narrowly," explains Csikszentmihalyi.[11] "[T]he important thing is not to attach a numerical value to this frequency, but to use the results comparatively, both within individuals and within groups, to assess where flowlike experiences are most likely to exist."

When a study suggests that 50% of their participants reported experiencing flow a mere 1x/week, that simply means that the study must have looked at very intense flow states only. When a study suggests that 80% of their participants reported experiencing flow when watching Netflix, that simply means that the study must have counted even mild instances of flow. As I've mentioned before, there's no official cutoff: There's no official boundary between what counts as flow and what doesn't. The frequency numbers of flow always depend on where the boundary is made, and that is somewhat arbitrary. When it comes to flow, we always look at relative, not absolute, frequencies.

Given these caveats, what can we say about where people most reliably find flow in their lives? In general, they find flow in active, productive, effortful, and challenging activities where moderate to high skills are involved. While flow is typically experienced most frequently at work, the most intense and satisfying flow experiences occur in active leisure, specifically in sports, games, arts, creative activities, and hobbies of all kinds. Moderate amounts of flow can be experienced when socializing and in everyday activities like cooking, cleaning, shopping, or driving a vehicle. The least amount of flow occurs in passive leisure activities like watching television or listening to music.

Chapter 9

The Brain and Body in Flow

You can't ruminate about yourself while you're absorbed in a challenging task. This is one reason people love dangerous sports like mountain climbing, a situation where you have to be totally focused. But when you come down the mountain, the self-referencing network brings your worries and cares right back.[1]

—RICHARD DAVIDSON

Imagine you're engaged in your favorite flow activity. You're completely absorbed in what you're doing. You feel confident, strong, and in control. You're zoned in and switched on. Everything feels easy, light, and spontaneous. It feels like you're floating from one moment to the next. You feel ecstatic.

In this final chapter of Part 1, we'll see what's happening in your brain and body as you're experiencing the total involvement, feeling of control, loss of self-consciousness, and other characteristics of the flow experience. This will further advance your knowledge of flow and help you better understand some of the flow-enhancing strategies described in later chapters.

A Wandering Mind

Have you ever caught yourself thinking about something completely unrelated to what you were doing? Perhaps while reading this very book, you may have wondered what's for dinner. Or, while watching television, you may have imagined a vacation with your spouse. Or, while trying to focus on some work task, you may have recalled an unpleasant conversation with a co-worker.

This experience—attention drifting away from the task and toward task-unrelated thoughts—goes by many names, including *mind wandering, daydreaming, self-generated thinking*, or *stimulus-independent thinking*.

Jonathan Smallwood and Jonathan Schooler, two leading researchers on this topic, define mind wandering as "a shift in the contents of thought away from an ongoing task and/or from events in the external environment to self-generated thoughts and feelings."[2] During mind wandering, we are mentally away from the "here and now."

The experience is incredibly common. In a 2010 study, researchers used a version of the experience sampling method to gauge how frequently people's minds wandered in everyday life.[3] They developed an iPhone app that contacted participants at random moments during their waking hours and asked them what they were doing and if they were thinking about something other than what they were currently doing. If the answer to the latter question was a yes, then the researchers concluded that participants' minds had been wandering.

And indeed, they had been wandering. The study found that participants' minds were off-task a whopping 47% of the time during everyday life—during half of their waking hours, participants were thinking about things completely unrelated to whatever they happened to be doing. Minds wandered most frequently during conditions that demand little conscious attention. Easy and mundane activities can mostly be done on autopilot, leaving the mind free to think about something else. That's why people's minds wandered 65% of the time when taking a shower or brushing their teeth. During more challenging and engaging activities, minds wandered less frequently, though still a lot. Rates of mind wandering were 50% when working, 40% when exercising, and 10% when having sex.

Other studies have come to similar rates of mind wandering. Smallwood and Schooler suggest that people spend between 25–50% of the time they are awake engaged in thoughts unrelated to the present moment.[4]

Given this massive time investment, you might wonder: What are we thinking about all the time? Where are our minds wandering to so frequently? What topics are so important?

Turns out we are thinking mostly all about ourselves. I'm thinking about *me* and *my* personal problems, *my* relationships with other people, *my* past, and *my* future. I'm thinking about the things *I* have to do today, the goals *I* want to accomplish, the wrong thing *I* have said, and what *I* should have said instead.

For most of us, this self-referential, me-focused thinking is geared toward the negative. Our minds tend to wander to our shortcomings, failings, missteps, and fears rather than to our victories, good deeds, strengths, or pleasant memories. "While the mind sometimes wanders to pleasant thoughts or fantasy, it more often seems to gravitate to rumination and worry," explains science journalist Daniel Goleman.[5] Rumination (compulsively rehashing past events) and worry (anxiously imagining future events) are forms of mind wandering.

Because the mind gravitates toward negative thoughts, mind wandering is often an unpleasant experience. A 2014 study made some interesting findings to attest to this point. The study found that "participants typically did not enjoy spending 6 to 15 minutes in a room by themselves with nothing to do but think, that they enjoyed doing mundane external activities much more, and that many preferred to administer electric shocks to themselves instead of being left alone with their thoughts."[6] The researchers hypothesized that being left alone with their thoughts was difficult because "participants focused on their own shortcomings and got caught in ruminative thought cycles."

The 2010 study mentioned earlier found that "people were less happy when their minds were wandering than when they were not, and this was true during all activities, including the least enjoyable." People were no happier when thinking about pleasant topics than when focused on their current activity. And they were considerably unhappier when thinking about neutral or negative topics than when focused on their activity. The researchers concluded: "[A] human mind is a wandering mind, and a wandering mind is an unhappy mind. The ability to think about what is not happening is a cognitive achievement that comes at an emotional cost."

In the long run, excessive mind wandering (e.g., in the form of worry or rumination) can contribute to the development of various mental health issues such as depression and anxiety. People with depression, for example, are known to get stuck in negative, self-focused, ruminative trains of thought. As one study puts it, "Depression is associated with significant difficulty staying 'in the moment' as the mind tends to wander away from current activity to focus instead on personal concerns."[7] Another study writes: "[T]he depressed state is characterized by an increase in self-focus, and an inability to disengage from self-referential ruminative thought."[8]

In short, mind wandering is an often unpleasant experience that can lead to serious health issues.[9] Well then, why don't we just stop? Why do we spend so much time engaged in self-referential thinking? The answer: Because we can't help ourselves; we can't stop our minds from wandering. If you've ever tried to meditate, you've experienced this firsthand. The mind seems to want to think, even if that thinking makes us miserable or gets in the way of accomplishing another task. Self-referential thinking seems to be our brain's preferred state.

When I tell you to lie down and not do anything, your mind will not go quiet or blank but will instead naturally begin to wander. When given nothing else to do, the human brain defaults to thinking about the person it's embedded in. In fact, as we've seen, even when given some other task, part of the brain wants to pull us out of that task and into task-unrelated thoughts. That's why concentration can be so effortful at times—we have to constantly pull our attention back from distracted me-focused thinking. Mind wandering is the brain's default or go-to state.

Default Mode

Because mind wandering is our default state, researchers refer to the collective of brain areas responsible for generating it as the *default mode network* (DMN).[10] In brain scanning studies, neuroscientists reliably see increased activation in this network when people report bouts of mind wandering, and they reliably see decreased activation when people report that their minds have not been wandering. While the exact functions of the DMN are still debated, one of its core roles is to generate the kind of self-referential thinking we've been discussing. This network of brain regions can be viewed as the neural correlate of mind wandering.

Whenever you're in a state of worry, rumination, self-doubt, lost in some personal melodrama, daydreaming, or fantasizing, you can thank or blame your DMN. When your mind wanders away from these pages, that's your DMN in action.

Since its discovery in 2001, a lot of research has been done on this fascinating brain network. The findings dovetail nicely with our discussion on mind wandering and the brain in flow.

One relevant discovery is that failures to downregulate or deactivate the DMN are associated with distractedness, lapses in attention, and decreased performance during tasks that require focused concentration.[11] When we wish to give our full attention to a task, the DMN is supposed to go quiet and make room for task-relevant networks to take over. Me-focused attention is supposed to make room for task-focused attention. Concentration requires a quieting of our inner chatter, a calming of the DMN. Failure to deactivate the DMN thus translates into difficulty concentrating; we get distracted by our own thinking, our daydreams, fantasies, worries, doubts, and fears.

Mind wandering and DMN activity predict performance in a number of tasks.[12] The stronger the DMN activity and the higher the rate of mind wandering, the poorer you'll perform on reading comprehension tasks, attention tests, or general intelligence tests. As one study puts it, "During mind-wandering, cognitive resources become occupied by internal activity unrelated to the external environment. Given this mental state, it is little surprise that mind-wandering can significantly interfere with the individuals' primary task performance."[13]

One of the hallmarks of ADHD seems to be excessive mind wandering caused by difficulty turning off the DMN.[14] Edward Hallowell, a psychiatrist who specializes in ADHD, refers to the DMN as the "demon of ADHD."[15]

Another finding is that an overactive DMN is associated with depression.[16] Depressed individuals get stuck in repetitive and destructive loops of rumination produced by the DMN. Some research suggests that selective serotonin reuptake inhibitors (SSRIs), a major class of antidepressants, work by lowering DMN hyperactivity.[17]

Other research shows that the DMN quiets down during meditation.[18] In long-term meditators, DMN activity during meditation calms down more strongly than in novice meditators. Long-term meditators also show lower baseline DMN activity and show less mind wandering and a better ability to focus in general. This makes sense, given the fact that the general instruction during meditation is to bring attention back to an object of focus (e.g., the breath) whenever the mind has wandered. Perhaps unsurprisingly, meditation has also been shown to improve symptoms of ADHD and depression.[19]

Research by psychiatrist and neuroscientist Judson Brewer suggests that the subjective experiences during meditation line up with the activity of the DMN.[20]

When participants' brains show decreases in DMN activity, they report: feeling relaxed, calm, tranquil, and content; having no struggle preventing their minds from wandering; noticing and observing sensory experience but not being distracted by it; a sense of unforced concentration; acceptance of things as they are; feelings of ease, equanimity, or bliss; no struggling or striving; effortless experience.

When participants' brains show increases in DMN activity during meditation, they report: being distracted and lacking concentration; feeling hazy, unclear, or muddled; thinking, deliberating, remembering, trying to understand experience; trying to control and change the way things are, often associated with dissatisfaction with current experience; trying to make something happen; feeling unhappy, uncomfortable, dissatisfied or displeased, frustrated, wanting the meditation to end; struggling; effortful experience.

Brewer suggests that the DMN is at least partly responsible for the experience of getting in our own way.[21]

Other research links activity in the DMN to our sense of self or ego. When researchers give participants a list of adjectives and ask them to consider how they apply to them, the DMN leaps into action.[22] It also activates when we receive "likes" on social media, and the more "likes" we receive, the stronger it activates.[23] Because of its prominence in self-referential processing, Brewer refers to the DMN as the "me" network.

Psychedelic drugs like psilocybin (the active ingredient in magic mushrooms) and LSD reliably produce experiences of self-transcendence or *ego dissolution*, defined as a reduction in self-referential awareness, disruption of self-world boundaries, and increasing feelings of unity with others and one's surroundings.[24] During these self-transcendent states, researchers see a big drop in DMN activity. Interestingly, the therapeutic utility of psychedelic substances in treating anxiety, addiction, and mood disorders has received increased attention in recent years.

The same drop in DMN activity is likely seen during other experiences of oneness or ego dissolution, such as during deep meditative states or near-death experiences.[25] To a lesser extent, such a drop in activity is likely seen in everyday absorbing activities, giving new meaning to the metaphor of "losing one's self in one's work."

To sum up, it seems that when activity in the DMN falls off sharply, internal chatter calms down, focused attention goes up, feelings of relaxation, ease, calm, and equanimity ensue, the sense of self vanishes, and experience takes on an effortless and enjoyable character.

Are you beginning to see the connection to flow?

The Brain in Flow

If you see a lot of commonalities between DMN downregulation and flow, you're absolutely spot on. In the brain, during flow, we see a deactivation or *hypo*activation of the DMN, and the more pronounced it is, the deeper the flow state.[26]

During flow, the chatter zone goes quiet. The worry and rumination centers turn off. The "me" goes offline and takes our negative self-talk, our fears, worries, insecurities, and self-doubts, and our sense of separation with it. The inner critic takes a backseat as we get out of our own way. This might be the neural explanation for why flow is such an enjoyable and functional state. Liberated from ourselves, our limitations are gone, and we are free to perform to the best of our abilities. Bruce Lee once said, "The consciousness of self is the greatest hindrance to the proper execution of all physical action."[27]

Flow and the DMN share a kind of seesaw, an either-or reciprocal relationship. When DMN activation goes up, flow goes down; when flow goes up, DMN activation goes down.

Flow and DMN Activation

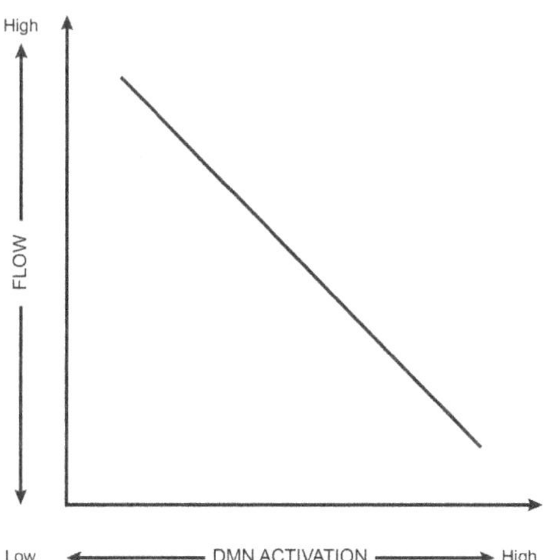

FIGURE 6: The seesaw relationship between flow and the default mode network (DMN). As one goes up, the other goes down. Flow seems to result, at least in part, from decreased activity in the DMN. Adapted from Peifer and Tan (2021).[28]

Remember that flow can be described as the state between boredom and anxiety. Research suggests that during both of these states, the DMN sees an increase in activity.[29] When tasks are either too easy or too difficult, attention focuses on the "me" instead of on the task in front of me. That's why the challenge-skills balance is perhaps the most important condition or antecedent of flow.

While research on the brain in flow is still in its infancy, DMN downregulation seems to be the most robust finding to date. Given everything we've learned about the DMN, it makes a lot of sense that it would go quiet during flow. It should be noted, though, that the DMN is a network made up of multiple brain regions. Future research might reveal that only some parts of the network are downregulated during flow but not others.

It should also be noted that deactivation of the DMN is not the only change taking place in the brain during flow. In general, we can assume that task-relevant brain areas see an increase in activation, while task-irrelevant brain regions (like the DMN) see a decrease in activation. Precisely which areas see changes in which direction, we don't know yet.

Some research shows that activity in the so-called "multiple-demand (MD) system," which is involved in various task-relevant cognitive functions, is increased during flow.[30] Other research suggests that neural structures related to cognitive control, specifically the dorsolateral prefrontal cortex (DLPFC), see greater activation during flow.[31] This would make sense, given that *cognitive control* includes various processes necessary for engaging in an activity, such as planning, goal maintenance, performance monitoring, and suppression of inappropriate thoughts, emotions, and behaviors. It has also been suggested that activity in areas related to reward, such as the nucleus accumbens, putamen, and caudate nucleus, see increased activation during flow.[32] Given the intrinsically rewarding nature of flow, this would also make sense. The so-called Synchronization Theory hypothesizes that during flow, neural areas that are task-relevant and involved in cognitive control become synchronized with reward structures, resulting in an energetically optimized state.[33]

So far in our discussion, we have only looked at the brain through the lens of neuroanatomy. But the brain also goes through changes in brainwave frequencies and neurochemistry, though less is known about these. It is strongly assumed that dopamine plays a key role in flow.[34] Dopamine is heavily involved in reward processing and addiction, two themes that certainly connect strongly to flow (we'll discuss addiction in chapter 12). Steven Kotler, who has been trying to pin down the neuroscience of flow for more than 20 years, suggests that flow might involve a whole host of neurochemicals, including not just dopamine but also endorphins, anandamide, norepinephrine, serotonin, and oxytocin.[35] Precisely how these chemicals interact to produce the state of flow, research might be a long way from knowing.

As far as brainwaves are concerned, a 2018 study suggested that the flow state is "characterized by increased theta activities in the frontal areas and moderate alpha activities in the frontal and central areas."[36] If that doesn't do much to further your understanding of flow, you're certainly not alone.

At this point, I should also note that different flow states may have different neurological profiles. Flow during sports may be different from flow during intellectual endeavors, which may be different from flow during meditation, which may, again, be different from flow during social interactions. We can strongly assume that all flow states share some common patterns both in the brain and the body. But we don't know yet what that shared physiology is. And neither do we know about the potential differences between distinct flow states.

The Body in Flow

While still relatively little is known about the brain in flow, even less is known about the body in flow. That being said, the little we know makes an important contribution to our understanding of it.

From the perspective of the body, boredom is a state of low arousal, while anxiety is a state of high arousal. Flow, at the intersection of the two, is a state of moderate or optimal arousal; we're just aroused enough to be alert, attentive, and stimulated but not so much to be jittery and nervous.

This is in line with what's known as the *Yerkes-Dodson law*, which states that performance increases with physiological or mental arousal, but only up to a point. When levels of arousal become too high, performance decreases. This relationship is often illustrated as an inverted U curve which first increases and then decreases as arousal levels go up (Figure 7).

Researchers have investigated the relationship between arousal and flow using a variety of bodily markers, including cortisol, heart rate, heart rate variability, and galvanic skin response.

Cortisol is often referred to as the *stress hormone* because it's secreted in large quantities during stressful situations. It supports us in coping with stress by heightening arousal and triggering the release of glucose, thus providing us with additional energy. It also influences our attention, focusing it on stress-relevant stimuli and shielding it from distractions. Too little cortisol means we lack the energy and focus to optimally deal with a stressor. Too much cortisol means trouble, too, leading to decreased cognitive functioning.

Flow and Arousal

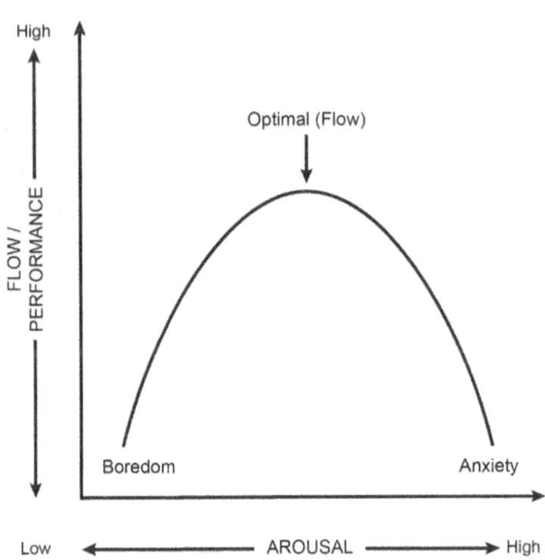

FIGURE 7: Flow as a state of moderate physiological arousal and optimal performance. As stated by the *Yerkes-Dodson law*, both under- and over-arousal reduce task performance. Low arousal can be said to coincide with boredom; high arousal with anxiety. Adapted from Peifer and Tan (2021).[37]

We would therefore expect cortisol levels to be moderate during flow, as this seems ideal for performance. According to Corinna Peifer, a flow researcher who has done multiple studies on the psychophysiology of flow, this is exactly what's happening. She suggests that "the relation of cortisol and flow-experience follows an inverted-u-shaped function: As long as cortisol values are in a normal day-to-day range, a positive relation between cortisol and flow is expected. When cortisol is further increased, as in consequence of a strong and enduring stressor, a negative relation of cortisol and flow would result."[38]

Another way to measure arousal is via the two branches of the autonomic nervous system. The sympathetic nervous system increases heart rate and arousal while the parasympathetic nervous system decreases them. When parasympathetic influence dominates, this results in a state of low arousal (e.g., boredom). When the sympathetic influence dominates, this results in a state of high arousal (e.g., anxiety). As expected, there is some evidence that during flow, both branches are moderately activated. Put differently, there is a co-activation of the sympathetic "fight or flight" system and the parasympathetic "rest and digest" system.

According to Peifer, such a co-activation "can be described as a *relaxed alertness* and is linked to many desired outcomes: evidence shows that this pattern is associated with better adaptation to demanding situations and to active coping during high workload. Accordingly, the particular co-activation pattern provides optimal conditions for successfully dealing with demanding situations."[39] This gives yet more meaning to the term "optimal" that is so connected with flow.

Investigations into other markers of arousal came to the same conclusion: Flow indeed seems to be a state of moderately heightened arousal.

This finding makes an important contribution to our understanding of flow: The effortlessness characteristic of flow is a subjective experience rather than an objective reality. While flow feels effortless, there is still actual effort on the part of the body and brain involved. The physiological costs may be masked during flow, but they accumulate nonetheless. Depending on the type of activity bringing forth the flow state and depending on the intensity of the state, the costs will vary. But they will be there, and this we should take into account. In the words of Peifer: "Despite the pleasant and rewarding nature of flow, literature suggests that it is still a state of heightened physiological arousal that needs to be counterbalanced by phases of relaxation."

Conclusion—A Brain-Body Definition of Flow

When we enter a state of flow, a number of changes take place in both the brain and body (Figure 8). In the brain, we see a decrease or hypoactivation of task-irrelevant brain regions (most notably the DMN) and an increase or hyperactivation of task-relevant brain regions. We also see the release of powerful neurochemicals such as dopamine and a shift in brainwave activity.

In the body, flow seems to be a state of heightened but not excessive arousal, marked by moderate levels of cortisol and a co-activation of the sympathetic and parasympathetic branches of the autonomic nervous system.

In summing up the research on the psychophysiology of flow, Peifer and colleagues refer to flow as a state of *optimized physiological activation* characterized by: (1) moderate levels of sympathetic activation, (2) moderate levels of cortisol, (3) decreased activation in default networks of the brain, (4) high synchronization of brain regions involved in cognitive control and in reward, (5) high activation of the brain's multiple-demand system, which is involved in task-relevant cognitive functions, (6) moderate levels of parasympathetic activation.[40]

Discussing the underlying physiological mechanisms of flow is not just intellectually entertaining; the information can also be translated into practical ways to experience flow more frequently. For example, you could meditate prior to a challenging task in order to calm down the DMN and reduce subsequent mind wandering. Or you could take up a regular meditation practice to make these changes more permanent. As we'll see in chapter 18, regular meditation helps you become more prone to experiencing flow, period.

The Brain and Body in Flow

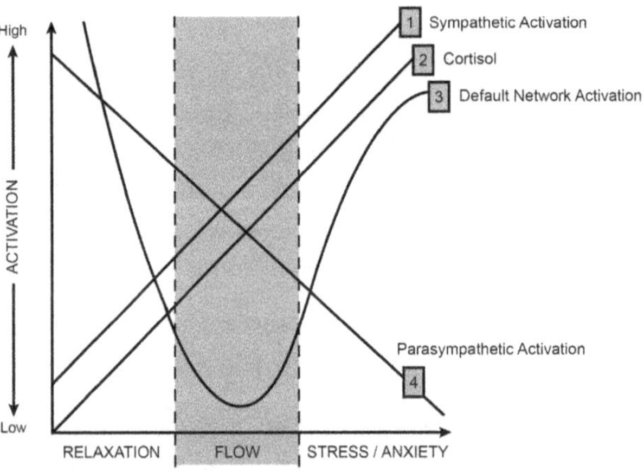

FIGURE 8. A summary of what's going on in the brain and body during flow. Adapted from Peifer and Tan (2021).[41]

Given that psychedelic substances can reduce activity in the DMN, you could play with microdosing as a way to facilitate flow. Microdosing has gained traction over recent years, with anecdotal evidence suggesting it can decrease anxiety, improve mood, and enhance attention, memory, and sociability.[42] You could also play with other substances that reduce overthinking, calm an overly anxious mind, or increase focus.

You could also consider the current physiological arousal in a given moment. If under-aroused, you could go for a walk, turn up the lights in the environment, or drink a cup of coffee to increase sympathetic activation. If over-aroused, you could perform some relaxation exercises, do deep breathing, or meditate to increase parasympathetic activation.

Part 2

The Benefits and Dangers of Flow

Chapter 10

Feeling Your Best

While sleeping, we have good dreams and bad dreams; while taking psychedelics, we have good trips and bad trips. Flow, on the other hand, is always a positive experience. No one ever has a bad time in a flow state.[1]

—STEVEN KOTLER

Remember how I felt on the sledding trip with my father and brothers? Fully alive, energized, euphoric, and like my system had just been flooded with a bunch of feel-good hormones. That's how incredible flow can feel.

In this chapter, we'll explore the relationship between flow and well-being. First, we'll establish once more that flow is a deeply enjoyable in-the-moment experience. We'll see that flow can feel so good that people are willing to die for it. Then, we'll turn our attention to the long term. Does flow bring benefits that go beyond positive but fleeting feelings? Can flow make us happier? Can it help us grow as individuals? Can it give meaning to our lives? Let's find out.

The Fun Factor

As we've discussed, flow exists on a spectrum. On the shallow end, the experience doesn't necessarily feel spectacular. But it feels good and certainly far better than experiences of boredom, anxiety, or apathy. In everyday experiences of flow, people report feeling alert, strong, cheerful, involved, excited, free, creative, energetic, and motivated.[2] They also report feeling good about themselves; self-esteem peaks during flow.[3]

Any activity feels better when done in flow, even if it's a relatively mild instance of the state. In one study, researchers brought people into the lab and allowed them to play Tetris.[4] They found that participants enjoyed the game significantly more when they were in a flow state.

As the experience becomes more intense, so do the positive feelings. We feel even more alert, strong, cheerful, etc. On the very deep end of the spectrum, flow is frequently described as ecstatic, exhilarating, blissful, euphoric, out-of-this-world, or mystical.

The experience feels so good that people are going to great lengths to seek it out. The amount of time, nerves, and money it takes to go skiing offers an example. It typically involves packing, getting ready, driving to the ski resort, wearing uncomfortable gear all day long, and putting down a considerable amount of money, too. Oh, but once you're skiing down the mountain, all is forgotten because you've just entered a most exquisite state of consciousness. The same could be said for snowboarding, mountain biking, surfing, kayaking, hiking, kitesurfing, and other popular hobbies.

Perhaps the greatest attest to the bliss flow provides is that some people are willing to pay the ultimate price for it. In his 2014 book, *The Rise of Superman*, Steven Kotler depicts a number of the world's most successful and revered action and adventure sports athletes.[5] The reason they engage in skydiving, BASE jumping, mountaineering, or any other extreme sport is to experience the flow at the very deep end of the spectrum.

"I take the easy way," said American free climber, alpinist, BASE jumper, and highliner Dean Potter.[6] "I can sit on my ass and meditate for two hours to get a fifteen-second glimpse of this state. Or I can risk my life and get there instantly—and it lasts for hours." Potter died in a wingsuit flying accident in Yosemite National Park in 2015. Shane McConkey, a professional skier and BASE jumper who was also depicted in the book, once said, "I'm getting maximum enjoyment out of life and I'll never stop."[7] He died during a ski-BASE jump in the Italian Dolomites in 2009. As these examples illustrate, flow can perhaps feel a little too good for some people.

Before going into more detail on the risks, for now, the point is this: Flow feels good on the shallow end of the spectrum and out-of-this-world on the deep end. It's a feel-good experience par excellence; a deeply enjoyable in-the-moment experience. But what about the long term? What are the consequences once the experience is over? What happens beyond the here and now?

Brief Descriptions of Ecstatic Flow Experiences

Flow can feel ecstatic. As Csikszentmihalyi once wrote, "When the experience is over, people report having been in as positive a state as it is possible to feel."[8] Here are three quotes that illustrate that point.

"You are in an ecstatic state to such a point that you feel as though you almost don't exist. I have experienced this time and time again. My hand seems devoid of myself, and I have nothing to do with what is happening. I just sit there watching in a state of awe and wonderment. And the music just flows out by itself."[9] — Composer, cited in Csikszentmihalyi, *Beyond Boredom and Anxiety*

"It was just one of those programs that clicked. I mean everything went right, everything felt good. . . . It's just such a rush, like you feel it could go on and on and on, like you don't want it to stop because it's going so well."[10] —Figure skater, cited in Csikszentmihalyi, *Flow, The Secret to Happiness*

"You feel like . . . there's nothing that will be able to stop you or get in your way. And you're ready to tackle anything, and you don't fear any possibility happening, and it's just exhilarating."[11] — Cyclist, cited in Csikszentmihalyi, *Living in Flow—The Secret of Happiness*

Enjoyment, Pleasure, and Personal Growth

There is an important difference between flow and other "feel-good activities" (e.g., watching television, drinking wine, eating doughnuts, smoking weed, or taking other drugs). After all, if good feelings are all we're after, those can come at a far lower cost.

As mentioned in chapter 3, Csikszentmihalyi differentiated between enjoyment and pleasure. In his lingo, flow activities are enjoyable, while the other feel-good activities are pleasurable. "Playing a close game of tennis that stretches one's ability is enjoyable, as is reading a book that reveals things in a new light, as is having a conversation that leads us to express ideas we didn't know we had. Closing a contested business deal, or any piece of work well done, is enjoyable. None of these experiences may be particularly pleasurable at the time they are taking place, but afterward, we think back on them and say, 'That really was fun' and wish they would happen again."[12]

The pleasures come easily, require little or no effort, and pose no risk of failure. They are easy thrills. On the flipside, the good feelings associated with them are also fleeting and short-lived. Remove the stimulus, and you are right back to where you started. Potentially worse off if you've over-indulged. You may have compromised your health or other aspects of your life, and you may feel guilty, frustrated, or ashamed for doing so.

Enjoyment, on the other hand, is typically hard-won. Experiencing flow requires skill and effort, and because it involves meeting challenges, there is the possibility of failing. Flow takes work. It usually requires initial effort before the feeling of effortlessness arises.

And flow activities can be stressful. "A mountain climber may be close to freezing, utterly exhausted, in danger of falling into a bottomless crevasse," explains Csikszentmihalyi.[13] But then again, this is all well worth it. The climber wouldn't want to be anywhere else. "Sipping a cocktail under a palm tree at the edge of the turquoise ocean is nice, but it just doesn't compare to the exhilaration he feels on that freezing ridge."

The pleasures are nice. They feel good. They provide an excellent means to treat oneself to something. But when it comes to excitement, bliss, and exhilaration, the pleasures pale in comparison to flow.

And while the pleasures can leave you feeling guilty, unmotivated, mildly depressed, and perhaps ashamed, flow tends to leave you feeling strong, confident, and satisfied with yourself. You're basking in a sense of pride and accomplishment. In the words of a rock climber: "You look back in awe at the self, at what you've done, it just blows your mind."[14]

And it gets better still for flow. Not only do these experiences feel great during and after the experience, but they also tend to contribute to long-term growth. In flow, we're pushing ourselves to the limits of our capabilities. We're fully engaged. We're using skills. Concentration soars. Investing energy and attention, we're yielding growth and development. A person who frequently experiences flow grows into a more mature and complex being. "By stretching skills, by reaching toward higher challenges, such a person becomes an increasingly extraordinary individual," explains Csikszentmihalyi.[15]

The obvious development is in skill. The chess player in flow becomes better at playing chess, the writer better at writing, the pianist better at playing the piano. Sub-skills and related skills get improved, too. A math student in flow improves his reasoning abilities, problem-solving, abstract thinking, spatial sense, concentration, and much more.

And then there is the other kind of development, that which concerns psychological growth. Completing challenging tasks and improving skills help you feel competent and in control of your life. Frequent flow experiences can lead to greater self-belief, self-esteem, self-efficacy, agency, optimism, mental toughness, and intrinsic motivation.

This principle of growth doesn't apply to the pleasures. When we watch television, eat a feastful dinner, or watch one Instagram story after another, we're just passively consuming. We're taking pleasure in the comforts of the modern world. We're extracting good feelings from what we've built. But we're not building anything new.

There is a time and a place for the pleasures. But in designing one's life, they shouldn't dominate. By investing time and energy into flow activities, we will be more satisfied and possessing of rarer skills. And, as we're about to see, we'll find more happiness and meaning.

Happiness and the Meaning of Life

Happiness suffers from a similar issue as flow: it's hard to define and measure. What exactly does it mean to be happy? How can you tell if someone is happy? How can you tell how happy someone is compared to others?

Researchers agree that we need to differ between how we feel at any given moment (our so-called *affective state*) and how we cognitively evaluate our overall happiness or quality of life (our so-called *life satisfaction*). We can feel sad in the moment but still rate our lives as happy, or we can feel joyful in the moment but rate our overall happiness as low.

Flow is a highly positive affective state; we have clearly seen that. It's enjoyable as an event-specific, moment-by-moment experience. But what about our overall sense of happiness? Can momentary experiences of flow contribute to general life satisfaction?

The evidence certainly suggests so. Flow is associated with greater life satisfaction in countless studies across various demographics.

In a 2020 study titled *Living Well by Flowing Well,* researchers followed participants over a period of ten days and investigated daily fluctuations in flow, affect, and flourishing (a measure of purpose in life, good social relationships, meaningful social contributions, optimism, and other elements of good mental health).[16] They found that individuals who experienced more flow had better well-being, as indicated by higher levels of daily flourishing and higher levels of positive daily affect. A similar study, also published in 2020, followed participants over two weeks and found that the frequency of flow at work was positively associated with well-being in the same period of time.[17]

A 2013 study with Italian teenagers showed that adolescents who experienced more flow also reported higher life satisfaction, *hedonic balance*, and *psychological well-being* than their peers.[18] (Hedonic balance is a measure of the prevalence of positive over negative feelings. Psychological well-being is a combined measure of purpose in life, autonomy, mastery, positive relations, personal growth, and self-acceptance.)

A 2010 study with Japanese students showed that those who experienced flow more often in their daily lives reported greater life satisfaction and more *Jujitsu-kan*, a Japanese sense of fulfillment.[19] They also reported higher self-esteem, lower anxiety, more active commitments to college life, search for future career, and daily activities in general.

Studies with elderly Koreans, school teachers, elite musicians, top athletes, and other individuals from all walks of life come to the same conclusion.[20] More flow goes hand in hand with greater life satisfaction.

As I've mentioned, Csikszentmihalyi himself studied flow and happiness for over 40 years. He suggested that "flow not only improves momentary experiences, but helps build a better quality of life in its entirety."[21] He said that "happiness depends on whether a person is able to derive flow from whatever he or she does."[22] He also said that flow experiences "add up to a sense of mastery—or perhaps better, a sense of participation in determining the content of life—that comes as close to what is usually meant by happiness as anything else we can conceivably imagine."[23] He even went as far as calling flow "the bottom line of existence (because) without it there would be little purpose in living."[24]

Other prominent researchers in this field agree. Sonja Lyubomirsky, author of countless studies and several books on the topic of happiness, says that "the experience of flow leads us to be involved in life (rather than be alienated from it), to enjoy activities (rather than to find them dreary), to have a sense of control (rather than helplessness), and to feel a strong sense of self (rather than unworthiness). All these factors imbue life with meaning and lend it a richness and intensity. And happiness."[25]

Martin Seligman, another renowned well-being researcher, lists flow as one of the five main factors that contribute to well-being in his PERMA model.[26] The factors are Positive Emotions, Engagement (flow), Relationships, Meaning, and Accomplishments.

Given everything we've learned so far, it makes sense that flow would make us happier. Frequent flow experiences lead to greater self-esteem and self-confidence. By turning off the "me" centers in the brain, flow experiences give us much-needed breaks from, well, ourselves—our worries, shortcomings, and insecurities. The full engagement on the task at hand means that flow allows us to live in the present moment, free from the anxiety of the future and the regrets of the past. *Self-focused attention*, which is strongly related to clinical depression and anxiety, is replaced by *task-focused attention*.[27]

Compared with their less flowy peers, high-flow individuals likely have greater skills and more accomplishments to be proud of. They are constantly growing, learning, and thus experiencing a sense of progress. The fact that they are engaged with life and fulfilling their potential means that they are less likely to struggle with guilt, shame, and regret. Regularly having enjoyable flow experiences gives them something to look forward to.

Flow also gives meaning to people's lives. Elite athletes find flow and meaning in their sports. Extreme sports athletes find flow and meaning in big waves, big rivers, or big mountains. Scientists find flow and meaning in their research. Surgeons find flow and meaning in the operating room. Teachers find flow and meaning in the classroom.

All things being equal, individuals who find flow easily and frequently will be happier than those who find themselves bored, anxious, or apathetic a lot of the time. Flow is clearly a potent pathway to greater happiness.

Caveat

I have made three major points in this chapter: 1) flow is a positive affective experience, 2) flow leads to long-term growth, and 3) flow makes us happier. While the first point is always true, there are exceptions for the latter two.

As we'll see in chapter 12, flow does not always lead to growth and happiness. For example, when a person neglects important areas of life because they are overly occupied by their pursuit of flow, the consequences can be negative. Or when a person becomes addicted to a flow activity, the addiction can cause a lot of harm.

Chapter 11

Performing Your Best

When in flow, the individual operates at full capacity.[1]

—MIHALY CSIKSZENTMIHALYI

Flow is powerful. It can save lives, and it allows people to push the human body beyond the limits of what we thought was possible. . . . People are better when they're in flow. They seem to have more time. They make better decisions, and they make them faster. . . . Flow can boost creativity for days. . . . Athletes in flow take in more data and process it more efficiently.[2]

—AMIT KATWALA

Think about the most productive and creative moments of your life—the times when you're performing at full capacity. You're able to access your complete repertoire of skills and knowledge. You're fully on, and you're being the best you're capable of being. You're in flow during these moments, aren't you?

For me, it's very obvious: Whether I'm writing, running, reading, playing tennis, or acing an exam—I perform at my best when I'm in flow; when the voice in my head is quiet, and I'm confident, focused, and fully engaged in what I'm doing.

In this chapter, we'll look at the evidence of flow's performance-enhancing benefits. We'll first consider the anecdotal evidence. We'll see that everyone from top athletes and successful coaches to world-class creatives, famous artists, and major companies like Toyota, Patagonia, and Ericsson are singing the praises of flow. We'll then look at the science. We'll see that research from all over the world has confirmed that flow boosts performance across various fields, including sports, music, academia, and work. Finally, we'll cover why flow is so beneficial for both short-term performance and long-term achievement. We'll see precisely how flow brings out the best in us.

"When you get in that zone…"

During half-time at the Super Bowl of 1992, Jimmy Johnson, the coach of the Dallas Cowboys, was asked what he did to prepare his team for this supreme test. Johnson held up a copy of Csikszentmihalyi's *Flow* in response. After winning back-to-back Super Bowls in 1992 and 1993, he explained that he had built his team around the concept of flow: "For many years, I've admired Dr. Csikszentmihalyi's pioneering work and tried to apply his concepts on the football field. Some people have labeled my approach as 'intense,' but the more accurate term might be 'in flow.' Being totally absorbed in the task at hand is essential to becoming a sports champion."[3]

Legendary basketball player Bill Russell, a key player for the Boston Celtics during the period when they won 11 championships in 13 years, is one such sports champion who credits flow for raising his performance: "When it happened, I could feel my play rise to a new level. . . . At that special level, all sorts of odd things happened. The game would be in the white heat of competition, and yet somehow I wouldn't feel competitive. . . . I'd be putting out the maximum effort . . . and yet I never felt the pain."[4]

Fellow basketball legend Kobe Bryant famously scored a career-high 81 points in 2006, the second-highest score in a single game in NBA history. His interviews were often littered with references to being in the zone. He once said: "When you get in that zone, it's just this supreme confidence; you know it's going in. It's not a matter of if . . . it's just that it's going in. Things just slow down. You know, everything just slows down, and you just have supreme confidence. And when that happens, you know, you don't really try to focus on it at all because you can lose it in a second . . . you try not to let anything break that river. You're oblivious to everything that is going on."[5]

"Teams at the highest level prioritize flow," says Steve Kerr, head coach of the Golden State Warriors.[6] "There's nothing else that can match group flow. That's what I'm constantly hoping our team achieves." Kerr started with the Warriors in 2014 and led the team to its most successful period in history, reaching six NBA Finals and winning four championships in 2015, 2017, 2018, and 2022. In the 2015–16 season, they won an unprecedented 73 games, breaking the record for the most wins in an NBA season.

Lewis Hamilton is one of the most successful Formula One drivers in history. He has won a joint-record seven Championship titles (tied with Michael Schumacher) and holds the records for the most wins (104), pole positions (104), and podium finishes (199). According to sports journalist Amit Katwala, who has interviewed Hamilton multiple times, it's all about flow for the Brit.[7] After winning the Spanish Grand Prix in 2020, Hamilton said in an interview, "I felt like I was in the most . . . It was like a clear zone. . . . The clarity I had when I was driving . . . Honestly, I felt fantastic in the car. It was physically challenging, but in terms of not making any mistakes, delivering lap upon lap upon lap, I was in the perfect zone. And that's the zone I dream of being in. . . . There were all these elements perfectly in place. I was very centered in my core and I've got to try to get there every day. . . . I always like to talk about trying to be our higher selves, because each of us has an unlimited capacity. It just felt like I was at a high plane. I am always talking about perfect races and that was one of them. We all try for perfection and it is not always easy to deliver like that but today, for me and the car, I was ecstatic. When I came across the line I didn't realize it was the last lap. I was still going. I was like a horse with blinkers on. I was going to keep going."[8]

Football icon Pele mentioned "a strange calmness" and "a type of euphoria" during his best performances: "I felt I could run all day without tiring, that I could dribble through any of their team or all of them, that I could almost pass through them physically. I felt I could not be hurt. It was a very strange feeling and one I had not felt before. Perhaps it was merely confidence, but I have felt confident many times without that strange feeling of invincibility."[9]

Sports psychologist Michael Sachs hypothesizes that in "every gold medal or world championship that's ever been won, most likely, we now know, there's a flow state behind the victory."[10]

In the world of extreme sports, meanwhile, accessing flow isn't merely the difference between setting a new record or falling short, between winning the title or coming in second or third; it can be the difference between life and death. "While finding flow may be the goal of every athlete on the planet, for action and adventure sports athletes it's a necessity," explains Steven Kotler.[11] "In all other activities, flow is the hallmark of high performance, but in situations where the slightest error could be fatal, then perfection is the only choice — and flow is the only guarantee of perfection. Thus, flow is the only way to survive in the fluid, life-threatening conditions of big waves, big rivers, and big-mountains." As legendary skateboarder Danny Way put it: "It's either find the zone or suffer the consequences—there's no other choice available."[12]

For writers, flow is viewed by many as the ideal writing state. "While there is no scientific proof that flow necessarily produces top-quality writing, research has found that many writers are convinced they produce much of their best work while they are in such an altered situation," explains Susan K. Perry, author of *Writing in Flow*.[13] "When you're in flow, scenes and images almost seem to concoct themselves. As one writer told me, 'I have to keep reminding myself that all I have to do is get into that place and the language will furnish itself.'"

Flow "connects you to the joy of writing," explains Anne Janzer in her book *The Writer's Process*.[14] "When flow happens, it's worth the work. For many people, the experience itself is reason enough to write. Look for ways to structure your process to increase the opportunities for flow."

Novelist Zadie Smith describes a highly productive state of magical thinking, during which "you sit down to write at 9 am, you blink, the evening news is on and four thousand words are written."[15] John Steinbeck, a Nobel Prize in Literature winner, once remarked in one of his journal entries: "Not an early start today but it doesn't matter at all because the unity feeling is back. That is the fine thing. That makes it easy and fun to work."[16] For Australian singer-songwriter Tash Sultana, flow is so integral to everything she does that she named her debut album after it. The album is called "Flow State."

These sentiments ring very true for me. Without flow, writing is slow, hard, frustrating, and demotivating. With flow, writing is fast, easy, fun, and rewarding. When flow shows up, I make progress today, and I gain momentum and motivation to come back tomorrow. Flow is, in many ways, the fuel that powers my writing. If I wasn't able to access flow somewhat regularly during my writing, you probably wouldn't be reading this book right now.

In the corporate world, top executives report being up to five times more productive during flow, according to a ten-year McKinsey study: "When we ask executives during the peak-performance exercise how much more productive they were at their peak than they were on average, for example, we get a range of answers, but the most common at senior levels is an increase of five times."[17]

Venture capitalist James Slavet lists "flow state percentage"—the amount of time people spend in flow—as one of his five most important management metrics.[18] Jim Clifton, former CEO of the Gallup Organization, once said, "People with high flow never miss a day. They never get sick. They never wreck their cars. Their lives just work better."[19]

When Stefan Falk, a former vice president of strategic business innovation at Ericsson, moved to Green Cargo in mid-2003, the company had been losing money for 120 years. After Falk, who had studied flow and applied it previously at Ericsson, instituted a new management program based on flow, the company made its first profit, and Falk was credited with the turnaround.[20]

"In all our studies of extreme performance improvement, the people and organizations who covered the most distance in the shortest time were always the ones who were tapping into passion and finding flow,"[21] says John Hagel, founder of the Deloitte Center for the Edge, an organization researching the future of work in a changing world.

Former Patagonia CEO Michael Crooke completed a Ph.D. thesis under the tutelage of Csikszentmihalyi on the topic of creating a workplace environment conducive to flow. "Flow was at the center of everything I was doing at Patagonia, and remains at the heart of all my professional activities since," Crooke explains.[22] "[Flow] manifests itself in focused, on-time, on-spec products that win in the marketplace because they were developed in a system in which the customers and the internal people all know what they want and need."

Patagonia, whose corporate headquarters are on the California coast, "have a policy that when the surf comes up, you drop work and you go surfing," says Yvon Chouinard, the owner and founder of the company.[23] The idea is that if employees get into a flow state in the water, the productivity and creativity boosts will carry over into their work.[24]

As you can see, there's plenty of anecdotal evidence that flow is great for performance. Top performers from all walks of life praise and seek out flow for its performance-enhancing benefits. Next up, let's see what the science has to say on the matter.

The Science

The link between flow and performance is well-established in the scientific literature. Flow is positively associated with creativity, intrinsic motivation, skill development, and peak performance in various fields, including academia, sports, music, and the workplace.

In academic contexts, flow is consistently linked with improved learning, higher grades, and development of skills, commitment, and achievement.

A study by Csikszentmihalyi and colleagues followed talented teenagers over a period of four years.[25] They found that those who experienced more flow at age thirteen went on to outperform their less flowy peers in various areas of talent (e.g., math, music, or football) at age seventeen. More flow at age 13 predicted greater performance four years later, at age 17. In a similar, albeit shorter, study with math students, those who experienced more flow in the first part of a course performed better in the second half.[26] A 2008 study, which measured flow experience during a French course and a statistics course, found the same thing.[27] Those students who scored higher on levels of flow during lessons at the beginning of the semester performed better on their exams at the end of the semester.

More flow today equals better performance tomorrow.

In the area of game-based learning, flow has also been shown to predict performance. So-called *serious games* are games that may be enjoyable but are designed primarily for the purpose of training or education. A 2010 study brought people into the lab, gave them a serious game to play, and then tested them on how much they had learned.[28] Lo and behold, those who experienced more flow while playing the game learned more and scored better on the test.

In the area of sports, a study with college athletes in a broad range of individual sports (including swimming, golf, gymnastics, running, field and track athletics, and tennis) found that self-reported flow scores were significantly higher when athletes referred to their best performances than when rating their general performances.[29]

A study with runners came to the conclusion that flow enhances marathon performance in an indirect way.[30] Runners who experienced flow during training or in previous races found the experience more enjoyable and were thus more motivated to continue, which led to increased training. Performance in marathon races was not significantly influenced by flow during the race in question but by pre-race training. By positively influencing pre-race training, flow boosts race performance indirectly.

Work productivity and creativity get a boost, too. Jef van den Hout and Orin Davis, two experts on flow in the workplace, assert that finding flow is the "holy grail of business success for individual employees, teams, and companies."[31] They explain: "Flow experiences are extremely valuable to companies, because the more employees experience flow, the more they will love their jobs, perform well, come up with more creative solutions, and put their all into their work. . . . When people experience flow at work, they experience their jobs more as meaningful callings, and are willing to go above and beyond their job descriptions. In addition, they are more likely to develop their skills, becoming better able to perform complex tasks and create value."

A 2019 field study with office workers found a positive relationship between flow and self-reported work performance.[32] When participants reported experiencing relatively high flow, they were more likely to report "being productive," "finishing many things," and "not making any mistakes."

A 2010 survey of customer service personnel in 20 tech companies in Taiwan found that participants who reported more flow at work also reported delivering higher quality customer service (e.g., being more reliable, responsive, caring, trustworthy, knowledgeable, empathetic, and polite).[33] On a side note, the study also found that employees with meditation experience reported more flow. We'll come back to meditation in later chapters.

A 2014 study investigated the effects of team flow on performance during a project management simulation.[34] Students met in teams of four to six and were instructed to build a scale model of a goods vehicle. After 6½ hours, the vehicle had to be able to travel two routes varying in difficulty. Team performance was measured on a scale from 1 (the vehicle did not start) to 6 (the vehicle completed two routes). As expected, teams who experienced more flow performed better than those who experienced less flow. "The results of this study corroborate the importance of fostering flow experience among work team members," concluded the researchers. "More specifically, this study shows that flow is not only a determinant of individual performance, but also a determinant of team performance. Hence, team managers should put in place ways to foster flow in their teams."

A 2006 study investigated flow and creativity in musical composition.[35] Forty-five music students were split into groups of three and given the task of composing a musical masterpiece. When each group's composition was rated on measures of creativity, those groups with higher average flow scored better than those reporting less flow. "It is clear from the results that increased levels of flow are indeed related to increased levels of creativity," concluded the researchers.

In a 2012 study, researchers used a brain stimulation technique called transcranial direct current stimulation (tDCS) to artificially induce a state similar to flow in their participants. They then gave them the nine-dot problem to solve, a classic test of creative problem solving that in most studies is not solved by any of the participants.[36] This was true again in this experiment—

without tDCS, nobody solved it. With the stimulation, however, more than 40% did. "Whereas no participant solved this extremely difficult problem before stimulation or with sham stimulation," the researchers explain, "14 out of 33 participants did so with cathodal stimulation."

According to investigative journalist Sally Adee, this type of invasive brain technology has been found to "more than double the rate at which people learn a wide range of tasks such as object recognition, maths skills, and marksmanship."[37]

Adee got to try out tDCS herself in the course of investigating a story for the *New Scientist magazine*.[38] In a lab in Carlsbad, California, she participated in an "accelerated marksmanship training" simulation. "It's the very simulation that trains US troops to take their first steps with a rifle, and everything about it has been engineered to feel like an overpowering assault," she explains. "I spent a few hours learning how to shoot a modified M4 close-range assault rifle, first without tDCS and then with."

Without it, she was terrible; with it, she was excellent. "The 20 minutes I spent hitting targets while electricity coursed through my brain were far from transcendent. I only remember feeling like I had just had an excellent cup of coffee, but without the caffeine jitters. I felt clear-headed and like myself, just sharper. Calmer. Without fear and without doubt. From there on, I just spent the time waiting for a problem to appear so that I could solve it. It was only when they turned off the current that I grasped what had just happened. Relieved of the minefield of self-doubt that constitutes my basic personality, I was a hell of a shot." The feeling that emerged as soon as the current switched on was "markedly similar to the flow state."

Michael Weisend, the researcher who hooked up Adee's brain with the electrodes, explains that her experience was fairly common. "The number one thing I hear people say after tDCS is that time passed unduly fast."[39] Movements become more automatic, people report calm, focused concentration, and performance improves immediately.

Weisend has been doing research with tDCS for years and points out that not all forms of it bring about the flow state. The one he used with Adee, however, does. And it reliably boosts performance as well. In one study, it boosted the speed with which wannabe snipers could detect a threat by a factor of 2.3.[40] That's a 230% improvement.

And this isn't the only brain technology used to artificially blow up performance and accelerate learning by inducing flow states.[41] Chris Berka of Advanced Brain Monitoring uses a technology called *neurofeedback* to help novices achieve brain states similar to those of experts—brain states more closely to flow than struggle.[42] Berka is able to cut the time it takes novice archers to shoot like a pro by more than half.

No matter where we look, flow and performance go together.[43]

How Does Flow Improve Performance?

Flow is said to improve performance in two ways: (1) "direct," which refers to flow being a highly functional state that directly boosts performance on the spot, during the activity itself; (2) "indirect," which means that flow enhances other factors, which then boost performance.

Flow and Performance

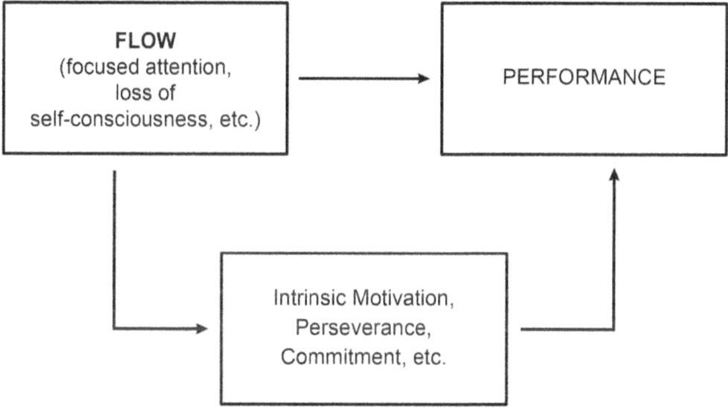

FIGURE 9: Direct and indirect effects of flow on performance. Direct: flow is a highly functional state that itself results in better performance. Indirect: flow improves intrinsic motivation, perseverance, commitment, and other variables that also result in performance benefits. Adapted from Barthelmäs and Keller (2021)[44].

Let's begin with the direct pathway. All things being equal, the person in flow will outperform the person who isn't. Someone who enjoys what they are doing, is highly motivated, deeply focused, free from worries and doubts, and feeling confident and in control will perform better than someone who's distracted, overthinking, worrying, anxious or bored.

Many of flow's characteristics facilitate performance themselves. If combined during flow, it's no wonder, really, that performance goes up.

Consider "focused attention." Research on elite athletes consistently shows that they possess greater concentration abilities than their average peers.[45] Poor performances and failures are typically ascribed to being unable to concentrate effectively. Research on reading comprehension proves the obvious: The more focused you are while reading, the greater your comprehension; the more your mind wanders away from the text, the worse your comprehension.[46]

"Concentration is essential for performing one's best whether the performer is an athlete, student, surgeon, musician, or something else," explains a group of sports psychologists.[47] "When I'm focused, there is not one single thing, person, anything that can stand in the way of my doing something," says Michael Phelps, the most decorated Olympian of all time with a total of 28 medals.[48]

Or consider "loss of self-consciousness." If we are free from self-conscious thoughts, we find it much easier to concentrate on the task at hand. Once the nagging inner voice goes offline, self-doubts disappear, and we are free to perform to the best of our abilities. The opposite experience—getting caught up in self-referential thinking to the detriment of performance—goes by the names of choking, the yips, bottling it, or simply getting in one's own way. Clearly, being able to turn off self-consciousness is vital for performing at our best.

The same spiel could be made with the other common characteristics of flow. The point is: Flow is a highly functional state that directly enhances performance whenever it shows up.

The indirect pathway comes down to flow's inherently enjoyable nature. Because the flow experience is intrinsically rewarding, we naturally seek to repeat any activity that provides it; what gets rewarded gets repeated. The person who experiences flow while doing math and thus finds the activity enjoyable will be at an advantage compared with the person who finds math boring or anxiety-provoking. The former will be more motivated to do math, will "practice" more, and will improve more.

Flow creates the motivation that keeps us coming back to an activity, which leads to long-term skill development. "Experiencing flow encourages a person to persist at and return to an activity because of the experiential rewards it promises, and thereby fosters the growth of skills over time," explains Csikszentmihalyi.[49]

When we come back to an activity, we often do so a little more skilled. To experience flow again, we thus need to up the challenge so as to not feel bored. We then get better again, up the challenge again, and so on (Figure 10). "The relation between flow and the realization of potential is this," explains flow researcher Jeanne Nakamura, "Flow is achieved when an activity challenges the individual to fully engage his or her capacities; as these capacities grow, staying in flow requires taking on increasingly greater challenges."[50] Thanks to the rewarding nature of flow, we keep getting better and better over time.

Flow and Skill Development

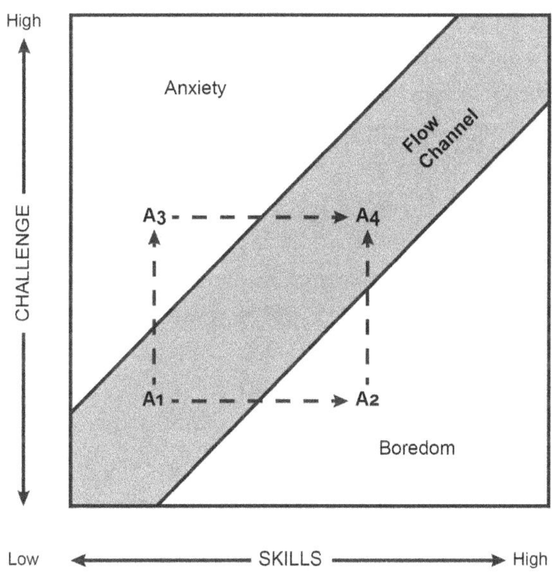

FIGURE 10: Why flow leads to skill improvement. Adapted from Csikszentmihalyi (1990).[51]

Consider Figure 10, which represents a specific activity, such as playing tennis.[52] When you play for the first couple of times, you find yourself at point A1. You have very little skill, and the only challenge is hitting the ball over the net. You find yourself in a flow situation because the level of difficulty is just right for your level of skill. As you keep practicing, your skills improve, and you grow bored just hitting the ball over the net (A2). Or, if you play a practice match against a superior opponent, you're likely to experience some anxiety because you're over-challenged (A3).

Neither boredom nor anxiety are nearly as enjoyable as flow. Because you remember how much fun it was when you were in flow, you feel motivated to get back to flow again. If you're in A2, the only way to get back to flow is by increasing the challenge (you can't reduce your skills). If you're in A3, the way to get back to flow is by either increasing your skills or reducing the challenge. The latter would temporarily bring you back to A1, and then, as you keep practicing, to A2, and then via A2 to A4. Either way, sooner or later, you'll end up in A4, which represents a deeper flow experience than A1. (Greater challenges and skills usually bring forth more intense flow experiences.)

In A4, playing tennis is fun. However, as you keep playing, you're bound to get bored or anxious again, and you'll feel motivated to again increase the challenge or increase your skills. Over time, you continue to move toward the top right-hand corner of Figure 10. If you keep playing, you can't help but improve your skills. And what keeps you playing? What keeps you excited and motivated to play? The rewarding experience of flow.

If you never experience flow during a specific activity, you're highly unlikely to feel motivated to engage in that activity again. This is a major reason why flow at an earlier point in time results in greater performance at a later point. It's why, in Csikszentmihalyi's study on talented teenagers, those who experienced more flow at age 13 performed better than their peers at age 17.[53] Flow ignites and continually fuels the fire of intrinsic motivation and thereby results in long-term commitment, perseverance, and, ultimately, achievement. If you're unable to experience flow, you're unable to fulfill your potential.

Bottom line: We need flow to perform our best. It is necessary for acing a one-off test, tournament, race, or game. And it's necessary for long-term motivation and skill development, and thus achievement. Without flow, we simply can't perform to the best of our abilities. Without flow, we can't reach our full potential.

Chapter 12

The Dark Side of Flow

Not all is sunshine and roses in flow land. While flow is always a positive (as in enjoyable) experience, it doesn't always have positive consequences. Yes, it typically leads to growth, development, and greater life satisfaction. But that isn't always the case. And even if it is, there can be costs involved.

Csikszentmihalyi himself hinted at the idea of costs in one of his more popular descriptions of flow as the state "in which people are so involved in an activity that nothing else seems to matter; the experience itself is so enjoyable that people will do it even at great cost, for the sheer sake of doing it."[1]

There can be financial costs, such as performing an expensive hobby; time costs, as in spending night after night playing video games; health costs, like getting injured; and all kinds of costs that result from neglecting other domains of life while in the pursuit of flow (e.g., neglecting one's job, education, or friends and family).

If we consider the characteristics of flow, the potential dangers are, in fact, glaringly obvious. Deep involvement and intense concentration on the task come with being oblivious to everything else, for better and for worse. Loss of self-consciousness means flow can be used to escape from one's problems instead of dealing with them. Distortion of time can result in missed appointments or not having enough time for other people and projects. The sense of being in control of the situation is subjective rather than objective— as the deaths of so many extreme sports athletes have shown, flow can make you feel in control until you're not. The feel-good nature, especially the exhilarating highs experienced at the deep end of the spectrum, make flow activities an obvious target for excessive use.

Having delved deep into all the positive aspects of flow, it's imperative to shed light on potential dangers and downsides: addiction, risk-taking, and flow in anti-social contexts.

Flow and Addiction

Because flow is such a rewarding experience, we want to repeat whatever activity provided it. If you just had an ecstatic experience while on a run, you'll feel compelled to go running again. If you felt completely at one with yourself, full of energy, intensely alive, in control, excited and peaceful—you'll want to experience that again.

What gets rewarded gets repeated, and flow experiences are among the most rewarding experiences we can have as human beings. As Csikszentmihalyi said: "The metaphor of flow is one that many people have used to describe the sense of effortless action they feel in moments that stand out as the best in their lives."[2]

On the bright side, this mechanism allows us to improve our skills and perform at higher and higher levels because we are constantly adjusting the difficulty of the task to our skills in order to stay in the flow channel (see Figure 10 in chapter 11).

On the dark side, we may feel compelled to repeat rewarding activities even if they come at great costs. We may excessively engage in activities that feel good in the moment but lead to negative consequences down the road. In such cases, we may then speak of addiction or, if that goes too far for you, addiction-related problems.

We may suffer from withdrawal, feeling anxious, depressed, miserable, frustrated, and irritable when away from the flow activity in question. We may feel bored by everything else and lose interest in other activities. We may compromise our health, neglect our loved ones, and jeopardize our careers and finances. Addiction, behavioral or substance-related, can cause all kinds of problems.

Continued use despite adverse consequences—the hallmark of addiction—is common in various flow activities, especially in extreme sports, internet use, and video gaming.

Flow and Extreme Sports Addiction

Extreme sports athletes are often referred to as "adrenaline junkies." A junkie can be defined as "a person with a compulsive habit or obsessive dependency on something."[3] Continued use despite adverse consequences is a staple in these sports; participants frequently get injured or lose their lives when skydiving, BASE jumping, downhill skiing, kayaking, or rock climbing.

Addiction is very real in these sports, and flow lies at the heart of it. Interviews with some of the world's best big wave surfers revealed that experiencing flow was one of the key reasons for engaging in the sport.[4] Participants didn't necessarily use the term flow, but they certainly described the experience. Here's an example:

> ". . . when you surf the best, you are in the zone. You are there alone. It is you, the wind, the waves, the salt in your mouth and the vision of the bumps and the chop and the sucking phase. There is nothing else there. There is nothing else in your mind. There is nothing else that matters. For a moment in time, time stands still and you are able to control the most uncontrollable because everything becomes slow motion and that's when you know you are surfing the best."

The interviews highlighted various features of addiction, such as tolerance, withdrawal, social conflicts, and continuation despite injuries. Many surfers used drug analogies and straight-up used the term "addiction." The authors of the study concluded that the surfers showed various characteristics of dependence on surfing.

Flow and addiction are common in extreme sports.

Rock climbing has been shown to produce both deep flow states and symptoms of dependency. One study concluded that rock climbers experience withdrawal symptoms comparable to people with substance and behavioral addictions.[5] Participants mentioned that climbing heightens their threshold for enjoyment, making other activities seem mundane and boring by comparison. They mentioned a "need" to go climbing and likened their cravings to those of smokers. Some mentioned feeling "restless," "miserable," "agitated," or "frustrated" when not being able to climb. Others referred to climbing as a "good stress reliever" that can provide "total escapism." Drug analogies were also frequently used. "The general feeling when you're held off it (climbing) would be exactly the same as drug takers, frustrated, driven to get it whatever it is and elation when you actually manage it."[6] "It's like for a drug user, they will take cocaine to get high. For me it's my addiction, I have to go to the mountains to get high."[7]

Flow and Addiction in Big Wave Surfing

Here are some quotes from big wave surfers highlighting various aspects of addiction. The quotes are from Partington et al. (2009).[8]

"We actually get high off it."

"It's like a drug or something."

"You just get a taste of it and I think it becomes addictive almost. It's something you can't quench, you can't satisfy and you chase it . . . It's there for a period of time and then you kinda hang your guns up for a while, dry out and then think when can I do it again?"

"My husband like wants to have babies. I kinda don't cause I want to keep surfing you know? Gosh it's kinda like once you are in it, you are almost stuck in it almost, you know? It's like you are in the club and in order to keep doing it, you have to keep doing it all the time."

"There is a risk of dying, of breaking bones, but the feeling you get off it (flow) is like no other feeling in the world. The best drugs cannot get you the same level of ecstasy, feeling of really good adrenaline. Once you get familiar with that feeling it's an addiction."

A study with skydivers found the same thing.[9] Skydivers freely state that they are "adrenaline junkies" who are "addicted to the high," that their "relationships suffer," that they "spend all of their money on skydiving," that they "can't get enough," that they "lose interest in other activities and things," and that they "suffer withdrawal" when they haven't jumped for a while. A small percentage of them graduate to BASE jumping, which is much riskier but even "more thrilling." As one participant put it, "Everyday jumping was becoming boring, you need to throw a little spice into it." The researchers also confirm that skydiving readily produces flow and that flow plays a key role in the addictive pull of skydiving.

The following quote from the researchers describes well the addictive potential of flow: "As a benefit or end state, flow is cathartic, leaving individuals both satisfied and exhilarated, with a sense of self-authentication. . . . Zen-like, individuals attain and sustain a period of accomplishment that transcends their normal level of efficiency; physical and mental activity are one. In this sense, flow is spell-like and has addictive qualities that summon individuals back over and over again."

Kotler's *The Rise of Superman* was entirely written around flow in action and adventure sports.[10] He spent years hanging around and interviewing some of the world's best athletes. In the book, Kotler refers to them as "flow junkies" who use extreme sports to "get their fix."

He quotes wingsuit and climbing legend Dean Potter to underscore the serious withdrawal extreme sports athletes can suffer from. "When I feel that really draining side of not being able to enter into the flow, it's horrible. I feel helpless, lethargic, restless, disturbed. The positive here is I hate that feeling so much it makes me more focused. I take all the necessary steps to get out of it as soon as I can. Sometimes, though, I end up sunk in a really bad place. True depression, trapped for quite some time."

Great highs, it seems, are capable of producing great lows. Snowboarder JP Schlick puts it well: "Thinking about the flow experience as a pendulum is perhaps most appropriate — in swinging to the highest of highs, it must also swing back."[11]

As mentioned earlier, Potter died in a wingsuit flying accident in 2015. His story highlights well the bright and dark sides of flow. On the one hand, he lived fully and experienced ecstatic and transcendent states most of us will likely never experience. On the other hand, he also experienced great despair and, in the end, paid the ultimate price in the pursuit of flow.

Less extreme sports can be mildly addictive as well. The prevalence of *exercise addiction* in the general population is said to be around 3%.[12] The number is higher for endurance athletes (14.2%), soccer, basketball, volleyball, and other ball sports enthusiasts (10.4%), fitness center attendees (8.2%), and weightlifters, bodybuilders, and crossfitters (6.4%).[13]

In general, the more intense the "high" experienced in any given sport, the greater the risk for addiction. All things being equal, the better an activity feels, the greater its addictive pull.

Flow and Internet Addiction

Flow on the internet, sometimes called *online flow*, is common. That's because various aspects of the internet (e.g., controllability, immediate feedback, ease of use, immersiveness, stimulation, interactivity, novelty, and access to entertainment) make it highly conducive to flow.

The internet is, in fact, designed to induce flow in its users. As one group of scientists explains: "As the internet gained popularity, researchers attempted to improve the use and experience of the World Wide Web by endeavoring to induce psychological states of immersive pleasure, by accommodating online flow. There has been an ongoing interest to better identify, understand and even optimize the role of online flow in various internet activities ranging from e-health and ecommerce to internet related entertainment."[14]

It's easy to get absorbed in even simple online activities like reading and sending email, seeking information, texting, watching videos, or scrolling through social media feeds. It's probably even easier to experience flow in activities like online shopping, gaming, gambling, watching pornography, or participating in cybersex.

Put shortly, the internet provides easy access to flow, available 24–7, at the push of a button, with little effort involved. If that sounds like an addictive recipe to you, that's absolutely right.

Internet addiction can be defined as "a state where an individual has lost control of the internet use and keeps using internet excessively to the point where he/she experiences problematic outcomes that negatively affects his/her life."[15] Symptoms include being preoccupied with the internet, frequently staying online longer than intended, having repeatedly yet unsuccessfully tried to control or cut back internet use, feeling restless, moody, depressed, or irritable when attempting to control use, and having jeopardized or risked the loss of a significant relationship, job, educational, or career opportunity because of the internet.

Does flow play a part in this phenomenon? It sure does. A 2014 study with high schoolers concluded that flow can increase high school students' addiction to the internet.[16] A 2018 study showed that participants who reported experiencing more flow on the internet were more likely to also report experiencing symptoms of internet addiction.[17]

Many other studies point to the same conclusion: The more a person finds using the internet interesting, enjoyable, exciting, and fun, is deeply engrossed, fully concentrated, and totally absorbed when using the internet, and loses track of time and forgets about their immediate surroundings when on the internet, the more at risk they are to suffer from internet addiction.

A 2014 study showed that flow can significantly predict compulsive smartphone use.[18] Participants who reported experiencing more flow when using the smartphone were more likely to report having made unsuccessful attempts to reduce the time using smartphone, finding it difficult to control smartphone use, and having a hard time trying to resist the urge to use it.

Another study looked at flow and media addiction and found that experiences of flow significantly influenced addiction to the internet, mobile phones, and video games.[19] The researchers concluded that individuals who experience more flow are more likely to struggle with addictive media use behaviors.

All things being equal, more flow equals more compulsive, excessive, and problematic use. As mentioned earlier, the more rewarding an activity is for a given person, the more likely he or she is to fall prey to addiction.

This doesn't mean everyone who finds great enjoyment in an activity gets addicted; other factors like personality and social support play a huge role as well. But it does mean that flow poses a risk factor for either full-blown addiction or addiction-related issues.

Flow and Gaming Addiction

During my high school years, I played an online game called *Demigod*. I've never engaged in an activity that so reliably put me in a flow state as this game. Within a few minutes of playing, I was gone from the real world and utterly and totally catapulted into the game. I entered a kind of trance-like state, characterized by being completely zoned into the game and oblivious to my surroundings. It was a state of full involvement, of pure and total absorption. It was riveting. If you were to look at me from the outside, you'd think to yourself, *Whoah, this kid is off in another world.* On the inside, it felt thrilling and exciting, kind of like an ongoing adrenaline rush.

The game had me hooked. Its allure was so powerful that I couldn't keep myself away from it. I played and played and played, and within a couple of weeks or months, I was showing clear signs of addiction. There were many days when I played upwards of 14 hours, just taking enough time away from gaming to eat, drink, and take care of my bodily needs. I often played until three or four o'clock in the morning. The next day, I was usually so tired that I skipped the morning classes. I remember one of my teachers telling me, "Nils, you haven't attended any Thursday morning classes for several weeks now. I don't buy your excuses anymore. You better show up next time." Even if I managed to get up in the morning, I was so tired in class that I could barely stay awake. It was seriously hard not to fall asleep at times, let alone concentrate on the subject being discussed.

During the height of my addiction, the game completely took over my world. The first thing I thought about upon getting up in the morning was Demigod, and the last thing I thought about before I went to sleep was Demigod. Most of what I thought about throughout the day was also Demigod. How could I get even better? What might I have overlooked in the last games? Which tactics could I try next time? When I got home from school, the first thing I did was walk upstairs, turn on the laptop, load the game, grab a bottle of milk from the fridge, and start playing. Most of the time I didn't even bother taking off my shoes or, to my mother's annoyance, put away my school bag. Oh, and when I wasn't playing, I was reading on the forums or watching replays. In total, the statistics suggest that I played well over 100,000 minutes (the equivalent of 1,666 hours or roughly 70 days).

I was obsessed with the game and neglected everything else at its expense—studying, exercising, sleeping, spending time with family and friends, or helping out in the household. It was a rough time for me and my family. Why my family? Let's just say I wasn't exactly the nicest person when someone interrupted me during gaming or when someone suggested I was addicted or wasn't able to stop. I was embarrassed by my lack of discipline and inability to resist playing. I tried to keep how much I played a secret and lied about it. I denied that I had lost control. I was irritated, angry, defensive, and uninterested a lot of the time.

As you can see, I showed many characteristics of addiction. Continuation despite adverse consequences? Check. Withdrawal? Check. Secrecy and denial? Check. Obsession and preoccupation? Check. Inability to stop? Check.

Thankfully, after multiple failed attempts at quitting, I eventually kicked the habit. I moved to Brighton, England, for a 4-month stay abroad after high school, and I was able to use that change of scenery as a catalyst to quit for good.

Gaming addiction is perhaps the best-known and most prevalent behavioral addiction. It is said that between 1–5% of the general population are affected.[20] Video games, even more so than the internet, are designed to induce flow in players. "It is standard in the game community to desire gameplay that puts players into the zone or flow," explains game scholar Brian Schrank.[21]

More flow equals greater enjoyment and longer playtime, which equals more money for game producers. "Game developers today understand that games become hits and make money in direct proportion to how much satisfaction they provide and how much positive emotion they provoke," explains game designer Jane McGonigal.[22] "As a result, game designers have been taught to relentlessly pursue happiness outcomes, including flow…"

In his popular design manual, *The Art of Game Design*, Jesse Schell writes: "[I]t pays for game designers to make a careful study of flow. . . . When observing a player, flow can be easy to miss—you must learn to recognize it. . . . Once you notice a player going into flow during your game, you need to watch them closely—they won't stay there forever. You must watch for that crucial moment—the event that moves them out of the flow channel, so you can figure out how to make sure that event doesn't happen in your next prototype of the game."[23]

Flow is said to hold "a position of almost paradigmatic power in game studies."[24] It is touted by some as the "holy grail of game design."[25] No other field, some argue, has been more influenced by the quest for flow than the study and design of video games.

According to McGonigal, the advent of video games "made it possible to experience flow almost immediately… From zero to peak experience in thirty seconds flat—no wonder video games caught on. Never before in human history could this kind of optimal, emotional activation be accessed so cheaply, so reliably, so quickly."[26] No wonder, either, that excessive and compulsive use is so widespread.

Addiction to video games goes by many names, including problem video game playing, problematic online game use, video game addiction, online gaming addiction, and internet gaming addiction.[27]

One of the more popular terms is *internet gaming disorder,* or *IGD* for short. Criteria include continued excessive use of games despite knowledge of psychosocial problems, unsuccessful attempts to reduce gaming, loss of interest in previous hobbies, deceiving family members, therapists, or others regarding the amount of gaming, and jeopardizing or losing a significant relationship, job, or education or career opportunity because of participation in gaming.[28] IGD is associated with various negative consequences, such as increased depression, loneliness, conduct problems, lower academic achievement, maladaptive coping, substance use, suicidal ideation and attempt, and loss of relationship with partner and family.[29]

Flow is a key culprit in the development of this phenomenon. A 2019 study on flow and IGD concluded: "The results of the present study are consistent with the findings of past studies which investigated the relationship between online flow and IGD. In two studies, gamers who reported experiencing higher flow (immersive pleasure) were also found to spend more time playing games. Clearly, the experience of online flow is attractive to gamers. Thus, a desire to attain the feeling of flow (immersive pleasure), might affect the frequency and duration of gaming, and therefore be implicated in the development and persistence of IGD behaviors."[30] Another study concluded that online gaming addiction can be explained by the flow experience.[31] Meanwhile, a 2022 study concluded that "the higher the flow experience experienced by online game players, the more likely it is to lead to online gaming addiction."[32]

Countless studies show the same thing. Video games produce lots of flow and are highly addictive. How big of a role flow plays in the addiction is hard to say, but it's definitely a risk factor.

Flow is likely to play a role in other behavioral addictions as well, for example, in sex addiction, porn addiction, shopping addiction, work addiction (workaholism), or gambling addiction. As we're about to see, it may even play a role in drug addiction.

Flow and Drug Addiction

"Besides substance-related variations, most drugs induce extremely positive experiences," explain Italian flow researchers Antonella Delle Fave, Fausto Massimini, and Marta Bassi.[33] "A perception of complete absorption, deep involvement, isolation from the surrounding world, and psychophysical well-being are commonly described." Many drugs induce flow-like experiences.

A study of flow in cannabis users concluded: "Cannabis contributes to wellbeing or optimal experience of consciousness for users. Consistent with descriptions found in other applications of the flow experience (e.g., with reference to athletes, artists, or musicians, or otherwise creative individuals), cannabis enhances the ability of users to meet and manage challenges arising from impairment due to chronic physical or mental health conditions… users experience a state of mind or spiritual connection marked by a sense of harmony, autonomy, empowerment, order, and control over their actions and surroundings."[34]

Methamphetamine can produce feelings of euphoria, arousal, reduced fatigue, loss of inhibition, increased sociability, and greater self-confidence.[35] Fentanyl, heroin, and other opioids can induce intense and euphoric highs.[36] Cocaine, too, can create a high, characterized by feelings of alertness, power, energy, confidence, and excitement.[37]

The psychedelic states induced by LSD, MDMA, magic mushrooms, and other substances are marked by the same selflessness, timelessness, effortlessness, and richness as flow. As I've briefly mentioned in chapter 3, flow and psychedelic states share some of the same neurobiology and can both be defined as non-ordinary states of consciousness.

When drug users were asked about their flow experiences, all of them mentioned drug consumption as one of their most frequent flow activities.[38] This means that all of them associated drug experiences with flow, speaking to the fact that drugs induce flow-like states.

A 2003 study investigated flow in addicts undergoing treatment and ex-addicts living in detoxification communities.[39] The goal was to assess similarities and differences between flow during drug intake and during other activities. Both experiences shared high levels of involvement, concentration, enjoyment, and excitement. However, participants reported feeling less relaxed and less in control during drug-induced flow, compared to flow in productive and leisure activities.

An additional difference noted by the researchers is that the chemically induced flow can leave people feeling anxious, depressed, and weary once the experience is over. In the long-run, it can have further negative consequences, especially if people get addicted. Addicts can "become progressively disengaged from daily life and activities, physically weak, and marginalized from the social context." This is in stark contrast to "real" flow experiences, which tend to leave people feeling strong, content, proud, accomplished, and capable and tend to lead to growth and greater life satisfaction (with exceptions, as we're learning in this chapter).

These differences led the researchers to suggest that drugs induce *mimetic flow* or *pseudo-optimal experiences*. According to this view, substance-induced flow is a kind of fake flow—drugs merely "deceive consciousness with an ephemeral perception of well-being, while entailing substantially maladaptive implications."

While this is true in many cases, there are important exceptions and caveats. Not all drugs are the same, and not all users are the same either. Some substances are clearly more addictive and potentially destructive than others. Some users no doubt abuse and overuse certain substances to their own detriment. Other users are able to use drugs constructively and benefit greatly from them.

So, does flow play a role in drug addiction? It sure does. "In our opinion the real problem of drug intake, which generates addiction, is the subjective experience associated with it," explains the Italian research team.[40] It's the flow-like experiences—experiences that provide both the presence of pleasure (the ecstatic high) and the absence of pain (difficult thoughts, memories, emotions)—that make drugs so attractive. Drugs may be taken to get pleasure or to avoid pain. Either way, flow provides the fix.

What about substances that don't evoke flow-like states but are addictive nonetheless? In such cases, flow may play a different role. It may be that a substance becomes addictive because of its flow-facilitating effects.

Caffeine on its own doesn't produce an intense, ecstatic, flow-like experience. But it does boost focus, alertness, and energy, which makes entry into flow more likely. Other substances have similar effects. Nicotine boosts concentration and reduces anxiety. Stimulants enhance alertness, energy, and attention. Alcohol, marijuana, and benzodiazepines reduce anxiety and overthinking and tone down self-consciousness. Pain killers free up attention and reduce internal interruptions by reducing pain.

Substances may thus hold some addictive power by virtue of facilitating the flow experience. Speaking for myself, I don't think I would use coffee and occasionally other stimulants, nicotine (in the form of lozenges), nootropic substances, and alcohol if I didn't see a benefit in taking them. All of them can make my experience more flow-like. While I wouldn't classify myself as addicted to these substances, I certainly see the addictive potential. I also see how these substances could cause more harm than gain if used excessively.

To sum up, drugs may be addictive in part via their relationship to flow: by either bringing about intense flow-like experiences all on their own or by facilitating entry into the state. Drugs are able to make our lives more flowy. This can be good but also dangerous.

Before moving on, I want to clarify that I'm not advocating for or against the use of drugs. In my opinion, drugs are neither good nor bad. They are tools and powerful ones at that. Drugs get people killed and can cause great destruction. But they also save lives and can cause great benefits.

Writers, poets, musicians, painters, and other artists have relied on nicotine, alcohol, marijuana, and other substances for ages—many great works of art would never have seen the light of day without them.[41] Our civilization likely wouldn't be as "advanced" if it weren't for coffee.[42] Preliminary evidence suggests that microdosing with psychedelics can improve mood, increase energy levels, boost work effectiveness, and confer a host of other benefits.[43]

Full-dose psychedelic trips show great promise for everything from opioid addiction, smoking cessation, depression, anxiety, Alzheimer's disease, post-traumatic stress disorder (PTSD), anorexia nervosa, and alcohol addiction.[44]

Drugs can heal, and drugs can destroy. They can bring more flow into our lives, for better and for worse.

Flow and Risk-Taking

As our depictions of big wave surfers, rock climbers, and skydivers have shown, the pursuit of flow can lead to risky behavior. Extreme sports athletes are willing to endanger their health and risk their lives for the sake of experiencing flow. "The joy I get from skiing, that's worth dying for," said freeskiing pioneer C. R. Johnson who died skiing in 2010 at age 26.

Risk is one of Kotler's 22 flow triggers (see chapter 4). When your life is at stake, your whole being is instantly pulled into the present moment. The full array of your resources becomes available. Adrenaline and other high-performance hormones flood your system. Your senses grow sharper. You become hyper-alert, hyper-sensitive, and hyper-focused. The nagging voice within goes quiet—your shortcomings don't take precedence right now. You are completely and totally involved in overcoming the challenge at hand.

Risk provides easy entry into flow. As Dean Potter said, "I take the easy way. I can sit on my ass and meditate for two hours to get a fifteen-second glimpse of this state. Or I can risk my life and get there instantly—and it lasts for hours."[45]

People select risky activities in order to experience flow. That's one aspect of the flow-risk relationship. There is another: During the experience of flow itself, further risk-taking may result from an altered risk perception. The loss of self-reflective awareness, the lost sense of time, the absence of anxiety, and the complete focus on a limited stimulus field combined with the feeling of having everything under control—these are elements of flow that might impair risk assessment.

And indeed, preliminary studies have found a relationship between flow and distorted risk perception. A study on white-water kayaking, a risky sport that involves the possibility of being seriously hurt or losing one's life through drowning, found that flow was associated with an underestimation of risks.[46] The study also confirmed that kayaking is an activity that easily brings about the experience of flow.

A later study with kayakers and rock climbers found the same negative effect of flow on risk perception, but only for inexperienced participants.[47] The researchers concluded: "Experienced athletes can get the most out of flow. They feel effective, but their experience in the sport situation does not lead them to underestimate risk or engage in risky behavior. In short, their expertise protects them from risks. Inexperienced persons lack such protection. They too may experience flow while engaging in their sport... However, having less information that could help them to judge the situation (in particular, knowledge about which situations are potentially dangerous) they are mostly guided by these feelings, which may betray them into underestimating and taking risks."

It's too early to say anything conclusive about flow's relationship to risk perception. What we can say for sure is that flow can lead to risky behavior simply because risk strongly facilitates the experience. The fact that people get injured and die in the pursuit of flow certainly reflects a dark side of the phenomenon.

Flow in Antisocial Contexts

Flow "does not necessarily have positive ethical or social consequences," explain Csikszentmihalyi and a fellow researcher.[48] One of the dangers inherent in flow is "that it can be experienced in antisocial contexts. When lacking other opportunities for action, or if deprived of sufficient skills, people will seek flow in destructive activities like violence, gambling, excessive risks, or drugs. Many people derive intrinsic rewards from crime or warfare; that they enjoy it does not justify their actions."

Flow is defined as an enjoyable, transient experience. What happens to other people or the environment during the experience, or what happens afterward, is a different question. Flow is an optimal state that may or may not produce optimal outcomes for individuals and the world as a whole. While flow is always fun, its consequences can be everything but.

People experience flow in various activities (e.g., stealing, burglarizing, vandalizing, computer hacking, graffiti spraying, fighting, or speeding) that tend to produce tragic and socially undesirable consequences.

Most notably, people experience flow in combat situations. "Battle veterans often describe front-line war experiences with nostalgia, as the time when they felt most intensely alive," explains Csikszentmihalyi.[49] "Warfare is an excellent flow activity because it provides clear goals, unambiguous feedback, total involvement, and potentially matched challenges and skills."

According to Historian Yuval Noah Harari, so-called *combat flow* "may have been central to military training and military performance throughout history."[50]

War veterans frequently describe that they felt "completely alive," "ecstatic," "absorbed in the moment," "strangely calm," and "free from fear" during combat. They refer to states of "complete mental and physical awareness," "zest," and "sheer delight." They mention how these states increased efficiency and enabled them to maximize their abilities.[51]

Philip Caputo was a Marine Lieutenant in the Vietnam war. In his memoir *A Rumor of War,* he describes how he led a platoon and encountered a Vietcong unit.[52] At first, he felt paralyzed and found the experience of being in battle suffocating. Then, all of a sudden, he became completely absorbed in the present moment; irrelevant thoughts disappeared, reflection ceased, and he entered the zone.

> "An eerie sense of calm came over me. My mind was working with a speed and clarity I would have found remarkable if I had had the time to reflect upon it. I knew what I was going to do. . . . The whole plan of attack flashed through my mind in a matter of seconds."

Leading his platoon to victory was one of the most enjoyable experiences of his life.

> "I felt a drunken elation. . . . I had never experienced anything like it before... an ache as profound as the ache of orgasm passed through me."

Back home, Caputo experienced the low of flow. Normal life paled in comparison to the exhilaration of the battlefield. He must have felt similar to how extreme sports athletes feel when away from their sport.

"Within a year I began growing nostalgic for the war. . . . I could protest [against the war] as loudly as the most convinced activist, but I could not deny the grip the war had on me, nor the fact that it had been an experience as fascinating as it was repulsive, as exhilarating as it was sad. . . . Anyone who fought in Vietnam, if he is honest about himself, will have to admit he enjoyed the compelling attractiveness of combat."

"Under fire, a man's powers of life heightened in proportion to the proximity of death. His senses quickened, he attained an acuity of consciousness at once pleasurable and excruciating. It was something like the elevated state of awareness induced by drugs. And it could be just as addictive, for it made whatever else life offered in the way of delights or torments seem pedestrian."

Caputo's experience is common. "I do not think there was any time of my life that I enjoyed more than that at the Siege of Sebastopol," said William Martin, a British veteran of the siege of Sebastopol (1854–1855).[53] "It was good weather, and though those who went into the trenches never all came back, this did not cast any shade of gloom on our lives; but, on the contrary, the danger we daily and hourly encountered gave a zest to life that nothing else can give."

In *War and Peace*, Leo Tolstoy, who himself fought in the Crimean War, describes the experience of an artillery battery commander: The commander "did not experience the slightest qualm of fear, and the idea that he might be killed or badly wounded never entered his head. On the contrary, he grew more and more elated... Though he forgot nothing, thought of everything, did everything the best of officers could have done in his position, he was in a state akin to feverish delirium or intoxication."[54]

In *Battle as an Inner Experience*, Ernst Jünger, who fought in the first World War, describes the combat experience as ecstatic.[55] "The condition of the holy man, of great poets and of great love," he writes, "is also granted to those of great courage. The enthusiasm of manliness bursts beyond itself to such an extent that the blood boils as it surges through the veins and glows as it foams through the heart . . . [I]t is an intoxication beyond all intoxication, an unleashing that breaks all bonds."

Flow may have played a role in countless war crimes and other violent and antisocial acts. By temporarily turning off reflective thinking and thus canceling morality, flow may "allow" people to commit crimes they would never consciously intend to commit. Swept away by a trance-like experience, soldiers may brutalize civilians and kill innocents. Perpetrators may only fully realize what they've done upon waking up from their delirium. I'll spare you the real-life examples, but make no doubt about it, they exist.[56]

Even more chilling is the notion that flow can make criminal acts enjoyable. People may be so attracted to the highs of hacking, stealing, speeding, or fighting that they are willing to pursue such activities at the expense of other people. A soldier may choose to fight another battle not for the sake of winning the war but for the sake of being in battle—for the sheer enjoyment of it.

It's a disturbing prospect, but research suggests there's some truth in it. "A large proportion of peacetime crimes are not motivated by want but by the enjoyable experience the criminal derives from the act," explains Csikszentmihalyi.[57] He quotes a young burglar: "If you can show me something to do that's as much fun as getting into a house at night, and lifting all the loot while the people stay asleep, I'll be glad to switch."[58]

Csikszentmihalyi saw both the problem and the solution to antisocial flow in the school system.[59] The problem is that school fails to provide flow experiences, which means "the only source of flow that students find is the negative opportunity to hurt or destroy. . . . The inability of schools to provide engaging action systems helps to create bored, frustrated, dissatisfied people. Since they lack opportunities for enjoyable involvement through school, students seek alternate structures of challenges to obtain flow experiences."

The solution is to provide students with more access to prosocial and constructive flow experiences within the school system. It is to "teach children to experience flow in settings that are not harmful to self and others," to "teach youths how to find pleasure in action which strengthens the bonds of human solidarity instead of weakening them."

Final Thoughts

As with most things in life, flow is neither good nor bad in an absolute sense. While the experience always feels "good"—enjoyable, fun, and even ecstatic—the consequences of that optimal inner state can be good or bad, creative or destructive.

Flow in extreme sports can lead to addiction, withdrawal, injury, and death. But it can also contribute to meaning, rapture, joy, bliss, and a life worth living. C.R. Johnson said the joy of skiing was worth dying for. He died doing what he loved the most after spending much of his life also doing what he had loved the most. Extreme sports athletes are said to die too early. But they are also said to "live life to the fullest" and "live thousands of lifetimes" in the short span of a few years or decades.[60]

Flow can make other sports addictive as well. But it also makes them enjoyable, and by doing that, it helps us become healthier and happier. Harvard scientist John Ratey explains in his book *Spark* that physical exercise positively impacts learning, attention, stress, anxiety, depression, aging, and more.[61] He suggests that "exercise is the single most powerful tool you have to optimize your brain function. . . . [E]xercise has a profound impact on cognitive abilities and mental health."

Designing games so that they lend themselves to flow makes these games highly addictive. People may jeopardize their health, careers, and relationships as a result. But flow also makes games enjoyable and fun to play. Gaming can provide learning, health, and social benefits.[62] In e-learning, gamification can make learning both more fun and effective. When researchers upgraded a university course to include gamification features, the students' understanding, engagement, and course grades all improved.[63]

Flow enhances competencies, making people better at performing surgery, driving ambulances, making medical diagnoses, writing, singing, dancing, and making comedy. But it also makes people better at designing new weapons, shooting down enemy planes, marketing and selling shady products, stealing, or fighting.

Flow provides escape from negative thoughts and emotions, which can be adaptive when occasionally used as a form of healthy distraction. But it can also be maladaptive if used excessively as a way to avoid facing difficult issues and problems.

Flow is best viewed as a tool, much like a hammer. Whether the hammer builds or destroys depends on the person using it; it depends on that person's motivations, values, ethics, and moral convictions.

Csikszentmihalyi likened flow to a form of energy, which "can be used either to help or to destroy. Fire warms or burns; atomic energy can generate electricity, or it can obliterate the world. Energy is power, but power is only a means. The goals to which it is applied can make life either richer or more painful."[64] It is therefore vital to "distinguish the useful and the harmful forms of flow, and then making the most of the former while placing limits on the latter."

Whether flow will be a net-positive or net-negative in your life is entirely up to you—the wielder of the tool. Use it well, and you'll be happier, healthier, and more successful for it. Use it badly, and you might go down a path of addiction, crime, moral dilemma, injury, or even death.

Flow is powerful. It's up to you to use that power responsibly.

Part 3

Making it Happen

Chapter 13

Flow(ing) at Work

*Forget the money, because if you say that getting the money is the most
important thing, you will spend your life completely wasting your time.
You'll be doing things you don't like doing in order to go on living—
that is, to go on doing things you don't like doing. Which is stupid.*

—ALAN WATTS

In the summer of 2020, I worked three different jobs. I worked first as a
construction worker, then as an employee in a wood working factory, and
finally as an employee in a rehabilitation center.

On the first job, I experienced little to no flow. My co-workers had a
terrible attitude and were moaning and complaining constantly. They were
disengaged, cold, and distant. I had almost no autonomy and felt insecure,
tense, and out of place most of the time. Some of the tasks would actually
have been quite interesting and engaging. But because the whole atmosphere
was so stifling, I had a hard time letting loose and relaxing into task-focused
attention. I was stuck in my head. My days were marked by watching the
clock and hoping for the workday to end.

On the second job, the co-workers were much nicer. They were positive,
motivated, and engaged. I felt more autonomous and confident and more
ready to experience flow. But despite these more advantageous circumstances,
I again experienced very little flow. Why? Because the tasks I had to perform
were so monotonous and easy that they weren't able to hold my attention.
Action and awareness were split. I was working but my mind was somewhere
else. I was under-challenged and bored. And so again, I was often watching
the clock and hoping for the day to end.

On the third job, things finally took a turn for the better. My co-workers
were friendly and supportive and the atmosphere was lighthearted and fun. I
felt appreciated, comfortable, and at home. The tasks I was able to perform

provided variety and suited me well. I was able to use many of my strengths and was directly involved in helping patients. The contrast to the previous two jobs was stark. Time went by much faster, the work was more rewarding and meaningful, and I experienced much more flow.

As these examples illustrate, some jobs are more conducive to flow than others. If you experience plenty of flow at your current job, that's great. If not, switching jobs may be one of the most impactful ways for you to experience more flow in your life.

But what should you look for in a job? What determines whether a job is conducive to flow or not? That's what we'll find out in this chapter. We'll discuss the many different factors that make jobs more or less conducive to flow. This knowledge will help you evaluate your current job and help you decide if making a change might be worth the trouble. It will also help you choose the most flow-conducive job on your next job search. If you are in a leadership role, it will help you create a more flow-supportive environment for yourself and your colleagues.

Flow-Conducive Work Activities

The activities you perform on the job clearly have the biggest impact on how much flow you'll experience. If what you do is boring, repetitive, monotonous, or overly stressful, you will struggle to find flow. That's true even if the money is great, the company's mission is inspiring, and the co-workers are wonderful.

So what would you ideally be doing at work? What kind of tasks help you experience flow?

If you can engage in activities you're good at and allow you to use your strengths, that's a big plus. As we'll see in chapter 14, using your strengths is exciting, meaningful, and highly conducive to flow.

It's also helpful if you can engage in activities you find interesting.[1] Whenever you find something interesting, your attention is naturally and effortlessly captured. You don't need to expend energy to concentrate; concentration happens on its own. Interest makes it easy to enter the kind of focused attention necessary for flow. This is why complex tasks are generally more conducive to flow than mundane ones.[2]

If you're able to perform a variety of different tasks and are able to use multiple skills and talents, that's also helpful. [3] Doing the same things over and over can become repetitive, dull, and boring. Being allowed to work on a complete process rather than just small and isolated parts, that's also advantageous.[4] Being involved in the entire process helps us feel more responsible, invested, engaged, and motivated.

If you're able to directly help another person or are able to see how you're benefitting the greater good in some way, that's also helpful. As we'll learn later on, the kind of motivation that comes from making a positive impact is highly conducive to flow.

Lastly, tasks should be appropriate for your skill level. Flow is most likely to occur when there's a balance between your skills and the difficulty of an activity. If tasks are too easy, you'll feel bored. If too difficult, you'll feel anxious. You're looking for a job or position that provides just the right challenge for you.

A job that provides all of these elements to some degree is highly conducive to flow.

Flow-Conducive Work Relationships

Next up, let's consider some of the social factors that make flow more or less likely on the job.

In general, workplaces with high *social capital* are more conducive to flow.[5] These are workplaces characterized by positive social relationships, cooperation and mutual support, trust and reciprocity, and the open sharing of information and resources between colleagues and supervisors.

Workplaces with high levels of *social support* are also more conducive to flow. When you feel valued by colleagues, are able to ask for and receive help, and can count on others when facing difficulties, you are more likely to experience flow. A 2021 review on flow in the work context writes: "Knowing that colleagues are at our side when things get tight has a beneficial effect on the frequency of flow in the workplace."[6]

Fun among colleagues is another factor that fosters flow.[7] How? By enabling restful breaks and creating positive emotions, which subsequently make it easier to enter flow.

Supervisors and managers also play a crucial role. Employees who get performance feedback (e.g., receive sufficient information about the results and satisfactoriness of their work) tend to experience more flow.[8] Employees who feel valued and adequately coached and who feel that their superior uses their influence to help them solve problems at work also tend to experience more flow.[9]

Leadership matters too. Good leaders support work environments conducive to flow by providing support, feedback, autonomy, encouragement, and opportunities for growth, facilitating trust among employees, and creating a safe climate. Two specific leadership styles have been found to be positively related to flow: *authentic leadership* and *transformational leadership* [10]

The former is a style in which the manager is aware of their own values, is reliable and open in their thinking, promotes the strengths of employees, and tries to create an overall positive and pleasant working environment. The latter involves communicating a clear vision (and walking the talk by behaving in ways consistent with that vision), expressing genuine concern about employees, encouraging workers to take risks and solve problems creatively, and instilling confidence and motivation in their followers.

The last factor is how much flow the other people in a work environment experience. A high-flow workplace increases your chances of experiencing flow via flow contagion. Your superiors and co-workers will transfer their flow, or their lack thereof, over to you.

Flow Contagion

Have you ever worked alongside people who truly enjoyed their work and who were engaged, energized, and excited about what they did? Such attitudes are contagious, and so are attitudes that communicate dread, disinterest, and disengagement.

The transfer of emotions and attitudes from one person to another is called *emotional contagion*. It's formally defined as the "tendency to automatically mimic and synchronize facial expressions, vocalizations, postures and movements with those of another person and, consequently, to converge emotionally."[11]

Several studies now suggest that the experience of flow is also contagious. One study showed that when music teachers reported higher levels of flow, their students also reported higher levels of flow.[12] The researchers hypothesize that students catch the flow of their teachers by unconsciously imitating their cheerfulness and positive mood and by consciously adopting their dedication to their work. Another study showed that both the flow of teachers and the flow of fellow classmates influenced how much flow a student experienced during class.[13]

People transfer their flow, or their lack thereof, over to you. High-flow workplaces, classrooms, and teams will increase your chances of experiencing flow.

A Flow-Conducive Organization

The organization as a whole, with its culture, mission, values, and policies, also plays a critical role. For example, employees are more likely to experience flow in an organization that provides a climate of innovation and safety and offers opportunities for growth.[14] It also makes intuitive sense that when a company's mission is inspiring, and its values are congruent with your personal values, you are more likely to see work as meaningful and to experience flow.

Companies can do a lot to support or hinder your chances of experiencing flow.

In chapter 18, we'll discuss the importance of switching off after work and getting sufficient recovery. Some organizations explicitly communicate that no emails should be read or answered during leisure time and that work should not be taken home. The German car company Volkswagen goes a step further and switches off mail servers for smartphones overnight.[15] Other companies offer free gym memberships, yoga classes, or nap rooms to promote rest and recovery.

Some organizations deliberately design fun in their workplaces, providing refreshing breaks and increasing the probability of flow in subsequent activities. Companies may employ a director of fun, provide ping-pong tables, or organize gamedays.

Companies can also promote trust and positive relationships in various ways, such as through team trainings, joint after-work activities, or by providing shared kitchens and other places where joint breaks can occur. Some companies provide training in authentic and transformational leadership or training in management methods designed to facilitate flow in employees.

As these examples show, the company as a whole can make a big difference in how much flow you experience.

The Dream-Job Elixir

One of the most important things a company can do to support your flow is to give you control over how, when, where, and with whom you perform your work. In other words, they can provide you with plenty of *autonomy*, a job characteristic deserving of special attention.

Autonomy has to do with freedom and self-determination. It's about making authentic and self-endorsed choices. It's about feeling in control, as opposed to feeling controlled or pressured by outside forces.

Autonomy is something we all strive for, (knowingly or unknowingly), and for good reason. More than just a nice-to-have, autonomy turns out to be fundamental to human well-being and flourishing. It is described by some psychologists as a basic psychological need in the sense that it's essential to human health.[16] If you deprive a plant of water, it will shrivel and die prematurely. If you deprive a human being of autonomy, it will also shrivel and die prematurely.

This idea is supported by a large body of research. For example, kids with autonomy-supportive parents are better adjusted and more self-motivated in school, are more committed to school, show more positive attitudes toward school, achieve better grades, and have better mental health and well-being.[17] (Autonomy-supportive parenting involves offering choice about how to go about doing things, supporting the child's initiative, providing meaningful rationale when making demands, acknowledging negative feelings, and using noncontrolling language.)

Infants of autonomy-supportive parents are more explorative and curious and persist longer in independent play.[18] When parents are autonomy-supportive during the first three years of life, children are better able to delay gratification, direct their attention, and inhibit impulses.[19] If you're familiar with the *marshmallow experiments*, you know that this type of self-regulation predicts future educational achievement, income, body mass index, life satisfaction, and much more.[20]

During teenage years, children who receive autonomy support are more likely to turn to their parents for help and guidance, more likely to internalize their parents' values, more likely to show good adjustment and achievement in school, less likely to engage in deviant behavior, and generally less problematic in their relationships.[21]

In schools, autonomy-supportive classrooms produce better results than more controlling classrooms. A 2015 review on this topic concluded: "In classrooms where teachers support autonomy, students improve their academic performance, are more creative and better adjusted, engage more in school, and feel less stress."[22] Students in such classrooms are also better able to concentrate and show greater well-being.

At work, having a sense of autonomy boosts employees' productivity and helps them experience their work as more meaningful and satisfying.[23] When employees have autonomy-supportive managers, they have better mental and physical health, are less stressed and less often absent from work, score higher on performance evaluations, stay on the job longer, are more committed to the organization, feel more trust in the organization, and are more satisfied with their job and with the pay and benefits they receive.[24]

Autonomy is "so powerful and so essential" to work satisfaction that Cal Newport, an expert on career building, refers to it as the *dream-job elixir*.[25]

When it comes to flow, autonomy matters, too. Employees who feel like they can decide how their job gets done, who feel free to express their ideas and opinions, and who feel like their feelings are taken into consideration experience more flow than employees who feel pressured at work and feel like they have to simply do what they're told.[26] Autonomy fuels intrinsic motivation, leads to positive emotions, and allows you to work in ways that best suit you. These are all factors that make flow more likely.

When looking for a job, autonomy should be near the top of your wishlist. You want a job that gives you control over how, when, where, and with whom you fulfill your duties. You want to be in an environment that acknowledges your perspective, encourages self-initiation, offers opportunities for choice and input, communicates in an informational rather than controlling manner, and avoids the use of rewards or sanctions to motivate behavior. If you can find such a work environment, you will no doubt thrive and experience plenty of flow.

What About Money or Prestige?

If your goal is to experience flow, there are factors far more important than earning a big salary or occupying a prestigious position. No amount of money or prestige will help you experience flow if your job fails to provide meaning, engaging challenges, or interesting activities.

Money and prestige only really play a role if they are so unsatisfactory as to get in the way of flow. If you're extremely unhappy with your salary or position at work, the resulting negativity can hijack your attention in ways that undermine flow. That being said, above a certain satisfactory threshold, more money and prestige will not result in more flow.

In Summary

So, what's a flow-conducive job? It's a job that allows you to use your strengths, express your values, help others, make a positive impact, and have fun. It's a job that allows you to do things you find interesting and enjoyable. It's a job where the company grants you plenty of autonomy, supports your recovery, employs good people, and provides a culture of safety, openness, innovation, and growth.

If you can find a job that provides even a subset of these factors, you'll experience plenty of flow.

What if Changing Jobs isn't an Option?

I get it. Not everyone is in the position to change jobs. If you think you're stuck in a job that doesn't allow you to experience as much flow as you'd like, that's okay. There are many things you can do to experience more flow on *any* job.

For example, you can make the job more meaningful by thinking about it differently or by finding ways to use your strengths (see chapter 14). Or you can gamify certain aspects of your job (see chapter 15) or adjust certain aspects of your workspace (see chapter 20).

The next chapters will provide you with plenty of ways to experience more flow, both on the job and in your free time.

Chapter 14

The Power of Meaning

Work is about a search for daily meaning as well as daily bread, for recognition as well as cash, for astonishment rather than torpor; in short, for a sort of life rather than a Monday through Friday sort of dying.

—*STUDS TERKEL*

Once upon a time, a person walked past a construction site. The person, ever curious, asked a group of three builders what they were doing. The first builder, seemingly annoyed, barked back that he was laying bricks. The second, with indifference, stated that he was building a wall. The third, with a huge smile on his face, explained that he was erecting a cathedral for the glory of God.

What about you? Do you feel like you're laying bricks? Or do you feel like you're erecting a cathedral?

How you feel about your work makes a big difference in how you show up and how likely you are to experience flow. If you view your work as meaningless, that is likely to make you feel unmotivated, frustrated, indifferent, and disengaged. If what you do feels pointless, you're unlikely to muster the kind of energy and focus supportive of flow. Viewing your work as worthwhile and valuable, on the other hand, tends to foster the kind of motivation and mindset conducive to flow.

Research shows that finding your work meaningful is good for you and for the organization you work for. A 2019 study concluded: "People with meaningful work *feel* better and *work* better."[1] Other studies show that experiencing one's work as significant is associated with job satisfaction, work engagement, organizational commitment, decreased turnover intentions and absenteeism, supervisor-rated performance, and many other positive outcomes.[2]

But what determines whether we experience our work as meaningful or not?

Obviously, the job itself makes a difference. It's surely relatively easy to experience meaning as a doctor who saves lives and receives ample appreciation from patients and loved-ones. It's probably a lot harder as a janitor who removes chewing gum from under tables. Some jobs are simply easier to experience as meaningful than others.

But the job is just one factor. Another factor is how you approach the job and how you view it in your own mind. As the introductory parable has illustrated, the same job can be meaningful for one person and meaningless for another.

A study with hospital cleaners, each having the same official job description, highlights this beautifully.[3] Some of them viewed their job as menial and boring, judged the skill level of the work to be low, disliked cleaning, and did only the minimum that was required of them. Others interpreted their job as bettering the lives of patients, nurses, and visitors. They reported enjoying their work and judged it as highly skilled. They challenged themselves to get the job accomplished in maximally efficient ways and made it their mission to help patients heal faster. They didn't see their work as just mopping floors and emptying trash cans but as improving the lives of others.

Objectively, the hospital cleaners all did the same thing. But how they approached and viewed it was different. And as a result, their experiences were different, too.

So, if you want to experience more meaning at work, you have two main options. First, you can look for a job that is objectively meaningful—a job that makes it easy to feel significant, valued, and motivated. Alternatively, you can create greater meaning by finding ways to approach and interpret what you do in ways that make it feel more meaningful.

This chapter is about the second option. We'll discuss three proven ways to experience *any* job as more meaningful: (1) using your strengths, (2) connecting work with your values, and (3) focusing on helping others. Let's address each of these in turn.

1. Find Ways to Use Your Strengths

Personal strengths can be defined as "specific individual characteristics, traits, and abilities that, when employed, are energizing and allow a person to perform at his or her personal best."[4] Your strengths are an integral part of who you are as a human being. They are what allow you to be at your best, to the benefit of yourself and others.

Jobs, Careers, and Callings

Some researchers suggest that people view their work as either a job, a career, or a calling.[5] People who view their work as a *job* perceive it as a necessary evil, a means to an end. Work isn't enjoyable or otherwise rewarding; it's just a means to make money. A *career* is not just about money but also about advancement. Work is seen as an opportunity to bring rewards such as higher social status, prestige, self-esteem, and power. People who perceive their occupation as a *calling* don't work primarily for money or other external rewards but because they enjoy working and find what they do fulfilling and meaningful. They see their work as contributing to the greater good, to something larger than themselves. They feel like they are making a difference and would continue even in the absence of pay.

Callings are not reserved for prestigious or "noble" endeavors. "Any honest and legitimate area of work can potentially be a calling, even jobs that may not appear to enhance the common good in any obvious way, and jobs that people may have entered without having much of a choice," explain organizational psychologists Bryan J. Djk and Ryan D. Duffy.[6] "A calling has little to do, in fact, with a person's actual job, and everything to do with how that person approaches that job. Research evidence supports this claim; groups of administrative assistants, hospital janitorial staff, hairdressers, and restaurant kitchen employees are among those in low-prestige jobs who nevertheless indicate they experience their work as meaningful, and as one way to improve the well-being of others. Meaningful work indicative of callings also has been found among individuals with highly repetitive jobs and those in 'dirty' (i.e., extremely undesirable or stigmatized) jobs."

People who view their work as callings are better off than those who view it as a job or career. They are more motivated and engaged, more satisfied at work, and more committed to their organizations. They are also happier, better able to cope with stress and challenges, are less likely to suffer from depression, and express a stronger sense of purpose in their lives.[7]

The strategies in this chapter will help you view your work more as a calling rather than just a job or career.

Using your strengths at work is one of the keys to experiencing greater meaning. Studies show that strengths use leads to greater work engagement, self-efficacy, proactive behavior, higher levels of in-role and extra-role performance, better ability to cope with job demands, and lower levels of sickness absenteeism.[8] In one study, workers who reported high strengths use were a whopping 18 times more likely to flourish at work than those who reported low strengths use.[9]

As far as flow is concerned, a 2021 study showed that the more an employee reported using their strengths during a given period, the more likely they were to experience flow.[10] In short, the more you're able to use your strengths, the more flow you're likely to experience.

The question is, how can you use your strengths more often?

It's actually easier than you might think. Research suggests it's as simple as learning more about your strengths and then actively contemplating ways to use them more often. This approach works because many of us lack an in-depth awareness of our strengths and have probably never considered ways to use them.

In the following section, I invite you to learn more and subsequently make greater use of a particularly important type of strength: your strengths of character, which can be defined as "the positive parts of your personality that impact how you think, feel, and behave."[11]

Identify and Use Your Character Strengths

According to one line of research, there are 24 character strengths that have been valued and cherished in cultures across the globe for millennia—traits like Creativity, Bravery, Honesty, Kindness, Leadership, Forgiveness, and Humor.

These character strengths are seen as the inner determinant of a happy and successful life, complementing external factors like good education, financial security, or a stable social environment. Every person is thought to possess all 24 strengths to different degrees. Some strengths are more strongly developed than others, but nonetheless, they are all already a part of us.

The strengths that are most pronounced in us, that feel most essential to us, that we feel we can enact naturally and effortlessly, that uplift and energize us the most, that leave us feeling happy, in balance, and ready to take on more— these are our so-called *signature strengths*. Using our signature character strengths helps us experience greater happiness and well-being, find meaning and purpose, improve relationships, manage stress and health, and accomplish important goals.[12]

You can identify your signature strengths by taking the free 15-minute *VIA (Virtues-in-Action) Character Strengths Survey*.[13] Upon completion, it will give you an ordered list of the 24 character strengths, ranked from your strongest to weakest. Looking at the top of your list, consider which 3–7 strengths might be your signature strengths—those that feel most essential, effortless, energizing, and authentic to you.

If you're curious to know, I regard the following as my signature strengths:

- **Judgment** – "Thinking things through and examining them from all sides; not jumping to conclusions; being able to change one's mind in light of evidence; weighing all evidence fairly."

- **Humility** – "Letting one's accomplishments speak for themselves; not regarding oneself as more special than one is."

- **Love of Learning** – "Mastering new skills, topics, and bodies of knowledge, whether on one's own or formally; related to the strength of curiosity but goes beyond it to describe the tendency to add systematically to what one knows."

- **Perspective** – "Being able to provide wise counsel to others; having ways of looking at the world that make sense to oneself/others."

- **Social Intelligence** – "Being aware of the motives/feelings of others and oneself; knowing what to do to fit into different social situations; knowing what makes other people tick."

- **Prudence** – "Being careful about one's choices; not taking undue risks; not saying or doing things that might later be regretted."

Once you have your signature strengths, make a conscious effort to use them more often, and in new ways, in your job every day for the next week or so.

If Curiosity is one of your signature strengths, maybe consider switching up some of your routines, trying different activities during your breaks, asking co-workers about their weekend, or turning off your phone for an entire morning and see what happens.

If Love is one of your signature strengths, you could surprise a co-worker with a small gift, such as a book, flowers, or a cup of coffee. Or you could commit to listening more attentively to others in the workplace.

If Leadership is a signature strength, you may plan an out-of-work getaway for you and your team, consider ways to be more empathetic, supportive, and attentive to the needs of others, or consider how to walk the talk and be more inspiring and more of a role model for others.

This simple intervention—taking the survey and making a deliberate effort to use your signature strengths more often—has been shown to help people experience more meaning at work and view their occupation more as a calling rather than just a means to make money or gain other external rewards.[14] It has also been shown in multiple studies to enhance people's happiness and reduce their symptoms of depression at the end of the week, as well as 1 month, 3 months, and 6 months after the completion of the intervention.[15] I'm convinced that the intervention can also help you experience more flow.

2. Re-Connect With Your Values and Express Them at Work

Your core values—the things you deem most important in life—are another important part of who you are as a human being. Research suggests that living in ways that are consistent with your values helps you experience greater meaning, authenticity, and life satisfaction.[16]

If brought to the forefront of our attention, values imbue our life with tranquility and meaning. In light of what's truly near and dear to our hearts, many things lose their power over us. Trivial and petty things no longer disturb us. Activities we find otherwise boring or dreadful take on entirely new qualities when accomplished in pursuit of our most deeply held values.

Unfortunately, many of us lose touch of our values in day-to-day life. We get so caught up in everyday problems and with getting to some future goal that we lose connection to what is important to us today, in the present. When that happens, meaning and well-being take a hit.

Thankfully, re-connecting with your values can be a quick and enjoyable process. If you want to give it a try, here's an exercise that you can do in as little as five to ten minutes.

- **Step 1:** List five to ten values that are deeply meaningful to you. You can pick from a list of common values (e.g., friendship, family, caring, connection, courage, forgiveness, fun, honesty, humility, industry, patience, persistence, responsibility, self-control, and trust), or you can come up with your own values by answering the following questions: Who are you at your best? What do you want to stand for in life? What are the principles you want to live by? Which personal qualities would you like to cultivate? How do you want to behave as a human being?

- **Step 2:** Pick one or more values and explain why they are important to you and how you can express them more frequently at work or in life in general.

I'll elaborate on some of my own values to provide examples. (As you're about to see, this exercise shares considerable overlap with the strengths exercise.)

For me, *Kindness* is an important value because being kind is good for my benefactors, myself, and the world as a whole. Being kind feels nourishing and deeply fulfilling. To me, kindness is an expression of respect and cherishment toward life. It's soft, tender, and somehow just beautiful. I can express it by being open, loving, accepting, tolerant, compassionate, and understanding toward others. I can let people know that I appreciate them. I can offer people my time and attention. I can perform all kinds of acts of kindness (e.g., give someone a compliment, offer my help, write a "thank you" note, or bring a gift).

Excellence is another value that I cherish. I think it's worthwhile and beautiful to produce something of high quality. It's inspiring and reflects care and attentiveness. I can express this value by performing my work to the best of my abilities, with the utmost care, attention to detail, and extraordinary focus.

As a third example, *Self-Discipline* is important to me because it helps me improve, build skills, and become a better version of myself. It helps me make progress toward my goals, and by doing that, it provides me with motivation, self-respect, and a feeling of accomplishment. I can express self-discipline by following through on the things I know are beneficial and important to me. For example, I can continue working on this book, even if I don't feel motivated. Or I can take a cold shower even if I dread it.

This simple exercise has been used in countless studies and has been shown to lead to surprisingly impressive results.[17] In the short term, it helps people feel more connected, loving, and compassionate toward others. It helps people feel more strong and powerful, increases pain tolerance, boosts self-control, and reduces rumination. In the long term, it has been shown to boost grades, improve mental health, reduce doctor visits, and help with everything from quitting smoking to reducing problem drinking and losing excess body weight.

You may find it helpful to repeat this exercise regularly as a way to bring your values back to the forefront of your attention and experience a boost in meaning. If you have a journaling practice, you may want to add it to your routine.

Alternatively, you may write down your most important values on a piece of paper and carry it with you. Or you may create a bracelet or keychain to remind yourself of your most dearly held value(s). Me, I wear a bracelet with the word "Surrender" engraved in it. It reminds me to surrender to what happens—to be in acceptance rather than resistance and to yield to life rather than fight with it.

3. Focus on Helping Others

The third way to experience greater meaning at work is via *perceived social impact*—the sense of making a positive contribution to the lives of others. The more strongly we feel like we're having a positive impact, the more meaning, motivation, and satisfaction we experience.[18]

A field experiment with call-center fundraisers seeking donations for a scholarship fund at a university highlights this beautifully.[19] The fundraisers' work consisted of calling people, giving them information about the scholarship fund, and asking for a donation. As part of the experiment, one group got to spend five minutes interacting with a real recipient of the scholarship, who expressed gratitude and shared how the scholarship had made a big difference in helping him earn a degree and pursue his goals in life. The control group did not get to spend time with the recipient and instead engaged in a five-minute discussion with fellow fundraisers.

When the researchers later compared the work output of the employees in both groups, they found that the fundraisers in the first group spent more than double the amount of time making calls and raised almost three times the amount of money. Face-to-face contact with a benefactor of their work had increased the perceived social impact they were having and, in turn, increased their motivation and performance.

When lifeguards read stories about other lifeguards rescuing swimmers—an activity that increases their sense of making a difference in people's lives and a sense that others appreciate and value their contributions—they work for longer hours and are rated by their supervisors as being more helpful to guests in general, more likely to go out of their way to protect the safety of guests, and more likely to help orient new guests even though it is not required as part of their job.[20]

When students reflect on how learning in school will help them make a positive contribution to other people, they get a boost in motivation, put more time and energy into learning, and earn higher end-of-semester GPAs.[21] When students are made aware of the prosocial impact they could have in a biomedical research career, they feel more positive and motivated about pursuing such a career.[22] When workers reflect on a real-world task they completed at work for the benefit of others, they judge their work as more meaningful than if they reflect on a task they completed to benefit themselves.[23]

In a 2018 study, participants were asked to complete a typing task (entering the alternating letters of X and Z on a computer keypad as many times as possible within 5 minutes) to earn money for themselves, a charity, or someone they knew would directly benefit from their work.[24] Those who worked to benefit someone else rather than themselves reported greater task meaningfulness. "Our findings indicate that even the most meaningless task can be imbued with meaning when it is attached to a significant, prosocial cause," conclude the study authors. "Future research and interventions that help employees connect their work to a greater, prosocial cause may allow employees to feel a greater sense of meaningfulness, and in turn promote work-related and general well-being."

You may not be able to change what you do at work, but you can change the meaning of what you do by focusing on the positive impact you're having on other people. Let's consider some specific ideas for doing that.

Identify and focus on the impact you're already having
Even if your job isn't directly about helping others, you still benefit other people in some way; you just have to become aware of it.

Ask yourself: In what indirect ways are you contributing to the lives of others? Reflect on tasks you've completed at work for the benefit of others. Or ask yourself how you're making a positive difference, no matter how small, in the lives of your co-workers.

Count your good deeds

An easy way to become more aware of how you're already making a difference in other people's lives is to simply count the ways.

In one study, researchers asked participants to become aware of their own kind behavior toward other people every day for a week.[25] Specifically, participants were asked to keep track of each and every act of kindness they performed and to report the daily number of these acts. After a week of doing this, all participants felt significantly happier than they were at the start of the study.

The researchers suggest that counting kindnesses improves people's happiness for three reasons. By becoming more conscious of their kind behavior, people develop a stronger desire to be kind to others, more strongly recognize themselves as kind people, and more frequently enact kind behaviors toward others.

If you want to give it a try, here's how I suggest you do it: At the end of the day, simply write down all the kind things, big or small, you did on that day (e.g., remembering someone's birthday, listening to a co-worker's problems, helping a friend with a chore, or cooking for your family). Make a list of your acts of kindness.

Whenever I do this for a couple of days in a row, I notice the positive changes the researchers noted—I feel a greater desire to be kind, identify myself as a kinder person, and naturally find myself performing more acts of kindness. It's a quick, easy, and surprisingly effective way to support my well-being.

View your job from a prosocial perspective

A last way to immediately experience your job as more meaningful is to look at it through a prosocial lens: Your job isn't about the tasks you're doing; it's about somehow making a positive difference in other people's lives—the lives of your supervisors, co-workers, and customers. Your job isn't to clean stables, collect garbage, nurse patients, or write code. It's to keep the horses healthy, beautify the surroundings for everyone who walks by, support patients in their healing process, help bring forth the vision of your boss, or support your family.

As a bus driver, your job may be about keeping passengers safe and making them feel comfortable and welcomed. As such, it may involve greeting customers, making eye contact, and just generally trying to make them feel seen and heard.

As a hairdresser, your job might be about providing customers with an energizing, joyful, and relaxing break from their everyday lives. It may include listening actively and empathically to what people are saying, being considerate, understanding, tolerant, and supportive, and being a source of presence, love, and connection. It may also be, of course, about making your customers look and feel beautiful.

Re-imagine your job from the perspective of making a positive impact. How are you contributing to the well-being of others? Shift your perspective from just doing a job to making a positive difference in the lives of others.

If you lack meaning in your current job, you can change your job or change how you approach and view your job.

Viktor Frankl, a Jewish-Austrian psychiatrist and Holocaust survivor, once wrote: "Everything can be taken from a man but one thing: the last of the human freedoms—to choose one's attitude in any given set of circumstances, to choose one's own way."[26]

If you feel like you're stuck in a suboptimal job, exercise your human freedom to choose your attitude. Use the strategies outlined in this chapter to create greater meaning for yourself. You'll feel better, perform better, and will no doubt experience more flow.

Chapter 15

Humor, Fun, and Play

Good humor is a tonic for mind and body. It is the best antidote for anxiety and depression. It is a business asset. It attracts and keeps friends. It lightens human burdens. It is the direct route to serenity and contentment.

—GRENVILLE KLEISER

When I was in high school, I had an exceptionally funny history teacher. He would constantly make our entire class chuckle and burst out laughing. I still remember that his lectures always seemed to go by quickly. The frequent laughing and the lighthearted atmosphere were so refreshing and energizing that it somehow made it easy to stay focused and engaged. Now that I think of it, I understand why his lectures felt so smooth and enjoyable: His humor helped us be in flow.

You've surely experienced this yourself. When you're having a good time, the whole experience just feels lighter, more fluid, effortless, and flowy.

As we're about to see, the science backs this up. Humor and fun are powerful allies in our attempt to experience more flow. In this chapter, we'll discuss the evidence for this claim and learn about several ways to use humor, fun, and play to experience more flow.

The Humor Advantage

Humor is good for you. It's a character strength that is just as valuable as some of the more "noble" ones, like bravery, humility, or honesty.

People with a sense of humor report lower levels of depression, stress, and anxiety, have bigger social networks, are better able to tolerate pain, and live longer lives than their less humorous peers.[1] They also score higher on social functioning, positive emotions, optimism, self-esteem, and hope.[2]

Why is humor good for us? One reason is because it helps us cope with stress and adversity. Research consistently shows that individuals who score high on sense of humor are less affected by stressful events and situations than individuals who score low on sense of humor.[3] Laughter and positive emotions reduce the stress hormone cortisol and reduce muscle tension.[4] The lightheartedness and non-seriousness that come with humor allow us to keep things in perspective and keep an optimistic outlook on life.

Clergyman Henry Ward Beecher (1813–1887) once put it well, "A person without a sense of humor is like a wagon without springs. It's jolted by every pebble on the road." Humor provides the springs to cope with the many pebbles along the road of life.

Humor is also good for us because it helps us build and maintain positive social connections. At the beginning of a relationship, humor can work as an icebreaker and help us establish open and genuine communication. Shared humorous experiences have been shown to create feelings of closeness and trust between strangers.[5] Humor and the accompanying laughter are sources of pleasure, and we like people who are able to cause us pleasure. Indeed, research suggests we tend to like and trust the people who make us laugh.[6]

A 2017 study suggests that shared laughter holds profound implications for one's relationships.[7] When we laugh with someone, it signals that we see the world in the same way, it momentarily boosts our sense of connection, and it increases how much we like the other person and want to affiliate with them. As Danish-American comedian Victor Borge once said, "Laughter is the closest distance between two people."

Humor is also beneficial for our physical health. Humor and laughter have been shown to boost the immune system, relieve physical tension, enhance blood flow, and regulate hormones that help us feel happier and more motivated (dopamine), more trusting (oxytocin), less stressed (cortisol), and even somewhat euphoric (endorphins).[8]

Even in the workplace, humor is now recognized as a powerful tool and sought-after skill. A 2012 review on humor at work concluded: "Results suggest employee humor is associated with enhanced work performance, satisfaction, workgroup cohesion, health, and coping effectiveness, as well as decreased burnout, stress, and work withdrawal. Supervisor use of humor is associated with enhanced subordinate work performance, satisfaction, perception of supervisor performance, satisfaction with supervisor, and workgroup cohesion, as well as reduced work withdrawal."[9]

Humor and Flow

Can humor help you experience more flow? Indeed it can.

A 2021 study showed that a three-hour humor intervention could increase nurses' sense of humor, which could subsequently increase their frequency of flow experiences.[10] Another study showed that nurses experienced a decline in flow experiences during the Covid-19 pandemic, but this negative effect was less strong for nurses scoring high on sense of humor.[11] A third study looked at the relationships between humor, stress, and flow and concluded that "humor increases the likelihood of flow experience."[12]

In the workplace, fun is said to contribute to flow in two main ways.[13] First, when employees experience their actual work tasks as fun, they are more likely to experience flow while performing these tasks. Second, when employees have fun during work breaks, they experience a release from pressure and a boost in mood, which helps them re-engage with tasks feeling more refreshed and energized, which helps them experience flow more easily.

Bottom line: Having a good time can help you experience more flow. In the remainder of this chapter, we'll discuss three ways to boost humor, have more fun, and experience more flow: (1) getting humor training, (2) letting go of humor myths, and (3) giving yourself permission to play.

1. Get Yourself Some Humor Training

Humor is a skill. When you practice shooting hoops, you get better at it. When you practice playing the piano, you get better at it. When you practice humor, you also get better at it.

Consider the 2021 study in which one group of nurses received a three-hour humor training, while a control group received no training.[14] Six months later, the nurses in the control group saw a decline in their sense of humor, while nurses who received the training saw no such decline. The study also showed that those individuals who scored higher on sense of humor reported greater work enjoyment and meaning and more flow at work.

The researchers concluded: "The results of this study confirm the effectiveness of humor interventions in promoting humor, and, through this, the meaningfulness of work, work enjoyment, and the frequency of flow experience."

In another study, participants went through an eight-week program designed to teach specific skills relating to the use and enjoyment of humor in everyday life.[15] Each week, a new skill was taught in a one-hour learning session presented by an instructor to a small group. After the eight weeks, participants reported increases in self-efficacy, positive affect, and optimism and decreases in stress, depression, and anxiety.

A seven-week humor training study published in 2018 came to the same conclusion: "Humor training was effective in decreasing perceived stress, depressiveness, and anxiety whilst increasing coping humor, cheerfulness, and well-being."[16]

Humor training works. It improves not only your humor skills but also boosts your emotional well-being and helps you experience more flow. So, get yourself some humor training. Join a class, read a book, or take up stand-up comedy.

If you want to go through a program that is proven and affordable, I recommend checking out Paul McGhee's 2010 book *Humor as Survival Training for a Stressed-Out World: The 7 Humor Habits Program.*[17] Many of the humor trainings mentioned above have used this very program (or slight variations thereof). As you can probably guess, I haven't read the book yet. If I had, there would probably have been more and better jokes in this book.

2. Let Go of The Four Humor Myths

In their book, *Humor, Seriously: Why Humor Is a Secret Weapon in Business and Life*, Jennifer Aaker and Naomi Bagdonas suggest that there are four myths holding people back from using humor at work.[18]

Letting go of these myths will help you feel more comfortable about using humor at work, which will allow you to have more fun and experience more flow. Let's tackle the myths one after another.

The Serious Business Myth

The first misconception is that humor has no place amid serious work. We may worry about harming our credibility and not being taken seriously. Yet, as we've already seen, humor is something to be cherished, not feared at work; it's a strength, not a weakness.

As Aaker and Bagdonas explain: "Humor can be one of the most powerful tools we have for accomplishing serious things. Studies show that humor makes us appear more competent and confident, strengthens relationships, unlocks creativity, and boosts our resilience during difficult times."

Surveys of executive leaders suggest that 98% prefer employees with a sense of humor, while 84% believe employees with a sense of humor do better work.[19] Showing your sense of humor makes your co-workers more likely to attribute higher status to you, view you as intelligent, and vote you into a leadership position.

In one study, participants were asked to rate testimonials for VisitSwitzerland, a fictional travel company.[20] Half of the testimonials were serious (e.g., "The mountains are great for skiing and hiking. It's amazing!"); the other half were funny (e.g., "The mountains are great for skiing and hiking, and the flag is a big plus!"). The humorous testimonials were rated as 5% more competent, 11% more confident, and 37% higher in status. When asked to choose a group leader for a subsequent task, creators of the funny testimonials were significantly more likely to be chosen.

If you're in a leadership position, humor works equally well. It allows you to humanize yourself to employees, break down barriers, and balance authority with approachability. One study showed that leaders who use self-deprecating humor are rated higher on measures of both trustworthiness and leadership ability by their employees.[21]

The Failure Myth
We're probably all familiar with the fear of telling a joke that falls flat or that unintentionally offends someone. We're afraid of humor failures.

However, according to Aaker and Bagdonas, we misunderstand what it means to fail at humor. It's not about whether a joke results in laughter or not; it's about whether a joke is perceived as appropriate or not. Humor only fails when it's regarded as inappropriate; only then can it do more harm than good (e.g., it can hurt your reputation).

As long as your attempts at humor are appropriate for the context, you can count them as a success. Even if humor doesn't generate laughter, it still leaves you better off by increasing others' perceptions of your confidence— you have the gumption to tell a joke.

As you've probably noticed by now, I've mostly shied away from making jokes or humorous remarks in this book. Why? Because I, too, have been afraid of humor failures. After learning about this myth, it's clear to me that I could have included more attempts at humor. If I manage to make you chuckle, that's a big plus. And even if you don't find my humor funny, it's still okay as long as it's appropriate and considerate.

The Being Funny Myth
We may think that in order to use humor in the workplace, we have to actually "be funny" and be able to make others laugh. According to Aaker and

Bagdonas, this isn't true: "Even if you're not comfortable being funny yourself, as long as you understand the value of humor at work, you can benefit from it. The mere act of signaling that your sense of humor has a heartbeat is enough to make a big difference—especially if you're in a leadership role."

Showing that you have a sense of humor is as simple as laughing at others' jokes, jumping on opportunities to lighten the mood, and just having a good time.

The Born With it Myth

Some of us think that humor is an innate ability; we're either funny, or we're not, and there's nothing we can do about it. As we've already seen, this is also a myth. Humor is a skill you can strengthen through training and use, much like you can strengthen your leg muscles by working out at the gym or climbing stairs. As Aaker and Bagdonas put it: "A sense of humor is like a muscle—it atrophies without regular use."

3. Give Yourself Permission to Play

Work and play were once considered mutually exclusive. In recent years, however, the trend has been to integrate the two—to bring play into the workplace and to make work more like play.[22]

When employees approach and perform their tasks as opportunities for play, researchers refer to this as *playful work design*. As the term suggests, this is about designing your work to be more playful. It's about "gamifying" work. Individuals accomplish this in two main ways: (1) *designing fun* is about using humor, fantasy, imagination, or creativity to generate lighthearted pleasure, amusement, and fun; (2) *designing competition* is about deriving pleasure from stretching one's skills and challenging oneself in different ways, such as by trying to perform tasks as quickly and flawlessly as possible.

Using these play strategies, employees make their work more interesting, meaningful, engaging, and fun. On days when they do this, they report feeling more energized, enthusiastic, inspired, challenged, resilient, and more absorbed, immersed, and happily engrossed in their work.[23] They also have more creative ideas, are more effective at dealing with stress and adversity, ruminate less, and perform better.[24] One study specifically showed that they are also more likely to experience flow.[25]

Designing your work to be more playful is good for you. Here are three ideas for making it happen.

Take Inspiration from Other "Players"
A 2020 study asked employees what they do to make their work more playful.[26] Here are some of their answers.

- An accountant said: "I try to reduce the number of emails by sending one email less than the day before—and I do this every day."

- A pilot: "I often try to save fuel by trying to minimize the impact of winds, turbulence, and other natural conditions that require my plane to use additional fuel. I also try to find out what the best practices are for flying into and out of airports."

- An HR manager: "When I need to work on a boring, bureaucratic task, I make it playful by building additional tasks into the boring task. One option is to fill out the form using the fewest words possible yet covering all the content that must be addressed. This makes it a writing challenge and as such, more interesting."

- A researcher: "I often make a list of very specific things I need to do, for example, answering emails, reading an article, designing a survey. I then estimate how much time each task should take, and set an alarm clock for the time allotted for a task and try to beat the clock. This is fun and efficient because I do not randomly stray to do something else because I know I must beat the clock."

Another study mentions a bus driver who frames every ride as a game to drive as smoothly as possible and with the least amount of sudden decelerations.[27] The study also mentions a server who compares work to performing as a ballerina on stage and a cashier who describes ringing groceries as playing the piano. In 2009, a flight attendant went viral after making flight safety more entertaining by communicating the safety procedure as a rap.[28]

Frame Work as Play
Research suggests that the mere act of framing tasks as play transforms their experiential qualities: "It suspends the instrumental, efficiency-oriented

qualities of a task, and promotes an intrinsic, process-oriented mindset and positive affective states."[29]

You can choose to look at work as a duty and obligation. Or you can choose to see it as a playground, a place to have fun, joke around, laugh, and have a good time. The truth is, you're not some robot who's condemned to work. You're a free human being.

Go to work thinking to yourself: *Today, I'm going to have some fun. I'm going to play. Let the games begin...*

Ask Yourself to Be Playful

A study asked participants to perform the same task either in a playful or non-playful manner.[30] One instruction read, "Please find a way of doing it, so that it feels playful and nothing but playful." The other read, "Please find a way of doing it, so that it feels not playful at all." The results showed that when asked to be playful, the majority of participants were able to enter a playful stance, suggesting it's possible for most of us to enter a playful state of mind on demand.

The results also showed that participants in the playful condition mentioned feeling excited, creative, free, autonomous, relieved of obligations, and encouraged to explore and enjoy themselves. They felt drawn in by the task and experienced the kind of effortless focus reminiscent of flow.

In the non-playful condition, participants mentioned feeling more stressed, rushed, and driven by pressure. They were worried about evaluation, felt like they had to fulfill expectations, and felt like they had to perform the task in the right way. They also reported actively trying to focus on the task, suggesting more effortful rather than effortless attention.

So, simply ask yourself: *How can I approach work so that it feels playful and nothing but playful?*

Whichever way you accomplish it, if you can experience work in a more playful way, you'll have more fun, and you'll experience more flow.

Not All Fun is Created Equal

It's probably obvious, but I'll mention it anyway: Not all types of humor and fun are beneficial. Humor that offends, victimizes, ridicules, or belittles others or that is otherwise inappropriate or hurtful isn't helping anyone. Fun that is perceived as loud, noisy, distracting, or as getting in the way of task-focused attention isn't the type of fun that facilitates flow.

Of course, these things are subjective. What's funny to me may be offending to you. The key is simply to be considerate of others, and to apologize if we said or did something inappropriate. As long as we do that, humor is usually a win-win for everyone involved.

Chapter 16

Mind Like Water

Mind Like Water: A mental and emotional state in which your head is clear, able to create and respond freely, unencumbered with distractions and split focus.

—DAVID ALLEN

Flow occurs when you invest your full and undivided attention in an activity. It's a state of complete absorption and intense yet effortless concentration. Anything that disturbs task-focused attention—anything that distracts you and pulls your focus away from what you're doing—gets in the way of flow.

Perhaps the most common type of distraction is our own thinking: We are focusing on the task at hand when, suddenly, a thought about something entirely different intrudes and captures our attention. Instead of concentrating on the task, we are now thinking about something else. The mind has wandered off. Action and awareness are split. At least for the moment, we are out of flow.

In the current chapter, we'll deal with one specific cause of intrusive thoughts: tasks, projects, goals, and obligations that are unfinished. As human beings, we're equipped with an innate need for completion. When things are complete, they are done and in the past. We can stop thinking about them. We can move on. We feel relaxed and at ease. When things are unfinished, they beg for completion. They continue to occupy mental real estate. They nag us and put us in a state of subtle tension and unease.

We are more likely to remember interrupted or incomplete tasks than tasks that have been completed; this is known as the Zeigarnik effect. We have a strong tendency to resume tasks that have been interrupted and left incomplete; this is known as the Ovsiankina effect. And we have a strong tendency, of course, to continue watching TV shows that end with a cliffhanger.

When it comes to intrusive thoughts, unfinished things are far more likely to disturb us than finished things. Incomplete things are far more likely to distract us from what we're doing, harm performance, and get in the way of flow. Social psychologists E. J. Masicampo and Roy F. Baumeister have recently demonstrated this in a set of studies.[1]

In one experiment, they asked participants to think of two important tasks or errands (e.g., completing homework assignments, studying for exams, grocery shopping, doing laundry, or attending doctor's appointments) they needed to complete in the next few days. In a control group, participants were asked to describe two important tasks they had completed in the last several days.

All participants then performed a reading comprehension task in which they read the first 3,200 words of a popular novel. They were told that they would later answer questions about the plot. They were also told to focus all their attention on the task but that it was normal if they zoned out occasionally. During reading, participants were interrupted four times and asked, "Prior to the appearance of this screen, was your attention on- or off-task?" One response option stated, "I was reading the text and was very much paying attention to the story." A second response stated, "I was reading the text, but my attention was elsewhere." The goal was to measure participants' rate of mind wandering or task-irrelevant thinking.

After the reading, participants indicated on scales from 1 (*not at all*) to 7 (*very*) how well they could focus on the story and to what extent they were distracted by thoughts of the tasks they had written about earlier. Participants also answered eight reading comprehension questions.

Results? Participants in the unfulfilled tasks group reported being significantly more distracted by intrusive thoughts than participants in the control group. Their attention wandered significantly more often from the story. They also performed worse on the reading comprehension assignment: they answered significantly fewer questions correctly than participants in the control group. In the words of the researchers: "Participants who reflected on two important but unfinished tasks were distracted during a later attempt to read a novel. They were more bothered by intrusive thoughts of their incomplete tasks than were control participants, and their reading comprehension suffered as a result."

In another experiment, participants were given a packet and told that it contained multiple tasks that they would have limited time to complete.

Before starting the packet, participants received written instructions about the final task, which was a brainstorming task.

Participants in the control condition were told that this task would require them to list as many examples as they could of a given category. They were told that the optimal method for performing well on this brainstorming task would be to work through each letter of the alphabet individually; they should brainstorm as many examples as possible for each letter, beginning with the letter A and continuing with each letter through Z. Participants in the unfulfilled goal condition were given the same instructions but were already told the specific topic of the brainstorming task. They were told they would have to list as many examples of sea creatures as they could.

Participants were then asked to open the packet and begin working on the tasks. The packet contained 25 anagram tasks and one brainstorming task. Participants were first given 5 minutes to solve as many anagrams as they could. Then, they were given 5 minutes to list as many sea creatures as they could.

The researchers expected that the incomplete goal of listing sea creatures would interfere with the ability to solve anagrams. And that's exactly what they found. Participants who had already been told the topic of the brainstorming task solved significantly fewer anagrams than participants in the control group—it's harder to stay focused on solving anagrams when part of the mind is already contemplating sea creatures. Both groups did equally well on the brainstorming task.

These findings are directly relevant to your experiences at work and after work. Staying focused on a task is harder when your inbox is overflowing with urgent emails. Finding flow on your evening run is harder when your mind nags you about an unfinished and overdue report. Being fully present with your family is harder when you're preoccupied with incomplete work projects. Unfinished tasks are a source of distraction, overwhelm, anxiety, stress, and unease. As such, they pose a major challenge to experiencing flow.

A 2020 study decided to test the assumption that unfinished tasks get in the way of flow.[2] The researchers conducted a short-term diary study to investigate whether unfinished tasks at work affected flow in the evening during a leisure activity and how this translates into well-being the next morning.

Participants were asked to answer surveys at three time points: (1) when they finished their workday, (2) in the evening before going to bed, and (3) the next morning before starting to work. The first questionnaire assessed unfinished tasks and flow experience during the respective workday. The second questionnaire asked for flow experience during the evening activity. The last questionnaire assessed well-being the next morning.

The results were in line with expectations. When participants indicated high amounts of unfinished tasks, they reported experiencing relatively little flow during the work day and also relatively little flow during the evening leisure activity. High amounts of unfinished tasks and little flow subsequently resulted in relatively lower well-being scores the next morning. Unfinished tasks, the researchers explain, "bind cognitive resources, trigger intrusive thoughts about the unfulfilled goal and facilitate mind-wandering, whereas flow experience requires that one's whole attention is focused on the task at hand. We assume that unfinished tasks lead to intrusive thoughts, which militate against flow in subsequent tasks."

The researchers conclude: "[O]ur research provides evidence that finishing tasks during the day and even more so every evening before leaving the workplace facilitates experiencing flow both at work and during non-work activities and fosters well-being."

It's harder to experience flow when part of your mind is constantly bombarding you with distracting thoughts. And it's not just flow that is negatively impacted. Other studies by the same researchers have shown that unfinished tasks impair recovery after work and sleep quality on the weekend.[3]

So, what can you do about this? In the remainder of this chapter, we'll discuss eight strategies to deal with this common issue.

1. Don't Take on Too Much

The more you take on, the more incomplete tasks are likely to pile up, and the more likely you are to suffer from distraction, stress, and overwhelm. If you want to experience more flow and greater peace of mind, stop burdening yourself with endless tasks and projects. Do less but better. Learn to say no. Go all in on the few projects you're truly excited about and ruthlessly eliminate the rest. Take your time and be very deliberate when committing to new endeavors.

The naturalist and philosopher Henry David Thoreau once wrote: "Simplicity, simplicity, simplicity! I say, let your affairs be as two or three, and not a hundred or a thousand; instead of a million count half a dozen, and keep your accounts on your thumb nail."[4]

Easier said than done, of course. For me, applying this idea requires considerable awareness and discipline. I need to be aware of the issues associated with overextending myself and aware of my tendency to want to do it anyway. I need to see, *"Oh, there's a part of me that wants to start reading yet another new book (even though I still haven't finished my last two)."* *"Wait a second, am I really on the verge of accepting yet another dinner invitation?"* *"Do I really want to plunge into yet another work project?"* Once I see that I'm about to jump into yet another commitment, I then need to inhibit that impulse. I need to be self-disciplined to keep myself from taking on too much.

2. Finish. Finish. Finish.

Do you often switch tasks when you feel stuck, frustrated, bored, or otherwise uncomfortable? Do you jump into new projects instead of finishing old ones because the new ones feel easier and more exciting? If you're anything like me, you would probably agree: that's a trap. It's a classic example of a choice that's easy in the moment but problematic in the long run.

If you want to reduce the issues associated with unfinished tasks, you need to become disciplined about finishing. You need to stop jumping ship at first sight of difficulty—you need to stay with tasks and projects, even when the going gets tough. Complete things and get them off your mind. Find joy in finishing.

Again, that's largely a matter of awareness and discipline. For me, I've become very aware of my tendency to abandon tasks and projects prematurely, and I've become disciplined about not doing so.

Let me give you an example. In the past, I would often start reading new books before finishing the ones I had already started. (Continuing on "old" books often feels harder and less exciting to me than starting new ones.) The problem with that approach was that some part of my mind didn't like having multiple books open at the same time. That part kept reminding me and nagging me about these open books and urging me to complete them. It may sound weird, but open books were a definite source of overwhelm and intrusive thoughts for me.

Nowadays, I very rarely read two books at once. In fact, I've become reluctant about starting new books in general. When I see a path to finishing the book soon, then sure, I'll get reading. But when I know that my schedule won't allow me to spend much time reading over the following days and weeks, I'll usually opt against starting the book. Why? Because I know how my mind works: It will keep track of that unfinished book and will urge me to complete it. (Your mind might be less of a bother in this regard.)

On a side note, "completing" a book, for me, doesn't necessitate reading all of it. I just have to get closure somehow. I have to let my mind know that it doesn't have to remind me about the book any longer. I can accomplish this by finishing reading it. Or I can accomplish it by making a note within the book itself, describing clearly which parts I've read, skimmed, or not looked at whatsoever, and by writing down why I'm moving on for now.

3. End Smartly

Don't begin anything new at the end of the workday unless you're sure you can finish it. Instead, use the last 30–60 minutes to get on top of things. Tackle any small tasks that have piled up over the day. Check your upcoming calendar. Review your to-do list. Get an overview of what's been done and what's coming. Clean up and declutter your workspace. Plan the next day.

The idea here is to empty your head before leaving work so you can detach from your job and move into your free time with a clear and relatively unencumbered mind.

4. Shield Yourself from Interruptions

Interruptions, whether face-to-face, through emails, or phone calls, initiated by colleagues, supervisors, subordinates, or clients, are ubiquitous in many of today's workplaces. Field studies suggest that nurses are interrupted every 5 to 10 minutes, while office workers are interrupted about every 3 to 11 minutes.[5]

One problem with interruptions is that they often cause us to leave tasks unfinished. The more frequently we get interrupted, the more unfinished tasks tend to pile up, and the stronger the detrimental effects of unfinished tasks become.

It is, therefore, advisable to shield yourself from interruptions as best you can. You may do this by disabling notifications, turning off your phone, setting expectations with your co-workers, or scheduling dedicated email time. We'll discuss these and other useful ideas in greater detail in chapter 18.

5. Make a Plan

Masicampo and Baumeister didn't just investigate the negative effects of unfinished tasks; they also investigated whether planning when and how one will tackle an unfinished task would act as a buffer against these negative effects. In both studies we discussed earlier, there was a third condition that was identical to the unfulfilled tasks condition, except that participants were also asked to make plans to complete each task.

In the first study, the planning group was told to think of two tasks or errands they needed to complete in the next few days and to also indicate in detail how, when, and where they would complete the tasks. This group did equally well on the reading comprehension task as the control group, which was told to think of two tasks they had completed last week. The researchers explain: "Unfulfilled tasks made people's minds wander, thereby reducing their ability to comprehend the novel. But participants who made a plan to get their personal tasks done were able to read with less mind wandering. Despite having had an unfulfilled goal activated, they were relatively well able to concentrate on material that had nothing to do with that goal."

In the second study, the planning condition was again identical to the unfulfilled goal condition, except that participants were asked to commit to a specific plan for their later performance on the brainstorming task. Specifically, participants in the planning group committed to the following statement: "I will try my best on the final task. When I get to the final task, I will write down the letters of the alphabet and will list sea creatures for each one." Participants thus committed to a plan that detailed exactly how they would execute the task. And again, individuals who made that plan did better than those who didn't.

Once a plan is made, the mind seems to no longer interfere so strongly with current concerns. It's as if the mind is able to relax, knowing that the goal is being taken care of. As a result, it no longer has to remind you and nag you about it.

There is a caveat, though. For plans to be effective at putting the mind at ease, they must be specific. At the very least, they should detail the next action to be taken: What exactly will you do, and how will you do it? Even better is if you can specify when and where you'll execute your plan of action. You'll also want to put the plan in writing rather than just keep it in your head. The mind is good at making plans but terrible at storing them. It's almost always a good idea to get things out of your head and into an "external brain." To-do lists, calendars, and daily planners are excellent tools in this regard.

In addition, here are two quick tips for implementing what we've just discussed:

- At the end of the workday, consider making a list of all your incomplete tasks of the day and specify when and how you will complete them (or when and how you will continue working on them). When workers were asked to do this in a 2015 study, they felt more relaxed, detached from work, and better able to enjoy their leisure.[6]

- When you are forced to abandon a task before finishing it, take a minute to write a so-called *ready-to-resume plan*: Jot down where you left off and how you'll continue upon returning to the task. This simple action has been shown to help individuals disengage from what they are doing and better concentrate on subsequent tasks.[7] One minute is all it takes. You can streamline and habitualize the process by specifying a set of questions that you always ask yourself before leaving a task that is not yet completed (e.g., "What's the last thing I did? What still needs to be done? What comes next?").

6. Implement a GYLIO Practice

Your mind isn't just preoccupied with all the incomplete tasks and projects from work. It's also stressed out about the unpaid bills, the dirty laundry, the defective dishwasher, and the long overdue doctor appointment that should be scheduled. Mundane chores tend to pile up and contribute to distractedness and the feeling of being overwhelmed.

One way to reduce this nag is by implementing a so-called GYLIO practice: an hour, morning, day, or even a full week dedicated to "Getting Your Life in Order."[8] It's about taking care of a large number of chores and other unfinished tasks in order to clear your mind and free up mental space. (Don't be discouraged by the name. You certainly don't need to get your entire life in order to reap the rewards. Even completing a few chores can help you feel less stressed and overwhelmed.)

Personally, I always notice a substantial improvement in my mood, focus, and peace of mind after doing some GYLIO. I also tend to feel more in control, relaxed, and on top of things. For me, it's a dose-response relationship: The more chores I can complete and tick off, the better I feel.

So, if you feel like small tasks have been piling up, consider scheduling some time for GYLIO. Getting these things done and off your mind will help you show up with greater energy and focus in your other endeavors.

7. Adopt the GTD System

I believe the best method for dealing with the issues discussed in this chapter is by adopting the Getting Things Done (GTD) productivity system developed by David Allen and explained in his book with the same title.[9]

GTD is a sophisticated set of tools and principles designed to help you arrive at a state called *mind like water*, which Allen defines as "a mental and emotional state in which your head is clear, able to create and respond freely, unencumbered with distractions and split focus."

The goal is to free your mind of everything that's clogging up mental real estate. You get everything that is nagging you out of your head and into a trusted external system. Knowing that it's all captured and under control, the mind no longer has a reason to distract you with intrusive thoughts. You are free to focus your full attention on whatever you happen to be doing. Your ability to concentrate and find flow is greatly enhanced.

In fact, this is something David Allen has observed in his clients. "Adopting GTD enables individuals to find flow more easily in their work and personal lives," he writes in the 2015 version of his book. "By getting tasks out of the mind and into an external system, they can more easily see and track progress, which is a form of feedback. Having a complete picture of one's commitments in work and life can help individuals make better decisions about what to pay attention to in any given moment, which, in turn, will allow them to engage more fully in the task at hand, making flow a more likely outcome."

Explaining the system in its entirety is beyond the scope of this book. If you're intrigued and want to learn more about it, David Allen's book *Getting Things Done* is the ideal place to start. It explains the system in detail and shows you step-by-step how to implement it.

8. Use the 2-Minute Rule

Invented by the aforementioned David Allen, the 2-minute rule states that if an action takes less than two minutes to complete, it should be done immediately. Instead of filling your mind or to-do list with an endless supply of small tasks, get in the habit of tackling small things the instant they appear.

It's a simple and elegant way to keep the number of unfinished tasks low and to prevent things from clogging up your mental machinery. Greater mental clarity, peace of mind, and focus are the result.

Keeping the number of unfinished tasks in check isn't easy. It takes awareness, discipline, and a set of tools and routines. The effort can be considerable. But that effort is well worth it when it comes to peace of mind and flow. Experiencing flow is simply a lot easier when your mind is clear rather than burdened by a gazillion nagging and distracting thoughts.

If flow is the goal, we're well advised to follow Thoreau's advice: Let our affairs be as two or three rather than a hundred or a thousand; instead of a million, count half a dozen.

Chapter 17

Sprint. Rest. Repeat.

The heart of achieving mastery is expanding the amplitude of the waves you make in your life. When you're working, give it everything you've got, for relatively short periods of time. When you're recovering, let go and truly refuel. Average is a steady state, free of highs and lows.

—*TONY SCHWARTZ*

All life on our planet is guided by rhythms. Think heart rhythms, brain waves, wake-sleep cycles, the daily rising and setting of the sun, or the ebb and flow of the tides. Rhythmic, wavelike movement represents strength, vitality, and life; linearity represents weakness, disease, old age, and death. At the point of death, we lose all rhythmicity, as illustrated by the flat line of the EKG machine when the heart stops beating.

High performance and good health tend to correspond to big waves while mediocre performance and bad health tend to correspond to linearity or small waves.

I first heard about this principle from performance experts Tony Schwartz and Jim Loehr who themselves first spotted it when studying world-class tennis players.[1] They found that the best competitors made bigger waves between energy expenditure and energy renewal than their lesser competitors. For example, the heart rates of the best players dropped as much as 20 beats per minute between points before shooting up again during play. Heart rates of lesser competitors didn't drop as much and stayed more elevated—a sign of less pronounced recovery.

Schwartz and Loehr also found that the more linear any one player's heart rate became as the match progressed, the worse they tended to play and the more likely they were to lose their match. Chronically elevated heart rates, they found, were a sign of exhaustion, while chronically low heart rates were a sign that the player had given up or was not committed enough. Heart rates needed to move in a wavelike fashion, and the bigger the waves, the better the performance.

This isn't an isolated finding; it's a common theme. Time and time again, we find that performance, health, and vitality correspond to big waves.

Consider, for example, a study on elite violin students at the prestigious Music Academy of West Berlin.[2] The goal of the study was to figure out what separated the best students from the merely good ones. The researchers found that the best students didn't necessarily practice more than their less skilled peers. But they practiced with greater intensity, concentration, and purpose. Because of the sheer intensity of their approach, they had to keep practice sessions to no longer than 80–90 minutes—they simply couldn't keep up the level of intensity for any longer than that. After going all out and exhausting themselves, they then moved into recovery, which they took more seriously and approached more deliberately than their less skilled peers. They often took naps—large recovery waves in the middle of the day—to fully recharge and fuel their afternoon practice. The naps also helped them get an additional five hours of sleep per week compared with the other students.

In short, the best students were more intense in their approach. They made bigger waves, both practicing and recovering more intensely than their peers. They were fully on or fully off, not something in between. Hot or cold, not lukewarm.

And again, this isn't an isolated finding. Decades of research into elite performance show that it's not so much the *quantity* of practice that separates the best from the rest. Instead, it's the *quality* of practice and the *quality* of recovery. This has been shown in countless fields, including ballet dance, chess, swimming, tennis, and long-distance running.[3] Elite performers practice intensely and recover equally intensely. They work hard and rest equally hard. They move rhythmically between energy expenditure and energy renewal, and they do it more consistently and powerfully than the rest of us.

This is perhaps most evident in the world of elite sports. Elite athletes train and compete with unmatched intensity, focus, and purpose. They're in no way sluggish, lackluster, or lethargic. They aren't wasting time. You don't see them checking their phones during training or competition. You don't see them mindlessly, halfheartedly going through the motions. They are fully on. And once they're done, they are fully off, going to great lengths to recover as profoundly as possible. Some athletes claim to sleep up to 12 hours a day to fuel their intense training regimes.[4] Many use ice baths, cryotherapy, massage therapy, infrared therapy, hyperbaric oxygen, pulsed electromagnetic field, self-myofascial release, neuromuscular electrical stimulation, and other special tools and techniques to get the most out of their recovery periods. They train hard, compete hard, and rest hard. Fully on. Fully off. Repeat.

We see the same pattern in intellectual domains. A study that followed a group of 38 scientists for thirty years highlights it beautifully.[5] Starting out, all scientists seemed equally likely to have highly productive careers. Over the years, however, their paths diverged. While some went on to have highly satisfying and scientifically successful careers (e.g., five of them won Nobel Prizes), others settled into less-distinguished and less satisfying careers. Why?

Questionnaires and interviews revealed that the best scientists were more aware of what allowed them to do their best work and were more deliberate in designing their lives accordingly. Many of them pursued active hobbies and exercised regularly because it helped them be more productive. It enabled them to detach from work and provided incubation periods for insights to occur. Most relevant for our discussion, they found it gave them the necessary physical and mental energy to go deep during their working hours. Many of them called themselves lazy because they didn't put in insane hours day by day but instead allowed or perhaps forced themselves to get plenty of rest. They balanced periods of intense and focused work with periods of recovery.

The less accomplished scientists viewed and did things differently. They didn't see leisure and work as part of a whole, as connected and mutually supportive. Instead, they seemed to view exercise and hobbies as taking away from time they could use for work. Many of them were convinced that they would be more successful if they could just devote more hours to their research. They felt time-pressed, pursued fewer active hobbies, engaged in less physical activity, and generally didn't value and prioritize rest as much as the top scientists. When working, they seemed to lack the clarity of mind, energy, and concentration necessary for breakthrough accomplishments.

In short, the top scientists made bigger waves. They moved rhythmically between hot and cold while their less accomplished peers followed a more lukewarm approach.

We see the same theme in the lives of revered scientists, engineers, and writers of the past and present.[6] Charles Darwin typically finished work by noon, proclaiming, "I've done a good day's work."[7] Afternoons and evenings were filled with long walks, naps, family dinners, and other recovery activities. Stephen King recommends reading and writing for no more than four to six hours a day, a schedule he describes as "strenuous."[8] Ernest Hemingway, when asked about his writing schedule, replied he started work at about six in the morning and finished before noon.[9] "It is the wait until the next day that is hard to get through," he once said. Thomas Mann, the German writer and Nobel laureate, worked on his most important writing for only three hours a day, from 9 am till noon. It was a time of intense focus, during which he tolerated no distractions, shut the door to his office, and made himself unavailable to visitors and his family. Mann said, "Afternoons are for reading, for my much too mountainous correspondence and for walks."[10] He was fond of taking hour-long naps to recover from his intense morning sessions.

These are but a few examples of highly productive individuals who accomplished great things yet invested relatively few hours into their most important work. They deliberately restricted working hours and filled the rest of their days with downtime, not out of laziness but as a way to be more productive. It's not just work, work, work, non-stop. It's a rhythmic movement between work and rest, work and rest, work and rest.

Tony Schwartz, one of the men who discovered this principle in elite tennis players, has adopted a similar schedule. It's characterized by relatively few but intense working hours, frequent breaks, and lots of recovery time.[11] He likes to write in 90-minute sessions with renewal breaks in between. He might eat breakfast after the first session, go for a run after the second, and eat lunch after the third. After three sessions, he's done with his most important work for the day. Afternoons are for less demanding work and recovery.

I followed a similar routine when writing the book you're holding in your hands. I would usually work for 60–90 minutes first thing in the morning, then go for a walk, then work for another 60–120 minutes, and then take another break—go for another walk, do some kind of a relaxation exercise (e.g., yoga nidra), or simply chat with my girlfriend. Then, it was either admin work or more writing. After lunch, it was usually another walk followed by another guided relaxation exercise or a nap. Then came maybe a cold shower followed by another writing session or more admin work. By 5 p.m., I was usually done with work for the day. Evenings were for hobbies, quality time with loved ones, and to prepare for a good night's sleep.

The details—break activities, length of writing sessions, etc.—change depending on the day, the season, interests, and motivation. What doesn't change is the underlying principle: working in relatively short but intense sessions with frequent breaks in between. Instead of sitting at my desk for hours on end, I try to move between deep work and deep recovery. It's a way of working and living that I find both enjoyable and efficient.

The principle applies to all types of work. Regardless of industry, job, or task, the highest levels of performance and health seem to result from frequently moving between periods of hard work and recovery.

An informal study by the time-tracking app *DeskTime* found that the most productive employees of a social networking company worked for 52 minutes and then took a break for 17 minutes.[12] The key to productivity, the study concluded, was working in short bursts with frequent breaks in between: "The reason the most productive 10% of our users are able to get the most done during the comparatively short periods of working time is that their working times are treated as sprints. They make the most of those 52 minutes by working with intense purpose, but then rest up to be ready for the next burst."

A study with assembly-line workers in a meat-processing plant found that giving employees more breaks increased productivity even though the total working time was reduced. [13] The experiment tested the effects of two break schedules, which both provided 36 minutes of extra break time over the regular schedule. The workers were given either twelve 3-minute breaks or four 9-minute breaks evenly distributed over the workday. Results? The extra breaks improved the total productive output despite the employees working for 36 minutes less.

A study with data entry workers produced similar results.[14] For this experiment, the company "gave away" four supplementary 5-minute breaks throughout the workday, for a total of 20 minutes of extra recovery time per day. Data entry performance neither increased nor decreased in this case. However, employees still benefitted greatly because eyestrain and aches and pains in several areas of the body were significantly lower under the supplementary breaks schedule.

A study on work-rest schedules during the operation of a rotary power tiller found that the highest productivity output was achieved by working for 75 minutes and then breaking for 15 minutes. The researchers concluded that alternating periods of intense effort with frequent breaks "maximizes the total quantity of physical work an individual can perform during the working day compared to working at a steady but lower level."[15]

Findings like these are supported by a growing number of studies highlighting the merits of so-called *microbreaks*, which refer to "short respite activities that are undertaken voluntarily on a need basis between series of task episodes."[16] Distinguished from lunch and other formal breaks, microbreaks are informal, unscheduled, a few seconds to several minutes long, and taken by employees at their discretion, according to their needs.

We intuitively engage in these breaks as a way to manage our energy and sustain our physical and psychological resources throughout the workday. It seems we have a natural tendency to intermittently recover throughout the workday and to move frequently between periods of energy expenditure and energy renewal.

And our intuition pays off. Microbreaks are associated with general employee well-being, lower levels of fatigue and exhaustion, lower levels of negative and higher levels of positive emotions both throughout and at the end of the workday, higher levels of engagement, and better work outcomes (e.g., sales performance).[17] Microbreaks are an excellent strategy for feeling better and performing better.

All of this evidence suggests that making waves—balancing intense activity with plenty of recovery—is critical to health and performance.

Making Waves: Every Hour, Every Day, Every Week, Etc.

The principle of making waves works both on a micro and macro level; it benefits you both over short and more extended periods.

Over the course of a few hours, workers who take microbreaks tend to do better than those who don't. Tennis players whose heart rates move more rhythmically outperform those whose heart rates move more linearly. Over the course of a workday, employees who take full advantage of lunch and other formal breaks do better than those who skip them.[18] Over the course of a full 24 hours, individuals who sleep well do better than those who sleep poorly. Over the course of a week, employees who fully detach and recharge on evenings and weekends do better than those who fail to do so.[19] Over the course of months and years, employees with more vacation time tend to do better than those with less vacation time.[20]

Bottom line: We do best by moving rhythmically between energy expenditure and energy renewal—on an hourly, daily, weekly, monthly, and yearly level. The principle holds equally true over short and long time spans. If you want to feel and perform at your best, make waves.

When it comes to flow, the principle is just as important. Make bigger waves, and you're more likely to experience flow. Why? Because engaging in an activity with great intensity for a relatively short period is far more conducive to flow than engaging halfheartedly for long periods. Tackling an activity with high energy, feeling refreshed and ready to go is likewise far more conducive to flow than arriving at an activity feeling tired and lethargic.

The practical advice following everything we just discussed is thus twofold. First, we want to approach life like a sprinter rather than a marathoner—we want to work in intense sprints with frequent breaks in between rather than in a continuous, linear, never-ending slog. Second, we want to prioritize and optimize our recovery so that we can arrive at flow activities with as much energy as possible.

In the remainder of this chapter, we'll have a closer look at working and living in sprints. In the next chapter, we'll pick up the topic of optimal recovery.

6 Tips to Sprint-Rest-Repeat Your Way to Flow

Whether at work or in leisure, you're more likely to experience flow by engaging fully for short periods than halfheartedly for long periods. You sprint, then rest, then sprint again, then rest again.

The exact activity-to-rest schedule isn't that relevant. It will no doubt differ from person to person and even from day to day, depending on energy levels, time constraints, the activity being performed, etc. What matters is the underlying principle: continually moving between energy expenditure and energy renewal. We'll now consider six practical strategies for implementing and getting the most out of your sprints.

1. Avoid the Grey Zone

The grey zone is the space between full engagement and full disengagement, between proper effort and proper rest. We've all been there. It's when we're kind of sort of doing something, or kind of sort of resting, but not really. It's a halfhearted approach, neither being fully on nor fully off. Given everything we've discussed, this partial engagement is precisely what we want to avoid.

Instead of lukewarm, pick hot or cold. When you're working, give it everything you've got. When you're taking a break, fully disengage and truly renew. There's no flow to be found in the grey zone.

2. Get Ready With a Pre-Sprint Routine

In chapter 9, I briefly mentioned that the default mode network (DMN) quiets down during meditation. You may recall that DMN activity is synonymous with mind wandering, me-focused thinking, and lapses in attention during task performance. DMN activity and flow exist in a seesaw relationship. In order to experience flow, the DMN needs to go offline—mind wandering needs to come to a halt, and self-focused attention needs to make way for task-focused attention.

By acutely reducing DMN activity and putting you in a calmer and more focused state, meditation before a sprint can help you ease into flow. The type of meditation doesn't matter as long as the instruction includes bringing attention back to an object of focus (e.g., the breath) whenever the mind has wandered.

How long should you meditate for? While longer sessions tend to have more pronounced effects, my experience suggests that as little as one minute can make a difference. In one study, a short 8-minute mindful breathing meditation reduced mind wandering and improved performance on a subsequent task of sustained attention.[21]

If meditation isn't your thing, you can try other pre-sprint routines. Another one that I like to use is called *Release Tension, Set Intention*. I believe it was invented by author and high performance coach Brendon Burchard.[22] Here's how it works:

- **Step 1: Release Tension:** Close your eyes and repeat the word "release" over and over in your mind. As you do, ask your body to release any tension you're holding. Move from top to bottom, releasing tension in your face and jaw, neck and shoulders, chest and back, belly and pelvic floor, legs, feet, and toes. Keep repeating the word "release" in your mind. Do this for a minute or two.

- **Step 2: Set Intention:** After having relieved some tension, think about how you want to feel and perform and what you want to achieve in your upcoming sprint. Ask yourself, "What energy do I want to bring to this activity? How do I want to feel? How can I perform with excellence? How can I enjoy the process?" You don't have to use these exact questions, but they are the kinds of prompts that will allow you to be more fully engaged in the activity you're about to perform.

That's it. This simple routine takes less than five minutes and can transform your performance during your next sprint.

3. Time-Limit Your Sprints

It can be helpful to set a timer at the beginning of a sprint and to commit to going all out until the time is up. You commit to engaging with as much intensity and focus as possible—no dillydallying or goofing off on social media—until the timer rings.

Psychologically, it's much easier to commit to short, time-limited bursts than to seemingly endless sessions. You can make a deal with yourself to give everything you've got and abstain from distractions for a short time; you can't really make the same deal if there's no end in sight.

What's the ideal length to set the timer for? I've heard people use as little as two minutes to as much as 90–120 minutes. For me, the sweet spot is 20–30 minutes. Too short, and I view it as pointless because how much progress can I really make in a couple of minutes? Too long, and I find it too hard to commit to the full length of time. When I'm in flow when the timer goes off, I can always just keep going. Sometimes, I set a new timer; other times, I don't. This is something everyone has to experiment with themselves.

4. Try the Pomodoro Technique

If you're into personal productivity, you've probably heard of the *pomodoro technique.* It's a popular time management method invented by Francesco Cirillo in the late 1980s.[23] Using a timer, work is broken up into multiple intervals of 25 minutes, separated by short breaks. Each interval is referred to as a *pomodoro,* which is Italian for tomato. When Cirillo developed the method, he used a red kitchen timer that was shaped like a tomato. Hence the name, the pomodoro technique.

Here's how it works:

1. Choose a task
2. Set a timer to 25 minutes
3. Work on your task until the timer rings
4. Take a short break (e.g., 5 minutes)
5. After four pomodoros, take a longer break (e.g., 15–30 minutes)

Why is the method so popular? For one thing, there's the gamification aspect—you get to count the number of pomodoros you have performed in a day, week, or month. The method also incorporates both the principle of working in sprints and the principle of time-limited sessions. This combination makes for a fun, rewarding, and effective method.

5. Expect Early Frustration—and Push Through it

The first few minutes of a sprint can often feel hard, uncomfortable, and frustrating. We rarely begin an activity and enter a state of complete focus and absorption from the get-go. Instead, it usually takes a while to settle in, get warmed up, and find our rhythm.

Think of it this way: When you first arrive at an activity, your DMN is likely to be in full swing. You're thinking about a million and one thing, and you must continuously bring your attention back to the task in front of you. It takes time and effort to focus a wandering mind. The good news: Things get easier once the DMN starts quieting down. You get more and more absorbed in the task, irrelevant thinking subsides, the negative voice in your head takes a backseat, and your experience begins to feel more focused and enjoyable. Concentration transforms from effortful to effortless. Once in flow, it's no longer hard. It's easy.

The point is that it often takes time to drop into flow. And in order to get there, we often need to push through an initial phase of struggle. Yes, there are tools and tricks to make this easier (e.g., with a pre-sprint routine or a time limit), but I don't think you can ever entirely circumvent the early difficulty. It's just part and parcel of the game. If you want to reap the rewards of flow, expect and embrace having to pay an initial price.

6. Eliminate Distractions

Your chances of experiencing flow depend on how frequently you get interrupted—either by yourself or external sources. The more you get interrupted, the less likely you are to enter and sustain flow. In an ideal scenario, you're able to give your full and undivided attention to the task in front of you for the entire duration of a sprint without getting interrupted. We'll discuss tips for reducing interruptions in chapter 19.

We experience more flow by emulating a sprinter rather than a marathoner. We do best by working in short but intense bursts followed by recovery periods. Sprint, then rest, then sprint again, then rest again. In this chapter, we discussed tools and strategies for getting the most out of your work sprints. In the next chapter, we'll discuss tools and strategies for getting the most out of your recovery periods. Optimize both your sprints and breaks, and you're well on your way to more flow.

Chapter 18

The Science of Recovery

Deliberate rest is not a negative space defined by the absence of work or something that we hope to get sometime. It is something positive, something worth cultivating in its own right.

—*ALEX SOOJUNG-KIM PANG*

In the previous chapter, I suggested that we're more likely to experience flow when we feel fresh and full of energy than when we feel sluggish and fatigued. In 2014, a group of researchers wanted to see if they could prove this with a scientific study. To do that, they surveyed workers' state of being recovered in the morning and its impact on flow throughout the day.[1]

The researchers sent participants (programmers, software engineers, and web designers) four daily surveys for an entire workweek from Monday through Friday. The first survey, filled out at the beginning of every workday, asked participants to indicate on a scale from 1 (*not true at all*) to 5 (*very true*) how much they agreed with the following four statements: ''This morning I feel well rested,'' ''This morning I feel physically refreshed,'' ''This morning I feel mentally refreshed,'' and ''This morning I am filled with new energy.'' This indicated the participants' state of being recovered.

The next three surveys were sent out throughout the rest of the workday: one in the morning, another around noon, and the last in the afternoon. These were experience sampling forms (see chapter 7) that asked participants what they were currently doing and tapped their level of flow.

The researchers found that participants reported higher levels of flow during programming activities (e.g., programming or fixing bugs) than administrative activities (e.g., bookkeeping or writing invoices) and personal activities (e.g., taking a break or chatting with a colleague). This confirms what we already know: Certain types of activities are more conducive to flow than others.

But what about the recovery aspect? As expected, the more recovered a person felt in the morning, the more flow they experienced during work that day. Better recovery translated into more flow.

This makes intuitive sense, of course. When we feel refreshed, mentally sharp, and full of energy, we are more likely to experience flow than when we feel tired. Feeling recovered, whether in the morning or at any other time of day, facilitates flow.

Therefore, if we want to get the most out of our flow activities, we must recover well in the periods between these activities. For example, if we want to experience more flow at work, we must recover well during nonwork time—during breaks, evenings, weekends, and vacations.

Well then, how do we accomplish that? What are the keys to recovery? How can we recharge deeply and efficiently? That's precisely what we'll find out in this chapter. We'll look at the type of activities, experiences, and environments that provide you with the deepest levels of recovery so you can return to your flow activities feeling refreshed and primed for flow.

Restorative Activities

Some activities are more restorative than others. In the following section, we'll discuss a list of activities that have been shown to foster deep recovery. Nonwork time that is high in these activities is highly restorative. If pursued regularly, many of these activities will even change your brain and body in ways that make you more flow-prone.

I suggest sprinkling these activities liberally into your work and lunch breaks, evenings, weekends, and vacations. As a result, you'll experience greater recovery and, subsequently, more flow and greater overall health and well-being.

Physical Activity

Sabine Sonnentag is one of the world's leading researchers in the field of work-related recovery. She refers to physical exercise as an activity with a "high recovery potential."[2] Sonnentag has done research showing that when people exercise during the evening they subsequently feel more energetic and less fatigued, and they report greater well-being and more positive emotions.[3] The positive effects last until the next day: On days with more physical activity after work, people report feeling more energetic and recovered the next morning.

Other research has shown that on days when employees exercise during their lunch breaks, they feel and perform better on afternoons, are better able to concentrate, and are better able to deal with stressful situations.[4] In one study, participants who went for a 15-minute park walk during lunch reported better concentration and reduced feelings of stress and tension in the afternoon.[5]

The exciting thing about exercise is that it provides immediate, short-term, and long-term benefits. One study found that exercise leads to immediate increases in mood that can last up to 12 hours.[6] In another study, a 15-minute brisk walk was able to shut down cravings for sugary snacks.[7] In a similar study, 15 minutes of moderate-intensity stationary cycling reduced the desire to smoke cigarettes in regular smokers.[8]

Learning, too, gets an immediate boost, and it doesn't take much. In one study, vocabulary learning was 20% faster after just six minutes of intense physical exercise.[9] A meta-analysis of the effects of acute exercise on cognitive performance found that a single exercise session can lead to immediate improvements in attention, information processing, and executive functions.[10]

John Ratey, one of the world's foremost authorities on the benefits of exercise and author of *Spark: The Revolutionary New Science of Exercise and the Brain,* suggests that exercise puts us in a state of heightened focus and attention, enhanced impulse control, improved mood, reduced tension, and greater calm, motivation, and alertness—an ideal state for learning, working, and experiencing flow.[11] Ratey likens exercise to taking a little bit of Prozac and a little bit of Ritalin; exercise, much like these drugs, improves mood and attention. (The immediate and short-term effects obviously differ depending on the intensity of exercise. If we completely exhaust ourselves, we probably won't be in a flow-ready state.)

The long-term effects are even more impressive. Exercise has been shown to have positive effects on cardiovascular fitness, obesity, diabetes, cancer, anxiety, depression, schizophrenia, and other physical and mental health issues. It induces powerful changes both in the body and the brain. Among other things, it reduces blood pressure and resting heart rate, improves insulin signaling, strengthens bones and muscles, speeds up metabolism, increases brain volume and blood flow to the brain, and even facilitates the growth of new brain cells. It's been shown to be more effective for depression than prescription medications like Zoloft and Prozac. "Exercise is the single most powerful tool you have to optimize your brain function," asserts Ratey. "The better your fitness level, the better your brain works."

Physical activity makes you more flow-prone both in the short and long term.

Therefore, it's a good idea to sprinkle bouts of movement into your nonwork time. Don't worry about breaking a sweat or pushing yourself to exhaustion if that's not your thing. Low-intensity exercise like walking is a fantastic option, too. You don't have to overdo it, either. As little as five minutes of exercise have been shown to produce positive effects.[12] In one study, a 12-minute walk was found to increase mood, attentiveness, and confidence.[13]

Don't worry about engaging in the right type of exercise, either. You don't need to lift weights or go running; research suggests it's best if you choose an activity you enjoy.[14] Walking, running, biking, hiking, stretching, jumping rope, playing basketball, gardening, dancing, yoga, swimming, playing with your pets or your kids—it doesn't matter as long as you get moving.

Personally, I like to sprinkle several short walks into my day to counterbalance all my sitting. I also love hiking in the summer, playing tennis and football on a semiregular basis, lifting weights approximately once a week, and going for the occasional run with my girlfriend. When I add any of these activities to my lunch break, I often notice a substantial boost in my afternoon mood and ability to concentrate.

Meditation

Almost anything that was said about physical activity can also be said about meditation. Just like physical activity, meditation produces profound immediate, short-term, and long-term benefits. And just like physical activity, meditation makes you more flow-prone both in the short and long term. It also helps you recover on a physical, mental, and emotional level.

Regarding the immediate benefits, one study showed that an 8-min meditation reduced mind wandering and improved performance on a subsequent task that required focused attention.[15] Another study showed that a similarly short meditation reduced aggressive behavior after a subsequent social rejection.[16] Within a few minutes of meditating, heart rate, blood pressure, and overall physiological arousal go down. Default mode network (DMN) activity, mind wandering, and me-focused thinking also go down, while present moment focus goes up. Meditation tends to put us in a more focused, calm, cool, and collected state. As mentioned in the previous chapter, meditation can put us in a more flow-ready state.

In the long run, a regular meditation practice can reduce stress, anxiety, depression, and pain, lower blood pressure, strengthen the immune system, and improve sleep, memory, attention, and overall well-being.[17] There is barely a physical, mental, or emotional condition that has not been shown to benefit from a meditation practice. Meditation is a kind of wonder pill, a cure for all ills.

As it relates to flow, meditation has been shown to have positive effects on many relevant skills, attitudes, and personality traits.[18] Meditation has been shown to make people more conscientious, optimistic, mentally tough, emotionally intelligent, self-disciplined, mindful, self-compassionate, and gritty. At the same time, meditation has been shown to reduce anxiety, self-critical perfectionism, mind wandering, worry, rumination, and baseline DMN activation.

Many studies have shown that meditation improves people's ability to experience flow.[19] Without a doubt, regular meditation will make you more flow-prone. (There is even some evidence that long-term meditators—people who have done tens of thousands of hours of meditation in their lifetime—live in a kind of perma-flow.[20])

In my opinion, having a regular meditation practice is the #1 thing you can do to improve your ability to experience flow. Because the benefits of meditation follow a dose-response relationship, it can be said that the more you meditate, the more flow-prone you'll become.

In short, adding meditation into your nonwork time can help you experience more flow in two major ways: (1) it puts you in a more flow-ready state, thereby increasing your chances of experiencing flow in the next activity; (2) it helps you build skills and adopt attitudes that make you more flow-prone.

I started meditating approximately ten years ago. I've read countless books on the subject, attended two 10-day retreats, and had a daily practice for years. While my practice is a bit more sporadic these days, I strongly intend to attend more retreats and establish a more regular practice again soon. Meditation has made me a better person on so many levels. My experience has taught me: If I want greater happiness, peace of mind, calm, tranquility, and joy, meditation can provide me with all of that. I know what it can do for me. It's just a matter of making it a priority.

Some practical considerations:

- Most meditation experts agree that it's better to meditate frequently for short periods than to do long sessions every once in a while. That's why a daily practice is often recommended. If you can do 10–20 minutes a day, research shows you can reap considerable rewards, and quickly. In one study, just five days of daily meditation (20 minutes per day) resulted in improvements in mood and concentration and "a significant decrease in stress-related cortisol, and an increase in immunoreactivity."[21] In another study, just four days of daily meditation (also 20 minutes per day) resulted in improvements in various cognitive skills and reductions in fatigue and anxiety.[22]

- If you're new to meditation, one of the best ways to get started is with a meditation app. These apps teach you how to meditate and help you establish a daily practice. They are easy and fun to use and make the process enjoyable and rewarding. I've started my own meditation journey with the Headspace app and was very happy with it. Many excellent apps, free and premium, exist. Of course, you can also read a book or attend a course or retreat to learn meditation. If you're looking for a book, I would recommend *The Mind Illuminated* by Culadasa, Matthew Immergut, and Jeremy Graves. It's my favorite meditation manual.

- The type of meditation is secondary, in my opinion. Whether it's mantra meditation, mindfulness, loving-kindness, or some other form—they have all been shown to work. They have been shown to produce mostly the same benefits with only minor differences. Do the type of meditation you enjoy the most—it will make it easier to establish a regular routine and stick with it.

Social Interactions

"We are wired to be social," argues psychologist Matthew Lieberman in his book *Social: Why Our Brains Are Wired to Connect*.[23] "We are driven by deep motivations to stay connected with friends and family." Staying socially connected, he says, is a need as important as food and shelter.

Research confirms Lieberman's assertions. Nothing seems to impact our well-being more strongly than our social lives. As psychologist Daniel Gilbert puts it, "We are happy when we have family, we are happy when we have friends and almost all the other things we think make us happy are actually just ways of getting more family and friends."[24] One illustrative study showed that the happiest 10% of participants were rated highest on good relationships by themselves and their friends.[25]

Loneliness and social isolation, on the other hand, are associated with everything from depression, anxiety, and suicide to drug and alcohol use, smoking, unhealthy diet, physical inactivity, unfavorable health behaviors, impaired memory and learning, poor decision-making, and all-cause mortality.[26] Feeling acutely lonely causes the nervous system to sort of panic and react as if it were under attack; among other things, a large amount of cortisol floods the system.[27]

When people are told to remember a time when they felt lonely and isolated, they experience reduced optimism, self-esteem, and positivity and increased anger, anxiety, negativity, and fear of negative evaluation.[28] When they are told to remember a time in which they felt a sense of belonging, the opposite happens.

Feeling lonely and isolated hampers recovery; feeling socially connected and supported facilitates recovery. The former puts us in a state of stress; the latter puts us at ease.

Social activities (e.g., meeting friends and family, sharing a meal with others, chatting over the phone, or exercising together) are thus profoundly restorative. Positive social interactions can restore our confidence and optimism and provide comfort, appreciation, advice, and understanding. On a biological level, positive social interactions release oxytocin and endogenous opioids and activate the calming part of the nervous system.[29]

Engaging in social activities after work is associated with an increase in well-being over the course of the evening, as well as a high level of vigor and a low level of exhaustion the next morning.[30] Social lunch breaks, during which people feel a sense of community and belonging, help workers feel more recovered, less exhausted, and more engaged throughout the afternoon.[31]

The best kind of social interaction is face-to-face. Phone calls are less deeply restorative but still good. Texting, email, and social media activities don't really count; when it comes to fulfilling your social needs, they don't do the trick.[32]

Before we move on, I'd like to point out that there's a difference between being lonely and being alone. The former refers to a subjective experience (e.g., feeling that you lack companionship, that there's nobody you can turn to, or that you don't have much in common with those around you). Loneliness is often defined as the painful feeling that results from a discrepancy between the quantity and/or quality of one's desired and actual social connections.[33] On the other hand, being alone simply means that no other people are around. You can *be* alone but not *feel* lonely. And you can *be* in the company of others but *feel* lonely.

It's loneliness, not aloneness, that is associated with so many negative outcomes. Being alone, depending on what you do and how you feel, can be very beneficial.

Relaxation

Relaxation exercises facilitate a wide variety of recovery processes. They activate the rest-and-digest branch of the nervous system, slow breathing rate and heart rate, reduce physical and psychological activation, release tension, and induce an overall state of relaxation and serenity.

One of the most studied techniques is *progressive muscle relaxation (PMR)*, which involves tensing and relaxing various muscles of the body. PMR has been shown to produce "many well-documented recovery effects."[34] It can reduce blood pressure, improve sleep, increase mood and physical well-being, raise pain thresholds, decrease tension and stress, reduce levels of the stress hormone cortisol, ease anxiety and depression, reduce physical and mental fatigue, and put people in a more energized state.[35]

In one study, call center agents were asked to engage in a 20-minute PMR session during lunch breaks every day for a period of six months.[36] Compared to a control group, the PMR group felt more relaxed, concentrated, energetic, and motivated in the afternoons. A PMR-based lunch break "may significantly reduce sleepiness for several hours," noted the researchers. The PMR group also showed reduced cortisol levels after lunch and at bedtime, and over time even reduced cortisol levels upon awakening in the morning—a sign of reduced stress and strain.

Another study showed that a 15-minute relaxation exercise (a combination of PMR, deep breathing, and acceptance of thoughts and experiences) during lunch breaks led to better concentration, less strain, and less fatigue in the afternoon.[37]

While relaxation exercises may be especially well suited for lunch breaks, they can, of course, be done at any time of day. Proven techniques include PMR, diaphragmatic breathing, body scan meditation, guided imagery, or yoga nidra. You can find guided sessions on YouTube and other platforms. If you fall asleep, that's fine. As we're about to see, naps provide similarly powerful recovery benefits.

Napping

"In an ideal world, all humans, including you, would nap."[38] That's according to leading nap scientist Sara Mednick, who suggests that "not only is napping beneficial for alertness, mental ability and overall health, but our brains are actually programmed for it."

Napping is an obvious and highly effective choice for recovery during the workday. A 2021 meta-analysis on the effects of daytime naps on cognitive performance concluded that napping improves all types of cognitive performance: "Napping is particularly beneficial to performance on tasks, such as addition, logical reasoning, reaction time, and symbol recognition. Napping appears beneficial for all types of memory, either procedural, declarative or short-term memory. Daytime napping offers various other benefits such as relaxation, reduced fatigue and improved mood. Napping can boost creativity and productivity, improve physical performance and help people to cope with fatigue related to shiftwork. Daytime sleep may also offer cardiovascular benefits in the form of greater cardiovascular recovery from psychological stress."[39]

Naps can also improve emotion regulation and self-control. In one study, participants who had napped were less likely to give up during a "Frustration Tolerance Task" than those who hadn't napped. They were less impulsive and were better able to deal with frustration.[40]

If you think all of these benefits might help facilitate flow, you're exactly right. A 2012 study showed that people who took a 20-minute nap experienced more flow and performed better in a subsequent cognitive task than people who read books or magazines in the same time.[41]

While the ideal length for a midday slumber is around 20 to 30 minutes, naps as short as six minutes have been shown to create positive effects. [42] Long naps (40 to 90 minutes) provide the most benefits but can result in sleep inertia (feeling groggy after waking up). If you can't fall asleep, that's fine. Quiet wakefulness—resting quietly with your eyes closed—will recharge you, too.[43]

Personally, I often lay down during my lunch break to do a guided 10 to 30-minute body scan meditation or yoga nidra session. Some days, I fall asleep; some days I don't. Either way is fine with me because both naps and relaxation exercises leave me feeling refreshed, relaxed, and ready to tackle the rest of the day.

Flow

Yes, you read that right. Experiencing flow has also been found to support recovery. Even though it can be energy-expensive (depending on the activity), research shows that flow helps employees return to their jobs feeling more positive, motivated, refreshed, and ready to go.[44]

The absorbing aspect of the experience helps you fully detach from work and forget about work-related issues. Flow tends to leave you feeling strong, confident, competent, efficacious, and optimistic. Flow can boost your mood and well-being for several hours or even days.

Sabine Sonnentag was once asked about the most valuable recovery activity she would recommend. Her response involved flow and physical activity: "Of course, there are always individual preferences, different hobbies, and so on. It seems that it is important to pursue an activity into which one gets fully immersed, and that helps to forget anything else for a while. And: Research tells us that physical exercise is an activity that usually has a high recovery potential."[45]

Finding flow on evenings, weekends, and vacations can help you experience more flow at your job. Flow in leisure facilitates experiencing flow at work.

Play

"A lack of play should be treated like malnutrition—it's a health risk to your body and mind."[46] These are the words of Stuart Brown, one of the world's leading researchers on the science of play. Brown suggests play is a biological drive as integral to our health as sleep and nutrition.

We've seen in chapter 15 that approaching tasks in a playful manner can help you experience more flow. But play doesn't just make work periods more flowy; it also makes nonwork periods more restorative. Play generates positive emotions, reduces stress, lets us forget about our problems, and usually puts us in at least a mild flow state. One study showed that playing a simple smartphone game called Sushi Cat 2 for five minutes could boost mood, reduce feelings of worry, and increase engagement in a subsequent task.[47]

So, find ways to add play to your nonwork time: Play board or card games, solve crosswords or sudokus, joke around with co-workers, play a round of darts or ping-pong, goof around with the kids, play a musical instrument, put together model airplanes—the options are endless.

Laughter

A 2014 study found that older adults who watched a funny video scored better on subsequent memory tests and showed reduced levels of cortisol compared to a control group.[48] As we've seen in chapter 15, the benefits of laughter are no joke. Laughter has been shown to relieve tension, strengthen the immune system, enhance blood flow, decrease pain, reduce stress, boost focus, and much more.[49]

Make a list of things that make you laugh—whether it's watching comedy shows, reading joke or comic books, or doing laughter yoga—and add them to your list of recovery activities.

What about Netflix and co.?

After a tough day at work, we don't always have the energy or motivation to pursue any of the previous activities. Sometimes, we just want to chill out in front of the television. Can Netflix and co. provide recovery, too?

It depends. While watching television is typically associated with an increase in relaxation and mood *during* viewing, these positive effects can fade quickly *after* the experience. After viewing, people often report feeling depleted, tired, less alert, and less able to concentrate.[50]

In extreme cases, watching television can cause profound feelings of despair, anxiety, and stress. One study found that people who watched six or more hours of television news about the Boston Marathon bombing in 2013 were more likely to develop post-traumatic stress disorder than people who were actually at the bombing.[51] In another study, the single best predictor of people's anxiety and fear was how much time they spent watching talk shows.[52] Psychologist Shawn Achor suggests that "the less negative TV we watch, specifically violent media, the happier we are."[53] (Violent media refers to movies, TV programs, and video games that display acts of physical aggression—acts intended to injure or irritate another being.)

The potential long-term effects of excessive watching are not exactly rosy, either. More than two decades ago, psychologist Tannis MacBeth Williams studied a mountain community in Canada that had no television until cable finally arrived.[54] This allowed Williams to compare these people's lives before and after the introduction of television. Over time, she found that both children and adults in the town became less able to persevere at tasks, less tolerant of unstructured time, and less creative in problem-solving. Williams concluded: "Television viewing may result in the following: increases in children's physical and verbal aggression; decreases in reading skills, varying by sex and grade level; decreases in some cognitive skills; formation of more traditional sex role attitudes; and decreases in participation in community activities."

Aric Sigman, a psychologist and author of *Remotely Controlled: How Television is Damaging Our Lives*, goes a step further and refers to television as "the greatest health scandal of our time."[55] His extensive research has convinced him that watching television contributes to a wide range of negative health outcomes, including obesity, Alzheimer's disease, autism, heart trouble, hormone imbalances, increased appetite, delayed healing, sleep difficulties, decreased attention span, decreased metabolism, cancer, limited brain growth, damaged eyesight, early puberty, and diabetes.

That being said, the effects, of course, depend on the amount of watching and the programs being watched. There is some evidence that watching entertaining media *can* be supportive of recovery.[56] There is also evidence that watching nature documentaries can reduce negative feelings like tiredness, anger, and stress while increasing positive feelings like awe, contentedness, joy, amusement, and curiosity.[57]

It's the experience you have during and after watching that matters most. Watching the Super Bowl with friends is a very different experience from binge-watching some Netflix series all by yourself. Watching an awe-inspiring documentary is different from watching a negative news program. Watching for 30 minutes is different from watching for several hours.

When I lived in an apartment with my younger brother Yanis, we often watched thought-provoking and philosophical TV series together and then talked about them afterward. TV time with him was always a social and enjoyable experience. It was something I could look forward to. As such, it was a very valuable recovery activity for me.

Bottom line: TV time shouldn't be excessive or come at the expense of other more restorative and beneficial activities. That said, it's a viable recovery option if you can truly enjoy the experience and feel good afterward.

The Importance of Having a Good Time

Getting the most out of your nonwork time isn't just about what you do; it's also about what you experience while doing it. Regardless of the activity, having a good time is more restorative than having a miserable time. Recovery works best when you do things you truly want to be doing and are able to enjoy yourself.

When you feel obligated or have to force yourself to do something, it requires more self-control, causes more strain, is less enjoyable, and thus less restorative. The same activity performed out of extrinsic motivation (feeling like you should or have to) can produce very different results than the same activity performed out of intrinsic motivation (you actually want to do it because it's fun or meaningful).

In one study, household and care activities caused exhaustion when these activities were extrinsically motivated but not when they were intrinsically motivated.[58] Similarly, on days when people felt unhappy during evening household activities, time spent on these activities was negatively related to recovery.[59] On days when people felt happy pursuing the same activities, there was no negative effect on recovery. A study with teachers showed that they recover more successfully when they spend their breaks doing things they find personally important and meaningful.[60] Forcing yourself to go for a run after work and dreading every moment of the experience is less restorative than having a blast playing football with friends.

In choosing how to spend your nonwork time, yes, favor activities with a high recovery potential. But also favor activities that provide you with enjoyable and meaningful experiences.

The Restorative Power of Nature

It doesn't just matter *what* you do, it also matters *where* you do it. Some environments are more restorative than others.

Where would you ideally engage in your recovery activities? In short, in an as natural environment as possible. The more nature an environment provides, the greater its recovery potential. For example, a number of studies have shown that walking in more natural settings provides superior results compared to walking in more urban settings.

In a 2008 study, two groups of undergraduate students went through an initial series of rigorous cognitive tasks.[61] Afterward, both groups were asked to take walks of equal length (2.8 miles). One group took the 50- to 55-minute walk in the Ann Arbor Arboretum (a park near campus); the other group in downtown Ann Arbor. The arboretum walk was tree-lined and secluded from traffic, while the downtown walk was largely on a traffic-heavy street lined with university and office buildings. After the walk, participants returned to the lab and performed the cognitive tasks again. Results? The nature walkers improved their performance, but the urban walkers didn't. The natural environment was superior at restoring cognitive function. When the same group of researchers repeated their experiment four years later, they showed that the nature walkers also experienced greater increases in mood than the urban walkers.[62]

In 2015, researchers at Stanford University conducted a similar experiment. They sent participants on a 90-minute walk in either a natural or an urban environment in and around Stanford.[63] Before and after the walk, the researchers had individuals fill out a rumination questionnaire and scanned their brains. They were particularly interested in a brain area called the subgenual prefrontal cortex, a region that gets activated when people ruminate and that is also linked to sadness, withdrawal, and general grumpiness. Results? The nature walk significantly decreased both self-reported rumination and neural activity in the subgenual prefrontal cortex, whereas the urban walk had no such effects. Nature thus reduced the kind of self-conscious attention and overthinking that so often gets in the way of flow and contributes to so many mental health problems.

A small but intriguing 2013 study also looked at brain changes related to nature exposure.[64] The researchers asked volunteers to walk around Edinburgh, Scotland, for a total of 25 minutes. Their path took them through an urban shopping street, a city park, and a street in a busy commercial district. The walkers wore a mobile EEG able to transmit real-time information wirelessly to a laptop. The signals were run through an algorithm translating the brain wave patterns to various emotional states, including "excitement," "arousal," "frustration," "engagement," and "meditation." When participants entered the park, their brain waves showed reductions in "arousal" and "frustration" and an increase in "meditation." This bears repeating: The moment participants moved into the more natural setting, their brains responded by becoming more calm, relaxed, and at ease.

Other studies show that walking in nature (versus in urban settings) reduces blood pressure and heart rate, improves memory, and makes us feel more energetic, enthusiastic, focused, alert, alive, vital, and even more creative.[65] The benefits seem to follow a simple dose-response relationship:

the more natural the setting and the more time spent in it, the greater the rewards. Even when people are skeptical and don't expect to experience benefits from being in nature, they still reap the rewards.[66]

Of all the natural spaces available to us on this planet, one of the most restorative settings to walk or otherwise spend time in is the forest. The Japanese practice of forest bathing, or *shinrin-yoku,* has gained popularity over recent years. *Shinrin* in Japanese means "forest," and *yoku* means "bath." *Shinrin-yoku* means bathing in the forest atmosphere and taking in the forest through our senses. It's not about exercising, hiking, or jogging. It's simply about being in nature and connecting with it through our five senses. The benefits are profound. Forest bathing has been found to promote relaxation, reduce stress, lower cortisol levels and blood pressure, improve mood and emotional well-being, enhance sleep quality, strengthen immune function, boost attention, improve general cognitive functioning, and much more.[67] In some studies, as little as 15 minutes have been shown to have beneficial effects.[68]

To be clear, you don't need a forest to reap the benefits of nature. Urban parks, riverbanks, green patios, gardens, balconies, and even tree-lined streets can be fantastic options.

And if outdoor nature isn't on the menu, connecting with nature through images, videos, indoor plants, or even aquariums can do the trick. In one study, individuals who viewed pictures of natural areas for six minutes subsequently outperformed individuals who viewed pictures of urban areas on cognitive tests.[69] In another study, individuals who viewed slides of nature scenes for ten minutes prior to a stressful task were better able to cope with and recover from the stress than individuals who viewed slides of urban scenes.[70]

A 2015 study found that looking into an aquarium for five to ten minutes resulted in significant decreases in heart rate and blood pressure, improvements in mood, and decreases in arousal.[71] A similar study published in 2019 also showed decreases in heart rate, blood pressure, and anxiety as well as improvements in alertness, concentration, and creativity after ten minutes of aquarium watching.[72] When an aquarium was added to the home of seven non-institutionalized elderly people, these individuals experienced significant reductions in blood pressure and reported greater relaxation and overall leisure satisfaction.[73] When a fish tank was added to the activity and dining areas of patients with Alzheimer's disease, they reported similar benefits.[74]

Videos of nature work as well. In one study, participants were requested to watch video content for a period of ten minutes.[75] Three groups watched video clips of animals (fish, birds, and primates), one group watched parts of a soap opera, and another group just sat in front of a blank screen. After watching, participants were asked to read aloud for ten minutes from a relatively complex piece of text—a task designed to induce stress. After the reading, participants' heart rates and blood pressure (indicators of stress) were measured. Results? Individuals who watched the videotapes of birds, fish, and primates showed significantly lower levels of heart rate and blood pressure following the reading task than participants in the other two groups. The researchers concluded that the animal videos buffered the participants from the stressor.

In chapter 20, we'll see that indoor plants, window views of nature, and natural sounds and scents provide benefits as well. Nature, in any shape or form, helps you calm down, relax, and recover. As I've stated earlier, the more natural an environment, the greater its restorative potential.

Leaving Work at Work

There's one last factor that strongly influences how restorative your nonwork time is. Researchers refer to it as *psychological detachment* and define it as the subjective experience of leaving work behind—to forget about work and switch off during non-work time.[76] It describes the sense of being away and mentally disengaged from work.

The person who keeps engaging with work (e.g., through email) or keeps thinking about work during nonwork time recovers less well than the person who fully lets go of work-related activities and thoughts. Exercise, play, social interactions, and flow have all been shown to boost detachment, which is one reason why they work so well.

Psychologically detaching from work is so important that some researchers consider it "the most powerful driver of recovery."[77] On evenings when employees detach well from their work, they experience fewer negative emotions, more positive emotions, higher levels of serenity and vigor, and lower levels of work-family conflict.[78] They also sleep better and wake up the next day feeling more recovered, positive, motivated, energized, and less fatigued. The same goes for weekends and vacations.

In the long run, employees who consistently detach well from work report lower levels of psychological strain and exhaustion, fewer physical complaints, a lower need for recovery, higher levels of motivation and vigor at work, and higher overall life satisfaction. [79]

If you're serious about recovering from work, truly leave it behind. Don't bring work home with you. Don't check work-related emails on evenings, weekends, and vacations. Maintain strong boundaries between your work and your private life. Consider creating separate email accounts and using separate laptops and phones. Detach from work today, and you're more likely to experience flow tomorrow.

Chapter 19

One Thing at a Time

*Concentrate all your thoughts upon the work at hand. The sun's rays
do not burn until brought to a focus.*

—ALEXANDER GRAHAM BELL

The legendary management and productivity thinker Peter Drucker once said
that "real achiever[s] do one thing at a time." The Hindu monk Swami
Vivekananda similarly urged his disciples to do just one thing at a time and
"while doing it to put their whole soul into it to the exclusion of all else."

Self-help pioneers Og Mandino and Samuel Smiles shared the sentiment.
Mandino said, "It is those who concentrate on but one thing at a time who
advance in this world." Smiles suggested that "the shortest way to do many
things is to do one at a time."

Many others offer the same advice. But are they right? Is singletasking
superior to multitasking? Is doing one thing at a time more effective, and more
conducive to flow, than doing multiple things at once? That's what we're
going to find out in this chapter.

Multitasking Madness

Multitasking refers to the performance of multiple tasks at the same time.[1]
Two kinds exist: (1) *concurrent* (or *parallel*) multitasking and (2) *sequential*
(or *interleaved*) multitasking.

The former describes literally performing two or more tasks at the same
time, such as driving and holding a conversation, walking while writing a text
message, or folding clothes while chewing gum and following the plot of a
TV show. The latter describes performing two or more tasks in (rapid)
succession and in sequential order, such as frequently switching back and
forth between email, phone calls, social media, in-person conversations,

meetings, and other tasks—the kind of behavior every office worker is no doubt familiar with.

Both forms are widespread in today's world. A study that asked participants to track their media activities during a one-hour evening period showed that they switched between mobile phones, tablets, and laptops 21 times, and 95% of them did this with the television on for the entire hour.[2] Another study showed that 81% of Americans always or almost always engage in at least one additional activity while watching television.[3]

A 2013 study found that middle school, high school, and college students interrupted their learning sessions on average every six minutes.[4] "Even during a short 15-min observation period, and aware that they were being observed, participants were only capable of maintaining on-task behavior for a short time, averaging less than 6 min on task before switching," explain the researchers. Students mostly switched to digital distractions like instant messaging, social media, or watching television.

A study from 2004 showed that office workers switch tasks on average every three minutes, or 20 times per hour. [5] A study from 2016 found that the average online screen focus of office workers was a mere 40 seconds.[6] A similar study with college students found that task switching occurred on average every 48 seconds when participants were on their computers—the equivalent of 1.2 switches per minute, or over 70 switches per hour.[7]

If Drucker and co. were still alive, they would think we've all gone mad.

Your Brain on Multitasking

For your brain, both forms of multitasking are actually the same. That's because the brain doesn't really multitask. Neither in concurrent nor in sequential multitasking does the brain process two or more tasks at the same time. Instead, it switches back and forth between the tasks. Multitasking is an adequate description of behavior, but it doesn't reflect what the brain does.

To be more precise, the brain *can* engage in multiple processes at the same time. It does it all the time, of course. But only for processes that are unconscious, reflexive, and fully automated, such as breathing, moving blood throughout the body, maintaining heart rate, or digesting food. When tasks require some form of conscious attention, the brain can't process them at the same time; it has to switch back and forth between them. As multitasking expert and researcher Anthony D. Wagner notes: "The human mind and brain lack the architecture to perform two or more tasks simultaneously."[8]

We know this because of neuroimaging studies that look at what's happening in the brain as we attempt to multitask. When participants lie in brain scanners and are asked to perform two or more tasks at the same time, their brains switch between the neural networks responsible for the different tasks.[9] If two tasks are involved, the brain switches back and forth between task-A-network and task-B-network. The neural networks are not active at the same time. It's a constant switching between the networks, a constant on-off, on-off, on-off.

If that sounds like an energy-expensive process to you, that's absolutely correct. On a neuronal level, multitasking is more expensive than singletasking; it takes energy to orchestrate and execute the constant back-and-forth switching between neural networks. As Wagner puts it: "Our minds are taxed by multitasking. When we attempt it, we must engage in task switching, placing increased demands on neurocognitive systems that support, control and sustain attention. . . . Multitasking is not free—we pay a price in increased demands on these systems and some performance deficit typically occurs."[10]

Switching Costs

The performance deficits Wagner mentions are typically referred to as *switching costs*.[11] The most straightforward costs are higher error rates, reduced quality, and longer completion rates. In terms of completion times, these can increase by as much as 25–100% when people switch between tasks compared to when they complete one after the other.

The extent of the costs depends on factors like switch frequency, task complexity, age, and cognitive abilities of the person attempting to multitask.[12] In general, the more frequently we switch, the more complex the tasks involved, and the older the person, the higher the costs will be. That being said, the costs are there for everyone. Switching is inefficient, period. In the words of Wagner: "The behavioral costs of task switching are typically unavoidable: individuals almost always take longer to complete a task and do so with more errors when switching between tasks than when they stay with one task."[13]

Consider a 2012 experiment in which participants had to perform a Sudoku and a Word Search puzzle.[14] All participants first played a singletasking round, in which they worked on the tasks sequentially for 12 minutes each. This was done so that subjects were familiar with the tasks and wouldn't switch for curiosity's sake. The real experiment happened in the second round, for which participants were split into three groups.

The singletasking group worked again on the tasks sequentially for 12 minutes each. The multitasking group was forced to switch between the two tasks approximately every four minutes. The "choice" group could alternate between the tasks at their discretion—they could either singletask or multitask with the only constraint that they had to spend 12 minutes on each of the tasks. The amount of time spent on each task was identical for all groups; performance differences, therefore, reflected the effect of task switching.

Results? The singletasking group did substantially better than the forced multitasking group: They filled in significantly more Sudoku cells and found more words. What about the third group? These participants chose to switch an average of 2.16 times between both tasks. Most of them switched at least once (71%), but some (29%) decided not to switch at all. As a group, they performed slightly better than the forced multitaskers but still far worse than the singletaskers. Within the group, those who switched more often performed worse than those who switched less often or didn't switch at all.

To conclude, the study showed that more switching equaled greater switching costs; multitasking lowered performance compared to singletasking.

The study produced one more noteworthy finding. In the post-experimental questionnaire, subjects in the choice group were asked about their reasons for switching. Turns out they switched because they wrongly thought it would improve their performance. Many participants mentioned switching in order to look at the problem with a fresh eye, which they expected would help improve their performance. This might be one reason why multitasking is so prevalent these days: We think we're being efficient when in reality, we're not.

Let's consider a second experiment. Three groups of students were asked to read a book chapter and take a comprehension test.[15] The first group simply read the chapter and took the test. The second group first had an instant message conversation with the experimenter and then read the chapter and took the test. The last group was interrupted by the same conversation (delivered in pieces at various times during the reading) and then took the test, simulating the typical behavior of college students. All groups performed equally well on the test, but the interrupted group took substantially longer to read the chapter. Even when the time spent on instant messaging was removed, they required 22–59% more time than the non-multitaskers.

Bottom line: Multitasking is less efficient than singletasking.

Multitasking and (No) Flow

Is singletasking more conducive to flow than multitasking? If so, that would be another explanation of why the former is more efficient than the latter. After all, we know we're generally more productive in flow states than non-flow states.

In 2019, a group of researchers conducted an experience sampling study to test whether singletasking is indeed more conducive to flow than multitasking.[16] Office workers from various fields were beeped twice daily, once in the morning and once in the afternoon, for an entire workweek from Monday to Friday. When beeped, participants filled out an experience sampling form regarding the 30 minutes prior to the beep, inquiring about flow (e.g., *"I did not notice time passing"*) and multitasking behavior (e.g., *"I worked on several tasks in parallel"*).

Lo and behold, the researchers found that multitasking was negatively associated with flow. When participants indicated high multitasking in the previous 30 minutes, they reported relatively low levels of flow. When they indicated less multitasking, they reported higher levels of flow.

Multitasking impairs flow; singletasking fosters flow. Doing one thing after another is more conducive to flow than doing multiple things at once. The more you switch between tasks, the less likely you are to experience flow. And the less flow you experience, the less productive you tend to be. There's no doubt that flow, or the lack thereof, at least partly explains singletasking's superiority over multitasking.

Potential Long-Term Costs of Multitasking

Performing one task after another is more efficient and more conducive to flow than frequently switching between tasks; the immediate and short-term consequences of multitasking are reduced productivity and less flow.

But what about the long-term consequences? Does multitasking today influence your ability to experience flow tomorrow or weeks, months, and years into the future?

There is indeed some preliminary evidence to suggest this. Most of this research is done on *media multitasking*, which occurs when two types of media (e.g., print media, television, video, audio, instant messaging, email, or web surfing) are being used simultaneously or when one type of media is being used while doing another task. Examples include texting while talking face-to-face with another person, watching television while scrolling through social media, or listening to music while also sending emails.

A now-famous 2009 study divided people into heavy media multitaskers and light media multitaskers and compared their performance on various cognitive tests.[17] It was found that heavy multitaskers had less control over their working memory, were more easily distracted by irrelevant stimuli, and were less able to maintain focus on any given task.

The researchers' comments were eye-opening and alarming. One of them commented about heavy multitaskers: "When they're in situations where there are multiple sources of information coming from the external world or emerging out of memory, they're not able to filter out what's not relevant to their current goal. That failure to filter means they're slowed down by that irrelevant information." Another researcher added: "They couldn't help thinking about the task they weren't doing. The high multitaskers are always drawing from all the information in front of them. They can't keep things separate in their minds."

The third and last co-author of the study, Clifford Nass, painted an even bleaker picture, calling heavy multitaskers "suckers for irrelevancy" who are "distracted by everything." In an interview about his research, he said: "People who chronically multitask show an enormous range of deficits. They're basically terrible at all sorts of cognitive tasks, including multitasking. . . . People who multitask all the time can't filter out irrelevancy. They can't manage a working memory. They're chronically distracted. They initiate much larger parts of their brain that are irrelevant to the task at hand. And even . . . they're even terrible at multitasking. When we ask them to multitask, they're actually worse at it. So they're pretty much mental wrecks."[18]

Heavy multitaskers, he continued, have "developed habits of mind that make it impossible for them to be laser-focused. They're suckers for irrelevancy. They just can't keep on task." When asked if multitasking had caused these people to lose their ability to focus on one thing, he emphatically agreed: "That's precisely right. Our brains have to be retrained to multitask and our brains, if we do it all the time . . . brains are remarkably plastic, remarkably adaptable. We train our brains to a new way of thinking. And then when we try to revert our brains back, our brains are plastic but they're not elastic. They don't just snap back into shape."

Even more mind-boggling, Nass explained that multitaskers tend to believe themselves to be incredibly productive. He said it might be possible to retrain these people's ability to concentrate by forcing them to quit multitasking for a few weeks—but the heavy multitaskers flat-out refused to do it.

Since that preliminary study, many others have followed. A 2017 study does an excellent job of summarizing the findings: Heavy media multitaskers have increased self-reported mind-wandering and more everyday lapses of attention, greater self-reported impulsivity, increased distractibility, reduced self-control, reduced attentional control, and reduced ability to delay gratification.[19] (These skills are all highly relevant to experiencing flow.)

This research suggests that multitasking may, in the long run, decrease our ability to experience flow. That being said, it should be clearly noted that all of these studies are correlational only. It could be that frequent media multitasking creates the aforementioned changes (increased mind-wandering, more lapses of attention, etc.). Or it could be that individuals with greater impulsivity, higher distractibility, or reduced self-control are more likely to engage in media multitasking. It could also be both. We don't know.

What we do know is that our brains are plastic and are constantly changing in response to our everyday behavior.[20] Frequent multitasking for sure changes our brains. Do the brain changes involve higher distractibility, increased mind-wandering, impaired ability to concentrate, reduced self-control, greater impulsivity, and reduced ability to delay gratification? Maybe. Personally, I find this research scary enough to reduce my multitasking, with or without media, as best I can.

12 Ways to Reduce Multitasking

If you want to experience more flow, ditch multitasking in favor of singletasking. Reduce the number of switches between tasks. Even seemingly inconsequential switches (e.g., quickly checking email or glancing at social media or your favorite news website) can prevent or disrupt flow. Stay with one and the same task for an extended stretch of time. Work in a focused rather than fragmented fashion. Here are 12 strategies for making it happen.

1. Disable Alerts

Notifications from digital devices can be a major driver of task switching. We often interrupt what we're doing to check and potentially engage with whatever alerted us. Studies are now beginning to show the disruptive effects of notifications.

A 2016 study suggested that smartphone alerts could reduce productivity and well-being by causing symptoms of ADHD in the general population.[21] These symptoms include inattention (having difficulty focusing on one task at a time, being easily distracted, and getting easily bored when trying to focus) and hyperactivity (fidgeting, a sense of restlessness, difficulty sitting still, and difficulty doing quiet tasks and activities). If any of these symptoms feel familiar to you, know that notifications may be at least partly responsible.

It's important to note that alerts can be disruptive even if not attended to. In one study, the mere buzz of a new notification was enough to reduce performance on a cognitively demanding task.[22] Even when participants did not check the content of the notification, they still got distracted by the mere fact of knowing there was a notification waiting for them. When we get alerted about a notification, a part of us wants to know what it's all about. That part is distracting us by telling us to have a look—*who knows, it might be something important!*

Disabling notifications can make a big difference. In one study, participants who turned off alerts on all devices for 24 hours reported engaging with their devices less often and feeling significantly more productive and less distracted.[23]

If you're serious about flow, consider disabling alerts. Engage with your work for an extended period without getting disrupted. Then, at your discretion, check alerts at the end of a focused work session. This approach goes well with the sprint-rest-repeat recommendation from chapter 17. Sprint with as much focus as possible, then check alerts at the beginning of the rest period. That's how I do it whenever possible.

2. Know Your VIPs

You may want to (or have to) be reachable at all times for some individuals like your boss, supervisor, certain co-workers, your spouse, or your kids. If that's the case, you can use the settings on your devices to allow alerts for these VIPs. Yes, it's a bit annoying and time-consuming to set it up. But it's a one-time job that can benefit you for weeks, months, or even years.

3. Know Yourself

Studies that ask participants to disable notifications tend to find two things.[24] On the one hand, turning off alerts can make people feel *less* stressed and distracted and more focused and productive. On the other hand, it can also make some people feel *more* stressed because they're afraid of missing important information or violating the expectations of others.

For example, one study asked office workers to turn off their email notifications for one week. While some workers reduced their email checking compared to baseline, others ended up checking more frequently in order to avoid missing important messages.[25]

If you belong to the group that feels overly anxious without notifications, either skip this strategy or give yourself time to get used to it; know that the anxiety will almost certainly become more manageable over time. Alternatively, turn off notifications but make a deal with yourself to check in after thirty or sixty minutes.

4. Set Expectations

Let people know about your intentions to work in a more focused way. Explain why this is important to you and how you plan to do it. Tell them that you may reply less quickly to texts and emails. Tell them that early mornings (or any other times) are "flow periods" during which you prefer as little communication as possible.

5. Use "Don't Interrupt" Signals

Find ways to let others know when you wish not to get disturbed. Put a "Do Not Disturb" sign on your desk or office door. Or wear headphones so that people are less likely to disturb you even if you're not listening to music. Over time, your co-workers will come to understand and hopefully respect your signals.

Again, it's helpful to communicate your intentions. It's not that you don't want to talk to others; it's just that you would like to work with as few distractions as possible.

6. Block Distracting Websites

Do you frequently interrupt what you're doing to look at your email inbox, scroll through social media feeds, or check your favorite news website? One way to deal with this issue is to block the distracting websites.

A 2018 field study highlights the merits and potential pitfalls of this approach.[26] The study asked office workers to install the website blocking software *Freedom* and to block all distracting, non-work-related websites. These sites got blocked for a full workweek during working hours.

Results? During this week, participants reported greater focus and productivity and more flow. They mentioned that "work became less fragmented," that they "multitasked less," that they "did less task switching," that "tasks moved to longer durations," that the "duration of focus increased," and that they "worked in longer chunks of time without getting distracted."

One participant said: "Yes, I was more productive this week. I'm thinking about something, then I get distracted, then I have to start over; but now I didn't have to take a step back and start over.... I think I was more deeply concentrated this week than previously; it was easier for me to concentrate more, I had more deep concentration for sure."

In short, participants described precisely the kind of interruption-free working that facilitates flow.

Participants also reported that the software prevented *rabbit-holing*, which helped them save time and remain more focused. Rabbit-holing means losing yourself in internet distractions without noticing how much time is passing. One participant described it well: "When my head gets a little tired then I go and open Facebook, then read a message or two, and that would often lead to an article, and then I would write a rant; and that's 5 or 7 or 10 minutes." Blocking websites reduced this type of behavior.

Two more findings deserve our attention. First, some participants reported feeling more tired during the distraction-free week. That's likely because non-work related sites usually provide an easy break for office workers. Participants who replaced these breaks with more physical breaks (e.g., taking a walk, doing some yoga, stretching, or visiting others at their desks) reported no increase in fatigue. Only those who kept working without taking breaks felt more tired at the end of the day.

Second, not everyone found the website-blocking approach helpful. People who were high in self-control and already good at limiting interruptions themselves felt the software was unnecessary and controlling. They said they could shut out non-essential sites themselves and preferred being in control. The approach was thus most successful for those individuals who were most susceptible to distractions.

This lines up perfectly with my own experience. I benefitted greatly from blocking websites when I was younger and had less self-control. Now that I'm more disciplined, I feel that I no longer need to control myself like that. I can grant myself more flexibility and freedom and still perform and stay focused in a satisfactory manner.

If you feel like you might benefit from blocking certain websites, you have plenty of software options to choose from, including *Freedom*, *RescueTime*, *FocusMe*, *Cold Turkey*, and many more. I personally used both FocusMe and Cold Turkey in the past and have been very satisfied with them. These tools keep getting better and more sophisticated. You should be able to find a good fit quite easily.

7. Schedule Dedicated Email Time

Email can be another major source of task switching. A 2015 study showed that office workers check email on average 74 times a day, or roughly 11 times per hour.[27] Another study suggested that 70% of emails are attended to within a mere six seconds of arriving.[28]

Instead of checking and replying to emails intermittently throughout the day, schedule periods when you deal with email. For example, give yourself one hour at 11 am and another at 4 pm. Decide on pre-determined blocks and stick with them. In one study, when office workers were asked to check email only three times a day, they reported less stress, which predicted better overall well-being, greater self-reported productivity, and even improved sleep quality.[29]

Again, set expectations and let people know ahead of time that you'll be slower to respond. You can set up an automated response, saying, *"Hey there, just letting you know that I've received your email. In an attempt to be less distracted and more deliberate about using my time, I've decided only to check email at 11 am and 4 pm. If this is urgent, please call my office."*

8. Remove Visual Cues

Research on *priming* shows that sensory stimuli in our environment unconsciously activate goals and behaviors in us. The sight of an apple can trigger the goal of being healthy or losing weight. Walking past the gym can trigger an urge to exercise or feelings of guilt. Seeing an act of kindness can make us act more kindly.

In one study, putting sweets on a secretary's desk in a clear rather than opaque bowl (thereby making them more visible but not more available) increased snacking by 46%.[30] In another study, participants who were given sandwich quarters wrapped in transparent wrap ate more than those given sandwiches in nontransparent wraps.[31]

A particularly relevant study suggested that the amount of distracting technology available within an environment predicted task switching and on-task performance.[32]

Removing visible cues from your physical and digital environments is thus an easy and painless way to self-interrupt less frequently. Leave your phone in another room or a drawer. Close tabs of distracting websites. Remove the bookmarks bar in your browser. Install a browser extension that displays a blank page instead of thumbnails when you open a new tab. Delete all or most quick launch icons from your taskbar. Move all or most quick-launch icons on your desktop to one folder. "Out of sight, out of mind" truly works in this case.

9. Track Your Behavior

Research on behavior change consistently shows that enhanced awareness promotes better behavior. When dieters keep track of their food intake, they eat more healthily and lose more weight.[33] When people keep track of their exercise, they exercise more often.[34] The mere act of using a pedometer has been shown to lead to an increase in physical activity and decreases in body mass index and blood pressure.[35]

Apply this knowledge to your advantage. Consider keeping track of how frequently you switch between tasks. Or how long you can stay with the same task before getting interrupted. Or how many different tasks you work on during a given amount of time (e.g., in the morning).

I sometimes keep a "Last Checked" list on my desk. I simply write down on a piece of paper when I last checked my phone, social media, email, or any other distraction. When I then feel the urge to check again, I look at the sheet and realize, "Oh wait, I've only just checked my phone 22 minutes ago. Not much can have happened in such a short period." I can then put aside my anxiety of missing something and get back to whatever I was doing. This kind of tracking considerably reduces my check-in behavior and task switching. Importantly, I don't have to keep it up to retain the benefits. Doing this tracking every once in a while, for a day or two, is enough to remind me of my tendency to want to look at distracting tools and devices too frequently. This awareness then automatically improves my behavior for days and weeks to come.

If you work on a computer, you can use an online time-tracking application like *RescueTime*, *Harvest*, or *Toggl*. These tools provide you with feedback on your online behavior, giving detailed statistics on how much time you spend on various websites and applications. Similar apps exist for smartphones and other digital devices.

Preliminary research suggests that such tools are valuable. A 2016 study showed that an application showing users how they spent the last 30 minutes reduced the use of social media, email, browsing, and total time online.[36] A 2020 study examined whether showing people how long they switched away from a task increased their productivity by reducing the number and length of their switches. Lo and behold, participants who used the tool made shorter switches, were faster at completing the task, and made fewer errors.[37]

10. Use Collection Buckets

Do you sometimes switch from a task because you remember to do something else (e.g., call a friend or make an appointment)? Or because you remember that you wanted to check up on something (e.g., whether a movie is still in the cinema)? Or because you get the sudden insight to google some exciting topic (e.g., strategies to reduce multitasking)?

A simple remedy for such task switches are *collection buckets*—trusted places to store all the thoughts, ideas, and to-dos that come up while you're engaged in an activity. Instead of pursuing something immediately, you store it for later. Instead of switching tasks, you keep working on what you're already doing.

When I'm researching a topic on the Internet, I don't read articles or watch videos on the spot. I add relevant articles to Instapaper (a read-later app) so I can read them later, and I add relevant videos to a watch-later playlist so I can watch them later. I don't constantly switch between researching, reading, and watching. I do one thing at a time.

Collection buckets can be notes on your phone or computer, notebooks in Evernote, simple pieces of paper, read-later apps like Pocket or Instapaper, or watch-later playlists on YouTube and other video streaming sites.

I should note here that for a bucket to be effective, it has to be checked regularly. If you store stuff without ever taking care of it, you'll run into the issues associated with unfinished tasks (chapter 16). A part of your mind will know that your bucket can't be trusted and will feel like it has to remind you of whatever you stored there. If you check the bucket regularly, that part of your mind will come to trust it and will generate fewer intrusive thoughts.

11. Train Yourself to Deal With Discomfort

Another common reason for task switching is discomfort. We tend to abandon tasks when we feel stuck, frustrated, bored, annoyed, or otherwise uncomfortable. We switch to an easier task or our favorite distraction in an attempt to make ourselves feel better. Switching is often an escape from negative feelings.

If we want more flow, we must learn to handle these feelings differently and not abandon tasks at first sight of difficulty. If we switch every time we feel uncomfortable, we drastically limit how much flow we can experience.

What can you do when you experience discomfort? For starters, don't run away. Instead, simply stay put and allow the uncomfortable feelings to be there. Observe the feelings in an open, curious, and accepting way. Don't judge them, and don't try to control or change them. If you watch and welcome your feelings, they will become weaker and move on naturally. Within a minute or so, you'll likely feel that you can re-engage with the task. If you want a more step-by-step approach, try the RAIN-R technique described at the very end of chapter 21. (We'll discuss how to deal with difficult inner experiences in detail in chapter 21.)

12. Take Proper Breaks

Another common reason for task switching is fatigue. It's relatively easy to stay focused when we're fresh and full of energy. It's a lot harder when we're running out of steam. When our energy levels decline, we're at the greatest risk of leaving tasks unfinished, switching too frequently, and giving in to distractions.

If you feel fatigue kicking in, finish strong and take a real break. Make a clean cut. You've fully engaged, now fully disengage. Don't allow yourself to get sucked into the grey zone of working halfheartedly without real intensity and focus. Remember what we discussed in chapter 17: We perform best when we sprint-rest-repeat—when we move between periods of energy expenditure and energy renewal. Fully on or fully off. There's no flow to be found in the gray zone.

We started this chapter with Drucker, Vivekananda, Mandino, and Smiles, who all suggested that doing one thing at a time is more effective than doing multiple things at once. To me, there's no doubt they were right. Singletasking is far superior to multitasking.

If you want to experience more flow, stop the multitasking madness. Keep task switching to a minimum. Do one thing at a time, and do that thing with as much focus as you can muster.

Chapter 20

Flow-Supportive Sights, Sounds, Smells, and Co.

You are a product of your environment. So choose the environment that will best develop you toward your objective. Analyze your life in terms of its environment. Are the things around you helping you toward success—or are they holding you back?

—W. CLEMENT STONE

Your environment greatly influences how you think, feel, and behave. That's not news. You're reminded of it every day of your life.

When a bulldozer wreaks havoc near your office, you notice that the noise is distracting and frustrating. When it's 30°C (86°F) in your bedroom, you can't help but notice that the heat is keeping you awake. When the people around you are in a shitty mood, you can't help but notice that it's pulling you down as well.

Many environmental influences are so strong you can't help but notice their effect on you. But there are also more subtle influences. So subtle, in fact, that they escape your conscious detection. There are sights, sounds, scents, and other elements in your environment that influence you without you necessarily being aware that they influence you. Let me share some examples.

When wine shoppers pass by a display of wines from different countries, they are more likely to pick up a French bottle when French music is being played and more likely to pick up a German bottle when German music is being played.[1]

Living close to a fast-food restaurant can significantly increase your risk of obesity.[2] Living in a wealthy neighborhood can make you more materialistic.[3] Walking past a jewelry store can make you more selfish and less kind.[4] Holding a warm rather than cold cup can make you perceive strangers as "warmer" and more trustworthy.[5] Competing in red rather than blue outfits can give you an edge in combat sports.[6] Eating out of bigger containers can cause you to eat more food when compared to eating out of smaller containers—the bigger the plate, bowl, or food packaging, the more we eat. [7] It's a well-established finding.

The scent of citrus, when diffused into the air, can make you keep your surroundings cleaner. In one study, participants exposed to this clean-smelling scent made three times as many hand movements to clean crumbs off the table after eating a biscuit compared to participants who weren't exposed to the scent.[8] In another study, medical students were more likely to comply with hand hygiene regulations when the smell of citrus was in the air.[9]

The common theme in these examples is that people are being influenced without recognizing that they're being influenced. When asked if a certain environmental stimulus had an effect on them, most participants denied it. *No, the music had no impact on my wine choice. No, the plate size had nothing to do with how much I ate.*

This chapter is about becoming more aware of some of the subtle environmental factors that influence you. Once you know about these factors, you can tweak them and design your environments to make them as conducive to flow as possible.

Let the Light in

Light strongly influences your health and well-being; junk light, just like junk food, can make you miserable and sick. A 2016 review on light and indoor productivity and well-being concluded that among the many factors that impact building occupants, lighting seems to have the biggest influence.[10]

When it comes to indoor lighting, the best choice is *daylight*—the natural light of the sun coming in through windows or other transparent media and reflective surfaces. Daylight is far superior to artificial, man-made light. It provides us with the full spectrum of light, gives us important cues about the time of day, and adjusts our circadian rhythm in an ideal way. The natural light of the sun is what we've evolved under for the entirety of our history as a species. It's the light we know, the light we're adapted to, and the light we thrive under.

Compared with artificial light, daylight has been shown to boost mood and cognitive performance, enhance sleep quality and learning, lower blood pressure, speed healing processes, and improve our overall health and well-being.[11]

In schools, daylight has been shown to impact kids' test performance and sleep. One study found that students in classrooms with the most window area and daylight had 7–18% higher scores on standardized tests than those with the least window area and daylight.[12] Another study found that children exposed to plenty of daylight through large windows slept on average 36 minutes longer than children exposed to little daylight in their classroom.[13] Daylight is said to improve sleep by positively impacting our circadian rhythm. Precisely how it works is beyond the scope of this book. But more daylight translates into better sleep; it's a robust finding.

In the workplace, the benefits are equally profound. A 2017 study found that optimizing the amount of natural light in an office significantly improved workers' health, wellness, and productivity.[14] The researchers suggest that placing employees in office spaces with optimal natural light should be one of companies' first considerations. Another study concluded that organizations that pay attention to the importance of daylighting achieve higher productivity in their workplaces.[15] The study mentions companies that have reported a 47% increase in attendance in buildings designed to provide maximum daylight for their occupants.

In another eye-opening study, researchers compared the well-being and sleep quality of two groups of office workers. One group had minimal exposure to daylight at their workstations; the other group had windows and plenty of daylight at their workstations.[16] Results? On average, the group with windows slept a whopping 46 minutes longer per night than the group without windows. They also reported greater vitality, fewer physical complaints, and higher activity levels. The researchers summarized their findings: "Office workers with more light exposure at the workplace tended to have longer sleep duration, better sleep quality, more physical activity, and better quality of life compared to office workers with less light exposure at the workplace."

The most impressive study to date has been published in 2020.[17] Thirty office workers spent one week working in each of two office environments. They conducted their normal office work from 9 am to 5 pm in office A for a week and in office B for another week. Both offices were made to be as identical as possible. They had the same layouts, furnishings, and near-identical temperature, relative humidity, air quality, and noise levels. They were located in the same building, adjacent to one another. The only difference was that one setup provided significantly more daylight.

Participants wore devices on their wrists to measure sleep and completed cognitive assessments on the Friday of each test week.

Results? In the better lighting condition, participants slept on average 37 minutes longer per night. They also scored 79% higher on the cognitive tests. These are big differences. I strongly suspect that being in the better-lit office would put you in a far better position to experience flow.

There's also some fascinating research on how hospital stay is influenced by daylight. One study found that patients situated in beds near the window can leave the hospital sooner than those in beds near the door.[18] In another study, patients housed on the "bright" side of a hospital (and thus exposed to more daylight) experienced less stress and less pain, took 22% less analgesic medication per hour, and had 21% lower pain medication costs compared to patients housed on the "dim" side of the same hospital.[19] A study with nurses showed that those who had access to natural light enjoyed lower blood pressure, communicated more often with their colleagues, laughed more, and served their patients in better moods than nurses who had to settle for large amounts of artificial light.[20]

As you can see, the effects of light can be profound. If you have the choice, pick environments that provide plenty of daylight. It doesn't matter whether the light comes in through windows, glass doors, transparent roofs, or any other way. If you can spend time outdoors, all the better, of course.

If you are stuck in a windowless or otherwise dim space, consider the following tips:

- Invest in high-quality artificial lights that mimic the full spectrum light of the sun. Your best options are incandescent, halogen, or full-spectrum LED bulbs; these are far superior to fluorescent bulbs or regular LEDs.[21]

- Place a small lightbox, made for the treatment of seasonal affective disorder, on your desk and turn it on whenever you need an energy and alertness boost. (Don't do this close to bedtime as the bright light will interfere with sleep.)

- Get outside during lunch and other breaks. The time under natural light will help offset some of the adverse effects of poor indoor lighting.

Light influences mood, alertness, sleep quality, and other factors that subsequently influence your likelihood of experiencing flow. A well-lit environment will support you in experiencing flow.

Turn Down the Noise

Noise is a prevalent issue in many work and living spaces. In office environments, noise frequently comes from street and air traffic, co-worker conversations, office equipment, heating, ventilation, and air-conditioning systems.

A 2017 Gallup Poll suggested that 75% of office workers complain about noise in the workplace and 38% report that they would change their jobs just to have an office with a door.[22] In one survey, 99% of participants reported that their concentration was impaired by various components of office noise, especially people talking in the background and telephones left ringing at vacant desks.[23]

Excessive noise is stressful and can seriously get in the way of performance and flow. Workers in noisier environments show reduced memory and math performance, more tiredness, lower motivation, more health problems, and higher stress levels.[24] Children in urban areas living in noisier apartments have lower reading scores than those living in quieter apartments in the same building.[25] Reading comprehension scores in quiet classrooms are higher than in noisier classrooms.[26]

If noise is an issue for you, consider investing in a pair of noise-canceling headphones; these have been shown to improve task performance in noisy environments.[27] In one study, the best results came when active noise canceling was paired with sounds of nature; with these settings, performance in the noisy environment was as good as in the quiet environment.[28]

Find Your Temperature Sweet Spot

We've probably all had the experience of working in environments where we felt either too hot or too cold. Temperature has a noticeable effect on comfort, concentration, and overall well-being. Interestingly, research finds that performance suffers more when it's too warm than when it's too cold.[29] Perhaps less surprisingly, temperature affects complex tasks more strongly than simple tasks.[30]

If you're able to set the temperature in your environment, aim for somewhere between 20°C (68°F) and 22°C (72°F). According to a meta-analysis of 24 studies, that's the temperature that maximizes mental performance and productivity.[31] It's probably also the temperature that's most conducive to flow.

That said, what's more important than temperature per se is that you feel comfortable. So-called *thermal comfort* is influenced not just by temperature but also by air velocity, relative humidity, clothing, and metabolic rate. Individual differences matter a lot here. For example, my preferred temperature is quite a bit lower than that of my girlfriend. At a temperature where she feels perfectly comfortable, I might get hot and sweaty, making me uncomfortable and interfering with my concentration. Thermal comfort is highly individual, so you'll have to find your own sweet spot.

Mind the Air You Breathe

In modern society, many of us spend 80–90% of our time indoors.[32] Indoor air quality is an often neglected but crucial influence on our health, well-being, and productivity.

Unfortunately, indoor air quality is often less than ideal. Research suggests that air pollution indoors is between two and five times—and occasionally more than 100 times—greater than outdoors.[33] That's because indoor air contains whatever pollution is outside, plus the pollution created inside.

Indoor air pollution is a serious issue, causing a high prevalence of allergies, airway infections, asthma, and *sick building syndrome* (SBS) —dry, itchy, sore, and burning eyes, irritated noise and sinusitis symptoms, respiratory irritation, headaches, lethargy, and mental fatigue.[34] Indoor air pollution has also been shown to negatively impact diabetes, neurodevelopment deficits, dementia, adverse birth outcomes, and much more.[35] According to the Lancet Commission on pollution and health, 800,000 people die every year due to poor air quality in their workplace.[36]

While the problem is more severe in developing countries, it's also an issue in developed countries. In the latter, chemicals from cleaning and consumer products, furniture and construction materials, electronic equipment, and inadequate ventilation and air conditioning deteriorate indoor air quality.[37]

The major key to indoor air quality is *ventilation,* which refers to replacing indoor air with fresh outdoor air to dilute and remove air pollutants from inside the building. High ventilation rates result in good indoor air quality.

Many studies have shown that low ventilation rates in schools are associated with increased absenteeism, more respiratory symptoms, poor test performance, and poor health outcomes.[38] When ventilation rates are increased, all of these outcomes see significant improvements.[39]

In the workplace, the same is true. A 2019 study stated that "there is a very large literature base on the effects of office ventilation on productivity and health" and that "removing common indoor sources of air pollution and increasing ventilation is associated with increased productivity, reduced short-term sick leave, SBS symptoms, inflammation, respiratory infections, asthma and allergy."[40] One study showed that doubling the ventilation rate reduced short-term sick leave by 35%.[41] In another study, doubling the ventilation rate improved employees' productivity by 8%.[42]

A 2016 review of studies on productivity and office environment quality concluded that indoor air quality greatly impacts office productivity; workplaces with good air quality have higher work performance in office tasks such as text typing, proof-reading, and mathematical tasks.[43]

How can you improve the air quality in your indoor environment? Here are some suggestions:

- Clean the space regularly, using natural rather than chemical cleaning products and a high-quality vacuum cleaner with HEPA filtration.

- Get an air cleaner or purifier.

- Manually increase the ventilation rate by opening windows on opposite sides of the room so the air can move through.

- Increase the ventilation rate of whatever ventilation system is already in place.

- Invest in a more sophisticated ventilation system.

Personally, I focus mostly on points #1 and #3. I do my best to keep my work and living spaces clean by vacuuming regularly and cleaning other surfaces with natural products. I manually ventilate for 5–10 minutes first thing in the morning, right before going to bed, and every couple of hours throughout the day. When I'm in the office, I usually do this during breaks.

If you want to test the air quality in your environment, you can purchase an air quality monitor. That way, you'll see how severe the issue is and how far you'll want to go to remedy it. A monitor will also allow you to see how big of a difference the various air-purifying attempts make.

Tidy Up… or Don't

Another factor to consider is how cluttered or neat your environment is. A 2014 study found that people sitting at messy desks were less self-disciplined and persistent and more impulsive, easily frustrated, and weary than those sitting at neat desks.[44]

For their experiment, the researchers exposed participants either to an orderly space or to a work area where papers, folders, and cups were scattered over the desk, shelves, and floor. Each participant was then presented with a list of ten items (e.g., a high-end HDTV, a mini fridge, an air conditioner, a desk lamp, or a vacation package for a ski trip) and asked to indicate the highest price they were willing to pay in order to buy it. Those in the disorganized room gave higher prices than those in the neat room—a sign of greater impulsivity and lower self-control.

In another version of the experiment, participants were asked to undertake what was described as a challenging task that was, in reality, unsolvable. Those in the neat environment stuck with the task for an average of almost 19 minutes before giving up, more than 1.5 times as long as those in the messy space (11 minutes). Persistence in a frustrating task is a classic measure of self-control, which was again shown to be higher in the orderly environment.

After these experiments, participants were asked how they felt. Those who sat in the disorganized room reported feeling more depleted, burned-out, overworked, and weary compared with those who sat in the neat room. Messy environments, the researchers suggested, can deplete mental resources, leading to reduced self-control.

A study from 2013 came to a similar conclusion.[45] Participants in a neat room donated considerably more money and chose healthier snacks than those in an untidy room. The researchers concluded that "an orderly (vs. disorderly) environment leads to more desirable, normatively good behaviors."

That being said, this study did find a benefit to a disordered environment. In one version of their experiment, participants in the messy room came up with more creative ideas for new uses of ping-pong balls than those in the orderly room. Disorder, the researchers suspect, helps people break from convention and be more creative.

Neatness in your workspace is a factor you may wish to experiment with. Personally, I prefer orderly spaces. Clutter and disorder seem to overwhelm my senses and negatively impact my concentration.

Remove Your Phone

You would probably experience more flow if you removed your phone from your workspace. Why? Because the phone is a major source of task switching and because the sounds and buzzes of notifications are distracting even if not attended to. (We've discussed these issues in chapter 19.) And there's another reason. Recent research suggests that the mere presence of a phone can be disruptive, even in the absence of ringing, buzzing, or being used.

A 2017 study asked participants to sit at a computer and take a series of tests to measure attention and cognitive capacity (the brain's ability to hold and process data).[46] Before the test, all participants were told to put their phones to silent. Then, participants were randomly assigned to place their phones on the desk, in their pocket or personal bag, or in another room.

Results? Participants with their phones in another room significantly outperformed the other two groups. (Those who had their phone in their pocket or personal bag performed slightly better than those who had it on the desk. Whether smartphones were turned on or off, or lying face up or face down, didn't make a difference.)

These findings suggest that the mere presence of your smartphone can reduce your cognitive resources. Lead researcher Adrian Ward explains: "We see a linear trend that suggests that as the smartphone becomes more noticeable, participants' available cognitive capacity decreases." Ward refers to the mere presence of a phone as a "brain drain."

Ward and his colleagues made two more interesting findings. First, most participants were unaware of the negative impact the mere presence of their phones had on their cognitive abilities. Participants were asked after the experiment if they thought the position of their phones had affected performance. The vast majority of them indicated that where the phone was neither helped nor hurt their performance.

Second, not all participants were equally impacted by the phone's presence. The study measured participants' *smartphone dependence*—how strongly a person feels they need the phone in order to get through a typical day. All participants, regardless of the degree of smartphone dependence, performed equally well on the cognitive tests when smartphones were placed in another room. However, when phones were on the desk or in the pocket or personal bag, the highly phone-dependent participants scored worse than their less dependent peers. If you view yourself as highly dependent on your phone, removing it from your immediate surroundings may yield especially profound benefits.

Other experiments have produced similar results. One study found that the mere presence of a phone negatively affected learning and memory.[47] Another found that the presence of a phone was distracting for drivers, especially for those who are highly dependent on their phone, which may place them at a greater risk of a crash.[48] In yet another study, the presence of a phone was distracting and impaired cognitive performance, even if it wasn't the participant's phone but that of the experimenter.[49]

The presence of a phone can also reduce the quality of face-to-face social interactions. A 2012 study showed that the mere presence of a phone (not belonging to any of the participants, placed on a nearby table within full view but not in direct line of sight) inhibited the development of interpersonal trust and closeness between strangers and reduced the extent to which individuals felt empathy and understanding from their partners.[50] A similar study found that conversations in the absence of phones were rated as significantly superior compared with those in the presence of a phone.[51]

Bottom line: Phones are distracting. Whenever possible, consider removing your phone from your environment. Leave it in another room, a distant locker, a bag, or maybe even your car. Remember that its presence can have an impact even if you're not aware of that impact.

Bring Nature Inside

Exposure to the natural world is good for us. We've seen in chapter 18 that natural environments are more restorative than artificial ones, and we've seen in the current chapter that natural light is better for us than artificial light.

Wouldn't it make sense to bring more nature into our offices, schools, and homes? To make these places more natural and thus healthier and more restorative for us?

That's precisely the belief behind *biophilic design*, a design philosophy that incorporates natural features and systems into the built environment in order to provide human beings with exposure to nature.[52] Biophilic design brings nature into our indoor spaces by using plants, aquariums, fountains, gardens, animal feeders, and green roofs, by using natural materials, shapes, and colors, and by relying on daylight rather than artificial light.

The philosophy is based on the *Biophilia hypothesis*, which suggests that humans have an innate connection with the natural world and that exposure to the natural world is important for human well-being.

Though research on biophilic design is still relatively sparse, preliminary findings indicate great potential. A 2015 paper suggests that biophilic design results in a wide spectrum of benefits, including enhanced physical fitness, lower blood pressure, increased comfort and satisfaction, fewer illness symptoms, improved health, increased satisfaction and motivation, less stress and anxiety, improved problem-solving and creativity, enhanced attention and concentration, improved social interaction, and less hostility and aggression.[53]

In the workplace, biophilic-designed office buildings will likely become ever more popular in the coming years. In one study, the transformation from a regular to a more biophilic office resulted in increased productivity, reductions in stress, enhanced well-being, a more collaborative work environment, and greater workplace satisfaction.[54]

In the remainder of this chapter, we'll discuss various ways to bring more nature into your work and living spaces.

Potted Plants

The easiest way to bring green, living nature into your indoor environment is with potted plants. Not only do they look pleasant, but they have also been shown to reduce stress and improve productivity, workplace satisfaction, health, air quality, and overall well-being.[55]

In a 2011 study, participants were split into two groups.[56] One group was put into an office with plants, while the other was put into the same office but with no plants. Participants were then given tests to measure attention. The first test, administered immediately upon entering the room, showed no difference between the two groups; this means there were no pre-experimental differences between the plant and no-plant groups.

After the initial test, the researchers asked participants to perform a challenging proofreading task designed to increase mental fatigue. Then, they administered the attention test a second time. Results? Those who sat in the office with plants improved their performance in the second round, whereas those in the other room did not. This experiment suggests that the presence of plants is beneficial for attention and cognitive performance.

A study from Taiwan tested the effect of indoor plants in a different way.[57] They showed participants six different images of workplaces, each with a different combination of window views and plants: (1) no window, no plants; (2) no window, with plants; (3) window view of city, no plants; (4) window view of city, with plants; (5) window view of nature, no plants; (6) window view of nature, with plants.

While the participants looked at the images, the researchers measured various physiological stress parameters and asked participants to indicate how anxious they felt. Each image was shown for fifteen seconds. Of all the images, the one with the window view of nature plus indoor plants had the most beneficial effect: Both self-reported anxiety and objectively measured stress (e.g., muscle tension and sympathetic arousal) were lowest. The opposite was the case for the images showing an office with no view and no indoor plants: Both subjective anxiety and objective stress were highest.

So, consider getting some plants for your work and living spaces. Fresh flowers have been shown to produce similar benefits and are an excellent option as well.[58] If you feel like you're a complete newbie regarding plants, that's okay. Plant care fundamentals can be learned quickly and easily. I don't have a green thumb, either, and most of my plants are doing just fine. If you're unsure which plants will do well in your space, the workers at your local garden shop can help you figure that out.

Personally, I've added several additional plants to my spaces after reading this research. My office currently houses 11 small- to medium-sized plants. Obviously, I have no way of quantifying how much of a difference they make in terms of flow, productivity, or well-being. However, I do feel that they make a difference. It feels like they make the space more calm, relaxing, and overall pleasant. If nothing else, they're nice to look at.

Wooden Products

Another way to experience more nature is to use products made from natural materials such as wool, cotton, linen, wood, or stone rather than plastic or other synthetic materials. Using wooden products is an easy way to accomplish that, and there's some intriguing research on the topic.

The presence of wood has been shown to reduce stress, anxiety, blood pressure, heart rate, and cortisol levels and increase productivity, mental and physical health, and overall well-being.

One study compared the effects of spending 24 hours in near-identical hospital isolation rooms.[59] The only difference between the rooms was that one was redecorated with wood panels and rice straw paper on the walls, while the other still had its original concrete walls. On average, participants' cortisol levels were 20% lower in the redecorated room, indicating reduced stress levels. Participants also felt more thermally-comfortable in the wooden room compared to the control room.

In a year-long study, researchers examined the stress levels of high school students taught in either a wooden or non-wood conventional classroom.[60] Over the course of the school year, students taught in the wooden classroom showed lower heart rates and reduced stress. In another study, participants who performed a stressful mental task in a room with wood showed lower objective markers of stress than participants who performed the same task in a room without wood.[61]

Other studies show that wooden beds can improve sleep quality, wooden tables, chairs, and tableware can improve emotional states and relationships, and the presence of wood in workplaces can improve productivity, workplace satisfaction, mood, and overall well-being.[62]

In short, being surrounded by wood is good for you. If you want to reap some of the benefits, a simple thing you can do is to bring wooden objects into your work and living spaces. Most objects that surround us and most tools we use are available in wooden versions. There are wooden chairs, tables, shelves, desks, wardrobes, beds, cutlery, plates, bowls, laptop stands, keyboards, computer mice, picture frames, pens, patios, etc.

I've personally added a fair amount of wooden objects to my surroundings since learning about the benefits of wood. Has my life completely changed as a result of it? Am I in a permanent state of flow all the time? Of course not. But I do believe that the presence of wooden objects has a positive effect on me.

Sights of Nature

We've already discussed that rooms with windows are superior to rooms without windows. However, not all windows are equally beneficial; the content of the window view makes a difference. Views of nature tend to be more beneficial than views of built environments, such as other buildings, parking lots, or urban streets.

A 1984 study found that patients in hospital rooms with window views of trees recovered faster from surgery than patients with windows looking onto a brick wall.[63] Patients with the green views requested less pain medication, were described in nurses' notes as having better attitudes, and needed fewer postoperative days in the hospital. A 2019 study came to the same conclusion. It showed that higher satisfaction of window view decreased analgesic usage and reduced the scores of overall perceived pain, pain severity, and pain's interference with relationships, enjoyment of life, and mood.[64] More natural views were rated as more satisfying.

In the workplace, views of nature also show positive effects. One study found that workers sitting in offices with window views of a forest were less stressed and more satisfied with their jobs compared to workers who could not see a forest or any other natural setting from their windows.[65]

Obviously, many of us don't have the luxury of choosing the room or space we work in. If you don't have a window view of nature where you work, that's okay. You can rely more heavily on other natural elements, such as plants, flowers, wooden furniture, or pictures of nature. You can also make it a point to go into natural environments during breaks, as discussed in chapter 18.

Sounds of Nature

Sounds of nature are also beneficial. In a study titled *Of cricket chirps and car horns: The effect of nature sounds on cognitive performance*, researchers found that exposing participants to nature sounds as opposed to urban sounds led to significant improvements in cognitive performance.[66] The natural soundscapes primarily contained sounds of birdsong, insects (e.g., crickets), moving water (e.g., rainfall, ocean waves), and wind. The urban soundscapes primarily contained sounds of traffic, machinery (e.g., the "hum" of an air conditioner), and café ambiance (with unintelligible speech).

In a study conducted in Sweden, researchers investigated the effects of different sounds on stress recovery.[67] Participants were asked to perform a stressful arithmetic task while the researchers measured physiological indicators of stress. After the task, participants were given a recovery period during which they listened to one of four soundtracks: (1) nature sounds featuring tweeting birds and water sounds, (2) road traffic at high volume, (3) road traffic at low volume, and (4) ambient noise consisting of the soft whirring of a ventilation system. The physiological markers showed that stress recovery was fastest when participants heard the nature sounds. The researchers concluded that nature sounds facilitate recovery after a psychological stressor.

Another study examined the effect of sound on stress recovery and mood enhancement.[68] Participants were exposed to footage of a surgery in order to cause discomfort and negative mood. Before watching the video, participants completed a scale to measure their affective state; they indicated how happy, calm, energetic, lively, tired, gloomy, grumpy, loving, etc. they felt.

After viewing the disturbing video clip, participants were asked to listen to one of four audio tracks: (1) natural sounds of birdsong and rustling leaves, (2) natural sounds with motorized noises in the background, (3) natural sounds with human voices in the background, or (4) no sound. Then, they were again asked to fill out the mood questionnaire. Results? Those who listened to the pure nature sounds experienced the greatest mood and stress recovery benefits.

Nowadays, the internet provides free and unlimited access to nature sounds. Perhaps you can listen to bird sounds during specific tasks or after a particularly stressful situation. Or you can play ocean sounds when lying down for a nap, during a break, or on your ride home. Me, I often listen to bird sounds when cooking, cleaning, and during other everyday activities. I'm also considering purchasing a soundbox with a motion sensor for the bathroom—I like the idea of birds chirping while I shower or do my business.

Scents of Nature

I mentioned in the introduction that scents of citrus can make you care more about hygiene and cause you to keep your surroundings cleaner. Scents can also influence your mood, attention, and even athletic performance.

For example, several studies have shown that the aroma of rosemary essential oil can enhance mood and cognitive performance. In a study with schoolchildren, kids performed better on various tests of working memory when doing the tests in a rosemary-scented room than in a non-scented room.[69] In a similar study with healthy people aged 65 or older, those who were placed in a rosemary-scented room reported feeling more alert and scored 15% higher on prospective memory tests than those placed in a room with no aroma.[70]

Similar studies have been done with other scents, including peppermint. One study showed that performance on clerical tasks was greater in peppermint-scented rooms than in non-scented rooms.[71] Among other things, participants typed faster and more accurately in the presence of peppermint.

Athletic performance also gets a boost from peppermint. In one study, athletes undergoing a 15-minute treadmill stress test reported less fatigue, exertion, and frustration and greater vigor when in the presence of peppermint aroma compared to no aroma.[72] In a similar study, athletes in a peppermint-scented room ran faster, performed better on a handgrip strength test, and did more push-ups.[73] When rugby players use peppermint-flavored mouthguards, they report feeling more energized and motivated and performing better during games and practice.[74]

It's important to point out that different scents have different effects. If you're looking for a boost in athletic performance, peppermint is your best choice. If you're looking for a boost in general arousal and alertness, try peppermint or rosemary. If you're looking to calm down and reduce arousal, try jasmine, ylang-ylang, chamomile, or lavender.

If you want to give it a try, the most straightforward way is to use an essential oil diffuser. They are relatively inexpensive and come in different varieties. If you don't have a diffuser, add a few drops of essential oils to a bowl of hot water or simply apply a drop of essential oil to your wrist or inner elbows. If it irritates your skin, mix it with a carrier oil such as olive or coconut, and then apply it.

Another alternative is to use herbal teas or to add sprigs of rosemary, peppermint, or any other herb to a glass of water. In one study, consuming 330ml of rosemary water enhanced cognition in similar ways as inhaling the aroma of rosemary essential oil.[75] Drinking peppermint tea has been shown to increase arousal and alertness, while consuming chamomile tea has been shown to decrease arousal and have a more calming and sedating effect.[76]

I've been using essential oils and herbal teas for a while now, and I find it hard to say how much of an effect they're having. But again, just because we don't notice an effect doesn't mean there's no effect. While I can't claim that any scent or tea reliably puts me in a flow state, I do believe they are worth exploring and experimenting with.

Some environments are more conducive to flow than others. By using some of the ideas discussed in this chapter, you can tweak your surroundings in ways that make flow more likely. Of course, you can also just spend more time in environments that are already very conducive to flow. For example, you can engage in your flow activities in as natural environments as possible. If you go for a run, the nearby park or forest is likely more conducive to flow than the treadmill or neighborhood.

Chapter 21

Managing Flow-Disruptive Emotions

When force of circumstance upsets your equanimity, lose no time in recovering your self-control, and do not remain out of tune longer than you can help. Habitual recurrence to the harmony will increase your mastery of it.

—*MARCUS AURELIUS*

Mike and Melinda, two fictional co-workers, have a heated argument during lunch break. Both return to their work stations feeling angry and annoyed. Mike has a hard time moving on from the argument. He can't stop thinking about it and feels agitated all afternoon. As a result, he has trouble concentrating on his work and experiences very little flow. Melinda, on the other hand, is able to move on from the emotional upset and return to equanimity relatively quickly. As a result, she's able to focus on her work and experiences plenty of flow.

As this example illustrates, your ability to recover from difficult private experiences is crucial for flow. The more skilled you are at dealing with negative emotions, and the better you are at moving on from them, the more flow you tend to experience.

Why is that? Because negative thoughts and emotions tend to interfere with the kind of task-focused attention that is so characteristic of flow. You've undoubtedly experienced this yourself: It's hard to concentrate when feeling anxious, angry, or sad. On a neurological level, negative emotions are usually characterized by increased activation of the default mode network (DMN); as discussed in chapter 9, that's the very brain region that needs to deactivate for flow to happen.

It's simply a lot easier to transition into flow if you're in a state of positivity and inner harmony than a state of negativity and inner turmoil.

Research has shown that positive thoughts and emotions facilitate flow, while negative thoughts and emotions prevent and disrupt flow.[1]

This chapter aims to help you more effectively deal with anger, anxiety, sadness, and other negative emotions. This will allow you to spend less time in negative emotional states and more time in more flow-conducive states. As a result, you'll experience more flow.

"Positive" and "Negative" Emotions

"Positive" emotions tend to feel good, boost performance, and bring out the best in us; "negative" emotions tend to feel bad, lower performance, and bring out the worst in us. But that doesn't mean that negative emotions are all bad and positive emotions are all good. Both have their upsides and downsides. To live a healthy and meaningful life, we need both, as they serve different functions.

Among other things, negative emotions keep us safe and help us learn from our mistakes. Fear stops us from jumping off a cliff. Anxiety urges us to prepare for the future. Disgust alerts us to potential pathogens. The pain of guilt teaches us to respect our moral standards. Anger and frustration provide motivation to change.

It's normal and healthy to experience negative emotions in response to certain events. It's normal to experience fear in the face of imminent danger, anger when confronted with perceived injustice, guilt after falling short of personal standards, or grief following the death of a loved one.

Negative emotions per se aren't the problem; it's our mishandling of them. With the right skills, it's possible to "get the message" and "move on" from negative emotions without giving in to self-defeating behaviors, or compromising our moral standards. We can get the good from negative emotions without the bad.

Emotion Regulation

An entire field of research investigates how people deal with their emotions—how they try to increase, maintain, or decrease the intensity, duration, and trajectory of positive and negative emotions. This process is typically referred to as *emotion regulation*.[2] Emotion regulation is said to be part of the broader concept of emotional intelligence, which we briefly discussed in chapter 6.

Emotion regulation research has produced helpful and intriguing findings. Among other things, it has shown that some strategies for dealing with emotions work better than others, that people differ in the kind of strategies they habitually use, that people differ in how well they're able to regulate their emotions, and that this has wide-ranging consequences for their well-being.[3] People who are good at regulating their emotions do far better in life than those who struggle with this process. They are less likely to suffer from depression, anxiety, and other mental health issues, possess better physical health, have more positive interactions and relationships, and experience more flow.

The good news is that people can change the strategies they use to regulate their emotions and improve their overall emotion regulation ability. As they do so, their lives improve, and they experience more flow. Improving your emotion regulation skills—which is what this chapter is all about—will make you more flow-prone.

For me, learning and practicing the ideas we're about to discuss has been a game changer. It has helped me deal with my inner world more effectively and has made me a more productive, disciplined, calm, and overall better-functioning human being. Our entire lives are driven in large part by our emotions. We severely limit our potential and undermine our well-being if we never learn to deal with them appropriately; we'll thrive if we learn and practice to deal with them appropriately.

How do researchers study emotion regulation? How do they figure out which strategies work well and which don't? The most interesting method they use is the *mood induction experiment*. For these experiments, researchers bring participants into the lab and ask them to engage in tasks designed to make them feel bad; they have them watch negative film clips or images, work on frustrating tasks, recall painful autobiographical memories, or give impromptu speeches in front of a camera or other people.

Before participants perform their tasks, they are told the task may elicit negative emotions and that they should try to deal with their emotions in a specific way. Participants may be told to suppress their emotions, accept them, ignore them, or think about their causes or potential benefits. Researchers then compare participants' emotional and physiological experiences when using the different emotion regulation strategies.

Unhelpful strategies tend to increase the intensity of negative emotions and increase overall distress, agitation, and physiological arousal; in short, they exacerbate and prolong negative emotional experiences. Helpful strategies do the opposite, allowing participants to return to equanimity more quickly.

Let's look at an example study. In this experiment, participants listened to audiotapes, encouraging them to either accept or suppress their emotions.[4] Then, they were asked to apply the instructions while watching an emotion-provoking video clip. The clip was a 6-minute excerpt from *The Deer Hunter* in which captured soldiers were forced to play "Russian Roulette." The clip is known to induce anxiety and other negative emotions because viewers anticipate soldiers shooting themselves in the head and because the soldiers are depicted crying through much of the clip. Participants filled out mood questionnaires before, during, and 2 minutes after watching the clip.

Results? Participants in both groups scored equally high on negative emotion before and during watching the clip. However, 2 minutes after watching the clip, the acceptance group scored much lower on negative emotion than the suppression group—the negative emotions of accepters had subsided to a greater extent than those of suppressors. Put differently, the accepters showed greater recovery from the emotional upset. As we'll see later on, this is a common finding concerning these two strategies: Suppression tends to prolong negative emotional experiences, while acceptance tends to shorten them.

How to Deal With Negative Emotions—5 Do's and Don'ts

Now that you know what emotion regulation is and how it's studied, I want to share some of the most important lessons this research has brought forth. In the remainder of this chapter, I'll share with you five principles for dealing effectively with difficult emotions. Following these principles will improve your overall emotion regulation ability, make you more emotionally intelligent, and make you more flow-prone.

1. Don't Suppress

> *Again and again I have said to myself, on lying down at night, after a day embittered by some vexatious matter, 'I will not think of it any more! . . . It can do no good whatever to go through it again. I will think of something else!' And in another ten minutes I have found myself, once more, in the very thick of the miserable business, and torturing myself, to no purpose, with all the old troubles.*
>
> *—LEWIS CARROLL*

Suppression is about inhibiting whatever is going on inside of us.[5] It can refer to pushing emotions away, pushing them "deep down inside," holding them in, or otherwise trying not to experience them. It's a fighting stance—we fight, subtly or not so subtly, with our experience. We don't like what we're experiencing, so we're trying not to experience it. When you look for synonyms, you'll find words like defeating, conquering, triumphing over, crushing, quashing, squashing, extinguishing, putting down, or restraining.

Suppression is a common but counterproductive way of dealing with difficult private events.[6]

When researchers tell participants to suppress their emotions in mood induction studies, participants usually experience an ironic increase in the very emotions they're trying to suppress. Trying to suppress anger makes them more angry. Trying to suppress anxiety makes them more anxious. Trying to suppress sadness makes them more sad. Participants also usually experience increased heart rate, blood pressure, and overall physiological arousal. When we suppress, we become more agitated, distressed, and emotional.

As the saying goes, what you resist persists. Or as Carl Jung put it: "What you resist not only persists but will grow in size.''

The harder we try to squeeze out unwanted private experiences, the more dominant and intrusive they tend to become. Suppression tends to exacerbate and prolong negative emotional experiences. It's kind of like pouring gasoline on fire.

Quicksand offers another metaphor for what's happening when we suppress. When we land in quicksand, our natural reaction is to fight and struggle to get out, yet the more we do so, the more stuck we get. Something similar happens when we try to suppress our thoughts and emotions. The more we try to get rid of them, the stronger and more overwhelming we tend to make them, and the longer we tend to be stuck with them.

And there's another downside to suppression: it's exhausting. We all know that self-control takes effort—it takes effort to resist the cookie, to opt for the healthier choice, to not lash out at others, or to get a workout done when we don't feel like it. Trying to forcefully control our inner experience is just as tiring.

Many studies have shown that suppression depletes mental energy.[7]

Consider an experiment in which participants were instructed to suppress their emotions while watching a sad movie clip.[8] A control group was told to just watch the movie carefully without regulating their emotions in any specific way. The clip was a nine-minute excerpt from *The Champ*, in which a boy witnesses his father die after suffering a severe beating in the ring. After watching the clip, participants completed a 20-minute task designed to measure cognitive fatigue. Results? The suppression group performed worse on the subsequent cognitive task, indicating that suppressing was mentally taxing.

This isn't a trivial finding. We have limited supplies of mental energy, and if we've temporarily run out of it, we tend to lose the ability to control ourselves. When our energy reserves run on empty, we're more likely to cheat on our diet, drink too much, or procrastinate. By using up your mental energy, suppression can set you up for subsequent self-control failures. If you've ever wondered why some individuals are more disciplined than others, this research partly answers that question: Self-discipline and emotion regulation go hand in hand. If you want to become more disciplined, ditch suppression and learn to regulate your emotions in healthier ways.

The bottom line is this: We can't fight away unwanted private experiences. Suppression sets up an inner struggle that is both exhausting and counterproductive. The more we fight, the more turmoil we generate.

It makes intuitive sense: The very act of fighting runs counter to the harmonious nature of flow. The more you fight, the less flowy your life becomes. The opposite is also true: The less you fight with your inner world, the more harmonious and flowy your life becomes. Stop the inner war, and you'll find more flow.

The White Bear Experiments

Harvard scientist Daniel Wegner conducted the first major experiment on suppression in the 1980s. Wegner asked his participants not to think about a white bear for five minutes and to ring a bell each time the thought of a white bear nevertheless crossed their minds. Participants were told they could think about anything they wanted except for a white bear.

Results? No matter how hard they tried, participants couldn't keep the white bear out of their minds. They were unable to suppress thoughts about white bears. The following transcript from one participant thinking aloud reveals the difficulty: "I'm trying to think of a million things to make me think about everything but a white bear and I keep thinking of it over and over and over. So . . . ummm, hey, look at this brown wall. It's like, every time I try and not think about a white bear, I'm still thinking about one."[9]

Over the years, Wegner conducted many more experiments. He always found the same thing: It's impossible to just, on demand, exclude specific thoughts from consciousness. And the same is true for emotions, cravings, desires, physical sensations, and other private experiences. We can't just not think something, or not feel something, or not crave or desire something. We can't suppress these experiences.

In fact, Wegner made another discovery: The very attempt to suppress an experience has the paradoxical effect of making that experience more prominent. The act of trying not to think about something triggers the paradoxical effect of thinking about it more. The act of trying not to feel anxious has the paradoxical effect of making us more anxious. The more we try to suppress a thought, emotion, or craving, the more we're stuck with it and the more strongly we're influenced by it. Wegner concluded: "Suppression is not simply an ineffective tactic of mental control; it is counterproductive, helping assure the very state of mind one had hoped to avoid."[10]

Our inner world simply can't be controlled in the same way as the outer world. If I told you, "Cook me some dinner, or I'll shoot you," you'd immediately start cooking. If I said, "Fetch me some beer, or I'll shoot you," you'd immediately be on your way. But if I say, "Relax or I'll shoot you," or "Don't be afraid or I'll shoot you," or "Don't think of a white bear or I'll shoot you," you're in trouble.[11]

It's impossible to directly control our private experience. And the harder we try to do so, the more we tend to generate the very experience we're trying to avoid.

To be clear, it *is* possible to control our experience to some extent. But we can only do so indirectly. For example, we can take a drink to calm our nerves, talk to a friend to soothe our pain, or, as we're about to learn, observe our emotions to make them less overwhelming.

2. Don't Ruminate

She sat by the window, looking inward rather than looking out. Her thoughts were consumed with her sadness. She viewed her life as a broken one, and yet she could not place her finger on the exact moment it fell apart. "How did I get to feel this way?" she repeatedly asked herself. By asking, she hoped to transcend her depressed state; through understanding, she hoped to repair it. Instead, her questions led her

> *deeper and deeper inside herself—further away from the path that would lead to her recovery.*[12]
>
> *—ANONYMOUS*

Rumination can be defined as "repetitive thinking about the symptoms, causes, circumstances, meanings, implications, and consequences of depressed mood and distress."[13] It's often characterized by negative self-evaluative thinking, unfavorable social comparisons, and comparison of the current situation with some unachieved, perfectionistic standard.[14] If thinking turns into *over*thinking and becomes overly negative, repetitive, and hard to stop, that's rumination.

Just like suppression, rumination is a counterproductive way of dealing with inner experiences.

When researchers induce ruminative thinking in mood induction studies (e.g., by asking participants to think about the causes of a negative emotion repeatedly), they reliably find that rumination exacerbates any negative emotion currently active in an individual.[15] A sad person becomes sadder, an angry person becomes angrier, and an anxious person becomes more anxious. Some researchers refer to rumination as an "emotional magnifier" because it magnifies whatever negative emotion is already there.[16]

Rumination also interferes with concentration, reduces confidence, saps motivation, and increases self-criticism and pessimism. On the level of the body, it increases blood pressure, heart rate, cortisol levels, and other stress markers. Sonja Lyubomirsky, a leading rumination researcher who's been studying the topic for more than three decades, refers to the combination of rumination and negative emotions as "toxic."[17]

But at least you're getting to the bottom of things, right? Surely, you'll find a solution to your troubles if you just think about them hard and long enough. Unfortunately, that's rarely the case. Even though ruminators usually report that they think about their problems in an effort to solve them, evidence strongly suggests that rumination actually impedes problem-solving. That's because rumination makes us view our problems as more overwhelming and unsolvable, makes us less creative, and makes us less confident and motivated to carry out any solutions we come up with.[18] Lyubomirsky suggests that rather than gaining insights into our problems, what we gain is a distorted and pessimistic perspective on life.[19]

As it relates to flow, rumination is clearly unhelpful. Rumination exacerbates and prolongs negative thoughts and emotions and fuels self-criticism, pessimism, and other processes that get in the way of flow. You may also remember from chapter 9 that rumination is synonymous with DMN activation, a clear neurological sign that rumination acts against flow.

Thinking about our emotions can be helpful; *overthinking* isn't. *Reflection* can help us regulate our emotions; *rumination* does the opposite. Of course, I want to acknowledge that rumination isn't always a choice. For many of us, me included, it's a habit. We often can't stop ruminating even if we want to. The good news is that the ideas we're about to discuss can help us deal not only with negative emotions but also with ruminative thinking.

3. Find a Better Frame

There is nothing either good or bad, but thinking makes it so.

—WILLIAM SHAKESPEARE

Reframing, or *reappraising*, refers to changing the way you think about a situation in order to change its emotional impact. It's about viewing things (situations, emotions, sensations, etc.) in a more positive light—about finding a more positive interpretation of whatever is disturbing us.

Thomas Edison provides a good example. When his research lab was burning down and decades of work were being destroyed, he supposedly told his son, "Go get your mother and all her friends; they'll never see a fire like this again." "Don't worry," Edison calmed his son. "It's all right. We've just got rid of a lot of rubbish." Edison's interpretation was positive, and thus, his emotional experience was also positive. If his interpretation had been negative—that this was the worst thing that ever happened to anyone, he was so unlucky, his career was over, and the world was conspiring against him—he would have experienced great emotional turmoil (anger, rage, self-pity, etc.).

For many of us, our initial appraisals aren't as positive as Edison's. That's why we must make *re*-appraisals—we must change how we view the situation. If we manage to find a better interpretation, our emotions change for the better as well.

Reappraisal is one of the most effective emotion regulation strategies available to us.[20] In mood induction studies, reappraisal has been shown to reduce the intensity of negative emotions and help participants quickly return to equanimity. In some instances, reappraisal can move us from a negative emotional state to a positive state literally from one moment to the next. Consider a study that showed participants a photo of people crying outside a church, which elicited feelings of sadness.[21] They were then told to consider that the scene was a wedding and that the people were crying tears of joy. As soon as participants changed their appraisal of the photo, their emotional responses changed as well.

If your interpretation changes, your emotions follow suit. Feelings follow frame.

Reappraisal has also been shown to reduce heart rate, blood pressure, and other physiological markers of arousal, activate the more rational parts of our brain, and put the brakes on the more emotional parts. Reappraisal calms us down and moves us from a state of "hot" emotionality to a state of "cool" composure. When it comes to flow, reappraisal is a powerful ally.

So, how do you do it? How do you come up with helpful interpretations? You have plenty of options. You can simply look for the positive sides of a difficult situation. You can ask yourself: What's the upside here? What might I learn from this? What good unexpected outcomes might come from it?

You can remind yourself of the bigger picture and that, in the grand scheme of things, maybe this isn't a big deal. Or you can remind yourself that even though a situation may be painful, it could make your life better in the long run—facing difficulty can help you grow by adding depth to your being and making you more resilient, empathetic, understanding, and compassionate.

Another approach is to bring to mind helpful idioms and metaphors, such as: what doesn't kill you makes you stronger; every loss is a gain; a bad day for the ego is a good day for the soul; every cloud has a silver lining; what is to give light must endure burning; it's always darkest before the dawn; no rose without a thorn; this, too, shall pass.

Me, I often bring to mind the following story:

Once upon a time, there was a Chinese farmer who lost a horse. It ran away. All the neighbors came around that evening and said, "that's too bad." He said, "maybe." The next day, the horse came back and brought seven wild horses with it. All the neighbors came around and said, "why, that's great, isn't it?" He said, "maybe." The next day, his son was attempting to tame one of the wild horses. As he was riding it, the horse threw him off, and he broke his leg. All the neighbors came around and said, "that's too bad." He said, "maybe." The next day, the conscription officers came looking for people for the army. They rejected his son because he had a broken leg. All the neighbors came around and said, "isn't that wonderful?" He said, "maybe."[22]

This story immediately takes the sting out of a situation, calms me down, and sets me up to look for positive interpretations. Instead of whining, complaining, or wallowing in self-pity, I'm reappraising: *Maybe this isn't so bad. What's the upside here? How will I learn and grow from this?*

4. Accept and Observe With Mindfulness

> *[R]ather than trying to get rid of unpleasant feelings, we open up and accommodate them. We make room for them and allow them to come and go in their own good time. It doesn't mean we like them, want them or approve of them; we just stop investing our time and effort in fighting them. And the more space we can give those difficult feelings, the smaller their impact and influence on our lives.*
>
> *—RUSS HARRIS*

Mindfulness can be defined as nonjudgmental, moment-by-moment awareness of whatever is happening in the present moment. It is sometimes said to consist of two components, though the definition is a constant topic of debate.[23] The components are: (1) sustained attention to present experience and (2) an attitude of openness, curiosity, and acceptance toward that experience.

If we use mindfulness to deal with our emotions, it becomes an emotion regulation strategy. Researchers then refer to it as *mindful emotion regulation, mindful acceptance,* or *experiential acceptance.* These terms all mean the same thing; I'll use them interchangeably.

Mindful emotion regulation is all about accepting rather than resisting or fighting your emotions. It involves being aware of your emotions without judging them, identifying with them, interfering with them, or attempting to change them in any way. You adopt the role of an impartial (though compassionate) witness. Instead of struggling with your experience, you "let it be." Instead of trying to control or change private events, you allow them to be just as they are. You simply watch what's going on inside of you with openness, curiosity, and acceptance.

To be clear, this type of acceptance has nothing to do with accepting the status quo of a situation. A woman in an abusive relationship, for example, need not accept this as her fate; quite the opposite. As she takes steps to change the situation (e.g., by leaving her partner), she will likely experience anxiety and other negative emotions. It is the acceptance of these emotions and other difficult private experiences that constitutes mindful acceptance.[24]

Wisdom traditions like Buddhism, Hinduism, and Taoism have recommended this approach for thousands of years, and modern research is slowly catching up. Studies conducted over the past two decades have confirmed what wise humans have known for a long time: Accepting our inner world without trying to change it has the paradoxical effect of changing it for the better. By giving up trying to control our thoughts and emotions, we gain more control over them. What we resist persists. What we accept dissipates. It vanishes, goes away. Accepting troubling thoughts and emotions helps us recover and move on from them. Experiential acceptance is a counterintuitive but highly effective emotion regulation strategy.

In mood induction studies, participants who are instructed to mindfully accept their emotions tend to experience reductions in heart rate, blood pressure, and overall physiological arousal. They experience a decrease in the intensity of negative emotions and an overall reduction in agitation and inner turmoil. Just like reframing, acceptance helps us move from "hot" and emotional to "cool" and composed. It calms us down and allows us to return quickly to equanimity. Accepting negative emotions helps us move on from them.[25]

Intriguingly, experiential acceptance has been shown to cause a reduction in DMN activation.[26] As mentioned earlier, this is the exact brain region that must deactivate for flow to occur. Acceptance, in a very real way, facilitates flow by getting us into a more flow-ready state.

We have actually already seen these positive effects on DMN activity in chapter 9. Judson Brewer's brain scan experiments have shown a concomitant reduction in DMN activity when meditators report "just noticing and observing their experience," "acceptance of things as they are," or "no struggling, striving, or forcing." On the other hand, brain scans have shown increases in DMN activity when meditators report "trying to control and change the way things are," "trying to make something happen," or "struggling and fighting."

Acceptance leads to a decrease in DMN activity; non-acceptance (e.g., suppression) leads to an increase in DMN activity.

Another encouraging finding is that participants rate acceptance as relatively easy to learn and use.[27] It also doesn't require a great deal of energy or self-control. We've seen that suppression can be mentally taxing and result in temporary self-control depletion. The same has actually been shown for rumination and, to a lesser extent, reappraisal. But not for acceptance.

In one study, participants were asked to watch a sadness-inducing excerpt from the movie *Gladiator*, in which the protagonist finds his son and wife murdered when he arrives home.[28] Participants were asked to either accept or suppress their emotions while watching the clip. Participants in a control group received no instructions and were told just to watch the video. Subsequently, all participants performed a task designed to measure self-control. Results? Participants in the acceptance group outperformed both participants in the suppression and control groups. The researchers concluded that "acceptance-based coping is more efficient in terms of resource usage and relies less on self-control compared to suppression."

It's interesting that the acceptance group also outperformed the control group. We might speculate that participants in the control group naturally suppressed or otherwise tried to control their emotions during the movie clip. If that were the case, it would explain why they also depleted their self-control. Either way, the study showed that acceptance spares our mental resources and, by doing that, allows us to act with greater self-discipline in other areas of life.

There is a saying that "suffering = pain x resistance." While mindfulness can't keep pain and difficult private events from happening, it can eliminate or reduce their unnecessary exacerbation. It can keep us from experiencing additional distress on top of the initial pain. By removing the resistance, acceptance reduces our suffering. We may still land in quicksand, but we no longer make it worse by fighting and struggling against it. We may still feel disappointed, sad, angry, or anxious, but we no longer make it worse by suppressing, pushing away, or harshly judging ourselves and our emotions.

As it relates to flow, mindful acceptance is a wonderful friend. It protects us from prolonging and amplifying the kind of agitation that gets in the way of flow. It helps us move on from negative emotional states and return to more flow-conducive states quickly and efficiently. Experiential acceptance translates into less inner turmoil, less negativity, more energy, and less depleted willpower reserves, all of which translate into more flow.

Acceptance, inner harmony, and flow go hand in hand. The more accepting you are of your inner world, the more harmonious and flowy your life becomes. It comes as no surprise that mindful individuals have been shown to experience more flow than their less mindful peers.[29]

Acceptance Metaphors

One of the best ways to fully understand experiential acceptance is with metaphors. The two we're about to discuss are frequently used in *Acceptance and Commitment Therapy* (ACT), a form of therapy that heavily relies on acceptance in the treatment of depression, anxiety disorders, obsessive-compulsive disorder, eating disorders, substance use disorders, workplace stress, chronic pain, and other mental and physical conditions.

The Tug-Of-War With A Monster Metaphor

Imagine you're in an all-out tug-of-war with a powerful monster. The monster represents challenging inner experiences (e.g., depression, fear, guilt, or shame). Between you and the monster is a huge, apparently bottomless pit. You think that if you just pull hard enough, you can pull the monster into the pit and no longer have to struggle with any difficult experiences.

Despite your best efforts, though, it seems impossible to pull the monster into the pit. Even though you're expending massive amounts of energy, the monster isn't moving. The constant fighting is exhausting, but you feel like you have no choice. You must participate in the war; otherwise, the monster will pull you into the pit, and who knows what terrible things might lurk there.

So, what can you do? How do you get out of this seeming dilemma? Well, here's an alternative: drop the rope. End the fight and allow the monster to wander around freely. You might be surprised to learn that you can live your life just fine, even with the monster around. It's not actually as scary and destructive as you thought. And now that the fight is over, you find yourself with a lot more energy to focus on and approach the things you're actually excited and passionate about.

But beware: the monster will continue to taunt you and dare you to pick up the rope. Indeed, you are likely to find yourself over and over again with the rope in hand. The key is thus learning to recognize when you have inadvertently picked up the rope and then immediately dropping it again.

The Passengers on a Bus Metaphor

Imagine you're the driver of a bus. On your bus, there are a number of passengers. The passengers are your thoughts, emotions, physical sensations, and other aspects of experience. Let's further assume all of the passengers are intimidating and scary, and each is yelling directions about where you have to go. "You've got to turn right," "You've got to go left," and so on.

The threat they have over you is that if you don't do what they say, they will come up front from the back of the bus and start trouble. So you feel as though you must obey these passengers and follow their directions to stay safe.

You have a few options for dealing with this unsatisfactory and uncomfortable situation.

For one thing, you can just follow orders. That way, the troublemakers remain in the back of the bus, and you don't have to deal with them. The problem with this approach is that you give up control. There are places you might want to go but can't because you allow the passengers to determine where to go.

Another option is to throw the bad passengers off the bus. You stop the bus and go back to deal with the passengers. Notice, though, that you must stop in order to do that. You're no longer driving; you're busy dealing with passengers. Plus, they are strong. And it seems that despite your best efforts, you can't really get rid of them. And even if you could throw them off the bus, nothing is stopping them from hopping back on.

Thankfully, you have a third option: allowing unruly passengers to be on your bus without following their directions or fighting with them. Sure, they will come up occasionally, get really loud, threaten you, and so on. But if you don't engage in yelling matches or fights with them, they usually quiet down or even get off the bus on their own. Passengers come and go while you are riding toward your valued life goals.

5. Be A Good Friend to Yourself

Self-compassion is simply giving the same kindness to ourselves that we would give to others.

—*CHRISTOPHER GERMER*

The word "compassion" comes from the Latin "compati" and means "to suffer with."[30] *Compassion* can be defined as the feeling that arises when you see another's suffering and feel motivated to relieve that suffering.[31] It involves feelings of warmth, care, and concern toward the suffering being and a desire to help them. It may also involve an understanding that everyone suffers from time to time and that it's part of life. When we act on our instinct to help, we often do so by offering kindness, understanding, and perspective. We may lower our voice, speak in a soft and warm tone, and let the suffering being know they aren't alone in their pain.

Self-compassion is simply compassion directed at yourself. It's about being supportive of yourself when confronted with personal mistakes, failures, inadequacies, and painful life situations. It's about being a good friend to yourself.

Self-compassion is an important concept in Buddhist philosophy and has been valued and practiced for over 2,000 years. The scientific study of self-compassion began in 2003 when Kristin Neff introduced a way to define and measure the concept.[32] Neff is still the world's leading researcher on the topic and has probably done more to bring self-compassion to the world than anyone else. If Csikszentmihalyi is the father of flow, Neff is the mother of (modern) self-compassion.

According to Neff, self-compassion consists of three components: self-kindness, common humanity, and mindfulness. These elements combine and interact to create the experience of self-compassion.

- **Self-Kindness**. Being kind to ourselves entails being warm, caring, and understanding rather than cold, mean, judgmental, and condemning. Instead of beating ourselves up, making ourselves wrong, belittling, and punishing ourselves, we go in the opposite direction. Not only do we stop the self-bashing, but we actively comfort, soothe, nurture, and support ourselves. We take care of ourselves just like we would take care of a good friend. Kindness takes different forms depending on the situation. Sometimes it's warm, soft, and tender. Sometimes it's encouraging. Sometimes, it's tough love. But it's always considerate and well-meaning. Self-kindness means wanting what's best for us. It means being on our own side and not turning against ourselves when confronted with difficulty.

- **Common Humanity.** Suffering is often accompanied by a sense of isolation. I feel as if I'm the only person struggling in life. Common humanity means recognizing that suffering is part of the shared human experience—we all make mistakes, experience hardships, and feel inadequate, sad, depressed, frustrated, and disappointed at times. To comfort someone who has made a mistake, we sometimes say, "That's human." Self-compassion honors the fact that all people are fallible and imperfect. Bad decisions and challenging experiences are inevitable. That's the difference between self-pity and self-compassion. While self-pity says, "poor me," self-compassion remembers that everyone suffers. The pain I feel in difficult times is the same pain others feel in difficult times. The triggers and circumstances are different, and how much it hurts is different, but the pain is the same. You can't always get what you want. That's true for everyone.

- **Mindfulness.** As we've discussed, mindfulness means "stepping out" of experience and looking upon it with openness, acceptance, and curiosity. It means being aware of what's happening in the present moment, both in the inner and outer worlds, without judging it. It lets us see our thoughts and emotions as separate and distanced from us, allowing us to disidentify from them. Without mindfulness, we can't apply self-kindness and common humanity. If we don't see that we're suffering, we can't comfort ourselves. If we don't see that we're beating ourselves up, we can't stop. If we don't recognize that we feel isolated and are wallowing in self-pity, we can't do anything about it. Mindfulness allows us to step back and see what's going on. It allows us to disengage from the storyline of our inadequate and worthless selves. It allows us to choose a different approach—to make the conscious decision to be compassionate with ourselves.

Self-compassion is a kind of add-on to mindfulness; per Neff's definition, it adds self-kindness and common humanity. We're aware of our emotions and allow them to be as they are (mindfulness). But we also actively soothe and comfort ourselves (self-kindness) and remind ourselves that suffering is part of the shared human condition (common humanity).

Given that mindfulness by itself is already an excellent emotion regulation strategy, we can consider self-compassion an even more effective approach. Mood induction research on self-compassion has actually been very sparse, with researchers primarily focusing on suppression, rumination, reappraisal, and acceptance. That being said, the research so far suggests that self-compassion exerts some of the same benefits as mindfulness: It dampens emotional intensity, reduces arousal and overall distress, and decreases activity in the DMN.[33] If you treat yourself with warmth rather than harshness and accept rather than fight your experience, it's only natural that you'll feel less agitated, less overwhelmed, and less isolated by your emotions.

Other types of research have been much more abundant. Thousands of studies point to the many benefits of self-compassion. Among other things, self-compassionate individuals ruminate and suppress less, experience fewer negative emotions, respond to failures with less negativity, experience less fear of failure and less anxiety, are more emotionally intelligent, curious, optimistic, and less likely to commit suicide or abuse drugs and alcohol. They also sleep better, get sick less often, have stronger immune systems, and possess better overall physical health. Oh, and as a recent study has shown, they also tend to experience more flow.[34]

Bringing more self-compassion into your life will no doubt make you more flow-prone.

If you're unsure about exactly how you can use self-compassion to deal with difficult emotions, let me walk you through it. Self-compassionate emotion regulation starts with noticing that you're suffering in some way. Once you've noticed that, you then bring mindful acceptance to your experience. You simply watch what's going on inside of you without judging it or trying to change it. You accept and allow everything to be as it is.

Then, you bring to mind common humanity and direct self-kindness at yourself. You might say to yourself in a warm and soft tone, "This hurts, and that's okay. Difficult experiences are part of the shared human experience. Others struggle as well. It's natural and normal. I'm doing my best." You may put your hand on your heart, gently stroke your arms, give yourself a hug, or even hold your face tenderly in your hands (as long as no one's watching). Touch, whether from others or ourselves, can be very soothing.

You can then ask yourself what Neff calls the quintessential question of self-compassion: "What do I need right now?"[35] The answer will be unique to you and can change from situation to situation.

Sometimes, you may need to just be with your pain—to allow it to be there and hold it in a loving and accepting way. You may need to give yourself comfort, warmth, and understanding. Other times, you may need to encourage yourself, such as when you have to stand up for yourself, say no, draw boundaries, stay true to your values, or motivate yourself to make a change or pursue a goal. On other occasions, you may simply need some time to rest. You may need to just lie down, take some deep breaths, and allow yourself to calm down.

Self-compassion isn't complicated. It's about being a good friend to yourself. You already know how to be a good friend to others; now, treat yourself with the same love and understanding. Next time you're in distress, ask yourself, "What do I need right now to reduce my suffering?" and take it from there.

Meditation: Emotion Regulation Training at its Best

Reappraisal, mindfulness, self-compassion, and emotion regulation in general—these are skills that can be learned, practiced, and built up. The way you get better at these skills is by applying them in your life over and over and over again. Every negative emotional experience is an opportunity to practice.

If you want to improve your skills more quickly, you can engage in dedicated emotion regulation training. Just as you might go for a run to train your physical fitness, you can set aside time each day, or a couple of times per week, to train your emotion regulation fitness.

The best type of training for this purpose is meditation. A gigantic body of research has shown that meditation helps people get better at reappraisal and leads to impressive gains in mindfulness, self-compassion, and overall emotion regulation ability. Meditation reduces suppression, rumination, and self-criticism and lowers baseline DMN activity. That's right, meditation has favorable effects on all the Do's and Don'ts we've discussed in this chapter.[36]

But why does it work? How does meditation produce these changes?

Here's one way to explain it: In meditation, negative thoughts and emotions will show up sooner or later. It's almost inevitable that you'll feel agitated, bored, or frustrated and experience some discomfort and pain. During meditation, you can't run away from these difficult private events. You're forced to deal with them. And precisely because you're forced to deal with them, you'll learn, over time, how best to deal with them. You'll learn that fighting with them, resisting them, judging them, or screaming at them will only make things worse. You'll learn that beating yourself up also only makes things worse. You'll learn that all forms of judgment and resistance only make you more agitated and aroused. You'll learn that the way to remain relaxed, at peace, and focused is by accepting, non-resisting, non-judging, and being gentle and kind with yourself.

Meditation will prove to you that all the theory we've covered in this chapter is accurate. The more time you spend in meditation, the better you'll get at dealing with your inner world, and the more flow-prone you'll

> become. It's as simple as that. (For practical considerations, refer back to chapter 18.)

Bringing it All Together

Phew, we've covered a lot of ground. Let me recap and try to boil it down to the essence. The premise of this chapter is that emotion regulation is a critical flow-related skill. The better you are at dealing with negative emotions, the more flow you'll tend to experience.

So, what did we conclude is the best way to deal with negative emotions? For starters, don't judge, don't fight, and don't ruminate. Don't get into a war with yourself and your inner world. Don't overanalyze the causes and implications of your negative emotions.

Instead, step back and just observe what's happening inside of you. Step out of immediate experience and drop into the role of the impartial witness. Just watch without judging and without trying to control or change your experience. Welcome your feelings, give them space, and let them be there. Allow everything to be as it is. That's mindfulness. It's always the first step.

Once you have mindfulness, you can add common humanity, self-kindness, and reappraisal. Remind yourself that it's okay to struggle and that suffering is part of being human. Be kind, warm, understanding, and gentle with yourself—soothe and comfort yourself and consider asking, "What do I need right now?" Perhaps bring to mind the "maybe" story—the story of the Chinese farmer. Remind yourself that what's causing your negative emotions may not be that bad after all. Look for more helpful interpretations of the situation. Consider asking yourself, "How might this be a good thing? What's the upside? What can I learn from this?"

That's it. That, in my opinion, is how we best deal with negative emotions. As you can see, I like to use a combination of mindfulness, self-compassion, and reappraisal. For me, mindfulness is always the first step. It's the nonnegotiable. Then, I usually add self-compassion and reappraisal.

If you want an easy way to remember the process, use the acronym RAIN-R. "RAIN" stands for Recognize, Allow, Investigate, Nurture. Popularized by meditation teacher Tara Brach, it's designed to bring mindfulness and self-compassion to difficult emotions.[37] In order to also bring reappraisal into it, I've added an additional "R" at the end. RAIN-R has five steps. The first three correspond to mindfulness, the fourth to self-compassion, and the fifth to reappraisal.

- **R—Recognize What's Going On.** Become aware of thoughts, emotions, and sensations you're currently experiencing.

- **A—Allow the Experience to be There, Just as It Is.** Don't judge what you're experiencing, and don't try to change it. Don't get involved. Just observe. Be the impartial witness.

- **I—Investigate with Interest and Care.** Get curious about your present experience. Consider asking yourself, "What am I feeling right now? What's going on in my body? What occupies my attention?"

- **N—Nurture with Self-Compassion.** Treat yourself with warmth, understanding, compassion, and kindness. Bring to mind common humanity. Ask yourself, "What do I need right now?"

- **R—Reappraise your Experience.** Look for a positive interpretation. What's the upside here? How can you learn from this? What's the silver lining?

By their very nature, acceptance, attentiveness, compassion, and kindness are harmonious and flowy. By their very nature, resistance, judgment, criticism, and fighting are inharmonious and anti-flow. The principles discussed in this chapter don't just apply to emotions and their regulation. They apply to life in general.

The more acceptance, compassion, and kindness you can bring into your life, the more flow you'll bring into your life as well. The Chinese philosopher Lao Tzu wrote in the *Tao Te Ching*: "The gentle overcomes the rigid. The slow overcomes the fast. The weak overcomes the strong. . . . Everyone knows that the yielding overcomes the stiff, and the soft overcomes the hard."[38]

Be gentle with yourself and others. Be considerate, attentive, tolerant, understanding, loving, compassionate, and kind with yourself and others. More flow will be one of many rewards.

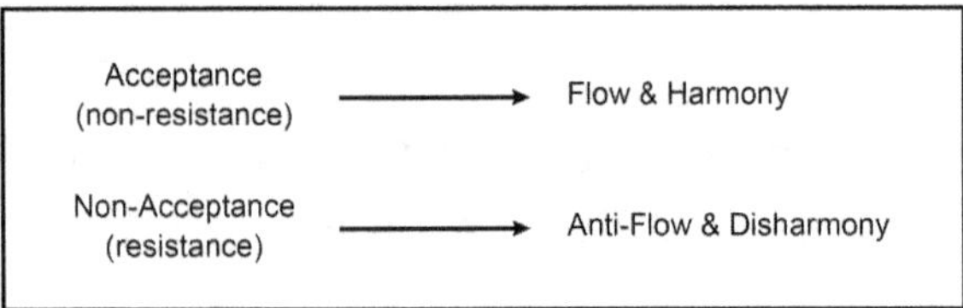

FIGURE 11: Acceptance leads to flow and harmony; non-acceptance leads to anti-flow and disharmony.

Chapter 22

Flow-Supportive Values

Perhaps the most significant thing a person can know about himself is to understand his own system of values. Almost every thing we do is a reflection of our own personal value system. What do we mean by values? Our values are what we want out of life.

—*JACQUES FRESCO*

The ideals which have lighted my way, and time after time have given me new courage to face life cheerfully, have been Kindness, Beauty, and Truth.

—*ALBERT EINSTEIN*

We all differ in what we view as important and valuable in life. For some of us, our careers are of paramount importance. For others, life is all about family, friendships, and community. Some care about amassing power and material wealth, while others are concerned with reaching enlightenment or preparing for the afterlife.

We refer to our beliefs about what is important in life as our *values*. These values guide our lives in subtle yet powerful ways, influencing our thoughts, emotions, actions, and much more.

If Christianity is important to you, you'll probably go to church on Sundays, pray regularly, read the Bible, and spend a lot of time thinking about God. If environmental protection is important to you, you may think about ways to reduce your energy use, avoid purchasing products with a lot of plastic and useless packaging, and be active in a pro-environment organization. For me, my health is important to me; as such, I make sure that I get enough high-quality sleep, make deliberate food choices, and overall spend a fair amount of time and money on taking care of my health.

We've seen in previous chapters that certain environments, activities, and personality traits are more conducive to flow than others. In this chapter, we'll see that certain values are also more conducive to flow than others. We'll see what those values are, how they operate within us, and how to shift them.

An Introduction to Values

Before we look at the specific values shown to influence flow, it's helpful to know how values operate in human beings. The most crucial thing to understand is that values are said to form an interconnected and dynamic system. Values don't function in isolation. Instead, each value stands in relative compatibility or conflict with other values.

For example, the values for material wealth and social status tend to be highly compatible. When you care about social status, it makes sense to also care about material wealth because material wealth is a strong indicator of social status. Actions congruent with one of these values are often also congruent with the other. Pursuing a prestigious career, working overtime, or accepting a promotion—these actions are usually in line with both material wealth and social status. On the other hand, the values for social status and spirituality are relatively incompatible. Most spiritual teachings emphasize not caring about how we are being perceived by others. Actions congruent with one of these values are often incongruent with the other. Spending an exorbitant amount of money on clothing and luxury goods is congruent with social status but conflicts with spirituality. Moving to a monastery is congruent with spirituality but conflicts with social status.

When it comes to conflicting values, you can't have your cake and eat it too. You can't place equal importance on both values. Yes, you can care about both social status and spirituality, but one will inevitably be more important than the other. When people say, and maybe even believe, that they care about two conflicting values equally, they are kidding themselves. Their true priority will be reflected in their actions. The pop star who keeps neglecting their partner and kids in favor of touring the world probably cares more about fame, admiration, or having fun than about family and parenthood. The food manufacturer who uses cheap and low-quality ingredients probably cares more about money than the welfare of his customers.

This brings up an important point: Prioritizing a specific value always also means de-prioritizing conflicting values. As one set of values becomes more prominent, another set of values gets crowded out and becomes less important.

As you care more and more about spirituality, you'll start to care less and less about social status, fame, and fortune. This isn't usually something we're consciously aware of. It isn't usually a conscious decision against something, either. If you choose to go north, you naturally move away from the south. It's not necessarily a decision *against* the south but *for* the north. Either way, you're moving away from the south. In this way, deciding *for* something means simultaneously deciding *against* something else. Giving importance to one thing means giving less importance to another.

A second crucial fact about values is that they are both dispositional and situational. This simply means that values are relatively stable over time (dispositional) but also fluctuate a bit depending on the circumstances (situational).

Each of us holds numerous values ordered in a hierarchical fashion; some values are more important to us than others. Our value hierarchies don't change much over weeks, months, and years. However, certain situational factors can make us care more about some values and less about others. Importantly, situational changes in values follow the dictum about conflicting values mentioned earlier: As one set of values becomes more prominent, the opposing set of values becomes less significant.

Equally important is that transient changes in values can, over time, lead to dispositional changes. If we're chronically placed in an environment that pushes certain values, we tend to move these values up in our hierarchy. We tend to copy and internalize whatever value hierarchy is most dominant in our environment. Over time, the values of the world around us become our dispositional values. They become part of our more stable personality. If you live among politicians of a right-wing party, you'll come to take on their values. If you live among politicians of a left-wing party, you'll come to internalize another set of values. People who grew up in Western countries usually have somewhat different values than those who grew up in Eastern countries.

Equipped with this understanding of values, we can now consider the values influencing our ability to experience flow.

Materialistic Values

> *To be materialistic means to have values that put a relatively high priority on making a lot of money and having many possessions, as well as on image and popularity, which are almost always expressed via money and possessions.*
>
> —*TIM KASSER*

The values that have been shown to influence flow and that are the subject of this chapter are referred to as *materialistic values.*[1] An individual with strong materialistic values places great importance on financial success, possessions, image, and status. Materialistic individuals care a great deal about making money, possessing nice things, and being perceived as attractive and successful. They tend to define success in terms of material wealth and social standing. They admire people with prestigious jobs, good looks, and expensive homes, cars, and clothes. They themselves pursue these ideals and, consciously or unconsciously, regard the accumulation of wealth and status as the keys to happiness.

It's important to note that being materialistic has nothing to do with a person's actual wealth or status but with their desire and concern for such things. People from all walks of life can be materialistic—the rich and the poor, the socially esteemed and despised, the handsome and the plain, those who have already achieved relative materialistic success, and those who have not. Likewise, being rich or popular doesn't mean a person is materialistic. They might be, but they also might not be.

It's also important to note that being materialistic isn't just about what a person cares much about but also what they care relatively little about. As we've discussed, prioritizing one set of values always also means de-prioritizing the conflicting set of values. In the case of materialism, research has shown that the opposing values include, among others: unity with nature, environmental protection, social justice, equality, family, affiliation, community, benevolence, helpfulness, tolerance, honesty, loyalty, and forgiveness.[2] These values are sometimes referred to as *self-transcendent values* because they transcend self-interest to consider the welfare of others. They are about protecting and enhancing the welfare of other people and the world as a whole. Materialistic values, on the other hand, are referred to as *self-enhancement values* because they promote self-interest; they are about enhancing the self.

To say that a person is materialistic is thus to say that they place great importance on becoming wealthy, having prestigious and luxurious possessions, and being attractive and popular. At the same time, they place less importance on contributing to the community, behaving in ecologically sustainable ways, helping others, and being honest, fair, and kind.

To be clear, and I know I'm repeating myself, being materialistic isn't about what we earn or have or how we're being perceived by others—it's about how much we care about such things. It's about what we deem most important in life, what we strive to achieve, and who we strive to become. Driving a nice car doesn't make you materialistic. Being poor doesn't make you non-materialistic. You can be rich, famous, and popular yet not very materialistic. You can be poor and have low social status yet be highly materialistic. And vice-versa.

Also, it's normal to care about money and status to some degree. We all want to be liked and respected, to be regarded as able and "successful," and to be viewed in a positive light by others. We all benefit from having money and possessions. Each of us is materialistic to one degree or another.

The question is: How materialistic are we? How strongly do we care about status, fame, and fortune? How strongly are we driven to accumulate more and more money and stuff and prestige? As we're about to see, if we put too much importance on materialistic values, that's neither good for us, nor our fellow men, nor the world as a whole.

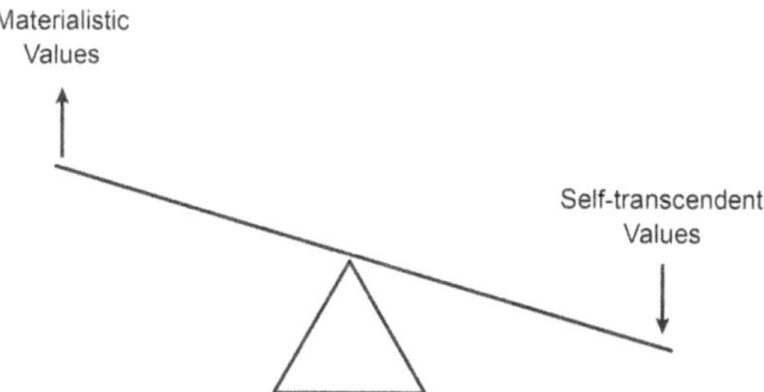

FIGURE 12: Materialistic values stand in relative opposition to self-transcendent values. The more people care about becoming rich and famous and climbing the social ladder, the less they tend to care about the welfare of others and their relationships with them. And vice-versa.

Materialistic Values and (No) Flow

Over the last 30–40 years, a lot of research has investigated the consequences of being overly materialistic. This research has shown that highly materialistic individuals are more likely to suffer from anxiety and depression, are less satisfied with their lives, have lower self-esteem, and have poorer overall well-being. They are also more likely to have racial and ethnic prejudicial attitudes, care less about corporate social responsibility, are more likely to act competitively rather than cooperatively, and are more Machiavellian—they're more willing to manipulate others to get ahead.

In short, the research has shown that the materialistic values are strongly associated with thoughts, feelings, and actions that are bad for the individual, society, and the world as a whole. On the flip side, the self-transcendent values are associated with thoughts, feelings, and actions that are good for the individual, society, and the world as a whole. (See the Notes section for more details and specific studies.)[3]

What about flow? Do materialistic values negatively influence our ability to experience flow? The research indeed suggests so. Several correlational studies have shown that highly materialistic individuals experience less flow than their less materialistic peers.[4] The more obsessed we are with money, stuff, and status, the less flow we tend to experience.

In 2021, an experimental study confirmed this assertion.[5] Researchers induced participants to either care more or less about materialistic aspirations and then assessed how much flow they experienced in a subsequent activity. Upon arriving at the lab, participants first filled out a materialism questionnaire. Then, they were asked to engage in an imagination task designed to either increase or decrease materialistic values. The high materialism group was asked to imagine visiting a luxury shopping center and winning a £20,000 voucher to spend within the center that day; they then had to list the items they imagined purchasing with their voucher. The low materialism group was asked to imagine visiting a countryside village; they then had to list the things they imagined themselves seeing or doing on their trip.

After the imagination task, participants completed the materialism questionnaire again to assess whether there had been any changes in values. And indeed, participants in the shopping center group experienced an increase in situational materialism, while the countryside group experienced a decrease in situational materialism. Participants were then allowed to play Tetris or do some artwork for 15 minutes. Both tasks had been shown in previous studies to be conducive to flow. Finally, participants filled out a questionnaire to assess how much flow they just experienced.

Results? Participants in the shopping center group reported less flow than participants in the countryside group. When researchers repeated their experiment with a different group of people, they replicated their findings: Participants who were made to care more about money and stuff experienced less flow than participants in the control group. The experiment thus showed that a materialistic mindset undermines our ability to experience flow.

There is something about materialistic values that gets in the way of flow. But what is it? Why are we less likely to experience flow when we are overly concerned with making lots of money and attaining a higher social status? There are several potential explanations:

- Materialism has been shown to reduce positive emotions and increase negative emotions. As seen in the last chapter, the former are flow-supportive, while the latter are flow-disruptive.

- Materialism makes us more self-conscious, which runs counter to the loss of self-consciousness that is characteristic of flow. Materialism is about enhancing the self, while flow requires letting go of the self. Thinking about stuff and status will likely put our default mode network (DMN) into high gear. Instead of ego dissolution, we get ego aggravation.

- Materialism corrupts our motivation. If we're primarily driven to accumulate wealth and status, we look at activities as a means to get these things. We're not interested in activities for the fun, interest, and challenge they provide but for the potential external rewards they might produce. Materialism reduces intrinsic motivation while fostering extrinsic motivation. As discussed in chapter 6, the latter is far less conducive to flow than the former.

- Materialism changes the kind of activities we pursue. If life becomes all about status and possessions, we're unwilling to engage in activities that don't help us get status and possessions; we're unwilling to engage in hobbies that provide flow but few external rewards. Sure, playing some football or basketball is fun, but how will it help you climb the materialistic ladder? Enjoyment for enjoyment's sake is pointless. In the materialistic worldview, it's all about getting rich and popular, not about having fun.

Bottom line: Materialistic values lead to thoughts, emotions, and actions that run counter to flow. As such, shifting our values from self-enhancement to self-transcendence will make us more flow-prone.

6 Ways to Shift Your Values

In his book *Lost Connections*, Johann Hari suggests that consumer culture puts us on a materialistic autopilot.[6] We are constantly bombarded with messages that we'll feel better if we become rich and popular and own the right products. We're constantly told that it matters a great deal how much money we make, how we look, and what others think of us. Consumer culture strongly pushes self-enhancement values. Unless we actively intervene, the healthier values get crowded out. The good news is that we *can* intervene: We can turn off the autopilot and re-orient ourselves toward the self-transcendent values. By doing so, we'll become healthier, happier, and more prone to experiencing flow. In the remainder of this chapter, we'll look at six ways to break free from the clutches of materialism.

1. End the Confusion

The essence of life is to serve others and do good.

—ARISTOTLE

Many of us succumb to materialism because we truly believe that more money and a higher status will reduce our suffering. We truly think, consciously or unconsciously, that we'd be happier if we had greater material success.

The assumption isn't that far-fetched, of course. It could be that material success and well-being go hand in hand. In reality, however, that doesn't seem to be the case. Researchers have investigated the connection between material wealth and well-being for decades, and what they reliably find is this: Once we can afford the basic necessities in life, it doesn't matter whether we earn $90k, $900k, or $90 million a year. Wealthy people *seem* to have more fun and be happier, but that isn't necessarily the case.

Martin Seligman, a leading well-being researcher, summarizes this research well: "In very poor nations, where poverty threatens life itself, being rich does predict greater well-being. In wealthier nations, however, where almost everyone has a basic safety net, increases in wealth have negligible effects on personal happiness. In the United States, the very poor are lower in happiness, but once a person is just barely comfortable, added money adds little or no happiness. Even the fabulously rich—the Forbes 100, with an average net worth of over 125 million dollars—are only slightly happier than the average American."[7]

Consider a study that followed the life satisfaction of almost 5,000 US adults over nine years.[8] Some of these individuals experienced large increases in materialistic wealth, some had moderate increases, and others simply kept up with the rising cost of living. In terms of well-being, it made no difference; those with large gains in money and stuff became no more or less satisfied with their lives than the others.

In another study, participants rated how much they felt they had achieved materialistic goals and nonmaterialistic goals.[9] The former are goals related to money, image, and status, while the latter are goals related to personal growth, community contribution, and close relationships. Whether participants reported high or low attainment of materialistic goals made little to no difference in terms of well-being and self-esteem. Attainment of nonmaterialistic goals, on the other hand, made a big difference: Those who reported high attainment of such goals scored much higher on well-being and self-esteem than those who reported low attainment of nonmaterialistic goals.

The same conclusion was reached when researchers tracked the progress people made in achieving materialistic or nonmaterialistic goals over the course of several months.[10] Making progress toward materialistic goals had little to no impact on daily, weekly, or monthly well-being. Making progress on nonmaterialistic goals, on the other hand, had a significant impact on well-being.

Such studies show that even the successful pursuit of materialistic ideals is often empty and unsatisfying. Of course, this is what religions and ancient sages have been telling us since forever. How much we *have* in terms of money, possessions, and status has little impact on our well-being. On the flipside, how much we *care* about money, possessions, and status greatly impacts our well-being.

If you're convinced that material success will make you happy, it's time to end the confusion. No amount of money, fame, or status will give you lasting happiness. True happiness is found in community, family, relationships, awe, gratitude, altruism, kindness, compassion, service, and... flow! It comes from self-transcendence, not self-enhancement; from turning down, not turning up the "me" centers in the brain. The hallmark of deeply fulfilled people is a *quiet ego,* not a *loud* and *overactive* one. When it comes to well-being, hypo-egoicism trumps egotism.[11]

2. Contemplate Death

Perhaps the most powerful way to break free from materialism is by having a near-death experience. Near-death experiencers often undergo profound shifts in values away from self-enhancement and toward self-transcendence.[12] Many of them come to view materialistic pursuits as empty and meaningless. They come to the realization that what truly matters in life is family, friends, community, the natural world, and our relationships with them.

Of course, we can't just have a near-death experience on demand. What we can do, however, is to engage in a reflection exercise designed to mimic such an experience. In 2004, a group of researchers created just such an exercise.[13] They called it *Death Reflection.* It tries to provide a "laboratory analog to the near-death experience." Participants are asked to imagine waking up in a friend's apartment on the 20th floor of an old downtown building to the sounds of screams and the choking smell of smoke. The scenario details futile attempts to escape from the burning building before finally giving in to the fire and eventually death. Participants are then asked to reflect on questions designed to activate common elements in near-death experiences. Several studies have shown that this exercise leads to the anticipated changes in values.[14] It also leads to an increased overall appreciation for life, and it makes participants behave in less selfish and more altruistic ways.

Contemplating your own death can provide the kind of food for thought that allows you to explore your values and reorganize them in positive ways. The Stoic philosopher Marcus Aurelius once wrote to himself in his journal: "You could leave life right now. Let that determine what you do and say and think."[15]

Death Reflection

Here are the instructions for the Death Reflection exercise mentioned in the main text. These are the exact instructions that are also used in the scientific studies.

Imagine that you are visiting a friend who lives on the 20th floor of an old, downtown apartment building. It's the middle of the night when you are suddenly awakened from a deep sleep by the sound of screams and the choking smell of smoke. You reach over to the nightstand and turn on the light. You are shocked to find the room filling fast with thick clouds of smoke. You run to the door and reach for the handle. You pull back in pain as the intense heat of the knob scalds you violently. Grabbing a blanket off the bed and using it as protection, you manage to turn the handle and open the door. Almost immediately, a huge wave of flame and smoke roars into the room, knocking you back and literally off your feet. There is no way to leave the room. It is getting very hard to breathe and the heat from the flames is almost unbearable. Panicked, you scramble to the only window in the room and try to open it. As you struggle, you realize the old window is virtually painted shut around all the edges. It doesn't budge. Your eyes are barely open now, filled with tears from the smoke. You try calling out for help but the air to form the words is not there. You drop to the floor hoping to escape the rising smoke, but it is too late. The room is filled top to bottom with thick fumes and nearly entirely in flames. With your heart pounding, it suddenly hits you, as time seems to stand still, that you are literally moments away from dying. The inevitable unknown that was always waiting for you has finally arrived. Out of breath and weak, you shut your eyes and wait for the end.

After reading the death scenario, answer the following questions:

- Please describe in detail the thoughts and emotions you felt while imagining the scenario.

- If you did experience this event, how do you think you would handle the final moments?

<blockquote>

- Again imagining it did happen to you, describe the life you led up to that point.

- How do you feel your family would react if it did happen to you?

Be sure to go through the exercise in a deep and involved manner.

</blockquote>

3. Reflect on the Regrets of the Dying

Bronnie Ware is an Australian author and former nurse who used to work in palliative care where she cared for patients in the last weeks of their lives. In her bestseller, *The Top Five Regrets of the Dying*, she shares the most common regrets that the people she had cared for had expressed to her.[16] None of her patients regretted that they hadn't bought, owned, or achieved more. Instead, they regretted that they had worked so much, had lost touch with friends, had neglected their family, and had focused their lives on superficial pursuits like status and validation.

Put differently, they regretted that they had lived their lives according to materialistic values. They regretted that they had cared so much about material wealth and what other people thought of them. If they could start anew, they would prioritize self-transcendent values and goals. Their primary focus would be on bringing happiness to the people they love, themselves, the community, and the world as a whole.

The words of a man named John, depicted in the book, illustrate well the regrets of the dying: "'Of course now as I sit here dying, I see that just being a good person is more than enough in life. Why do we depend so much on the material world to validate us?' John thought out loud, random sentences filled with sadness for both past and future generations who wanted everything, basing their importance on what they owned and what they did, rather than on who they were in their heart. 'There's nothing wrong in wanting a better life. Don't get me wrong,' he said. 'It's just that the chase for more, and the need to be recognized through our achievements and belongings, can hinder us from the real things, like time with those we love, time doing things we love ourselves, and balance.'"

Ask yourself: What would you do and think if this was your last day of life? Would you care about status, fame, and fortune? Or would you care about your loved-ones—about spending time with them, bringing a smile to their face, and letting them know they are loved, cherished, and appreciated?

We don't have to wait for death, a near-death experience, or some other traumatic experience to re-think our values. We can do it right now. We can ask ourselves right now: What is it that truly matters in life? What kind of values do we want to embody and let guide our life?

4. Reduce Your Exposure to Materialistic Messages

Materialistic messages are a major driver of materialism. These are messages suggesting that happy and successful people are wealthy, possess nice things, and are good-looking and popular. Examples include movies like *Pretty Woman* or *Wolf of Wallstreet*, documentaries like *The Fabulous Life of Billion Dollar Wall Street Ballers* or *The World's Most Extraordinary Homes*, or reality TV shows like *Keeping Up with the Kardashians* or *The Real Housewives*. Advertisements of all kinds also usually contain such messages. Ads tend to tell us: Right now, you're insecure, ugly, and worthless, but with our product, you'll be confident, loved, admired, happy, and successful. Materialistic messages have been shown to drive both situational and chronic materialism.[17] If you reduce your exposure to such messages, you'll experience a reduction in materialistic concerns.

But don't just avoid the bad, approach the good as well: Increase your exposure to more wholesome messages—messages that activate and reinforce the self-transcendent values. By orienting yourself toward healthier values, you'll naturally begin to crowd out the self-enhancement values.

Here are some suggestions:

- **Watch less (and better) television.** Research has shown that the more television we watch, the more materialistic we tend to be.[18] That doesn't mean we can't ever watch anything again. We just don't want to overdo it. In addition, we want to be mindful of what we consume. Movies and shows that glamorize a materialistic lifestyle probably aren't good for us. We want less drama, less glamour, more substance, and more of what's good in the world.

- **Less trips to the mall, more trips to nature.** Shopping centers are full of stimuli that tell us, in one way or another, that possessions and status are important. Nature, on the other hand, is devoid of these stimuli and has been shown to reduce materialism. (We'll discuss nature at the end of this chapter.)

- **Ditch reading materials that glorify exorbitant wealth, fame, and status.** Tabloid newspapers (e.g., *The Sun*, *The Daily Mail*, or *The New York Post*) and celebrity magazines (e.g., *Vogue*, *Cosmopolitan*, *GQ*, or *Esquire*) and websites (e.g., *E!Online*, *PopSugar*, or *TMZ*) have been shown to increase situational materialism.[19] Read actual books instead. Again, less drama, less glamour, more substance, and more of what's good in the world.

- **Quit social media, or use it less.** Social media is a source of advertising and a strong promoter of upward social comparisons—comparing ourselves to people we perceive to be superior. Such comparisons make us feel inadequate, resentful, envious, deprived, and dissatisfied, which, in turn, can make us more materialistic. Most of what we see on social media is curated, tweaked, enhanced, and designed to portray an image of perfection. We see perfect smiles, perfect bodies, and seemingly perfect lives everywhere. We see celebrities and influencers wearing luxurious outfits on luxurious vacations. We see photos of our peers at sporting events, having drinks, and smiling with friends. Everyone looks great and happy. It seems like they're all having the time of their life. It's easy to conclude that we're inferior. It's easy to feel deprived, resentful, and envious. Pastor Steve Furtick put it well: "The reason we struggle with insecurity is because we compare our behind-the-scenes with everyone else's highlight reel." Is it any wonder that social media use is associated with anxiety, depression, low self-esteem, suicide, materialistic values, and other adverse effects?[20]

5. Engage in Self-Transcendent Activities

Our values drive our actions. But our actions also drive our values. It's a two-way street. As such, we can change what we do in order to change what we care about. Just like we want to reduce exposure to materialistic messages, we also want to reduce the amount of time we spend in activities that reinforce materialistic values.

And again, don't just avoid what's making you sick, approach what's good for you. Pursue activities that nurture self-transcendent values and that allow you to experience flow. Spend more time with people and less time on social media. Spend time in nature rather than in shopping malls. Spend your money on experiences rather than things. Find ways to use your strengths. Do things you're good at. Pursue your interests and passions. Re-connect with old hobbies. Invest time in social relationships. Find meaningful work, even if it pays less.

Here are some other specific activities you can explore. They have in common that they transcend the self in one way or another. They have all been shown to reduce materialistic tendencies.

Try Meditation

We've discussed meditation in several previous chapters and have seen that it supports your ability to experience flow in numerous ways. Several studies have suggested that meditation is also a powerful strategy to reduce materialism.[21] There's plenty of evidence that a regular meditation practice leads to an enduring reduction of self-focus and ego-centricity, a greater propensity toward kindness and compassion, and an overall shift away from self-enhancement values and toward self-transcendent values.[22] Meditation is simply one of the best things you can do for personal growth and well-being. As I've mentioned, it's the #1 way to become more flow-prone. You can't go wrong with it.

Pick Up a Gratitude Practice

Gratitude practices (e.g., keeping a gratitude journal or writing gratitude letters) have received plenty of research attention over the last few years. These practices have been shown to create many positive changes, including improvements in life satisfaction, self-esteem, relationship quality, generosity, and compassion.[23] By making us feel supported by the goodwill of others, making us less self-centered and more humble, kind, and compassionate, gratitude can also reduce materialistic strivings. Several studies have shown that individuals who score higher on measures of gratitude tend to be less materialistic than their peers.[24]

A 2018 study showed that a daily gratitude journal can reduce materialism and boost generosity.[25] Participants were asked to keep a daily journal for two weeks. The gratitude group recorded who and what they were thankful for each day, while the control group recorded their daily activities. Before and after the two weeks, participants filled out questionnaires to measure materialism. After completing the questionnaires for the second time, participants received ten $1 bills for their participation. They were told they could either keep all the money or anonymously donate some or all of it to charity. Results? Participants who kept a gratitude journal were less materialistic at the end of the two weeks than their peers in the control group. They also behaved more generously, donating 60% more of their earnings than those who kept a daily activities journal. Fostering gratitude, the researchers conclude, is a simple, free, easy-to-implement, and effective strategy to reduce materialism.

If you want to try it yourself, an easy way to start is by simply writing down three things you're grateful for at the end of every day. Simple but surprisingly effective.

Explore Psychedelic Unselfing

Psychedelics can broadly be divided into *classic* and *non-classic* psychedelics. The former include psilocybin, DMT, LSD, and mescaline. Classic psychedelics can be defined as "a drug which, without causing physical addiction, craving, major physiological disturbances, delirium, disorientation, or amnesia, more or less reliably produces thought, mood, and perceptual changes otherwise rarely experienced except in dreams, contemplative and religious exaltation, flashes of vivid involuntary memory, and acute psychosis."[26]

If taken in moderate to high doses, these substances can reliably induce non-ordinary states of consciousness characterized by *ego dissolution*—a reduction in self-referential awareness, disruption of self-world boundaries, and increasing feelings of unity with others and one's surroundings.[27] Put differently, they can induce *psychedelic unselfing*.[28]

The peculiar thing about these transient experiences is that they can lead to lasting changes in values, behaviors, and well-being.[29] Single psychedelic experiences have been shown to induce long-term improvements in many clinical conditions, including depression, anxiety, obsessive-compulsive disorder, addiction, anorexia, and many others. Most relevant for our discussion, such one-off experiences can lead to enduring enhancements in empathy, altruism, and prosocial and pro-environmental behavior. People feel more connected to nature, are more concerned about the welfare of others and the planet, and are less interested in economic success. Psychedelics can shift us from a primarily egocentric perspective to a more allocentric (other-directed) and cosmocentric (universal) perspective. They can help us move away from self-enhancement values and toward self-transcendent values.

Albert Hofmann, the creator of LSD, provides an anecdote highlighting these changes.[30] In his autobiography, he writes about meeting a businessman:

"He thanked me for the creation of LSD, which had given his life another direction. He had been 100 percent a businessman with a purely materialistic world view. LSD had opened his eyes to the spiritual aspect of life. Now he possessed a sense for art, literature, and philosophy and was deeply concerned with religious and metaphysical questions."

Caveats: These substances are illegal in most places of the world. Even though they are among the safest drugs we know of, they still come with risks.[31] As such, they should be treated with great care and respect.

Do Volunteer Work

Volunteering refers to providing help without getting paid for it. It's about offering your time for free in order to help others and serve a greater good. The benefits of volunteering are profound, not just for the individual, organization, or community receiving help but also for the volunteer. In helping others, we help ourselves.

Working as a volunteer can reduce stress, loneliness, social isolation, depression, and various other mental health issues.[32] It can help you meet new people, feel part of a community, and feel more socially connected and appreciated. It can boost your self-esteem and confidence and give you a sense of accomplishment and purpose. In short, it can help you satisfy your psychological needs and powerfully enhance your well-being.

Volunteering is a way of going beyond egotistical concerns to consider the welfare of others. Because it's congruent with self-transcendent values, and because of its powerful effect on well-being, volunteering is likely to result in a decrease in materialistic tendencies. If you want to give it a try, a simple online search will provide you with plenty of organizations that actively seek volunteers.

6. Connect With Nature

And into the forest I go, to lose my mind and find my soul.

—JOHN MUIR

Nature is good for us. We've seen in previous chapters that exposure to nature can reduce stress, boost focus and productivity, improve mood and emotional well-being, enhance sleep quality, strengthen immune function, and much more. When it comes to reducing materialism, nature is once again a powerful ally.

Consider an experiment that asked participants to watch either four slides of nature scenes (e.g., depicting a desert canyon) or four slides of urban scenes (e.g., depicting a city street with buildings on either side).[33] Slides were shown for 2 minutes each and were coupled with an audio script encouraging participants to notice all aspects of their environments, pay attention to colors and textures and imagine any smells and sounds that may be present. Participants filled out questionnaires before and after the procedure to measure how much they cared about money, image, and status. Results? Participants in the nature group reported a decrease in materialistic tendencies, while those in the urban group reported an increase in materialistic tendencies.

In another experiment, participants were asked to sit in a room for five minutes.[34] One group sat in a room furnished with four plants, while the other sat in the same room but with no plants. After the 5-minute sitting period, participants were instructed to fill out several questionnaires and partake in a task designed to measure generosity. Results? Participants in the plant-filled room scored lower on a measure of materialism and acted more generously. Their values and behavior were less selfish and more self-transcendent. Multiple other experiments have come to the same conclusion: Exposure to nature reduces the importance people attach to materialistic values.[35]

Nature is thus a wonderful way to move from selfishness to selflessness, from self-enhancement to self-transcendence. Here are some suggestions for reconnecting with nature.

Indoor Plants, Forest Bathing, Green Exercise, and More…
I've made several recommendations for bringing more nature into your life in chapters 18 and 20. Here's a brief overview and summary:

- **Get some houseplants.** Fresh flowers are an excellent option as well. If you want to take it to the next level, turn your home into an *urban jungle* (a quick image search will reveal what I mean).

- **Spend time in nature.** Go hiking, kayaking, or skiing. Spend some time on the beach. Visit a nature reserve. Try forest bathing.

- **Use natural rather than synthetic materials.** Wool, cotton, linen, wood, or stone trump plastic. Most objects that surround us and most tools we use are available in versions that use natural materials.

- **Watch nature documentaries.** I thoroughly enjoyed the *Our Planet* series (7 episodes) and *My Octopus Teacher* on Netflix.

- **Surround yourself with imagery of nature.** Get some posters or other types of wall art. Update your screensavers and background images. Yes, merely looking at nature images offers benefits.

- **Instead of a coffee, doughnut, or bagel break, take a green break.** Go for a walk in a nearby park or sit by a tree. You'll return to work feeling refreshed and ready to fully concentrate on the tasks in front of you.

- **Exercise outdoors.** "Exercise in nature is exercise squared," suggests psychiatry professor John Ratey.[36] Green exercise is both healthier (better air quality and natural light, scents, smells, visuals, etc.) and more enjoyable. It also feels less strenuous because the natural setting—the trees, leaves, and bushes—draws the mind outside of the body, so it doesn't focus on feelings of fatigue, exertion, and pain. And because exercising in nature feels better and easier, you're more likely to stick with it.

- **Listen to sounds of nature.** Consider listening to the sounds of rainfall or birds when performing certain tasks, during breaks, on your ride home, or when lying down for a nap. The internet provides free and unlimited access to nature sounds.

- **Breathe in scents of nature.** Get an essential oil diffuser, add a few drops of essential oils to a bowl of hot water, make some herbal tea, or add sprigs of herbs to a glass of water. Peppermint and rosemary are stimulating, while jasmine, chamomile, and lavender are calming.

Move to the Country

Another way to increase your exposure to nature is by leaving the hustle and bustle of the city behind and moving to the country. That's what materialism researcher Tim Kasser did when he discovered the many adverse effects of materialistic values and consumer culture. With his wife and kids, he moved to a farm on ten acres of land in Illinois, where they live with a herd of goats, a flock of chickens, and a donkey named Earl.[37]

Urban environments abound with materialism-amplifying stimuli, such as corporate buildings, banks, shops, and billboards. Living in cities is associated with a higher risk for mental health issues, including anxiety, depression, post-traumatic stress disorder, schizophrenia, anger issues, and more.[38] Rural environments, conversely, are mostly devoid of messages that suggest it's important for individuals to attain riches, status, and popularity. Instead, rural settings provide natural stimuli that activate and reinforce the more self-transcendent values. A 2020 study showed that US states with more natural amenities and a higher percentage of national forest and wilderness areas score lower on materialism than less natural states.[39] Living in the country is also generally associated with better mental health.[40]

Me, I currently live in a small city with around 45,000 inhabitants. We're surrounded by mountains, have a lake, lots of greenspaces, and access to nearby forests. It's relatively quiet and green. Still, the move to a more rural, quiet, and slower-paced area appeals to me, and I'll probably make the move in a couple of years from now.

As we've seen, values guide our lives in subtle yet powerful ways. When self-transcendent values are situationally encouraged in us, flow becomes more likely—right then and there. When self-transcendent values move up on our stable value hierarchy (and materialistic values move down), flow becomes more likely at all times; we become more flow-prone, period.

If you want more flow in your life, find ways to orient yourself toward nature, community, helpfulness, honesty, forgiveness, and other healthy values.

Afterword: The Promise of Flow

Think about some of the best experiences in your life. The moments when you're at your best. Maybe you're acing an exam, setting a personal record in your sport of choice, confidently speaking up for yourself, sharing your deepest fears and desires with your spouse, or completing one task after another at work. You're in the zone. Fully engaged and completely absorbed in what you're doing. You feel confident, excited, and in control. You're having a blast.

Now think about some of the worst experiences in your life. Instead of acing your exam, you're paralyzed by test anxiety. Instead of sharing your true self, you're petrified by thoughts about what other people might think of you. Instead of feeling free and creative, you feel stuck and sterile. Nervous. Uncomfortable. Holding back. Instead of performing at your best, you crumble. You overthink. You stumble.

Now consider this: What if, during your worst experiences, you could flip a switch and move from fear to confidence, from distraction to focus, from stuck in your head to absorbed in the moment, from pessimism to optimism, from worry to excitement, and from dread to joy? What if you could feel strong and powerful in the most challenging moments of your life?

How much better would you feel? How much better would you like yourself? How much more could you accomplish? How much happier would you become?

That's the promise of flow.

Flow can help you become the best you can be. It can help you fulfill your potential. It can help you live the life you desire.

This book has given you the tools to make that happen. Now, go out there, and make it happen.

Thank you for reading, and may the flow be with you.

Enjoyed the Book?

Thank you so much for taking the time to read this book. I hope you enjoyed it and found it helpful.

If you have a minute, it would mean a lot to me if you could leave a review on Amazon, Goodreads, or other book platform of your choice. Reviews make a big difference in encouraging others to give the book a chance. Thank you in advance.

Also, if you find any mistakes in the book, please let me know by sending an email to nils@njlifehacks.com. Of course, I'm also happy to receive your feedback, questions, or remarks of any kind.

What's Next?

If you enjoyed *Mastering Flow*, here are a few additional resources you may enjoy.

Free Book Resources

I have put together several bonus resources for readers of this book, including:

- ***The Mastering Flow Reading List.*** Want to learn more about the autotelic personality, the brain in flow, emotion regulation, or how to arrive at a state of mind like water? Look no further! For each chapter, this reading list provides a number of books that expand on the topics discussed in the chapter.

- ***From Dread to Flow.*** Not all activities that allow us to experience flow are the same. There are activities we look forward to (e.g., hobbies) and there are those we dread (e.g., writing essays, studying for exams, preparing presentations, or fixing things around the house). For the latter, we often have to overcome resistance to begin with the activity. Yet, once we're engaged in it, it's actually quite fun and we often find ourselves in a flow state. This practical guide shares tips and strategies for overcoming resistance and moving from dread to flow.

I will add more resources in the future. You can get them for free at:

njlifehacks.com/mastering-flow-resources

NJlifehacks Blog and Newsletter

My brother Jonas and I publish articles on our website, NJlifehacks.com (the "N" stands for Nils; the "J" stands for Jonas). We write about anything that helps us live happier and healthier lives. Main topics include flow, procrastination, Positive Psychology, and Stoicism. If you enjoyed *Mastering Flow*, you'll probably enjoy our articles as well.

We also send out a weekly email newsletter. We share our latest articles, favorite quotes, book recommendations, and anything we find interesting and helpful. We also share what's going on in our lives, what we're currently working on, and what we're doing to live better.

If you'd like to join, you can sign up here:

njlifehacks.com/subscribe

Acknowledgements

Thank you, Nicole, my best friend, my future wife, and the love of my life. Thank you for your love and support. Thank you for your understanding, compassion, and acceptance. Thank you for cherishing me and loving me with all your heart. Thank you for sharing your life with me. I'm forever grateful for your existence.

Thank you, Jonas and Yanis, for the countless hours you put into reading and editing my first drafts; I know it was a heck of a lot of work. Thank you for your suggestions and support. Thank you for pointing out the good as well as the bad. Your involvement in this book means a lot to me.

Thank you, Dimitri, for your help with the book, for your ever-present interest in my life, and for always having my back. I feel seen and supported by you—what a gift, thank you.

Thank you Susanna and Roger, for bringing me into this world and for accompanying me on my journey through life. Thank you for everything.

Thank you, Simran, for your excitement, confidence, positivity, and love. Thank you for your respect and your appreciation of my being. Thank you for your honest and invaluable feedback. Thank you for helping and supporting me.

Thank you, Mihaly Csikszentmihalyi, for developing the concept and bringing flow to the world. Thank you, Steven Kotler, for doing a lot of the heavy lifting in making flow mainstream. The two of you introduced me to flow. You got me excited about it. You made me fall in love with it. I wouldn't have written this book if it wasn't for the two of you. Thank you.

Thank you to the countless flow researchers all over the world. You have never met me, but your work impacted me a lot. This book is littered with your insights. Thank you, Susan A. Jackson, Corinna Peifer, Stefan Engeser, Anja Schiepe-Tiska, Giovanni B. Moneta, Michael Barthelmäs, Johannes Keller, Sami Abuhamdeh, Julia Schüler, Jasmine Tan, Nicola Baumann,

Charles J. Walker, Gina Wolters, László Harmat, Örjan de Manzano, Fredrik Ullén, Falko Rheinberg, Antonella Delle Fave, Marta Bassi, Fausto Massimini, Jef J. J. van den Hout, Orin C. Davis, Christian Swann, Oliver Stoll, Jeanne Nakamura, Dwight C. K. Tse, and everyone else whom I'm forgetting. Thank you for the fascinating research—I loved reading your studies.

Thank you, Thibaut Meurisse, for your inspiration, support, advice, and friendship. It's nice sharing this author journey with you. Our chats always leave me feeling excited and motivated. Thank you.

Thank you, Shruti, for producing the graphics in this book and for teaching me about image formats, printing, and more. I was blown away by your professionalism and patience. It was a pleasure working with you.

Thank you to everyone else I forgot to mention here who supported me on this journey.

Finally, thank you to you, the reader. Thank you for your time; I hope it was worth it.

Notes

[1] Mihaly Csikszentmihalyi, *Beyond boredom and anxiety*, 25th Anniversary Edition (Jossey-Bass, 2000).

Introduction

[1] Steven Kotler, *The rise of superman: Decoding the science of ultimate human performance* (London: Quercus Editions Ltd, 2014).

[2] "Burden of selfhood" is a term used by Roy F. Baumeister in *Escaping the self: Alcoholism, spirituality, masochism, and other flights from the burden of selfhood* (New York: Basic Books, 1991).

[3] The term "unconscious" is not clearly defined and is the subject of considerable controversy. What I mean here is that during flow, your acquired skills and knowledge take over. You're able to use your skills and knowledge without conscious effort. You're able to perform to the best of your ability. You don't have to make conscious decisions; decision-making happens spontaneously.

[4] The idea of describing flow as "letting it happen" rather than "making it happen" comes from Christian Swann, Richard Keegan, Lee Crust, and David Piggott, "Psychological states underlying excellent performance in professional golfers: 'Letting it happen' vs. 'making it happen,'" *Psychology of Sport and Exercise* 23 (2016): 101-113.

Part 1: The Basics of Flow

[1] Susan A. Jackson and Mihaly Csikszentmihalyi, *Flow in sports* (Human Kinetics, 1999).

1 – The 10,000 Foot View

[1] "Frequently asked questions on flow," Steven Kotler, accessed November 3, 2023, https://www.stevenkotler.com/rabbit-hole/frequently-asked-questions-on-flow

2 – Flow's Origins

[1] Mihaly Csikszentmihalyi and Jeanne Nakamura, "Effortless attention in everyday life: a systematic phenomenology," in Brian Bruya, ed., *Effortless attention: A new perspective in the cognitive science of attention and action* (London: The MIT Press, 2010).

[2] The origin story I'm referring to here is explained in greater detail in Csikszentmihalyi, *Beyond boredom and anxiety*. All quotes in this chapter are from that book, unless otherwise referenced.

[3] Mihaly Csikszentmihalyi, *Flow: The psychology of optimal experience* (Harper Perennial, 1990).

[4] Csikszentmihalyi, *Beyond boredom and anxiety*.

[5] Ibid.

[6] Ibid.

[7] Ibid.

[8] Ibid.

[9] Csikszentmihalyi and colleagues had initially used the term *autotelic experience* rather than flow. "Autotelic" is another word for intrinsically motivated, while exotelic is another word for extrinsically motivated. When people pursue an autotelic activity, they have an autotelic experience—that was the original thinking. However, Csikszentmihalyi and co. quickly realized that the experience described by their interviewees could also happen during extrinsically motivated activities. You can experience flow even if you pursue external goals or receive external rewards. The term autotelic suggested that there were no extrinsic goals or rewards, and that wasn't true. That's why they changed the name to flow. Another reason was that the term flow is less awkward and more intuitive than the former label.

3 – Flow Defined

[1] Kotler, *The rise of superman.*

[2] See, for example, p.13 in Jef J. J. van den Hout and Orin C. Davis, *Team flow: The psychology of optimal collaboration* (Cham: Springer, 2019).

[3] Csikszentmihalyi, *Beyond boredom and anxiety.*

[4] Kotler, *The rise of superman.*

[5] "About Steven," Steven Kotler, accessed July 23, 2024, https://www.stevenkotler.com/about.

[6] Steven Kotler and Jamie Wheal, *Stealing fire: How silicon valley, the navy seals, and maverick scientists are revolutionizing the way we live and work* (New York: Dey Street Books, 2017).

[7] Quote is from "Ecstasy," Wikimedia Foundation, last modified 11 June 2023, at 20:23 (UTC), https://en.wikipedia.org/wiki/Ecstasy.

[8] Csikszentmihalyi, *Flow.*

[9] Jackson and Csikszentmihalyi, *Flow in sports.*

[10] For example, in *Flow in sports*, Jackson and Csikszentmihalyi literally write: "When people talk about their flow experiences, they mention two characteristics: that these special times are enjoyable and optimal. For this reason, the terms *enjoyment* and *optimal experience* will be used interchangeably with flow throughout the book. You can think of enjoyment and optimal experience as two points along a continuum. Enjoyment may be more descriptive of the lower to middle levels of flow, while optimal experience denotes the higher levels."

[11] First quote is from Csikszentmihalyi, *Beyond boredom and anxiety.* Second quote is from Csikszentmihalyi, *Flow.*

[12] Csikszentmihalyi, *Beyond boredom and anxiety.*

[13] For a thorough discussion of group flow, see R. Keith Sawyer, *Group genius: The creative power of collaboration* (New York: Basic Books, 2007).

[14] For a recent discussion on social flow, see, "Social flow," in Corinna Peifer and Stefan Engeser, eds., *Advances in flow research*, 2nd edition (Cham: Springer, 2021).

[15] For a recent discussion of different types of flow, see "Overview of extant research on interpersonal flow at work," and "How team flow relates to other flow constructs," in van den Hout and Davis, *Team flow.*

4 - The Three Conditions of Flow

[1] Quote is from Mihaly Csikszentmihalyi, *Finding flow: The psychology of engagement with everyday life* (New York: Basic Books, 1997).

[2] Csikszentmihalyi and Nakamura, "Effortless attention in everyday life," in Bruya, *Effortless attention*, 179-190.

[3] Ibid.

[4] Massimini, Fausto, Mihaly Csikszentmihalyi, and Massimo Carli, "The monitoring of optimal experience a tool for psychiatric rehabilitation," *The Journal of nervous and mental disease* 175, no. 9 (1987): 545-549.

[5] Kotler, *The rise of superman.*

[6] Quote is from Steven Kotler, *The art of impossible: A peak performance primer* (New York: Harper Wave, 2021).

[7] For a recent discussion of the 22 flow triggers, see Kotler, *The art of impossible.*

[8] Kotler, *The art of impossible.*

5 – The Six Experiential Characteristics of Flow

[1] Jackson and Csikszentmihalyi, *Flow in sports.*

[2] Ibid.

[3] Ibid.

[4] Jeanne Nakamura and Mihaly Csikszentmihalyi, "The concept of flow," *Handbook of positive psychology* 89 (2002): 105.

[5] Csikszentmihalyi, *Flow.*

[6] Csikszentmihalyi, *Beyond boredom and anxiety.*

[7] Csikszentmihalyi, *Flow.*

[8] Ibid.

[9] Barry Green and W. Timothy Gallwey, *The inner game of music* (New York: Doubleday, 1986).

[10] The quote is from a poem by William Butler Yeats titled, "Among school children."

[11] "Burden of selfhood" is a term used by Roy F. Baumeister in *Escaping the self: alcoholism, spirituality, masochism, and other flights from the burden of selfhood* (New York: Basic Books, 1991).

[12] Csikszentmihalyi, *Flow.*

[13] Ibid.

[14] Kotler, *The rise of superman.*

[15] Csikszentmihalyi, *Flow.*

[16] Ibid.

[17] Jackson and Csikszentmihalyi, *Flow in sports.*

[18] Kotler, *The rise of superman.*

[19] Jackson and Csikszentmihalyi, *Flow in sports.*

[20] Csikszentmihalyi, *Flow.*

[21] Jackson and Csikszentmihalyi, *Flow in sports.*

6 – The Autotelic Personality

[1] Nicola Baumann, "Autotelic personality," in Peifer and Engeser, *Advances in flow research,* 231-261.

[2] Flow proneness is usually measured with the Swedish Flow Proneness Questionnaire (SFPQ), a short 21-item questionnaire that measures flow proneness in three contexts (work, leisure, and maintenance activities). For each context, participants answer the same seven questions about how often they experience certain sensations (e.g., *"... it feels as if your ability to perform what you do completely matches how difficult it is"*). The seven questions are designed to capture the main dimensions of flow experience. For details on the SFPQ, see Fredrik Ullén, Örjan de Manzano, Rita Almeida, Patrik KE Magnusson, Nancy L. Pedersen, Jeanne Nakamura, Mihály Csíkszentmihályi, and Guy Madison, "Proneness for psychological flow in everyday life: Associations with personality and intelligence," *Personality and individual differences* 52, no. 2 (2012): 167-172.

[3] The term autotelic can cause some confusion. Originally, it seems that an autotelic personality was defined by Csikszentmihalyi as "an individual who generally does things for their own sake, rather than in order to achieve some later external goal." Such a person would indeed experience flow frequently. But it's not the same as saying that an autotelic personality denotes a person who possesses many attributes that facilitate the experience of flow in daily life. The two are related but not the same. A person who is autotelic (who generally does things for their own sake) is not the same thing as a person who experiences flow frequently because they possess flow-conducive attributes.

The following paragraph from Csikszentmihalyi, *Finding flow,* may clarify what I mean: "'Autotelic' is a word composed of two Greek roots: auto (self), and telos (goal). An autotelic activity is one we do for its own sake because to experience it is the main goal. For instance, if I played a game of chess primarily to enjoy the game, that game would be an autotelic experience for me; whereas if I played for money, or to achieve a competitive ranking in the chess world, the same game would be primarily exotelic, that is, motivated by an outside goal. Applied to personality, autotelic denotes an individual who generally does things for their own sake, rather than in order to achieve some later external goal. Of course no one is fully autotelic, because we all have to do things even if we don't enjoy them, either out of a sense of duty or necessity. But there is a gradation, ranging from individuals who almost never feel that what they do is worth doing for its own sake, to others who feel that most anything they do is important and valuable in its own right. It is to these latter individuals that the term autotelic applies."

To be clear, nowadays the term "autotelic personality" refers to individuals who possess relatively many attributes that faciliate flow and therefore are more likely to experience it.

[4] "Autotelic," Wikimedia Foundation, last modified 29 November 2023, at 07:47 (UTC), https://en.wikipedia.org/wiki/Autotelic.

[5] Dwight CK Tse, Vienne Wing-yan Lau, Rachael Perlman, and Michael McLaughlin, "The development and validation of the Autotelic Personality Questionnaire," *Journal of personality assessment* 102, no. 1 (2020): 88-101.

[6] Tse et al., "The development and validation"; Dwight CK Tse, Jeanne Nakamura, and Mihaly Csikszentmihalyi, "Living well by "flowing' well: The indirect effect of autotelic personality on well-being through flow experience," *The Journal of Positive Psychology* 16, no. 3 (2021): 310-321.

[7] Johannes Keller and Herbert Bless, "Flow and regulatory compatibility: An experimental approach to the flow model of intrinsic motivation," *Personality and social psychology bulletin* 34, no. 2 (2008): 196-209.

[8] A sample item reads, "When I am busy working on an interesting project: (A) I need to take frequent breaks and work on other projects. (B) I can keep working on the same project for a long time." Another one reads, "When I have learned a new and interesting game: (A) I quickly get tired of it and do something else. (B) I can really get into it for a long time." Options B represent the action-oriented responses and translate well into our idea of persistence.

[9] See, for example, Giovanni B. Moneta, "Opportunity for creativity in the job as a moderator of the relation between trait intrinsic motivation and flow in work," *Motivation and Emotion* 36, no. 4 (2012): 491-503; Susan A. Jackson, Stephen K. Ford, Jay C. Kimiecik, and Herbert W. Marsh, "Psychological correlates of flow in sport," *Journal of Sport and exercise Psychology* 20, no. 4 (1998): 358-378; Maura J. Mills and Clive J. Fullagar, "Motivation and flow: Toward an understanding of the dynamics of the relation in architecture students," *The Journal of psychology* 142, no. 5 (2008): 533-556.

[10] Fredrik Ullén, Örjan de Manzano, Töres Theorell, László Harmat, "The physiology of effortless attention: Correlates of state flow and flow proneness," in Bruya, *Effortless attention*, 205-218.

[11] Csikszentmihalyi, *Flow*.

[12] Ibid.

[13] This list includes the traits discussed in the main body of the text as well as other traits, including but not limited to self-efficacy, action orientation, need for achievement, hope for success versus fear of failure, mastery versus performance orientation, growth versus fixed mindset, shyness, self-handicapping, and more.

[14] See, for example, Ullén et al., "Proneness for psychological flow"; Fredrik Ullén, László Harmat, Töres Theorell, and Guy Madison, "Flow and individual differences—a phenotypic analysis of data from more than 10,000 twin individuals," in *Flow experience: Empirical research and applications* (Cham: Springer, 2016).

[15] Definition is from Psychology Today, "Conscientiousness," accessed September 28, 2023, https://www.psychologytoday.com/us/basics/conscientiousness.

[16] See, for example, Ullén et al., "Proneness for psychological flow"; Ullén et al., "Flow and individual differences."

[17] See, for example, Jackson et al., "Psychological correlates of flow"; Stefan Koehn, "Effects of confidence and anxiety on flow state in competition," *European journal of sport science* 13, no. 5 (2013): 543-550; Kiyoshi Asakawa, "Flow experience, culture, and well-being: How do autotelic Japanese college students feel, behave, and think in their daily lives?," *Journal of happiness studies* 11 (2010): 205-223.

[18] See, for example, Koehn, "Effects of confidence"; Christian Swann, Richard J. Keegan, David Piggott, and Lee Crust.,"A systematic review of the experience, occurrence, and controllability of flow states in elite sport," *Psychology of sport and exercise* 13, no. 6 (2012): 807-819.

[19] See, for example, Koehn, "Effects of confidence"; Jackson et al., "Psychological correlates of flow"; Nektarios A. Stavrou and Yannis Zervas, "Confirmatory factor analysis of the Flow State Scale in sports," *International Journal of Sport and Exercise Psychology* 2, no. 2 (2004): 161-181.

[20] Christian Swann, David Piggott, Lee Crust, Richard Keegan, and Brian Hemmings, "Exploring the interactions underlying flow states: A connecting analysis of flow occurrence in European Tour golfers," *Psychology of Sport and Exercise* 16 (2015): 60-69.

[21] For a research overview on optimism, see Martin Seligman, *Learned optimism: How to change your mind and your life* (New York: Knopf, 1991).

[22] Patricia C. Jackman, Christian Swann, and Lee Crust, "Exploring athletes' perceptions of the relationship between mental toughness and dispositional flow in sport," *Psychology of Sport and Exercise* 27 (2016): 56-65; Robin S. Vealey and Nicole C. Perritt, "Hardiness and optimism as predictors of the frequency of flow in collegiate athletes," *Journal of Sport Behavior* 38, no. 3 (2015): 321.

[23] Quote is from Doug Strycharczyk and Peter Clough, *Developing mental toughness: Coaching strategies to improve performance, resilience and wellbeing*, 2nd edition (London: Kogan Page, 2015).

[24] Ibid.

[25] The positive relationship between mental toughness and flow has been shown in many studies. See, for example, Patricia Jackman, Lee Crust, and Christian Swann, "The role of mental toughness in the occurrence of flow and clutch states in sport," *International journal of sport psychology* 51, no. 1 (2020): 1-27; Jackman et al., "Exploring athletes' perceptions"; Jenny Meggs, Mark A. Chen, and Stefan Koehn, "Relationships between flow, mental toughness, and subjective performance perception in various triathletes," *Perceptual and motor skills* 126, no. 2 (2019): 241-252.

[26] For studies on flow and perfectionism, see, for example, Tamar Kamushadze, Khatuna Martskvishvili, Maia Mestvirishvili, and Mariami Odilavadze, "Does perfectionism lead to well-being? The role of flow and personality traits," *Europe's Journal of Psychology* 17, no. 2 (2021): 43; Tajana Ljubin-Golub, Majda Rijavec, and Lana Jurčec, "Flow in the academic domain: The role of perfectionism and engagement," *The Asia-Pacific Education Researcher* 27 (2018): 99-107; Anida R. Fazlagić and Milena Belić, "The connection of perfectionism and flow with athletes of a different performance level," *Fizička kultura* 71, no. 2 (2017): 111-117; Arne Dietrich and Oliver Stoll, "Effortless attention, hypofrontality, and perfectionism," in Bruya, *Effortless attention*, 159-178.

[27] Interestingly, research has found that the two beliefs are independent of each other, so that people may possess both high internal as well as high external locus of control regarding a specific phenomenon. A person diagnosed with lung cancer, for example, may attribute the diagnosis to such internal factors as poor diet and a lifetime of smoking. At the same time, they might attribute it to such external causes as bad luck, punishment from God, or bad genes. In general, though, people possess a dominant orientation, and so are either generally internally or externally attributing.

[28] See, for example, Tse et al., "Development and validation"; Celeste M. Taylor, J. M. Schepers, and F. Crous, "Locus of control in relation to flow," *SA Journal of Industrial Psychology* 32, no. 3 (2006): 49-62; Johannes Keller and Frederik Blomann, "Locus of control and the flow experience: An experimental analysis," *European Journal of Personality* 22, no. 7 (2008): 589-607.

[29] This definition is from Psychology Today, "Emotional Intelligence," accessed September 28, 2023, https://www.psychologytoday.com/intl/basics/emotional-intelligence

[30] For a recent review on emotional intelligence, see Ilios Kotsou, Moïra Mikolajczak, Alexandre Heeren, Jacques Grégoire, and Christophe Leys, "Improving emotional intelligence: A

systematic review of existing work and future challenges," *Emotion Review* 11, no. 2 (2019): 151-165.

[31] See, for example, Valérian Cece, Emma Guillet-Descas, Kevin Juhel, and Guillaume Martinent, "Emotional determinants and consequences of flow experience of young elite athletes involved in intensive training centers across the competitive season," *International Journal of Sport and Exercise Psychology* 20, no. 3 (2022): 896-914; Amy Rakei, Jasmine Tan, and Joydeep Bhattacharya, "Flow in contemporary musicians: Individual differences in flow proneness, anxiety, and emotional intelligence," *PLoS One* 17, no. 3 (2022): e0265936; Manuela M. Marin and Joydeep Bhattacharya, "Getting into the musical zone: trait emotional intelligence and amount of practice predict flow in pianists," *Frontiers in psychology* 4 (2013): 853.

[32] See, for example, Ullén et al., "Proneness for psychological flow."; Ullén et al., "Flow and individual differences."

[33] For flow and self-esteem, see, Asakawa, "Flow experience, culture, and well-being"; Mihaly Csikszentmihalyi, Jennifer A. Schmidt, and David J. Shernoff, "Individual and situational factors related to the experience of flow in adolescence: A multilevel approach," in *Applications of flow in human development and education: The collected works of Mihaly Csikszentmihalyi* (2014): 379-405. For flow and grit, see, Jasmine Tan, Kelly Yap, and Joydeep Bhattacharya, "What does it take to flow? Investigating links between grit, growth mindset, and flow in musicians," *Music & Science* 4 (2021): 2059204321989529. For flow and self-compassion, see chapter 21 of this book. For flow and mindfulness, see chapter 21 of this book. For flow and self-control, see, Claudia Kuhnle, Manfred Hofer, and Britta Kilian, "Self-control as predictor of school grades, life balance, and flow in adolescents," *British Journal of Educational Psychology* 82, no. 4 (2012): 533-548.

[34] Ibid.

[35] Laura Moral-Bofill, Andrés López de la Llave, Mª Pérez-Llantada, and Francisco Pablo Holgado-Tello, "Development of flow state self-regulation skills and coping with musical performance anxiety: Design and evaluation of an electronically implemented psychological program," *Frontiers in Psychology* 13 (2022): 899621.

7 – Measuring and Researching Flow

[1] For detailed overviews of measurement methods, see, Giovanni B. Moneta, "On the conceptualization and measurement of flow," in Peifer and Engeser, *Advances in flow research*, 31-69; Antonella Delle Fave, Fausto Massimini, and Marta Bassi, "Instruments and methods in flow research," in *Psychological selection and optimal experience across cultures: social empowerment through personal growth* (Cham: Springer, 2011), 59-87.

[2] Methodology and findings of these interviews were presented in Csikszentmihalyi, *Beyond boredom and anxiety*.

[3] Susan A. Jackson, "Factors influencing the occurrence of flow state in elite athletes," *Journal of applied sport psychology* 7, no. 2 (1995): 138-166.

[4] Detailed in Susan K. Perry, *Writing in flow: Keys to enhanced creativity* (Cincinnati: Writer's Digest Books, 1999).

[5] Their first study using this methodology was Christian Swann, Richard Keegan, Lee Crust, and David Piggott, "Psychological states underlying excellent performance in professional golfers: 'Letting it happen' vs. 'making it happen,'" *Psychology of Sport and Exercise* 23 (2016): 101-113.

[6] The Flow Questionnaire (FQ) was first discussed in Csikszentmihalyi and Csikszentmihalyi, *Optimal experience*.

[7] Giovanni B. Moneta, "Flow in work as a function of trait intrinsic motivation, opportunity for creativity in the job, and work engagement," in Simon L. Albrecht, ed., *The Handbook of employee engagement: Perspectives, issues, research and practice*, (Bingley: Emerald Publishing Limited, 2010), 262-269.

[8] The quotes used for shallow flow were: (1) "My mind isn't wandering. I am totally involved in what I am doing and I am not thinking of anything else. My body feels good... the world seems to be cut off from me... I am less aware of myself and my problems." (2) "My

concentration is like breathing... I never think of it... When I start, I really do shut out the world." (3) "I am so involved in what I am doing... I don't see myself as separate from what I am doing."

The quotes used for deep flow were: (1) "I am really quite oblivious to my surroundings after I really get doing in this activity." (2) "I think that the phone could ring, and the doorbell could ring or the house burn down or something like that..." (3) "Once I stop I can let it back in again."

[9] For a recent and thorough explanation of the experience sampling method, see Mihaly Csikszentmihalyi and Reed Larson, "The experience sampling method," in Mihaly Csikszentmihalyi, ed., *Flow and the foundations of positive psychology: The collected works of Mihaly Csikszentmihalyi* (Cham: Springer, 2014), 21-34.

[10] This is explained in Csikszentmihalyi and Csikszentmihalyi, *Optimal experience.*

[11] For a detailed discussion, see, Michael Barthelmäs and Johannes Keller, "Antecedents, boundary conditions and consequences of flow," in Peifer and Engeser, *Advances in flow research*, 71-107.

[12] Mihaly Csikszentmihalyi and Judith LeFevre, "Optimal experience in work and leisure," *Journal of personality and social psychology* 56, no. 5 (1989): 815.

[13] Stefan Engeser and Nicola Baumann, "Fluctuation of flow and affect in everyday life: A second look at the paradox of work," *Journal of Happiness Studies* 17 (2016): 105-124.

[14] Susan A. Jackson and Robert C. Eklund, "Assessing flow in physical activity: The flow state scale–2 and dispositional flow scale–2," *Journal of sport and exercise psychology* 24, no. 2 (2002): 133-150. Both scales were originally created to measure flow in sports. Small tweaks allow them to be fruitfully applied in other areas as well.

[15] Ö. Blom and F. Ullén, "The psychophysiology of flow during music performance," In *IV European Conference on Positive Psychology*, p. 55. 2008.; Örjan De Manzano, Töres Theorell, László Harmat, and Fredrik Ullén, "The psychophysiology of flow during piano playing," *Emotion* 10, no. 3 (2010): 301.

8 – Activities and Contexts of Flow

[1] Quote is from Csikszentmihalyi and Csikszentmihalyi, *Optimal experience*, 366.

[2] For a full description of the study, see Fausto Massimi and Massimo Carli, "The systematic assessment of flow in daily experience," in Csikszentmihalyi and Csikszentmihalyi, *Optimal experience*, 266-287.

[3] To be more precise, the researchers actually used an 8-channel model in this study. As the researchers explain: "Flow refers to channel 2 (high challenges and high skills); boredom sums up situations referred to in channels 3, 4, 5 (skills prevalence); anxiety situations refer to channels 1, 8, 7 (challenges prevalence); apathy refers to channel 6 (low challenges and low skills)."

[4] Engeser and Baumann, "Fluctuation of flow and affect."

[5] For in-depth discussions of flow at work, see, "Work: A paradox in flow research," in Delle Fave et al., *Pschological selection and optimal experience*, 155-176; Mihalyi Csikszentmihalyi, "The paradox of work," in *Finding flow*, 49-63.

[6] Csikszentmihalyi and LeFevre, "Optimal experience in work and leisure."

[7] Judith LeFevre, "Flow and the quality of experience during work and leisure," in Csikszentmihalyi and Csikszentmihalyi, *Optimal Experience*, 307-318.

[8] I have stolen the idea of risks and opportunities from Csikszentmihalyi. Chapter 5 in *Finding flow* is titled, "The risks and opportunities of leisure."

[9] Csikszentmihalyi, *Finding flow.*

[10] For benefits of hobbies, see, for example, Sarah D. Pressman, Karen A. Matthews, Sheldon Cohen, Lynn M. Martire, Michael Scheier, Andrew Baum, and Richard Schulz, "Association of enjoyable leisure activities with psychological and physical well-being," *Psychosomatic medicine* 71, no. 7 (2009): 725.

[11] Joel M. Hektner, Jennifer Anne Schmidt, and Mihaly Csikszentmihalyi, *Experience sampling method: Measuring the quality of everyday life* (New York: SAGE Publications, 2007).

9 – The Brain and Body in Flow

[1] Quoted in Daniel Goleman, *Focus: The hidden driver of excellence* (New York: Harper Collins, 2013).

[2] Jonathan Smallwood and Jonathan W. Schooler, "The science of mind wandering: Empirically navigating the stream of consciousness," *Annual review of psychology* 66 (2015): 487-518.

[3] Matthew A. Killingsworth and Daniel T. Gilbert, "A wandering mind is an unhappy mind," *Science* 330, no. 6006 (2010): 932-932.

[4] Smallwood and Schooler, "Science of mind wandering."

[5] Daniel Goleman, *Focus*.

[6] Timothy D. Wilson, David A. Reinhard, Erin C. Westgate, Daniel T. Gilbert, Nicole Ellerbeck, Cheryl Hahn, Casey L. Brown, and Adi Shaked, "Just think: The challenges of the disengaged mind," *Science* 345, no. 6192 (2014): 75-77.

[7] Fionnuala Murphy, Kirsty Macpherson, Trisha Jeyabalasingham, Tom Manly, and Barnaby Dunn, "Modulating mind-wandering in dysphoria," *Frontiers in Psychology* 4 (2013): 888.

[8] Matthew M. Nour and Robin L. Carhart-Harris, "Psychedelics and the science of self-experience," *The British Journal of Psychiatry* 210, no. 3 (2017): 177-179.

[9] It should be noted that mind wandering isn't all bad. Research suggests that our non-stop mental chatter does provide its upsides. Some of the positive functions of mind wandering are creative problem solving, self-reflection, generating future scenarios, organizing our memories, or pondering what we're learning. Thoughts about current problems may help us solve them in creative ways. Thoughts about our past may help us come to terms with it. Thoughts about the future may help us plan for what's to come. Thoughts about other people may promote empathy and help us improve relationships.

Mind wandering per se thus isn't bad. While these thoughts rarely make us happy, they do serve useful functions. One might say that whether an episode of mind wandering is a net positive or negative depends on the types of thoughts we're thinking (content) and the situation we're thinking them in (context).

For a discussion on benefits and dangers of mind wandering, see, for example, Jonathan W. Schooler, Michael D. Mrazek, Michael S. Franklin, Benjamin Baird, Benjamin W. Mooneyham, Claire Zedelius, and James M. Broadway, "The middle way: Finding the balance between mindfulness and mind-wandering," *Psychology of learning and motivation* 60 (2014): 1-33.

[10] For a short introduction on the DMN, see Judson Brewer, *The craving mind: From cigarettes to smartphones to love—why we get hooked and how we can break bad habits* (New Haven: Yale University Press, 2017), 99-101.

[11] See, for example, Daniel H. Weissman, K. C. Roberts, K. M. Visscher, and M. G. Woldorff, "The neural bases of momentary lapses in attention," *Nature neuroscience* 9, no. 7 (2006): 971-978; Valerie Bonnelle, Robert Leech, Kirsi M. Kinnunen, Tim E. Ham, Cristian F. Beckmann, Xavier De Boissezon, Richard J. Greenwood, and David J. Sharp, "Default mode network connectivity predicts sustained attention deficits after traumatic brain injury," *Journal of Neuroscience* 31, no. 38 (2011): 13442-13451.

[12] For a discussion on mind wandering and task performance, see, Schooler et al., "The middle way."

[13] Ibid.

[14] See, for example, Athanasia M. Mowinckel, Dag Alnæs, Mads L. Pedersen, Sigurd Ziegler, Mats Fredriksen, Tobias Kaufmann, Edmund Sonuga-Barke, Tor Endestad, Lars T. Westlye, and Guido Biele, "Increased default-mode variability is related to reduced task-performance and is evident in adults with ADHD," *NeuroImage: Clinical* 16 (2017): 369-382.

[15] Edward M. Hallowell and John J. Ratey, *ADHD 2.0: New science and essential strategies for thriving with distraction - from childhood through adulthood*, (London: Hachette UK, 2023).

[16] For a recent study, see Hui-Xia Zhou, Xiao Chen, Yang-Qian Shen, Le Li, Ning-Xuan Chen, Zhi-Chen Zhu, Francisco Xavier Castellanos, and Chao-Gan Yan, "Rumination and the default mode network: Meta-analysis of brain imaging studies and implications for depression," *Neuroimage* 206 (2020): 116287.

[17] See, for example, Vincent van de Ven, Marleen Wingen, Kim PC Kuypers, Johannes G. Ramaekers, and Elia Formisano, "Escitalopram decreases cross-regional functional connectivity within the default-mode network," *PloS one* 8, no. 6 (2013): e68355.

[18] Brewer, *The craving mind.*

[19] For a recent research overview on meditation and ADHD, see Junhua Zhang, Amparo Díaz-Román, and Samuele Cortese, "Meditation-based therapies for attention-deficit/hyperactivity disorder in children, adolescents and adults: a systematic review and meta-analysis," *BMJ Ment Health* 21, no. 3 (2018): 87-94. For a recent research overview on meditation and depression, see Reangsing, Chuntana, Tanapa Rittiwong, and Joanne Kraenzle Schneider, "Effects of mindfulness meditation interventions on depression in older adults: A meta-analysis," *Aging & Mental Health* 25, no. 7 (2021): 1181-1190.

[20] Kathleen A. Garrison, Juan F. Santoyo, Jake H. Davis, Thomas A. Thornhill IV, Catherine E. Kerr, and Judson A. Brewer, "Effortless awareness: Using real time neurofeedback to investigate correlates of posterior cingulate cortex activity in meditators' self-report," *Frontiers in human neuroscience* 7 (2013): 440. It should be noted that Brewer usually refers to just one part of the DMN, the PCC.

[21] See Brewer, *The craving mind.*

[22] Brewer, *The craving mind*, 101.

[23] Brewer, *The craving mind*, 114.

[24] Matthew M. Nour, Lisa Evans, David Nutt, and Robin L. Carhart-Harris, "Ego-dissolution and psychedelics: validation of the ego-dissolution inventory (EDI)," *Frontiers in human neuroscience* (2016): 269.

[25] For a study on losing the self in near-death experiences, see Charlotte Martial, Géraldine Fontaine, Olivia Gosseries, Robin Carhart-Harris, Christopher Timmermann, Steven Laureys, and Héléna Cassol, "Losing the self in near-death experiences: The experience of ego-dissolution," *Brain Sciences* 11, no. 7 (2021): 929.

[26] This has been shown in various studies. For example, Martin Ulrich, Johannes Keller, Klaus Hoenig, Christiane Waller, and Georg Grön, "Neural correlates of experimentally induced flow experiences," *Neuroimage* 86 (2014): 194-202; Martin Ulrich, Johannes Keller, and Georg Grön, "Neural signatures of experimentally induced flow experiences identified in a typical fMRI block design with BOLD imaging," *Social cognitive and affective neuroscience* 11, no. 3 (2016): 496-507; Dimitri Van Der Linden, Mattie Tops, and Arnold B. Bakker, "Go with the flow: A neuroscientific view on being fully engaged," *European Journal of Neuroscience* 53, no. 4 (2021): 947-963.

[27] Bruce Lee, *Bruce Lee striking thoughts: Bruce Lee's wisdom for daily living* (North Clarendon: Tuttle Publishing, 2015).

[28] Corinna Peifer and Jasmine Tan, "The psychophysiology of flow experience," in Peifer and Engeser, *Advances in flow research*, 191-230.

[29] J. Van Oort, I. Tendolkar, E. J. Hermans, P. C. Mulders, C. F. Beckmann, A. H. Schene, G. Fernández, and P. F. van Eijndhoven, "How the brain connects in response to acute stress: A review at the human brain systems level," *Neuroscience & Biobehavioral Reviews* 83 (2017): 281-297; Ulrich et al., "Neural correlates."; van der Linden, Tops, and Bakker, "Go with the flow."

[30] Ulrich et al., „Neural signatures."

[31] Peifer and Tan, "Psychophysiology of flow."

[32] Ibid.

[33] René Weber, Ron Tamborini, Amber Westcott-Baker, and Benjamin Kantor, "Theorizing flow and media enjoyment as cognitive synchronization of attentional and reward networks," *Communication Theory* 19, no. 4 (2009): 397-422.

[34] For a discussion on dopamine and flow, see Peifer and Tan, "Psychophysiology of flow."

[35] For Kotler's thoughts on neurochemicals and flow, see Kotler, *The rise of superman*; Kotler, *The art of impossible.*

[36] Kenji Katahira, Yoichi Yamazaki, Chiaki Yamaoka, Hiroaki Ozaki, Sayaka Nakagawa, and Noriko Nagata, "EEG correlates of the flow state: A combination of increased frontal theta

and moderate frontocentral alpha rhythm in the mental arithmetic task," *Frontiers in psychology* 9 (2018): 300.

[37] Corinna Peifer and Jasmine Tan, "The psychophysiology of flow experience," in Peifer and Engeser, *Advances in flow research*, 191-230.

[38] Peifer and Tan, "Psychophysiology of flow."

[39] Ibid.

[40] Ibid.

[41] Corinna Peifer and Jasmine Tan, "The psychophysiology of flow experience," in Peifer and Engeser, *Advances in flow research*, 191-230.

[42] Lindsay P. Cameron, Angela Nazarian, and David E. Olson, "Psychedelic microdosing: Prevalence and subjective effects," *Journal of psychoactive drugs* 52, no. 2 (2020): 113-122.

[1] Kotler, *The rise of superman.*

[2] In ESM studies (see chapter 7), participants indicate on scales from one ("not at all") to seven ("very") how intensely they experience various subjective feelings. It is typically found that in the flow condition, most of the positive feelings are at their peak, meaning participants feel the most alert, cheerful, strong, etc..

[3] This has been found in many studies. See, for example, Anne J. Wells, "Self-esteem and optimal experience," in Csikszentmihalyi and Csikszentmihalyi, *Optimal Experience*, 327-341; Nakamura and Csikszentmihalyi, "Concept of flow."

[4] László Harmat, Örjan de Manzano, Töres Theorell, Lennart Högman, Håkan Fischer, and Fredrik Ullén, "Physiological correlates of the flow experience during computer game playing," *International Journal of Psychophysiology* 97, no. 1 (2015): 1-7.

[5] Kotler, *The rise of superman.*

[6] Ibid.

[7] Tim Sohn, "One life to live: Mcconkey film premieres at squaw valley," Huffpost, accessed November 3, 2023, https://www.huffpost.com/entry/one-life-to-live-mcconkey_b_4043664.

[8] Mihaly Csikszentmihalyi, "If we are so rich, why aren't we happy?," *American psychologist* 54, no. 10 (1999): 821.

[9] Csikszentmihalyi, *Beyond boredom and anxiety*, 44.

[10] Quote is from "Flow, the secret to happiness," TED Talk by Mihaly Csikszentmihalyi, accessed November 3, 2023, https://www.ted.com/talks/mihaly_csikszentmihalyi_flow_the_secret_to_happiness.

[11] Quote is from "Living in flow - the secret of happiness," YouTube video featuring Mihaly Csikszentmihalyi, accessed November 3, 2023, https://www.youtube.com/watch?v=TzPky5Xe1-s.

[12] Quote is from Csikszentmihalyi, *Flow.*

[13] Martin Seligman, *Authentic happiness: Using the new positive psychology to realize your potential for lasting fulfillment* (New York: Simon and Schuster, 2002).

[14] Csikszentmihalyi, *Flow.*

[15] Ibid.

[16] Tse et al., "Living well by 'flowing' well."

[17] Corinna Peifer, Christine Syrek, Vivian Ostwald, Eva Schuh, and Conny H. Antoni, "Thieves of flow: How unfinished tasks at work are related to flow experience and wellbeing," *Journal of Happiness Studies* 21 (2020): 1641-1660.

[18] Marta Bassi, Patrizia Steca, Dario Monzani, Andrea Greco, and Antonella Delle Fave, "Personality and optimal experience in adolescence: Implications for well-being and development," *Journal of Happiness Studies* 15 (2014): 829-843.

[19] Asakawa, "Flow Experience, Culture."

[20] See, for example, Seongyeul Han, "The relationship between life satisfaction and flow in elderly Korean immigrants," in Csikszentmihalyi and Csikszentmihalyi, *Optimal Experience*; Katarina Habe, Michele Biasutti, and Tanja Kajtna, "Flow and satisfaction with life in elite musicians and top athletes," *Frontiers in psychology* 10 (2019): 698; Diana Olčar, Majda Rijavec, and Tajana Ljubin Golub, "Primary school teachers' life satisfaction: The role of life goals, basic psychological needs and flow at work," *Current Psychology* 38 (2019): 320-329.

²¹ Mihaly Csikszentmihalyi, "The future of flow," in Csikszentmihalyi and Csikszentmihalyi, *Optimal experience*, 369.

²² Csikszentmihalyi, "If we are so rich."

²³ Csikszentmihalyi, *Flow*.

²⁴ Mihaly Csikszentmihalyi, "Toward a psychology of optimal experience," in Csikszentmihalyi *Flow and the foundations*, 209-226.

²⁵ Sonja Lyubomirsky, *The how of happiness: A new approach to getting the life you want* (New York: Penguin Books, 2007).

²⁶ For an explanation of the PERMA Theory of well-being, see Martin Seligman, *Flourish: A visionary new understanding of happiness and well-being* (New York: Free Press, 2011).

²⁷ A lot of research exists on the role of self-focused attention in depression and anxiety. For a recent discussion, see, Timo Brockmeyer, Johannes Zimmermann, Dominika Kulessa, Martin Hautzinger, Hinrich Bents, Hans-Christoph Friederich, Wolfgang Herzog, and Matthias Backenstrass, "Me, myself, and I: Self-referent word use as an indicator of self-focused attention in relation to depression and anxiety," *Frontiers in psychology* 6 (2015): 1564.

11 – Performing Your Best

¹ Nakamura and Csikszentmihalyi, "The concept of flow."

² Amit Katwala, *The athletic brain: How neuroscience is revolutionising sport and can help you perform better* (New York: Simon and Schuster, 2016).

³ Quote is from the backcover of Jackson and Csikszentmihalyi, *Flow in sports*.

⁴ William F. Russell, *Second wind: The memoirs of an opinionated man* (New York: Random House, 1979).

⁵ Quote is from Karen Grant, "In the zone," Who Are You? Blog, accessed November 3, 2023, https://www.whoareyou.blog/blog/2019/3/13/in-the-zone.

⁶ Michael Gervais, „The most optimal state for humans," Linkedin, accessed November 3, 2023, https://www.linkedin.com/pulse/most-optimal-state-humans-michael-gervais/; "Steve Kerr," podcast episode on Finding Mastery by Michael Gervais, accessed November 3, 2023, https://findingmastery.com/podcasts/steve-kerr/.

⁷ Amit Katwala, "The science behind sport's magic moments," Prospect Magazine, accessed November 3, 2023, https://www.prospectmagazine.co.uk/society/43171/the-science-behind-sports-magic-moments.

⁸ Andrew Benson, "'Lewis Hamilton touches perfection in Spanish Grand Prix victory,'" BBC, accessed November 3, 2023, https://www.bbc.com/sport/formula1/53800895.

⁹ Lawrence Shainberg, "Finding 'the zone,'" The New York Times, accessed November 3, 2023, https://www.nytimes.com/1989/04/09/magazine/finding-the-zone.html.

¹⁰ Quoted in Kotler, *The rise of superman*.

¹¹ Kotler, *The rise of superman*.

¹² Ibid.

¹³ Perry, *Writing in flow*.

¹⁴ Anne Janzer, *The writer's process: Getting your brain in gear* (San Francisco: Cuesta Park Consulting, 2016).

¹⁵ Quoted in Janzer, *Writer's process*.

¹⁶ Ibid.

¹⁷ Susie Cranston and Scott Keller, "Increasing the 'meaning quotient' of work," McKinsey, accessed November 3, 2023, https://www.mckinsey.com/capabilities/people-and-organizational-performance/our-insights/increasing-the-meaning-quotient-of-work.

¹⁸ James Slavet, "Five new management metrics you need to know," Forbes, accessed November 3, 2023, https://www.forbes.com/sites/bruceupbin/2011/12/13/five-new-management-metrics-you-need-to-know/#7c5b0568717d.

¹⁹ Ann Marsh, "The art of work," Fast Company, accessed November 3, 2023, https://www.fastcompany.com/53713/art-work.

²⁰ Ibid.

²¹ Peter H. Diamandis and Steven Kotler, *Bold: How to go big, create wealth and impact the world* (New York: Simon and Schuster, 2016).

22 Marsh, "Art of Work."

23 Catherine Clifford, "The founder of Patagonia fishes half the year and tells his employees to go surfing," CNBC, accessed November 3, 2023, https://www.cnbc.com/2016/12/23/founder-of-patagonia-fishes-half-the-year-tells-his-employees-to-surf.html.

24 Katwala, *Athletic brain*, 146.

25 Mihaly Csikszentmihalyi, Kevin Rathunde, Samuel Whalen, *Talented teenagers: The roots of success and failure* (Cambridge: Cambridge University Press, 1997).

26 Angela Heine, "Flow and achievement in mathematics," unpublished doctoral dissertation, University of Chicago.

27 Stefan Engeser and Falko Rheinberg, "Flow, performance and moderators of challenge-skill balance," *Motivation and emotion* 32 (2008): 158-172.

28 Davin Pavlas, Kyle Heyne, Wendy Bedwell, Elizabeth Lazzara, and Eduardo Salas, "Game-based learning: The impact of flow state and videogame self-efficacy," In *Proceedings of the human factors and ergonomics society annual meeting*, vol. 54, no. 28, pp. 2398-2402. Sage CA: Los Angeles, CA: SAGE Publications, 2010.

29 Susan A. Jackson and Glyn C. Roberts, "Positive performance states of athletes: Toward a conceptual understanding of peak performance," *The sport psychologist* 6, no. 2 (1992): 156-171.

30 Julia Schüler and Sibylle Brunner, "The rewarding effect of flow experience on performance in a marathon race," *Psychology of Sport and Exercise* 10, no. 1 (2009): 168-174.

31 van den Hout and Davis, *Team flow*.

32 Corinna Peifer, and Gina Zipp, "All at once? The effects of multitasking behavior on flow and subjective performance," *European Journal of Work and Organizational Psychology* 28, no. 5 (2019): 682-690.

33 Tsung-Hsien Kuo and Li-An Ho, "Individual difference and job performance: The relationships among personal factors, job characteristics, flow experience, and service quality," *Social Behavior and Personality: an international journal* 38, no. 4 (2010): 531-552.

34 Caroline Aubé, Eric Brunelle, and Vincent Rousseau, "Flow experience and team performance: The role of team goal commitment and information exchange," *Motivation and Emotion* 38, no. 1 (2014): 120-130.

35 Raymond MacDonald, Charles Byrne, and Lana Carlton, "Creativity and flow in musical composition: An empirical investigation," *Psychology of music* 34, no. 3 (2006): 292-306.

36 Richard P. Chi and Allan W. Snyder, "Brain stimulation enables the solution of an inherently difficult problem," *Neuroscience letters* 515, no. 2 (2012): 121-124.

37 Sally Adee, "Better living through electrochemistry," The Last Word on Nothing, accessed November 3, 2023, https://www.lastwordonnothing.com/2012/02/09/better-living-through-electrochemistry/.

38 Sally Adee, "Zap your brain into the zone: Fast track to pure focus," NewScientist, accessed November 3, 2023, https://www.newscientist.com/article/mg21328501-600-zap-your-brain-into-the-zone-fast-track-to-pure-focus/.

39 Ibid.

40 Ibid.

41 Whether we can bring about such strong flow states without the use of technology, and do it reliably and consistently, is another question.

42 Chris Berka, "TED talk: A window on the brain," Advanced Brain Monitoring, accessed November 3, 2023, https://www.advancedbrainmonitoring.com/news/ted-talk-a-window-on-the-brain-chris-berka.

43 It should be noted that there are varying degrees of flow and it's likely that the milder versions will have less of an impact on performance than the stronger ones. Most likely, the stronger the flow state, the bigger the performance improvements.

44 Barthelmäs and Keller, "Antecedents, boundary conditions and consequences of flow."

45 See, for example, Vikki Krane and Jean M. Williams, "Psychological characteristics of peak performance," in Jean M. Williams, ed., *Applied sport psychology: Personal growth to peak performance*, 6th edition (New York: McGraw-Hill Education, 2010).

[46] Amy A. Pachai, Anita Acai, Andrew B. LoGiudice, and Joseph A. Kim, "The mind that wanders: Challenges and potential benefits of mind wandering in education," *Scholarship of Teaching and Learning in Psychology* 2, no. 2 (2016): 134.

[47] Williams, *Applied sport psychology*, 336.

[48] Michael Phelps, *No limits: The will to succeed* (New York: Simon and Schuster, 2009).

[49] Nakamura and Csikszentmihalyi, "The concept of flow."

[50] Csikszentmihalyi and Csikszentmihalyi; *Optimal experience*, 320.

[51] Csikszentmihalyi, *Flow*.

[52] The following example is adapted from Csikszentmihalyi, *Flow*.

[53] Csikszentmihalyi et al., *Talented teenagers*.

12 – The Dark Side(s) of Flow

[1] Csikszentmihalyi, *Flow*, 4.

[2] Csikszentmihalyi, *Finding flow*.

[3] Definition per the Oxford Dictionary.

[4] Sarah Partington, Elizabeth Partington, and Steve Olivier, "The dark side of flow: A qualitative study of dependence in big wave surfing," *The sport psychologist* 23, no. 2 (2009): 170-185.

[5] Robert M. Heirene, David Shearer, Gareth Roderique-Davies, and Stephen D. Mellalieu, "Addiction in extreme sports: An exploration of withdrawal states in rock climbers," *Journal of behavioral addictions* 5, no. 2 (2016): 332-341.

[6] Ibid.

[7] Carla Willig, "A phenomenological investigation of the experience of taking part in extreme sports,'" *Journal of health psychology* 13, no. 5 (2008): 690-702.

[8] Partington et al., "The dark side of flow."

[9] Richard L. Celsi, Randall L. Rose, and Thomas W. Leigh, "An exploration of high-risk leisure consumption through skydiving," *Journal of consumer research* 20, no. 1 (1993): 1-23.

[10] Kotler, *The rise of superman*.

[11] JP Schlick, "Flow states, part 4: The darkside of flow," The Inertia, accessed November 3, 2023, https://www.theinertia.com/surf/flow-states-part-4-the-darkside-of-flow/.

[12] Marilyn Freimuth, Sandy Moniz, and Shari R. Kim, "Clarifying exercise addiction: Differential diagnosis, co-occurring disorders, and phases of addiction," *International journal of environmental research and public health* 8, no. 10 (2011): 4069-4081.

[13] Laura Di Lodovico, Ségolène Poulnais, and Philip Gorwood, "Which sports are more at risk of physical exercise addiction: A systematic review," *Addictive behaviors* 93 (2019): 257-262.

[14] Elwin Hu, Vasileios Stavropoulos, Alastair Anderson, Matthew Scerri, and James Collard, "Internet gaming disorder: Feeling the flow of social games," *Addictive behaviors reports* 9 (2019): 100140.

[15] Daniel Kardefelt-Winther, "A conceptual and methodological critique of internet addiction research: Towards a model of compensatory internet use," *Computers in human behavior* 31 (2014): 351-354.

[16] Shuiqing Yang, Yaobin Lu, Bin Wang, and Ling Zhao, "The benefits and dangers of flow experience in high school students' internet usage: The role of parental support," *Computers in Human Behavior* 41 (2014): 504-513.

[17] Vasileios Stavropoulos, Mark D. Griffiths, Tyrone L. Burleigh, Daria J. Kuss, Young Yim Doh, and Rapson Gomez, "Flow on the Internet: A longitudinal study of Internet addiction symptoms during adolescence," *Behaviour & Information Technology* 37, no. 2 (2018): 159-172.

[18] Kem ZK Zhang, Chongyang Chen, Sesia J. Zhao, and Matthew KO Lee, "Compulsive smartphone use: The roles of flow, reinforcement motives, and convenience," In *ICIS*. 2014.

[19] Hyoungkoo Khang, Jung Kyu Kim, and Yeojin Kim, "Self-traits and motivations as antecedents of digital media flow and addiction: The Internet, mobile phones, and video games," *Computers in Human Behavior* 29, no. 6 (2013): 2416-2424.

[20] The actual number depends on the study. The following studies showed a prevalence of 4.7%, 4.1%, and 0.3-1% respectively. Wendy Feng, Danielle E. Ramo, Steven R. Chan, and James A. Bourgeois, "Internet gaming disorder: Trends in prevalence 1998–2016," *Addictive*

behaviors 75 (2017): 17-24; Taiki Oka, Toshitaka Hamamura, Yuka Miyake, Nao Kobayashi, Masaru Honjo, Mitsuo Kawato, Takatomi Kubo, and Toshinori Chiba, "Prevalence and risk factors of internet gaming disorder and problematic internet use before and during the COVID-19 pandemic: A large online survey of Japanese adults," *Journal of Psychiatric Research* 142 (2021): 218-225; Andrew K. Przybylski, Netta Weinstein, and Kou Murayama, "Internet gaming disorder: Investigating the clinical relevance of a new phenomenon," *American Journal of Psychiatry* 174, no. 3 (2017): 230-236.

[21] Brian Schrank, *Avant-garde videogames: Playing with technoculture* (Cambridge: MIT Press, 2014).

[22] Jane McGonigal, *Reality is broken: Why games make us better and how they can change the world* (London: Penguin Books, 2011).

[23] Jesse Schell, *The art of game design: A book of lenses,* Third Edition (Boca Raton: CRC Press, 2019).

[24] Torill Mortensen, "Flow, seduction and mutual pleasure," paper presented at the *Other Players* conference, Center for Computer Game Research, IT university in Copenhagen, Denmark, 6-8 December, (2004).

[25] On video games as the holy grail of design, see Lennart E. Nacke and Craig A. Lindley, "Affective ludology, flow and immersion in a first-person shooter: Measurement of player experience," *arXiv preprint arXiv:1004.0248* (2010).

[26] McGonigal, *Reality is broken.*

[27] Mark D. Griffiths, Daria J Kuss, and Daniel L King, "Video game addiction: Past, present and future," *Current Psychiatry Reviews* 8, no. 4 (2012): 308-318.

[28] Orsolya Király, Mark D. Griffiths, and Zsolt Demetrovics, "Internet gaming disorder and the DSM-5: Conceptualization, debates, and controversies," *Current Addiction Reports* 2 (2015): 254-262.

[29] Hu et al., "Internet gaming disorder."

[30] Ibid.

[31] SungBok Park, and Ha Sung Hwang. "Understanding online game addiction: Connection between presence and flow," in *Human-Computer Interaction. Interacting in Various Application Domains: 13th International Conference, HCI International 2009, San Diego, CA, USA, July 19-24, 2009, Proceedings, Part IV 13*, pp. 378-386. Springer Berlin Heidelberg, 2009.

[32] Pinyapat Kiatsakared, and Kuan-Yu Chen, "The effect of flow experience on online game addiction during the COVID-19 pandemic: The moderating effect of activity passion," *Sustainability* 14, no. 19 (2022): 12364.

[33] Antonella Delle Fave, Fausto Massimini, Marta Bassi, "Psychosocial maladjustment and mimetic flow," in Delle Fave et al., *Psychological selection,* 321-356.

[34] Andrew D. Hathaway and Justin Sharpley, "The cannabis experience: An analysis of 'flow,'" in Dale Jacquette, ed., *Cannabis - philosophy for everyone: What were we just talking about?* (Hoboken: Wiley, 2010).

[35] "9 Facts about Meth," Drug Policy Alliance, accessed November 3, 2023, https://drugpolicy.org/drug-fact/meth/.

[36] Marisa Crane, "Fentanyl vs. heroin: An opioid comparison," American Addiction Centers, accessed November 3, 2023, https://americanaddictioncenters.org/fentanyl-treatment/similarities.

[37] "What is cocaine and what are the effects of cocaine on the body?," Drug Policy Alliance, accessed November 3, 2023, https://drugpolicy.org/drug-fact/cocaine/?fact=1.

[38] Delle Fave et al., "Psychological maladjustment."

[39] Ibid.

[40] Ibid.

[41] Mason Currey, *Daily rituals: How great minds make time, find inspiration, and get to work* (London: Pan Macmillan, 2013).

[42] Tim Carman, "Caffeine has been a boon for civilization, Michael Pollan says. But it has come at a cost," Washington Post, accessed November 3, 2023,

https://www.washingtonpost.com/news/voraciously/wp/2020/02/05/caffeine-has-been-a-boon-for-civilization-michael-pollan-says-but-it-has-come-at-a-cost/.

[43] James Fadiman, and Sophia Korb, "Might microdosing psychedelics be safe and beneficial? An initial exploration," *Journal of psychoactive drugs* 51, no. 2 (2019): 118-122.

[44] For a research overview, see "Research," Hopkins Psychedelic, accessed November 3, 2023, https://hopkinspsychedelic.org/index/#research.

[45] Kotler, *The rise of superman.*

[46] Julia Schüler and Mirjam Pfenninger, "Flow impairs risk perception in kayakers," *Sport psychology* (2011): 237-246.

[47] Julia Schüler and Jeanne Nakamura, "Does flow experience lead to risk? How and for whom," *Applied Psychology: Health and Well-Being* 5, no. 3 (2013): 311-331.

[48] Mihaly Csikszentmihalyi and Kevin Rathunde, "The measurement of flow in everyday life: toward a theory of emergent motivation," in Janis E. Jacobs, ed., *Developmental Perspectives on Motivation,* (Lincoln: University of Nebraska Press, 1993).

[49] Mihaly Csikszentmihalyi and Reed Larson, "Intrinsic rewards in school crime," *Crime & Delinquency* 24, no. 3 (1978): 322-335.

[50] Yuval Noah Harari, "Combat flow: Military, political, and ethical dimensions of subjective well-being in war," *Review of General Psychology* 12, no. 3 (2008): 253-264.

[51] Ibid.

[52] Philip Caputo, *A rumor of war* (New York: Holt, Rinehart and Winston, 1977).

[53] Quoted in Harari, *Combat flow.*

[54] Ibid.

[55] Ibid.

[56] Beth-Anne Canero and Naval War College Newport Ri Newport United States, "Deterring Combat Flow and Absorption: The Need for the COMMARFORCOM to Provide Ethics-and Morals-Based Training for Operational Leaders in Order to Deter the Effects of Combat Flow and Absorption on Their Decision-Making," (2018): 0027.

[57] Mihaly Csikszentmihalyi, "Reflections on enjoyment," *Perspectives in Biology and Medicine* 28, no. 4 (1985): 489-497.

[58] Ibid.

[59] Csikszentmihalyi and Larson, *Intrinsic rewards.*

[60] Kotler, *The rise of superman,* 157.

[61] John Ratey, *Spark: The revolutionary new science of exercise and the brain* (London: Hachette UK, 2008).

[62] Lisa Bowen, "Video game play may provide learning, health, social benefits, review finds," American Psychological Association, accessed November 3, 2023, https://www.apa.org/monitor/2014/02/video-game.

[63] Siobhan O'Donovan, James Gain, and Patrick Marais, "A case study in the gamification of a university-level games development course," In *Proceedings of the South African Institute for Computer Scientists and Information Technologists Conference*, pp. 242-251. 2013.

[64] Csikszentmihalyi, *Flow.*

13 – Flow(ing) at Work

[1] Céline Bricteux, Jose Navarro, Lucía Ceja, and Guillaume Fuerst, "Interest as a moderator in the relationship between challenge/skills balance and flow at work: An analysis at within-individual level," *Journal of Happiness Studies* 18 (2017): 861-880.

[2] That complex tasks are more conducive to flow than mundane tasks has been shown in many studies. See, for example, Maria T. Allison and Margaret Carlisle Duncan, "Women, work, and leisure: The days of our lives," *Leisure Sciences* 9, no. 3 (1987): 143-161.

[3] This is known as *skill variety.* See, for example, Clive J. Fullagar and E. Kevin Kelloway, "Flow at work: An experience sampling approach," *Journal of occupational and organizational psychology* 82, no. 3 (2009): 595-615.

[4] This is known as *task identity.* Its connection to flow at work is discussed in Corinna Peifer and Gina Wolters, "Flow in the context of work," in Peifer and Engeser, *Advances in flow research*, 287-321.

⁵ Anna-Carin Fagerlind, Maria Gustavsson, Gun Johansson, and Kerstin Ekberg, "Experience of work-related flow: Does high decision latitude enhance benefits gained from job resources?," *Journal of vocational behavior* 83, no. 2 (2013): 161-170.

⁶ Peifer and Wolters, "Flow in the context of work."

⁷ Barbara Plester and Ann Hutchison, "Fun times: The relationship between fun and workplace engagement," *Employee Relations* 38, no. 3 (2016): 332-350.

⁸ This is discussed in Peifer and Wolters, "Flow in the context of work," and Arnold B. Bakker and Marianne Van Woerkom, "Flow at work: A self-determination perspective," *Occupational Health Science* 1 (2017): 47-65.

⁹ Ibid.

¹⁰ This is discussed in Peifer and Wolters, "Flow in the context of work."

¹¹ Elaine Hatfield, John T. Cacioppo, and Richard L. Rapson, *Emotional contagion* (Cambridge: Cambridge University Press, 1993).

¹² Arnold B. Bakker, "Flow among music teachers and their students: The crossover of peak experiences," *Journal of vocational behavior* 66, no. 1 (2005): 26-44.

¹³ Satoris S. Culbertson, Clive J. Fullagar, Mathias J. Simmons, and Mengmeng Zhu, "Contagious flow: Antecedents and consequences of optimal experience in the classroom," *Journal of Management Education* 39, no. 3 (2015): 319-349.

¹⁴ See, for example, Fagerlind et al., "Experience of work-related flow." See, also, Peifer and Wolters, "Flow in the Context of Work."

¹⁵ Matthias Kaufmann, "Deutsche Konzerne kämpfen gegen den Handy-Wahn," Spiegel, accessed November 3, 2023, https://www.spiegel.de/karriere/erreichbar-nach-dienstschluss-massnahmen-der-konzerne-a-954029.html.

¹⁶ Autonomy is described as a basic psychological need in Self-Determination Theory (SDT).

¹⁷ For an overview, see Richard M. Ryan and Edward L. Deci, "Parenting and the facilitation of autonomy and wellbeing in development," in Richard M. Ryan and Edward L. Deci, eds., *Self-determination theory: Basic psychological needs in motivation, development and wellness* (New York: Guilford Publications, 2017), 319-450.

¹⁸ Wendy S. Grolnick, and Richard M. Ryan, "Parent styles associated with children's self-regulation and competence in school," *Journal of educational psychology* 81, no. 2 (1989): 143.

¹⁹ Samantha W. Bindman, Eva M. Pomerantz, and Glenn I. Roisman, "Do children's executive functions account for associations between early autonomy-supportive parenting and achievement through high school?," *Journal of educational psychology* 107, no. 3 (2015): 756.

²⁰ For a discussion on the marshmallow experiments, see Walter Mischel, *The marshmallow test: Understanding self-control and how to master it* (New York: Little Brown Spark, 2014).

²¹ For a recent study, see Elien Mabbe, Bart Soenens, Maarten Vansteenkiste, and Sarah De Pauw, "Is autonomy-supportive parenting beneficial only to adolescents with an autonomous personality? Two meanings of goodness of fit," *Merrill-Palmer Quarterly* 66, no. 3 (2020), 308-332.

²² Juan L. Núñez and Jaime León, "Autonomy support in the classroom: A review from self-determination theory," *European Psychologist* 20, no. 4 (2015), 275–283.

²³ See, for example, Frank Martela, Marcos Gómez, Wenceslao Unanue, Sofia Araya, Diego Bravo, and Alvaro Espejo, "What makes work meaningful? Longitudinal evidence for the importance of autonomy and beneficence for meaningful work," *Journal of vocational behavior* 131 (2021): 103631.

²⁴ For an overview, see Richard M. Ryan and Edward L. Deci, "Work and organizations: Promoting wellness and productivity," in Ryan and Deci, *Self-determination theory*, 532-558.

²⁵ Cal Newport, *So good they can't ignore you: Why skills trump passion in the quest for work you love* (New York: Grand Central Publishing, 2012).

²⁶ See, for example, Clive J. Fullagar and E. Kevin Kelloway, "Flow at work: An experience sampling approach," *Journal of occupational and organizational psychology* 82, no. 3 (2009): 595-615.

14 – The Power of Meaning

[1] Blake A. Allan, Cassondra Batz-Barbarich, Haley M. Sterling, and Louis Tay, "Outcomes of meaningful work: A meta-analysis," *Journal of management studies* 56, no. 3 (2019): 500-528.

[2] Martela et al., "What makes work meaningful?"

[3] Amy Wrzesniewski and Jane E. Dutton, "Crafting a job: Revisioning employees as active crafters of their work," *Academy of management review* 26, no. 2 (2001): 179-201.

[4] Wei Liu, Dimitri van der Linden, and Arnold B. Bakker, "Strengths use and work-related flow: An experience sampling study on implications for risk taking and attentional behaviors," *Journal of Managerial Psychology* 37, no. 1 (2022): 47-60.

[5] This framework was first mentioned in Amy Wrzesniewski, Clark McCauley, Paul Rozin, and Barry Schwartz, "Jobs, careers, and callings: People's relations to their work," *Journal of research in personality* 31, no. 1 (1997): 21-33.

[6] Bryan J. Dik, Ryan D. Duffy, *Make your job a calling: How the psychology of vocation can change your life at work* (Conshohocken: Templeton Press, 2012), 14.

[7] Ibid.

[8] Marianne van Woerkom, Wido Oerlemans, and Arnold B. Bakker, "Strengths use and work engagement: A weekly diary study," *European Journal of Work and Organizational Psychology* 25, no. 3 (2016): 384-397.

[9] Lucy C. Hone, Aaron Jarden, Scott Duncan, and Grant M. Schofield, "Flourishing in New Zealand Workers," *Journal of Occupational and Environmental Medicine* 57, no. 9 (2015): 973-983.

[10] Liu et al., "Strengths use and work-related flow."

[11] "Character Strengths," VIA Institute on Character, accessed November 3, 2023, https://www.viacharacter.org/character-strengths-via.

[12] "What the research says about character strengths," VIA Institute on Character, accessed November 3, 2023, https://www.viacharacter.org/research/findings.

[13] "The via character strengths survey," VIA Institute on Character, accessed November 3, 2023, https://www.viacharacter.org/account/register.

[14] Claudia Harzer and Willibald Ruch, "Your strengths are calling: Preliminary results of a web-based strengths intervention to increase calling," *Journal of happiness studies* 17 (2016): 2237-2256.

[15] For the first study using this intervention, see Martin Seligman, Tracy A. Steen, Nansook Park, and Christopher Peterson, "Positive psychology progress: Empirical validation of interventions," *American psychologist* 60, no. 5 (2005): 410.

[16] For a recent study discussing this idea, see Lucy Finkelstein-Fox, Jeffrey M. Pavlacic, Erin M. Buchanan, Stefan E. Schulenberg, and Crystal L. Park, "Valued living in daily experience: Relations with mindfulness, meaning, psychological flexibility, and stressors," *Cognitive Therapy and Research* 44 (2020): 300-310.

[17] See, for example, Geoffrey L. Cohen and David K. Sherman, "The psychology of change: Self-affirmation and social psychological intervention." *Annual review of psychology* 65, no. 1 (2014): 333-371; Zezhen Wu, Thees F. Spreckelsen, and Geoffrey L. Cohen, "A meta-analysis of the effect of values affirmation on academic achievement," *Journal of Social Issues* 77, no. 3 (2021): 702-750.

[18] For research on the importance of perceived social impact, see, for example, Adam M. Grant, "The significance of task significance: Job performance effects, relational mechanisms, and boundary conditions," *Journal of applied psychology* 93, no. 1 (2008): 108; Adam M. Grant, Elizabeth M. Campbell, Grace Chen, Keenan Cottone, David Lapedis, and Karen Lee, "Impact and the art of motivation maintenance: The effects of contact with beneficiaries on persistence behavior," *Organizational behavior and human decision processes* 103, no. 1 (2007): 53-67; Martela et al., "What makes work meaningful?"

[19] Grant et al., "Impact and the art of motivation maintenance."

[20] Grant, "The significance of task significance."

[21] David S. Yeager, Marlone D. Henderson, David Paunesku, Gregory M. Walton, Sidney D'Mello, Brian J. Spitzer, and Angela Lee Duckworth, "Boring but important: A self-

transcendent purpose for learning fosters academic self-regulation," *Journal of personality and social psychology* 107, no. 4 (2014): 559.

[22] Elizabeth R. Brown, Jessi L. Smith, Dustin B. Thoman, Jill M. Allen, and Gregg Muragishi, "From bench to bedside: A communal utility value intervention to enhance students' biomedical science motivation," *Journal of Educational Psychology* 107, no. 4 (2015): 1116.

[23] Blake A. Allan, Ryan D. Duffy, and Brian Collisson, "Helping others increases meaningful work: Evidence from three experiments," *Journal of Counseling Psychology* 65, no. 2 (2018): 155.

[24] Ibid.

[25] Keiko Otake, Satoshi Shimai, Junko Tanaka-Matsumi, Kanako Otsui, and Barbara L. Fredrickson, "Happy people become happier through kindness: A counting kindnesses intervention," *Journal of happiness studies* 7 (2006): 361-375.

[26] Viktor Frankl, *Man's search for meaning* (1946).

15 – Humor, Fun, and Play

[1] See, for example, Shelley A. Crawford and Nerina J. Caltabiano, "Promoting emotional well-being through the use of humour," *The Journal of Positive Psychology* 6, no. 3 (2011): 237-252.

[2] Ibid.

[3] Rod A. Martin and Herbert M. Lefcourt, "Sense of humor as a moderator of the relation between stressors and moods," *Journal of personality and social psychology* 45, no. 6 (1983): 1313.

[4] See, for example, Brandon M. Savage, Heidi L. Lujan, Raghavendar R. Thipparthi, and Stephen E. DiCarlo, "Humor, laughter, learning, and health! A brief review," *Advances in physiology education* (2017).

[5] Barbara Fraley and Arthur Aron, "The effect of a shared humorous experience on closeness in initial encounters," *Personal Relationships* 11, no. 1 (2004): 61-78.

[6] Avner Ziv, "The social function of humor in interpersonal relationships," *Society* 47 (2010): 11-18.

[7] Laura E. Kurtz and Sara B. Algoe, "When sharing a laugh means sharing more: Testing the role of shared laughter on short-term interpersonal consequences," *Journal of Nonverbal Behavior* 41 (2017): 45-65.

[8] For a research overview on the benefits of laughter, see Lawrence Robinson, Melinda Smith, M.A. and Jeanne Segal, "Laughter is the best medicine," Helpguide, accessed November 3, 2023, https://www.helpguide.org/articles/mental-health/laughter-is-the-best-medicine.htm.

[9] Jessica Mesmer-Magnus, David J. Glew, and Chockalingam Viswesvaran, "A meta-analysis of positive humor in the workplace," *Journal of Managerial Psychology* 27, no. 2 (2012): 155-190.

[10] Marek Bartzik, Andreas Bentrup, Susanne Hill, Maria Bley, Eckart von Hirschhausen, Gerrit Krause, Peter Ahaus, Angelika Dahl-Dichmann, and Corinna Peifer, "Care for joy: Evaluation of a humor intervention and its effects on stress, flow experience, work enjoyment, and meaningfulness of work," *Frontiers in Public Health* 9 (2021): 667821.

[11] Marek Bartzik, Fabienne Aust, and Corinna Peifer, "Negative effects of the COVID-19 pandemic on nurses can be buffered by a sense of humor and appreciation," *BMC nursing* 20, no. 1 (2021): 1-12.

[12] Marek Bartzik and Corinna Peifer, "On the relationships between humour, stress and flow experience—Introducing the humour-flow model," *The Palgrave Handbook of Humour Research* (2021): 479-496.

[13] Plester and Hutchison, "Fun times."

[14] Bartzik et al., "Care for joy."

[15] Crawford and Caltabiano, "Promoting emotional well-being."

[16] Nektaria Tagalidou, Viola Loderer, Eva Distlberger, and Anton-Rupert Laireiter, "Feasibility of a humor training to promote humor and decrease stress in a subclinical sample: A single-arm pilot study," *Frontiers in psychology* 9 (2018): 577.

[17] Paul McGhee, *Humor as survival training for a stressed-out world: The 7 humor habits program* (Bloomington: AuthorHouse, 2010).

[18] Jennifer Aaker and Naomi Bagdonas, *Humor, seriously: Why humor is a secret weapon in business and life (and how anyone can harness it. even you)* (New York: Crown, 2021).

[19] Survey results discussed in Aaker and Bagdonas, *Humor, seriously.*

[20] T. Bradford Bitterly, Alison Wood Brooks, and Maurice E. Schweitzer, "Risky business: When humor increases and decreases status," *Journal of personality and social psychology* 112, no. 3 (2017): 431.

[21] Ibid.

[22] For a recent discussion on this topic, see Yuri S. Scharp, Arnold B. Bakker, Kimberley Breevaart, Kaspar Kruup, and Andero Uusberg, "Playful work design: Conceptualization, measurement, and validity," *human relations* 76, no. 4 (2023): 509-550.

[23] Arnold B. Bakker, Jørn Hetland, Olav Kjellevold Olsen, Roar Espevik, and Juriena D. De Vries, "Job crafting and playful work design: Links with performance during busy and quiet days," *Journal of vocational behavior* 122 (2020): 103478; Yuri S. Scharp, Kimberley Breevaart, Arnold B. Bakker, and Dimitri van der Linden, "Daily playful work design: A trait activation perspective," *Journal of Research in Personality* 82 (2019): 103850.

[24] Arnold B. Bakker and Jessica van Wingerden, "Rumination about COVID-19 and employee well-being: The role of playful work design," *Canadian Psychology/Psychologie canadienne* 62, no. 1 (2021): 73; Scharp et al., "Playful work design."

[25] For a discussion on playful work design and flow, see, for example, Bakker and van Woerkom, "Flow at work."

[26] Arnold B. Bakker, Yuri S. Scharp, Kimberley Breevaart, and Juriena D. De Vries "Playful work design: Introduction of a new concept," *The Spanish Journal of Psychology* 23 (2020): e19. See also, Bakker and van Woerkom, "Flow at Work."

[27] Scharp et al., "Playful work design."

[28] "Rapping flight attendant," YouTube video, accessed November 3, 2023, https://www.youtube.com/watch?v=rhMOnr0GxU8.

[29] Scharp et al., "Playful work design."

[30] Katrin S. Heimann and Andreas Roepstorff, "How playfulness motivates–putative looping effects of autonomy and surprise revealed by micro-phenomenological investigations," *Frontiers in Psychology* 9 (2018): 1704.

16 – Mind Like Water

[1] E. J. Masicampo and Roy F. Baumeister, "Consider it done! Plan making can eliminate the cognitive effects of unfulfilled goals," *Journal of personality and social psychology* 101, no. 4 (2011): 667.

[2] Peifer et al., „Thieves of flow."

[3] Christine J. Syrek and Conny H. Antoni, "Unfinished tasks foster rumination and impair sleeping—Particularly if leaders have high performance expectations," *Journal of Occupational Health Psychology* 19, no. 4 (2014): 490; Christine J. Syrek, Oliver Weigelt, Corinna Peifer, and Conny H. Antoni, "Zeigarnik's sleepless nights: How unfinished tasks at the end of the week impair employee sleep on the weekend through rumination," *Journal of Occupational Health Psychology* 22, no. 2 (2017): 225.

[4] Henry David Thoreau, *Walden* (1854).

[5] For research with nurses, see, for example, Juliana J. Brixey, David J. Robinson, James P. Turley, and Jiajie Zhang, "The roles of MDs and RNs as initiators and recipients of interruptions in workflow," *International journal of medical informatics* 79, no. 6 (2010): e109-e115. For research with office workers, see, for example, Mary Czerwinski, Eric Horvitz, and Susan Wilhite, "A diary study of task switching and interruptions," in *Proceedings of the SIGCHI conference on Human factors in computing systems*, pp. 175-182. 2004; Gloria Mark, Victor M. Gonzalez, and Justin Harris, "No task left behind? Examining the nature of fragmented work," In *Proceedings of the SIGCHI conference on Human factors in computing systems*, pp. 321-330. 2005.

[6] Brandon W. Smit, "Successfully leaving work at work: The self-regulatory underpinnings of psychological detachment," *Journal of Occupational and Organizational Psychology* 89, no. 3 (2016): 493-514.

[7] Sophie Leroy and Theresa M. Glomb, "Tasks interrupted: How anticipating time pressure on resumption of an interrupted task causes attention residue and low performance on interrupting tasks and how a 'ready-to-resume' plan mitigates the effects," *Organization Science* 29, no. 3 (2018): 380-397.

[8] Madeleine Dore, "How to reduce 'attention residue' in your life," BBC, accessed November 3, 2023, https://www.bbc.com/worklife/article/20200130-the-life-hack-to-reduce-admin-and-carve-out-downtime.

[9] David Allen, *Getting things done: The art of stress-free productivity*, Revised Edition (Boston: Little, Brown Book Group, 2015).

17 – Sprint. Rest. Repeat.

[1] Schwartz and Loehr have written about this research in numerous places, including *The power of full engagement: Managing energy, not time, is the key to performance, health and happiness* (Crows Nest: Allen & Unwin, 2003).

[2] K. Anders Ericsson, Ralf T. Krampe, and Clemens Tesch-Römer, "The role of deliberate practice in the acquisition of expert performance," *Psychological review* 100, no. 3 (1993): 363.

[3] K. Anders Ericsson and Robert Pool, *Peak: Secrets from the new science of expertise* (Boston: Houghton Mifflin, 2016).

[4] See, for example, Zach McCann, "Sleep tracking brings new info to athletes," ESPN, accessed November 3, 2023, https://www.espn.com/blog/playbook/tech/post/_/id/797/sleep-tracking-brings-new-info-to-athletes.

[5] Robert S. Root-Bernstein, Maurine Bernstein, and Helen Garnier, "Correlations between avocations, scientific style, work habits, and professional impact of scientists," *Creativity Research Journal* 8, no. 2 (1995): 115-137.

[6] For an in-depth discussion on the working lives of creative people, see Currey, *Daily rituals*. Also see Alex Soojung-Kim Pang, *Rest: Why you get more done when you work less* (New York: Basic Books, 2016).

[7] Example taken from Pang, *Rest*.

[8] Stephen King, *On writing: A memoir of the craft* (London: Hodder & Stoughton, 2001).

[9] Example taken from Currey, *Daily rituals*.

[10] Example taken from Pang, *Rest*.

[11] Tony Schwartz, "Developing mastery through deliberate practice," in Jocelyn K. Glei, ed., *Maximize your potential: Grow your expertise, take bold risks & build an incredible career* (Las Vegas: Amazon Publishing, 2013). See also Tony Schwartz, "The 90-minute solution: Live like a sprinter!," Business Insider, accessed November 3, 2023, https://www.businessinsider.com/the-90-minute-solution-live-like-a-sprinter-2011-1?r=US&IR=T.

[12] Julia Gifford, "The secret of the 10% most productive people? Breaking!," Desktime, accessed November 3, 2023, https://desktime.com/blog/17-52-ratio-most-productive-people.

[13] Awwad J. Dababneh, Naomi Swanson, and Richard L. Shell, "Impact of added rest breaks on the productivity and well being of workers," *Ergonomics* 44, no. 2 (2001): 164-174.

[14] Traci L. Galinsky, Naomi G. Swanson, Steven L. Sauter, Joseph J. Hurrell, and Lawrence M. Schleifer, "A field study of supplementary rest breaks for data-entry operators," *Ergonomics* 43, no. 5 (2000): 622-638.

[15] P. S. Tiwari and L. P. Gite, "Evaluation of work-rest schedules during operation of a rotary power tiller," *International Journal of Industrial Ergonomics* 36, no. 3 (2006): 203-210.

[16] Sooyeol Kim, YoungAh Park, and Qikun Niu, "Micro-break activities at work to recover from daily work demands," *Journal of Organizational Behavior* 38, no. 1 (2017): 28-44.

[17] For research on microbreaks and their associated benefits, see, for example, Qi Nie, Jie Zhang, Jian Peng, and Xiao Chen, "Daily micro-break activities and workplace well-being: A recovery perspective," *Current Psychology* (2021): 1-14; Sooyeol Kim, YoungAh Park, and Lucille Headrick, "Daily micro-breaks and job performance: General work engagement as a cross-level moderator," Journal of Applied Psychology 103, no. 7 (2018): 772; Sooyeol Kim, Seonghee Cho, and YoungAh Park, "Daily microbreaks in a self-regulatory resources lens:

Perceived health climate as a contextual moderator via microbreak autonomy," *Journal of Applied Psychology* 107, no. 1 (2022): 60.

[18] Sabine Sonnentag, Laura Venz, and Anne Casper, "Advances in recovery research: What have we learned? What should be done next?," *Journal of occupational health psychology* 22, no. 3 (2017): 365.

[19] Ibid.

[20] Ibid.

[21] Michael D. Mrazek, Jonathan Smallwood, and Jonathan W. Schooler, "Mindfulness and mind-wandering: Finding convergence through opposing constructs," *Emotion* 12, no. 3 (2012): 442.

[22] Burchard writes about the technique in *High performance habits: How extraordinary people become that way* (Carlsbad: Hay House, 2017).

[23] For an in-depth discussion of the technique, see, Francesco Cirillo, *The pomodoro technique: The acclaimed time-management system that has transformed how we work* (New York: Currency, 2018).

18 – The Science of Recovery

[1] Maike E. Debus, Sabine Sonnentag, Werner Deutsch, and Fridtjof W. Nussbeck, "Making flow happen: The effects of being recovered on work-related flow between and within days," *Journal of applied psychology* 99, no. 4 (2014): 713.

[2] Sabine Sonnentag, Ute Stephan, Johannes Wendsche, Jessica De Bloom, Christine Syrek, and Tim Vahle-Hinz, "Recovery in occupational health psychology and human resource management research: An Interview with Prof. Sabine Sonnentag and Prof. Ute Stephan," German Journal of Human Resource Management 35, no. 2 (2021): 274-281.

[3] Sonnentag et al., "Advances in recovery research."

[4] Jo C. Coulson, Jim McKenna, and M. Field, "Exercising at work and self-reported work performance," *International Journal of Workplace Health Management* 1, no. 3 (2008): 176-197.

[5] Marjaana Sianoja, Christine J. Syrek, Jessica de Bloom, Kalevi Korpela, and Ulla Kinnunen, "Enhancing daily well-being at work through lunchtime park walks and relaxation exercises: Recovery experiences as mediators," *Journal of Occupational Health Psychology* 23, no. 3 (2018): 428.

[6] Jeremy S. Sibold and Kathleen M. Berg, "Mood enhancement persists for up to 12 hours following aerobic exercise: A pilot study," *Perceptual and motor skills* 111, no. 2 (2010): 333-342.

[7] Larissa Ledochowski, Gerhard Ruedl, Adrian H. Taylor, and Martin Kopp, "Acute effects of brisk walking on sugary snack cravings in overweight people, affect and responses to a manipulated stress situation and to a sugary snack cue: A crossover study," *PloS one* 10, no. 3 (2015): e0119278.

[8] Kate Janse Van Rensburg, Adrian Taylor, and Tim Hodgson, "The effects of acute exercise on attentional bias towards smoking-related stimuli during temporary abstinence from smoking," *Addiction* 104, no. 11 (2009): 1910-1917.

[9] Bernward Winter, Caterina Breitenstein, Frank C. Mooren, Klaus Voelker, Manfred Fobker, Anja Lechtermann, and Karsten Krueger, "High impact running improves learning," *Neurobiology of learning and memory* 87, no. 4 (2007): 597-609.

[10] Yu-Kai Chang, Jeffrey D. Labban, Jennifer I. Gapin, and Jennifer L. Etnier, "The effects of acute exercise on cognitive performance: A meta-analysis," *Brain research* 1453 (2012): 87-101.

[11] John Ratey, *Spark.*

[12] Jo Barton and Jules Pretty, "What is the best dose of nature and green exercise for improving mental health? A multi-study analysis," *Environmental science & technology* 44, no. 10 (2010): 3947-3955.

[13] Jeffrey Conrath Miller and Zlatan Krizan, "Walking facilitates positive affect (even when expecting the opposite)," *Emotion* 16, no. 5 (2016): 775.

[14] You are more likely to stick to it and experience greater benefits when you enjoy the activity. See, for example, Michelle Segar, *No sweat: How the simple science of motivation can bring you a lifetime of fitness* (New York: Amacom, 2015).

[15] Mrazek et al., "Mindfulness and mind-wandering."

[16] Whitney L. Heppner, Michael H. Kernis, Chad E. Lakey, W. Keith Campbell, Brian M. Goldman, Patti J. Davis, and Edward V. Cascio, "Mindfulness as a means of reducing aggressive behavior: Dispositional and situational evidence," *Aggressive Behavior: Official Journal of the International Society for Research on Aggression* 34, no. 5 (2008): 486-496.

[17] For an overview on the science of meditation, see Daniel Goleman and Richard J. Davidson, *Altered traits: Science reveals how meditation changes your mind, brain, and body* (New York: Avery, 2017).

[18] I don't cite any studies here because the list would be too long. If you search for meditation and rumination, optimism, self-compassion, and other mentioned factors, you'll find plenty of studies.

[19] Many studies have shown that meditation has a positive effect on flow. See, for example, Bruno Carrança, Sidónio Serpa, António Rosado, and Joan Palmi Guerrero, "A pilot study of a mindfulness-based program (MBSoccerP): The potential role of mindfulness, self-compassion and psychological flexibility on flow and elite performance in soccer athletes," *Revista Iberoamericana de psicologia del ejercicio y el deporte* 14, no. 1 (2019): 34-40; Fengbo Liu, Zhongqiu Zhang, Shuqiang Liu, and Nan Zhang, "Examining the effects of brief mindfulness training on athletes' flow: The mediating role of resilience," *Evidence-Based Complementary and Alternative Medicine* 2021, no. 1 (2021): 6633658; Mark A. Chen and Jennifer Meggs, "The effects of Mindful Sport Performance Enhancement (MSPE) training on mindfulness, and flow in national competitive swimmers," *Journal of Human Sport and Exercise* 16, no. 3 (2021): 517-527; Keith A. Kaufman, Carol R. Glass, and Diane B. Arnkoff, "Evaluation of Mindful Sport Performance Enhancement (MSPE): A new approach to promote flow in athletes," *Journal of clinical sport psychology* 3, no. 4 (2009): 334-356; Cian Aherne, Aidan P. Moran, and Chris Lonsdale, "The effect of mindfulness training on athletes' flow: An initial investigation," *The Sport Psychologist* 25, no. 2 (2011): 177-189.

[20] Interviews with long-term meditators suggest that these individuals have, through thousands of hours of practice, obtained a state of non-stop non-resistance, non-striving, and non-ambition. They don't fight with life. They don't struggle. They don't swim against the stream. They allow everything to be as it is. They allow life to unfold and to flow naturally. Their everyday experience seems to be much more harmonious and flowy than it is for the rest of us.

[21] Yi-Yuan Tang, Yinghua Ma, Junhong Wang, Yaxin Fan, Shigang Feng, Qilin Lu, Qingbao Yu et al, "Short-term meditation training improves attention and self-regulation," *Proceedings of the national Academy of Sciences* 104, no. 43 (2007): 17152-17156.

[22] Fadel Zeidan, Susan K. Johnson, Bruce J. Diamond, Zhanna David, and Paula Goolkasian, "Mindfulness meditation improves cognition: Evidence of brief mental training," Consciousness and cognition 19, no. 2 (2010): 597-605.

[23] Matthew Lieberman, *Social: Why our brains are wired to connect* (Oxford: Oxford University Press, 2013).

[24] Daniel Gilbert, *Stumbling on happiness* (New York: Vintage Books, 2006).

[25] This study is discussed in Martin Seligman, *Authentic happiness*.

[26] For a recent study, see Oliver Hämmig, "Health risks associated with social isolation in general and in young, middle and old age," PLoS One 14, no. 7 (2019): e0219663. For a more thorough discussion, see John T Cacioppo and William Patrick, *Loneliness: Human nature and the need for social connection* (New York: W. W. Norton & Company, 2009).

[27] This is discussed in Johann Hari, *Lost connections: Why you're depressed and how to find hope* (London: Bloomsberry Publishing, 2019).

[28] John T. Cacioppo, John M. Ernst, Mary H. Burleson, Martha K. McClintock, William B. Malarkey, Louise C. Hawkley, Ray B. Kowalewski et al., "Lonely traits and concomitant physiological processes: The MacArthur social neuroscience studies," *International Journal of Psychophysiology* 35, no. 2-3 (2000): 143-154.

[29] For more on this, see Lieberman, *Social*.

[30] Sonnentag et al., "Advances in recovery research."

[31] Christine Bosch, Sabine Sonnentag, and Anna Sophia Pinck, "What makes for a good break? A diary study on recovery experiences during lunch break," *Journal of Occupational and Organizational Psychology* 91, no. 1 (2018): 134-157.

[32] For more on this, see Sherry Turkle, *Reclaiming conversation: The power of talk in a digital age* (New York: Penguin Press, 2015).

[33] For a science-based discussion of loneliness, see Cacioppo and Patrick, *Loneliness*.

[34] Jarek Krajewski, Martin Sauerland, and Rainer Wieland, "Relaxation-induced cortisol changes within lunch breaks–an experimental longitudinal worksite field study," *Journal of Occupational and Organizational Psychology* 84, no. 2 (2011): 382-394.

[35] Ibid.

[36] Results from this study are presented in three different papers: Sianoja et al., "Enhancing daily well-being."; Krajewski et al., "Relaxation-induced cortisol changes."; Tobias Esch, Gregory L. Fricchione, Stefanie Joos, and Michael Teut, "Self-care, stress management, and primary care: from salutogenesis and health promotion to mind-body medicine," *Evidence-Based Complementary and Alternative Medicine* 2013 (2013).

[37] Sianoja et al., "Enhancing daily well-being."

[38] Sara C. Mednick and Mark Ehrman, *Take a nap! Change your life* (New York: Workman Publishing Company, 2006).

[39] Frédéric Dutheil, Benjamin Danini, Reza Bagheri, Maria Livia Fantini, Bruno Pereira, Farès Moustafa, Marion Trousselard, and Valentin Navel, "Effects of a short daytime nap on the cognitive performance: A systematic review and meta-analysis," *International Journal of Environmental Research and Public Health* 18, no. 19 (2021): 10212.

[40] Jennifer R. Goldschmied, Philip Cheng, Kathryn Kemp, Lauren Caccamo, Julia Roberts, and Patricia J. Deldin, "Napping to modulate frustration and impulsivity: A pilot study," *Personality and Individual Differences* 86 (2015): 164-167.

[41] Kosuke Kaida, Yuji Takeda, and Kazuyo Tsuzuki, "The relationship between flow, sleepiness and cognitive performance: The effects of short afternoon nap and bright light exposure," *Industrial Health* 50, no. 3 (2012): 189-196.

[42] Olaf Lahl, Christiane Wispel, Bernadette Willigens, and Reinhard Pietrowsky, "An ultra short episode of sleep is sufficient to promote declarative memory performance," Journal of sleep research 17, no. 1 (2008): 3-10.

[43] Cassie Shortsleeve, "Can't sleep? Try 'quiet wakefulness' instead," Medium, accessed November 3, 2023, https://elemental.medium.com/cant-sleep-try-quiet-wakefulness-instead-2b106e5b8e3c.

[44] Sonnentag et al., "Advances in recovery research."

[45] Sonnentag et al., "Recovery in occupational health psychology."

[46] Stuart Brown, *Play: How it shapes the brain, opens the imagination, and invigorates the soul* (London: Scribe Publications, 2010).

[47] Michael A. Rupp, Richard Sweetman, Alejandra E. Sosa, Janan A. Smither, and Daniel S. McConnell, "Searching for affective and cognitive restoration: Examining the restorative effects of casual video game play," *Human Factors* 59, no. 7 (2017): 1096-1107.

[48] Gurinder Singh Bains, Lee S. Berk, Noha Daher, Everett Lohman, Ernie Schwab, Jerrold Petrofsky, and Pooja Deshpande, "The effect of humor on short-term memory in older adults: A new component for whole-person wellness," *Advances in mind-body medicine* 28, no. 2 (2014): 16-24.

[49] For a research overview on the benefits of laughter, see Robinson et al, "Laughter is the best medicine."

[50] Robert Kubey and Mihaly Csikszentmihalyi, "Television addiction is no mere metaphor," *Scientific American* 286, no. 2 (2002): 74-80.

[51] E. Alison Holman, Dana Rose Garfin, and Roxane Cohen Silver, "Media's role in broadcasting acute stress following the Boston Marathon bombings," *Proceedings of the National Academy of Sciences* 111, no. 1 (2014): 93-98.

52 This study is mentioned in Kelly McGonigal, *The upside of stress: Why stress is good for you (and how to get good at it)* (London: Vermilion, 2015).

53 Shawn Achor, *The happiness advantage: How a positive brain fuels success in work and life* (New York: Currency, 2010).

54 Tannis MacBeth Williams, "The impact of television: A natural experiment involving three communities," (1979).

55 Aric Sigman, *Remotely controlled: How television is damaging our lives* (London: Vermilion, 2007).

56 Leonard Reinecke, Jennifer Klatt, and Nicole C. Krämer, "Entertaining media use and the satisfaction of recovery needs: Recovery outcomes associated with the use of interactive and noninteractive entertaining media," *Media Psychology* 14, no. 2 (2011): 192-215.

57 Dacher Keltner, Richard Bowman, and Harriet Richards, "Exploring the emotional state of 'real happiness'. A study into the effects of watching natural history television content," (2017). See also: N. L. Yeo, M. P. White, I. Alcock, R. Garside, S. G. Dean, A. J. Smalley, and B. Gatersleben, "What is the best way of delivering virtual nature for improving mood? An experimental comparison of high definition TV, 360 video, and computer generated virtual reality," *Journal of environmental psychology* 72 (2020): 101500.

58 Sonnentag et al., "Advances in recovery research."

59 Ibid.

60 Anniina Virtanen, Michelle Van Laethem, Jessica de Bloom, and Ulla Kinnunen, "Drammatic breaks: Break recovery experiences as mediators between job demands and affect in the afternoon and evening," *Stress and Health* 37, no. 4 (2021): 801-818.

61 Marc G. Berman, John Jonides, and Stephen Kaplan, "The cognitive benefits of interacting with nature," *Psychological science* 19, no. 12 (2008): 1207-1212.

62 Marc G. Berman, Ethan Kross, Katherine M. Krpan, Mary K. Askren, Aleah Burson, Patricia J. Deldin, Stephen Kaplan, Lindsey Sherdell, Ian H. Gotlib, and John Jonides, "Interacting with nature improves cognition and affect for individuals with depression," *Journal of affective disorders* 140, no. 3 (2012): 300-305.

63 Gregory N. Bratman, J. Paul Hamilton, Kevin S. Hahn, Gretchen C. Daily, and James J. Gross, "Nature experience reduces rumination and subgenual prefrontal cortex activation," *Proceedings of the national academy of sciences* 112, no. 28 (2015): 8567-8572.

64 Peter Aspinall, Panagiotis Mavros, Richard Coyne, and Jenny Roe, "The urban brain: Analysing outdoor physical activity with mobile EEG," *British journal of sports medicine* 49, no. 4 (2015): 272-276.

65 For more nature walking studies, see, for example, Ahmad Hassan, Jiang Tao, Guo Li, Mingyan Jiang, Liu Aii, Jiang Zhihui, Liu Zongfang, and Chen Qibing, "Effects of walking in bamboo forest and city environments on brainwave activity in young adults," *Evidence-Based Complementary and Alternative Medicine* 2018 (2018); Gregory N. Bratman, Gretchen C. Daily, Benjamin J. Levy, and James J. Gross, "The benefits of nature experience: Improved affect and cognition," *Landscape and Urban Planning* 138 (2015): 41-50.

66 See, for example, Elizabeth K. Nisbet and John M. Zelenski, "Underestimating nearby nature: Affective forecasting errors obscure the happy path to sustainability," *Psychological science* 22, no. 9 (2011): 1101-1106.

67 For a recent review, see Michele Antonelli, Davide Donelli, Lucrezia Carlone, Valentina Maggini, Fabio Firenzuoli, and Emanuela Bedeschi, "Effects of forest bathing (shinrin-yoku) on individual well-being: An umbrella review," *International Journal of Environmental Health Research* 32, no. 8 (2022): 1842-1867.

68 Ibid.

69 Berman et al., "Cognitive benefits."

70 Daniel K. Brown, Jo L. Barton, and Valerie F. Gladwell, "Viewing nature scenes positively affects recovery of autonomic function following acute-mental stress," *Environmental science & technology* 47, no. 11 (2013): 5562-5569.

71 Deborah Cracknell, Mathew P. White, Sabine Pahl, Wallace J. Nichols, and Michael H. Depledge, "Marine biota and psychological well-being: A preliminary examination of dose–

response effects in an aquarium setting," *Environment and behavior* 48, no. 10 (2016): 1242-1269.

[72] Akil Gordon-Beckford, "The therapeutic effect of an aquarium in the workplace," Videre Aquariums, accessed November 3, 2023, https://www.videreaquariums.com/post/the-therapeutic-effect-of-an-aquarium-in-the-workplace.

[73] Carol Cutler Riddick,"Health, aquariums, and the non-institutionalized elderly," *Marriage & family review* 8, no. 3-4 (1985): 163-173.

[74] Nancy E. Edwards and Alan M. Beck, "Animal-assisted therapy and nutrition in Alzheimer's disease," *Western journal of nursing research* 24, no. 6 (2002): 697-712.

[75] Deborah L. Wells, "The effect of videotapes of animals on cardiovascular responses to stress," *Stress and health* 21, no. 3 (2005): 209-213.

[76] Ibid.

[77] Tina Karabinski, Verena C. Haun, Annika Nübold, Johannes Wendsche, and Jürgen Wegge, "Interventions for improving psychological detachment from work: A meta-analysis," *Journal of occupational health psychology* 26, no. 3 (2021): 224.

[78] Sonnentag et al., "Advances in recovery research."

[79] Ibid.

19 – One Thing at a Time

[1] There is no official definition as to what counts as a "task," or what constitutes an interval of "time." Does chewing gum count as a task? Does doing two things within 30 seconds count as multitasking even if the actions are performed sequentially?

[2] Louise Ridley, "People swap devices 21 times an hour, says OMD," Campaign UK, accessed November 3, 2023, https://www.campaignlive.co.uk/article/people-swap-devices-21-times-hour-says-omd/1225960.

[3] "4 in 5 Americans multitask while watching tv," Marketing Charts, accessed November 3, 2023, https://www.marketingcharts.com/television-28025.

[4] Larry D. Rosen, L. Mark Carrier, and Nancy A. Cheever, "Facebook and texting made me do it: Media-induced task-switching while studying," *Computers in Human Behavior* 29, no. 3 (2013): 948-958.

[5] Victor M. González and Gloria Mark, "'Constant, constant, multi-tasking craziness': managing multiple working spheres," In *Proceedings of the SIGCHI conference on Human factors in computing systems*, pp. 113-120. 2004.

[6] Gloria Mark, Shamsi T. Iqbal, Mary Czerwinski, Paul Johns, and Akane Sano, "Neurotics can't focus: An in situ study of online multitasking in the workplace," In *Proceedings of the 2016 CHI conference on human factors in computing systems*, pp. 1739-1744. 2016.

[7] Gloria Mark, Yiran Wang, and Melissa Niiya, "Stress and multitasking in everyday college life: An empirical study of online activity," In *Proceedings of the SIGCHI conference on human factors in computing systems*, pp. 41-50. 2014.

[8] Kevin P. Madore and Anthony D. Wagner, " Multicosts of multitasking," in *Cerebrum: The Dana forum on brain science*, vol. 2019. Dana Foundation, 2019.

[9] See, for example, Wesley C. Clapp, Michael T. Rubens, and Adam Gazzaley, "Mechanisms of working memory disruption by external interference," *Cerebral cortex* 20, no. 4 (2010): 859-872; Paul E. Dux, Jason Ivanoff, Christopher L. Asplund, and René Marois, "Isolation of a central bottleneck of information processing with time-resolved fMRI," *Neuron* 52, no. 6 (2006): 1109-1120.

[10] Madore and Wagner, "Multicosts of multitasking."

[11] There are different types of costs. There is a general loss in efficiency as mentioned in the main text. But there's also a cost for learning (e.g., worse and less flexible memories) and other costs.

[12] See, for example, Edita Poljac, Andrea Kiesel, Iring Koch, and Hermann Müller, "New perspectives on human multitasking," *Psychological Research* 82, no. 1 (2018): 1-3.

[13] Madore and Wagner, "Multicosts of multitasking."

[14] Thomas Buser and Noemi Peter, "Multitasking," *Experimental Economics* 15, no. 4 (2012): 641-655.

[15] Laura L. Bowman, Laura E. Levine, Bradley M. Waite, and Michael Gendron, "Can students really multitask? An experimental study of instant messaging while reading," *Computers & Education* 54, no. 4 (2010): 927-931.

[16] Peifer and Zipp, "All at once?"

[17] Eyal Ophir, Clifford Nass, and Anthony D. Wagner, "Cognitive control in media multitaskers," *Proceedings of the national academy of sciences of the United States of America* 106, no. 37 (2009): 15583.

[18] Ira Flatow, "The myth of multitasking," NPR, accessed November 3, 2023, https://www.npr.org/2013/05/10/182861382/the-myth-of-multitasking.

[19] Dan Schutten, Kirk A. Stokes, and Karen M. Arnell, "I want to media multitask and I want to do it now: Individual differences in media multitasking predict delay of gratification and system-1 thinking," *Cognitive research: principles and implications* 2 (2017): 1-10.

[20] For an overview on brain plasticity, see, for example, Norman Doidge, *The brain that changes itself: Stories of personal triumph from the frontiers of brain science* (London: Penguin Books, 2007).

[21] Kostadin Kushlev, Jason Proulx, and Elizabeth W. Dunn, "'Silence your phones': Smartphone notifications increase inattention and hyperactivity symptoms," In *Proceedings of the 2016 CHI conference on human factors in computing systems*, pp. 1011-1020. 2016.

[22] Cary Stothart, Ainsley Mitchum, and Courtney Yehnert, "The attentional cost of receiving a cell phone notification," *Journal of experimental psychology: human perception and performance* 41, no. 4 (2015): 893.

[23] Martin Pielot and Luz Rello, "Productive, anxious, lonely: 24 hours without push notifications," In *Proceedings of the 19th International Conference on Human-Computer Interaction with Mobile Devices and Services*, pp. 1-11. 2017.

[24] Pielot and Rello, "Productive, anxious, lonely."; Martin Pielot and Luz Rello, "The do not disturb challenge: A day without notifications," In *Proceedings of the 33rd annual ACM conference extended abstracts on human factors in computing systems*, pp. 1761-1766. 2015.; Shamsi T. Iqbal and Eric Horvitz, "Notifications and awareness: A field study of alert usage and preferences," In *Proceedings of the 2010 ACM conference on Computer supported cooperative work*, pp. 27-30. 2010.

[25] Iqbal and Horvitz, "Notifications and awareness."

[26] Gloria Mark, Mary Czerwinski, and Shamsi T. Iqbal, "Effects of individual differences in blocking workplace distractions," In *Proceedings of the 2018 CHI Conference on Human Factors in Computing Systems*, pp. 1-12. 2018.

[27] Gloria Mark, Shamsi Iqbal, Mary Czerwinski, and Paul Johns, "Focused, aroused, but so distractible: Temporal perspectives on multitasking and communications," In *Proceedings of the 18th ACM Conference on Computer Supported Cooperative Work & Social Computing*, pp. 903-916. 2015.

[28] Thomas W. Jackson, Ray Dawson, and Darren Wilson, "Understanding email interaction increases organizational productivity," *Communications of the ACM* 46, no. 8 (2003): 80-84.

[29] Kostadin Kushlev and Elizabeth W. Dunn, "Checking email less frequently reduces stress," *Computers in Human Behavior* 43 (2015): 220-228.

[30] Brian Wansink, "Environmental factors that increase the food intake and consumption volume of unknowing consumers," *Annu. Rev. Nutr.* 24 (2004): 455-479.

[31] Ibid.

[32] Rosen et al., "Facebook and texting."

[33] Lora E. Burke, Jing Wang, and Mary Ann Sevick, "Self-monitoring in weight loss: A systematic review of the literature," *Journal of the American Dietetic Association* 111, no. 1 (2011): 92-102.

[34] Ibid.

[35] Dena M. Bravata, Crystal Smith-Spangler, Vandana Sundaram, Allison L. Gienger, Nancy Lin, Robyn Lewis, Christopher D. Stave, Ingram Olkin, and John R. Sirard, "Using pedometers to increase physical activity and improve health: A systematic review," *Jama* 298, no. 19 (2007): 2296-2304.

[36] Steve Whittaker, Vaiva Kalnikaite, Victoria Hollis, and Andrew Guydish, "'Don't waste my time' use of time information improves focus," In *Proceedings of the 2016 CHI Conference on Human Factors in Computing Systems*, pp. 1729-1738. 2016.

[37] Judith Borghouts, Duncan P. Brumby, and Anna L. Cox, "TimeToFocus: Feedback on interruption durations discourages distractions and shortens interruptions," *ACM Transactions on Computer-Human Interaction (TOCHI)* 27, no. 5 (2020): 1-31.

20 – Flow-Supportive Sights, Sounds, Smells, and Co.

[1] Adrian C. North, David J. Hargreaves, and Jennifer McKendrick, "The influence of in-store music on wine selections," *Journal of Applied psychology* 84, no. 2 (1999): 271.

[2] Janet Currie, Stefano DellaVigna, Enrico Moretti, and Vikram Pathania, "The effect of fast food restaurants on obesity and weight gain," *American Economic Journal: Economic Policy* 2, no. 3 (2010): 32-63.

[3] Jia Wei Zhang, Ryan T. Howell, and Colleen J. Howell, "Living in wealthy neighborhoods increases material desires and maladaptive consumption," *Journal of Consumer Culture* 16, no. 1 (2016): 297-316.

[4] Lubomir Lamy, Nicolas Guéguen, Jacques Fischer-Lokou, and Jérôme Guegan, "'Wrong place to get help': A field experiment on luxury stores and helping behavior," *Social Influence* 11, no. 2 (2016): 130-139.

[5] Lawrence E. Williams and John A. Bargh, "Experiencing physical warmth promotes interpersonal warmth," *Science* 322, no. 5901 (2008): 606-607.

[6] Russell A. Hill and Robert A. Barton, "Red enhances human performance in contests," *Nature* 435, no. 7040 (2005): 293-293.

[7] Brian Wansink and Jeffery Sobal, "Mindless eating: The 200 daily food decisions we overlook," *Environment and Behavior* 39, no. 1 (2007): 106-123.

[8] Rob W. Holland, Merel Hendriks, and Henk Aarts, "Smells like clean spirit: Nonconscious effects of scent on cognition and behavior," *Psychological science* 16, no. 9 (2005): 689-693.

[9] D. J. Birnbach, D. King, I. Vlaev, L. F. Rosen, and P. D. Harvey, "Impact of environmental olfactory cues on hand hygiene behaviour in a simulated hospital environment: A randomized study," *Journal of Hospital Infection* 85, no. 1 (2013): 79-81.

[10] Nastaran Shishegar and Mohamed Boubekri, "Natural light and productivity: Analyzing the impacts of daylighting on students' and workers' health and alertness," In *Proceedings of the International Conference on "health, Biological and life science"(HBLS-16), Istanbul, Turkey*, pp. 18-19. 2016.

[11] For an overview of the effects of daylight versus artificial light, see Mohamed Boubekri, *Daylighting, architecture and health* (London: Routledge, 2008).

[12] Lisa Heschong, "Daylighting and human performance," *ASHRAE journal* 44, no. 6 (2002): 65-67.

[13] M. Boubekri, J. Lee, K. Bub, and K. Curry, "Impact of daylight exposure on sleep time and quality of elementary school children," *European Journal of Teaching and Education* 2, no. 2 (2020): 10-17.

[14] "Study: Natural Light Is the Best Medicine for the Office," PR Newswire, accessed November 3, 2023, https://www.prnewswire.com/news-releases/study-natural-light-is-the-best-medicine-for-the-office-300590905.html.

[15] Yousef Al Horr, Mohammed Arif, Amit Kaushik, Ahmed Mazroei, Martha Katafygiotou, and Esam Elsarrag, "Occupant productivity and office indoor environment quality: A review of the literature," *Building and environment* 105 (2016): 369-389.

[16] Mohamed Boubekri, Ivy N. Cheung, Kathryn J. Reid, Chia-Hui Wang, and Phyllis C. Zee, "Impact of windows and daylight exposure on overall health and sleep quality of office workers: A case-control pilot study," *Journal of clinical sleep medicine* 10, no. 6 (2014): 603-611.

[17] Mohamed Boubekri, Jaewook Lee, Piers MacNaughton, May Woo, Lauren Schuyler, Brandon Tinianov, and Usha Satish, "The impact of optimized daylight and views on the sleep duration and cognitive performance of office workers," *International journal of environmental research and public health* 17, no. 9 (2020): 3219.

[18] Man Young Park, Choul-Gyun Chai, Hae-Kyung Lee, Hani Moon, and Jai Sung Noh, "The effects of natural daylight on length of hospital stay," *Environmental health insights* 12 (2018): 1178630218812817.

[19] Jeffrey M. Walch, Bruce S. Rabin, Richard Day, Jessica N. Williams, Krissy Choi, and James D. Kang, "The effect of sunlight on postoperative analgesic medication use: A prospective study of patients undergoing spinal surgery," *Psychosomatic medicine* 67, no. 1 (2005): 156-163.

[20] Rana Sagha Zadeh, Mardelle McCuskey Shepley, Gary Williams, and Susan Sung Eun Chung, "The impact of windows and daylight on acute-care nurses' physiological, psychological, and behavioral health," *HERD: Health Environments Research & Design Journal* 7, no. 4 (2014): 35-61.

[21] For the reasoning behind these recommendations, see the work of Dr. Alexander Wunsch.

[22] "State of the American workplace," Gallup, accessed November 3, 2023, https://www.gallup.com/workplace/238085/state-american-workplace-report-2017.aspx.

[23] Simon P. Banbury and Dianne C. Berry, "Office noise and employee concentration: Identifying causes of disruption and potential improvements," *Ergonomics* 48, no. 1 (2005): 25-37.

[24] Aram Seddigh, Cecilia Stenfors, Erik Berntsson, Rasmus Bååth, Sverker Sikström, and Hugo Westerlund, "The association between office design and performance on demanding cognitive tasks," *Journal of Environmental Psychology* 42 (2015): 172-181; Helena Jahncke, Staffan Hygge, Niklas Halin, Anne Marie Green, and Kenth Dimberg, "Open-plan office noise: Cognitive performance and restoration," *Journal of Environmental Psychology* 31, no. 4 (2011): 373-382; Gary W. Evans and Dana Johnson, "Stress and open-office noise," *Journal of applied psychology* 85, no. 5 (2000): 779.

[25] Sheldon Cohen, David C. Glass, and Jerome E. Singer, "Apartment noise, auditory discrimination, and reading ability in children," *Journal of experimental social psychology* 9, no. 5 (1973): 407-422.

[26] Rhiannon Thompson, Rachel B. Smith, Yasmin Bou Karim, Chen Shen, Kayleigh Drummond, Chloe Teng, and Mireille B. Toledano, "Noise pollution and human cognition: An updated systematic review and meta-analysis of recent evidence," *Environment international* 158 (2022): 106905.

[27] Brett RC Molesworth, Marion Burgess, Belinda Gunnell, Diana Löffler, and Antje Venjakob, "The effect on recognition memory of noise cancelling headphones in a noisy environment with native and nonnative speakers," *Noise and Health* 16, no. 71 (2014): 240.

[28] Helena Jahncke, Patrik Björkeholm, John E. Marsh, Johan Odelius, and Patrik Sörqvist, "Office noise: Can headphones and masking sound attenuate distraction by background speech?," *Work* 55, no. 3 (2016): 505-513.

[29] Amar Cheema and Vanessa M. Patrick, "Influence of warm versus cool temperatures on consumer choice: A resource depletion account," *Journal of Marketing Research* 49, no. 6 (2012): 984-995; Peter A. Hancock and Ioannis Vasmatzidis, "Effects of heat stress on cognitive performance: The current state of knowledge," *International Journal of Hyperthermia* 19, no. 3 (2003): 355-372.

[30] Ibid.

[31] Olli Seppanen, William J. Fisk, and Q. H. Lei, "Effect of temperature on task performance in office environment," (2006).

[32] Frank J. Kelly, and Julia C. Fussell, "Improving indoor air quality, health and performance within environments where people live, travel, learn and work," *Atmospheric Environment* 200 (2019): 90-109.

[33] See, for example, Lance A. Wallace, Edo D. Pellizzari, Tyler D. Hartwell, Roy Whitmore, Charles Sparacino, and Harvey Zelon, "Total Exposure Assessment Methodology (TEAM) Study: Personal exposures, indoor-outdoor relationships, and breath levels of volatile organic compounds in New Jersey," *Environment International* 12, no. 1-4 (1986): 369-387.

[34] Kelly and Fussell, "Improving indoor air quality."

[35] Ibid.

[36] "The Lancet Commission on pollution and health," The Lancet, accessed November 3, 2023, https://www.thelancet.com/commissions/pollution-and-health.

[37] Kelly and Fussell, "Improving indoor air quality."

[38] Ibid.

[39] Ibid.

[40] Ibid.

[41] Donald K. Milton, P. Mark Glencross, and Michael D. Walters, "Risk of sick leave associated with outdoor air supply rate, humidification, and occupant complaints," (2000).

[42] Ibid.

[43] Horr et al., "Occupant productivity."

[44] Boyoun Chae and Rui Zhu, "Environmental disorder leads to self-regulatory failure," *Journal of Consumer Research* 40, no. 6 (2014): 1203-1218.

[45] Kathleen D. Vohs, Joseph P. Redden, and Ryan Rahinel, "Physical order produces healthy choices, generosity, and conventionality, whereas disorder produces creativity," *Psychological Science* 24, no. 9 (2013): 1860-1867.

[46] Adrian F. Ward, Kristen Duke, Ayelet Gneezy, and Maarten W. Bos, "Brain drain: The mere presence of one's own smartphone reduces available cognitive capacity," *Journal of the Association for Consumer Research* 2, no. 2 (2017): 140-154.

[47] Clarissa Theodora Tanil and Min Hooi Yong, "Mobile phones: The effect of its presence on learning and memory," *PloS one* 15, no. 8 (2020): e0219233.

[48] Priscilla Chee, Julia Irwin, Joanne M. Bennett, and Ann J. Carrigan, "The mere presence of a mobile phone: Does it influence driving performance?," *Accident Analysis & Prevention* 159 (2021): 106226.

[49] Bill Thornton, Alyson Faires, Maija Robbins, and Eric Rollins, "The mere presence of a cell phone may be distracting," *Social Psychology* (2014).

[50] Andrew K. Przybylski and Netta Weinstein, "Can you connect with me now? How the presence of mobile communication technology influences face-to-face conversation quality," *Journal of Social and Personal Relationships* 30, no. 3 (2013): 237-246.

[51] Shalini Misra, Lulu Cheng, Jamie Genevie, and Miao Yuan, "The iPhone effect: The quality of in-person social interactions in the presence of mobile devices," *Environment and Behavior* 48, no. 2 (2016): 275-298.

[52] Kaitlyn Gillis and Birgitta Gatersleben, "A review of psychological literature on the health and wellbeing benefits of biophilic design," *Buildings* 5, no. 3 (2015): 948-963.

[53] Stephen Kellert and Elizabeth Calabrese, "The practice of biophilic design," *London: Terrapin Bright LLC* 3 (2015): 21-46.

[54] Tonia Gray and Carol Birrell, "Are biophilic-designed site office buildings linked to health benefits and high performing occupants?," *International journal of environmental research and public health* 11, no. 12 (2014): 12204-12222.

[55] For a recent review on the benefits of indoor plants, see, Ke-Tsung Han, Li-Wen Ruan, and Li-Shih Liao, "Effects of indoor plants on human functions: A systematic review with meta-analyses," *International journal of environmental research and public health* 19, no. 12 (2022): 7454.

[56] Ruth K. Raanaas, Katinka Horgen Evensen, Debra Rich, Gunn Sjøstrøm, and Grete Patil, "Benefits of indoor plants on attention capacity in an office setting," *Journal of Environmental Psychology* 31, no. 1 (2011): 99-105.

[57] Chen-Yen Chang and Ping-Kun Chen, "Human response to window views and indoor plants in the workplace," *HortScience* 40, no. 5 (2005): 1354-1359.

[58] For an overview of research on the benefits of fresh flowers, see "About flowers – health benefits research," Society of American Florists (SAF), accessed November 3, 2023, https://safnow.org/aboutflowers/quick-links/health-benefits-research/.

[59] Hiromi Ohta, Megumi Maruyama, Yoko Tanabe, Toshiko Hara, Yoshihiko Nishino, Yoshio Tsujino, Eishin Morita, Shotai Kobayashi, and Osamu Shido, "Effects of redecoration of a hospital isolation room with natural materials on stress levels of denizens in cold season," *International Journal of Biometeorology* 52 (2008): 331-340.

[60] Christina Kelz, Vincent Grote, and Maximilian Moser, "Interior wood use in classrooms reduces pupils' stress levels," In *Proceedings of the 9th Biennial Conference on Environmental Psychology*. 2011.

[61] "Wood as a restorative material in healthcare environments," naturally:wood, accessed July 23, 2024, https://www.naturallywood.com/resource/wood-as-a-restorative-material-in-healthcare-environments/.

[62] For wood and sleep quality, see "Positive health effects of stone pine furniture," Institute of Health Technology and Prevention Research Stone Pine. For wood and emotional states, see T. Anme, T. M. Watanabe, K. M. Tokutake, E. M. Tomisaki, H. M. Mochizuki, E. M. Tanaka, B. M. Wu et al., "Behavior changes in older persons caused by using wood products in assisted living," *Public Health Res* 2 (2012): 106-109. For wood and workplace benefits, see, Andrew Knox "Workplaces: wellness + wood = productivity," Pollinate, accessed November 3, 2023, https://puumarket.ee/wp-content/uploads/Workplaces-Wellness-and-Wood-Productivity.pdf.

[63] Roger S. Ulrich, "View through a window may influence recovery from surgery," *science* 224, no. 4647 (1984): 420-421.

[64] Chia-Hui Wang, Nai-Wen Kuo, and Kathryn Anthony, "Impact of window views on recovery—an example of post-cesarean section women," *International Journal for Quality in Health Care* 31, no. 10 (2019): 798-803.

[65] Won Sop Shin, "The influence of forest view through a window on job satisfaction and job stress," *Scandinavian journal of forest research* 22, no. 3 (2007): 248-253.

[66] Stephen C. Van Hedger, Howard C. Nusbaum, Luke Clohisy, Susanne M. Jaeggi, Martin Buschkuehl, and Marc G. Berman, "Of cricket chirps and car horns: The effect of nature sounds on cognitive performance," *Psychonomic bulletin & review* 26 (2019): 522-530.

[67] Jesper J. Alvarsson, Stefan Wiens, and Mats E. Nilsson, "Stress recovery during exposure to nature sound and environmental noise," *International journal of environmental research and public health* 7, no. 3 (2010): 1036-1046.

[68] Jacob A. Benfield, B. Derrick Taff, Peter Newman, and Joshua Smyth, "Natural sound facilitates mood recovery," *Ecopsychology* 6, no. 3 (2014): 183-188.

[69] Mark Moss, Victoria Earl, Lucy Moss, and Tom Heffernan, "Any sense in classroom scents? Aroma of rosemary essential oil significantly improves cognition in young school children," *Advances in Chemical Engineering and Science* 7, no. 04 (2017): 450-463.

[70] For a short discussion of the study, see "Herbs that can boost your mood and memory," Northumbria University Newcastle, accessed July 23, 2024, https://www.northumbria.ac.uk/about-us/news-events/news/2016/04/herbs-that-can-boost-your-mood-and-memory/

[71] Shannon Barker, Pamela Grayhem, Jerrod Koon, Jessica Perkins, Allison Whalen, and Bryan Raudenbush, "Improved performance on clerical tasks associated with administration of peppermint odor," *Perceptual and motor skills* 97, no. 3 (2003): 1007-1010.

[72] Bryan Raudenbush, Brian Meyer, and Bill Eppich, "The effects of odors on objective and subjective measures of athletic performance," *International Sports Journal* 6, no. 1 (2002): 14-27.

[73] Bryan Raudenbush, Nathan Corley, and William Eppich, "Enhancing athletic performance through the administration of peppermint odor," *Journal of Sport and Exercise Psychology* 23, no. 2 (2001): 156-160.

[74] "WJU Looks to Peppermint, Its Effect on Athletic Performance," The Intelligencer, accessed July 23, 2024, https://www.theintelligencer.net/news/community/2017/03/wju-looks-to-peppermint-its-effect-on-athletic-performance/

[75] Mark Moss, Ellen Smith, Matthew Milner, and Jemma McCready, "Acute ingestion of rosemary water: Evidence of cognitive and cerebrovascular effects in healthy adults," *Journal of Psychopharmacology* 32, no. 12 (2018): 1319-1329.

[76] Mark Moss, Robert Jones, Lucy Moss, Richard Cutter, and Keith Wesnes, "Acute consumption of peppermint and chamomile teas produce contrasting effects on cognition and mood in healthy young adults," *Plant Science Today* 3, no. 3 (2016): 327-336.

21 – Managing Flow-Disruptive Emotions

[1] See, for example, Christian Swann, Richard J. Keegan, David Piggott, and Lee Crust, "A systematic review of the experience, occurrence, and controllability of flow states in elite

sport," *Psychology of sport and exercise* 13, no. 6 (2012): 807-819; Leonard Tan and Hui Xing Sin, "Optimizing optimal experiences: Practical strategies to facilitate flow for 21st-Century music educators," *Music Educators Journal* 107, no. 2 (2020): 35-41; Christian Swann, David Piggott, Lee Crust, Richard Keegan, and Brian Hemmings, "Exploring the interactions underlying flow states: A connecting analysis of flow occurrence in European Tour golfers," *Psychology of Sport and Exercise* 16 (2015): 60-69.

[2] For a complete scientific guide on emotion regulation, see James J. Gross, ed., *Handbook of emotion regulation* (Guilford publications, 2013).

[3] Ibid.

[4] Laura Campbell-Sills, David H. Barlow, Timothy A. Brown, and Stefan G. Hofmann, "Effects of suppression and acceptance on emotional responses of individuals with anxiety and mood disorders," *Behaviour research and therapy* 44, no. 9 (2006): 1251-1263.

[5] Emotion regulation research differs between various types of suppression, including *experiential* and *expressive* suppression. The former refers to suppression of inner experiences, including emotions, thoughts, and physical sensations; it's the type of suppression I'm writing about in the main text. The latter refers to the suppression of the outward expression of emotions (e.g., keeping a poker face while holding a great hand during a card game). Both forms of suppression come with serious downsides.

[6] It should be noted that the negative effects of suppression depend on various factors. For example, suppression is especially problematic when individuals think it should be possible and easy to get rid of negative thoughts and emotions, when they think others can suppress easily, when they believe thoughts they're unable to suppress are especially important, when they view themselves as weak for being unable to get rid of thoughts, when they judge and criticize themselves, or when they think negative thoughts and emotions are the result of an unhappy mind.

[7] Hugo Alberts, Francine Schneider, and Carolien Martijn, "Dealing efficiently with emotions: Acceptance-based coping with negative emotions requires fewer resources than suppression," *Cognition & Emotion* 26, no. 5 (2012): 863-870; Michael Inzlicht, and Jennifer N. Gutsell, "Running on empty: Neural signals for self-control failure," *Psychological science* 18, no. 11 (2007): 933-937; Shian-Ling Keng, Elysia Li Yan Tan, Tory A. Eisenlohr-Moul, and Moria J. Smoski, "Effects of mindfulness, reappraisal, and suppression on sad mood and cognitive resources," *Behaviour research and therapy* 91 (2017): 33-42.

[8] Yan Wang, Lixia Yang, and Yan Wang, "Suppression (but not reappraisal) impairs subsequent error detection: An ERP study of emotion regulation's resource-depleting effect," *PloS one* 9, no. 4 (2014): e96339.

[9] Quote is from Daniel M. Wegner, *White bears and other unwanted thoughts: Suppression, obsession, and the psychology of mental control* (New York: Guilford, 1994).

[10] Richard M. Wenzlaff and Daniel M. Wegner, "Thought suppression," *Annual review of psychology* 51, no. 1 (2000): 59-91.

[11] Example inspired by Steven C. Hayes, Kirk D. Strosahl, and Kelly G. Wilson, *Acceptance and commitment therapy: The process and practice of mindful change* (New York: Guilford Press, 2011).

[12] Wendy Treynor, Richard Gonzalez, and Susan Nolen-Hoeksema, "Rumination reconsidered: A psychometric analysis," *Cognitive therapy and research* 27 (2003): 247-259.

[13] Edward R. Watkins and Henrietta Roberts, "Reflecting on rumination: Consequences, causes, mechanisms and treatment of rumination," *Behaviour research and therapy* 127 (2020): 103573.

[14] Treynor et al., "Rumination reconsidered"; Watkins and Roberts, "Reflecting on rumination."

[15] For a recent overview on rumination research, see Watkins and Roberts, "Reflecting on rumination."

[16] Ibid.

[17] Lyubomirsky, *The how of happiness*.

[18] Sonja Lyubomirsky, Kristin Layous, Joseph Chancellor, and S. Katherine Nelson, "Thinking about rumination: The scholarly contributions and intellectual legacy of Susan Nolen-Hoeksema," *Annual review of clinical psychology* 11, no. 1 (2015): 1-22.

[19] Lyubomirsky, *The how of happiness.*

[20] This has been shown in many studies. For a meta-analysis of different emotion regulation strategies, including cognitive reappraisal, see Thomas L. Webb, Eleanor Miles, and Paschal Sheeran, "Dealing with feeling: A meta-analysis of the effectiveness of strategies derived from the process model of emotion regulation," *Psychological bulletin* 138, no. 4 (2012): 775.

[21] This study is reported in David Rock, *Your brain at work: Strategies for overcoming distraction, regaining focus, and working smarter all day long* (New York: HarperCollins, 2009).

[22] This story has been told in different variations. Here, I'm using Alan Watts' recitation, "'A Chinese farmer story' ~ Alan Watts," YouTube, accessed July 3, 2024, https://www.youtube.com/watch?v=sWd6fNVZ20o.

[23] Scott R. Bishop, Mark Lau, Shauna Shapiro, Linda Carlson, Nicole D. Anderson, James Carmody, Zindel V. Segal et al., "Mindfulness: A proposed operational definition," *Clinical psychology: Science and practice* 11, no. 3 (2004): 230.

[24] James D. Herbert and Lynn L. Brandsma, "Understanding and enhancing psychological acceptance," in *Health, happiness, and well-being: Better living through psychological science* (2015): 62-88.

[25] Interestingly, a few studies have suggested that acceptance leads to an initial increase in the negative experience. That could be the case because acceptance involves welcoming, turning toward, and "being with" difficult thoughts and emotions, which may allow them to be perceived more fully and intensely. It's important to note that any initial increase in negative emotion found in these studies is then quickly followed by a decrease. Acceptance is said to allow for a natural and healthy emotional trajectory: The full experiencing of an emotion is followed by its subsequent dissipation. Just like waves start small, grow in size, peak, and dissipate, so do emotions. Acceptance doesn't interfere with this process and allows emotions to run their natural course.

[26] Irene Messina, Alessandro Grecucci, and Roberto Viviani, "Neurobiological models of emotion regulation: A meta-analysis of neuroimaging studies of acceptance as an emotion regulation strategy," *Social cognitive and affective neuroscience* 16, no. 3 (2021): 257-267.

[27] S. Troy Allison, Amanda J. Shallcross, Anna Brunner, Rachel Friedman, and Markera C. Jones, "Cognitive reappraisal and acceptance: Effects on emotion, physiology, and perceived cognitive costs," *Emotion* 18, no. 1 (2018): 58.

[28] Alberts et al., "Dealing effectively with emotions."

[29] See, for example, Stuart Cathcart, Matt McGregor, and Emma Groundwater, "Mindfulness and flow in elite athletes," *Journal of Clinical Sport Psychology* 8, no. 2 (2014): 119-141.

[30] Clara Strauss, Billie Lever Taylor, Jenny Gu, Willem Kuyken, Ruth Baer, Fergal Jones, and Kate Cavanagh, "What is compassion and how can we measure it? A review of definitions and measures," *Clinical psychology review* 47 (2016): 15-27.

[31] Ibid.

[32] Kristin D. Neff, "Self-compassion: An alternative conceptualization of a healthy attitude toward oneself," *Self and identity* 2, no. 2 (2003): 85-101; Kristin D. Neff, "The development and validation of a scale to measure self-compassion," *Self and identity* 2, no. 3 (2003): 223-250.

[33] For a recent review of studies on self-compassion, see Kristin D. Neff, "Self-compassion: Theory, method, research, and intervention," *Annual review of psychology* 74, no. 1 (2023): 193-218.

[34] Nicole Lyon and Mary Plisco, "The effects of self-compassion and mindfulness on performance anxiety and flow in elite athletes," *Journal of Sport Behavior* 43, no. 4 (2020).

[35] Kristin D. Neff, *Fierce self-compassion: How women can harness kindness to speak up, claim their power, and thrive* (New York: HarperCollins, 2021).

[36] I won't cite any specific studies here because the list would be too long. If you search for meditation and self-compassion, rumination, etc. you'll find a lot of research confirming what I've written in the main text.

[37] For an in-depth discussion of RAIN, see Tara Brach, *Radical compassion: Learning to love yourself and your world with the practice of RAIN* (New York: Viking, 2019).

[38] Lao Tzu, *Tao Te Ching* (New York: Vintage/Random House, 1997).

22 – Flow-Supportive Values

[1] For a detailed discussion of materialistic values, see Tim Kasser, *The high price of materialism* (Cambridge: The MIT Press, 2002); for a more recent discussion, see Tim Kasser, "Materialistic values and goals," *Annual review of psychology* 67, no. 1 (2016): 489-514.

[2] Kasser, "Materialistic values and goals"; Tim Kasser, "Materialism and living well," *Handbook of well-being* (2018): 860-871.

[3] Researchers usually investigate the consequences of materialistic values with either correlational or experimental studies. In correlational studies, researchers assess participants' level of materialism together with other measures of interest such as life satisfaction, depression, or ecological attitudes. They then compare the individuals scoring high on materialism with those scoring low on materialism to see if there are differences between the two groups. Do highly materialistic individuals feel and behave differently than their less materialistic peers?

In experimental studies, researchers subtly shift participants' values toward greater or lesser materialism and then watch what happens to their attitudes, feelings, and behaviors. Researchers have found many ways to increase participants' situational materialism: exposing them to advertisements of luxury products, asking them to write about unfulfilled material desires, having them read fashion magazines or rags-to-riches stories, or even just referring to them as "consumers" rather than "citizens" or "individuals." For an overview of the many ways researchers manipulate materialistic values, see Olaya Moldes and Lisbeth Ku, "Materialistic cues make us miserable: A meta-analysis of the experimental evidence for the effects of materialism on individual and societal well-being," *Psychology & Marketing* 37, no. 10 (2020): 1396-1419. Conversely, researchers can decrease participants' situational materialism by making them care more about the self-transcendent values we mentioned earlier. They can do this by exposing participants to nature or by having them read stories or watch videos expressing altruism, generosity, benevolence, etc..

Both kinds of studies point to the same conclusion: Materialistic values are bad for people's own well-being, and they lead people to behave in ways that are bad for the well-being of other people, the wider community, and the world as a whole. For recent overviews of the negative effects of materialism, see Kasser, "Materialistic values and goals"; Kasser, "Materialistic values and goals"; L. J. Shrum, Lan Nguyen Chaplin, and Tina M. Lowrey, "Psychological causes, correlates, and consequences of materialism," *Consumer Psychology Review* 5, no. 1 (2022): 69-86.

The correlational research shows that people who score high on materialism score higher on measures of depression and anxiety, are less satisfied with their lives, have lower self-esteem, are more likely to smoke and drink alcohol, and just have poorer overall well-being. They also have shorter, more conflictual, and overall lower-quality interpersonal relationships. Tim Kasser, one of the world's leading researchers on materialism, likes to say that when people spend a lot of time thinking about things, they end up treating people more like things as well. For an interview with Kasser, see "Materially False: A Q&A with Tim Kasser about the pursuit of the good life through goods," BEHAVIORAL scientist, accessed July 3, 2024, https://behavioralscientist.org/materially-false-qa-tim-kasser-pursuit-good-goods/.

Materialistic individuals also have, on average, more racial and ethnic prejudicial attitudes, care less about corporate social responsibility, engage in fewer prosocial behaviors, engage in more anti-social behaviors, treat others in less empathic ways, are more likely to act competitively rather than cooperatively, and are more Machiavellian—they're more willing to manipulate others to get ahead.

They also score higher on *social dominance orientation* (SDO)—the tendency to endorse group-based hierarchies. They believe it's good that certain groups in society have more power and resources than other groups and act in ways that keep high-status groups at the top and low-status groups at the bottom. They believe in a dog-eat-dog world. Given this worldview, it's unsurprising that people scoring high on materialism generally have worse ecological attitudes and higher ecological footprints and engage in fewer pro-environmental behaviors (e.g., recycling, using both sides of the paper, turning off lights, or riding a bike).

The experimental research supports these findings. When materialistic tendencies are momentarily amplified, individuals become unhappier and less satisfied with themselves. They become more selfish, competitive, and greedy, show a greater desire to outdo others, engage in less sustainable behaviors, and behave in less prosocial ways. For an overview of experimental research on negative effects of materialistic values, see Moldes and Ku, "Materialistic cues make us miserable."

In one study, when participants read magazines that increased their situational materialism, they subsequently behaved more selfishly in a simulation game—they donated less money to pro-environmental campaigns and spent more money shopping for themselves. Conversely, when participants read magazines that decreased their situational materialism, they subsequently behaved less selfishly in the simulation game—they donated more money to pro-environmental campaigns and spent less money shopping for themselves. The high materialism magazines contained a mixture of fashion and beauty news, coverage of the latest consumer goods like handbags and accessories, and articles and photographs of international luxury travel. The low materialism magazines contained articles and photographs about a charitable organization, a campaign against the consumption of shark fin soup in southeast China and Hong Kong, information about overseas work holiday opportunities, and articles centering on themes of altruism, affiliation, and self-acceptance. For the study, see Lisbeth Ku and Charles Zaroff, "How far is your money from your mouth? The effects of intrinsic relative to extrinsic values on willingness to pay and protect the environment," *Journal of Environmental Psychology* 40 (2014): 472-483.

In another study, when participants were referred to as "consumers" rather than "individuals" in a hypothetical resource dilemma, they felt less responsible for dealing with the problematic situation, reported less trust in the other parties, and were less likely to view the others as partners in facing the dilemma. For the study, see Monika A. Bauer, James EB Wilkie, Jung K. Kim, and Galen V. Bodenhausen, "Cuing consumerism: Situational materialism undermines personal and social well-being," *Psychological science* 23, no. 5 (2012): 517-523.

In short, as mentioned in the main text, the materialistic values are strongly associated with thoughts, feelings, and actions that are bad for the individual, society, and the world as a whole. On the flipside, the self-transcendent values are associated with thoughts, feelings, and actions that are good for the individual, society, and the world as a whole. Importantly, the adverse effects of materialistic values have been shown in poor and rich people alike. It's not the case that someone who has become rich and famous is then immune to the impact of materialism. Even a highly "successful" person will suffer the negative consequences of caring too much about themselves, their wealth, and their status. For a recent, short discussion on this finding, see Kasser, "Materialism and living well."

[4] Amy Isham, Birgitta Gatersleben, and Tim Jackson, "Materialism and the experience of flow," *Journal of Happiness Studies* 22 (2021): 1745-1768.; Amy Isham, Birgitta Gatersleben, and Tim Jackson, "Why do materialistic values undermine flow experiences? The role of self-regulatory resources," *European Journal of Applied Positive Psychology* 5 (2021).

[5] Isham et al., "Materialism and the experience of flow."

[6] Hari, *Lost connections.*

[7] Seligman, *Authentic happiness.*

[8] Ed Diener, Ed Sandvik, Larry Seidlitz, and Marissa Diener, "The relationship between income and subjective well-being: Relative or absolute?" *Social indicators research* 28 (1993): 195-223.

[9] Tim Kasser and Richard M. Ryan, "Be careful what you wish for: Optimal functioning and the relative attainment of intrinsic and extrinsic goals," in P. Schmuck and K. M. Sheldon, eds., *Life goals and well-being: Towards a positive psychology of human striving* (Hogrefe & Huber Publishers, 2001).

[10] Kennon M. Sheldon and Tim Kasser, "Pursuing personal goals: Skills enable progress, but not all progress is beneficial," *Personality and social psychology bulletin* 24, no. 12 (1998): 1319-1331.

[11] For a detailed discussion on the emerging science of hypo-egoicism, see Kirk Warren Brown and Mark R. Leary, eds., *The Oxford handbook of hypo-egoic phenomena* (Oxford: Oxford University Press, 2016*)*.

[12] Philip J. Cozzolino, Angela Dawn Staples, Lawrence S. Meyers, and Jamie Samboceti, "Greed, death, and values: From terror management to transcendence management theory," *Personality and Social Psychology Bulletin* 30, no. 3 (2004): 278-292.

[13] Ibid.

[14] Cozzolino et al., "Greed, death, and values"; Araceli Frias, Philip C. Watkins, Amy C. Webber, and Jeffrey J. Froh, "Death and gratitude: Death reflection enhances gratitude," *The Journal of Positive Psychology* 6, no. 2 (2011): 154-162; Emily LB Lykins, Suzanne C. Segerstrom, Alyssa J. Averill, Daniel R. Evans, and Margaret E. Kemeny, "Goal shifts following reminders of mortality: Reconciling posttraumatic growth and terror management theory," *Personality and Social Psychology Bulletin* 33, no. 8 (2007): 1088-1099; Mike Prentice, Tim Kasser, and Kennon M. Sheldon, "Openness to experience predicts intrinsic value shifts after deliberating one's own death," *Death studies* 42, no. 4 (2018): 205-215.

[15] Marcus Aurelius, *Meditations* (Penguin Books, 2006).

[16] Bronnie Ware, *Top five regrets of the dying: A life transformed by the dearly departing* (London: Hay House, 2012).

[17] See, for example, Moldes and Ku, "Materialistic cues make us miserable"; Shrum et al., "Psychological causes, correlates, and consequences of materialism"; Suzanna J. Opree, Moniek Buijzen, Eva A. van Reijmersdal, and Patti M. Valkenburg, "Children's advertising exposure, advertised product desire, and materialism: A longitudinal study," *Communication Research* 41, no. 5 (2014): 717-735; Moniek Buijzen and Patti M. Valkenburg, "The effects of television advertising on materialism, parent–child conflict, and unhappiness: A review of research," *Journal of applied developmental psychology* 24, no. 4 (2003): 437-456; Marsha L. Richins, "Materialism pathways: The processes that create and perpetuate materialism," *Journal of Consumer Psychology* 27, no. 4 (2017): 480-499; Jennifer Lewallen, Brandon Miller, and Elizabeth Behm-Morawitz, "Lifestyles of the rich and famous: Celebrity media diet and the cultivation of emerging adults' materialism," *Mass Communication and Society* 19, no. 3 (2016): 253-274; Rodolfo Leyva, "Experimental insights into the socio-cognitive effects of viewing materialistic media messages on welfare support," *Media Psychology* 22, no. 4 (2019): 601-625.

[18] See, for example, Buijzen and Valkenburg, "The effects of television advertising."

[19] See, for example, Lewallen et al., "Lifestyles of the rich and famous."

[20] For research on social media and materialism, see, for example, Marsha L. Richins and Lan Nguyen Chaplin, "Object attachment, transitory attachment, and materialism in childhood," *Current Opinion in Psychology* 39 (2021): 20-25.

[21] See, for example, Mauro Giacomantonio, Valeria De Cristofaro, Angelo Panno, Valerio Pellegrini, Marco Salvati, and Luigi Leone, "The mindful way out of materialism: Mindfulness mediates the association between regulatory modes and materialism," *Current Psychology* (2020): 1-11; David C Watson, "Self-compassion, the 'quiet ego' and materialism," *Heliyon* 4, no. 10 (2018); Amy Isham, Patrick Elf, and Tim Jackson, "Self-transcendent experiences and sustainable prosperity," (2022).

[22] See, for example, Ruth A Baer, "Self-focused attention and mechanisms of change in mindfulness-based treatment," *Cognitive behaviour therapy* 38, no. S1 (2009): 15-20; Michaël Dambrun, "When the dissolution of perceived body boundaries elicits happiness: The effect of selflessness induced by a body scan meditation," *Consciousness and cognition* 46 (2016): 89-98.

[23] For a review, see Don E. Davis, Elise Choe, Joel Meyers, Nathaniel Wade, Kristen Varjas, Allison Gifford, Amy Quinn et al., "Thankful for the little things: A meta-analysis of gratitude interventions," *Journal of counseling psychology* 63, no. 1 (2016): 20.

[24] For a recent discussion of these studies, see Lan Nguyen Chaplin, Deborah Roedder John, Aric Rindfleisch, and Jeffrey J. Froh, "The impact of gratitude on adolescent materialism and generosity," *The Journal of Positive Psychology* 14, no. 4 (2019): 502-511.

[25] Chaplin et al., "The impact of gratitude."

[26] Matthew W. Johnson, Peter S. Hendricks, Frederick S. Barrett, and Roland R. Griffiths, "Classic psychedelics: An integrative review of epidemiology, therapeutics, mystical experience, and brain network function," *Pharmacology & therapeutics* 197 (2019): 83-102.

[27] Matthew M. Nour, Lisa Evans, David Nutt, and Robin L. Carhart-Harris, "Ego-dissolution and psychedelics: Validation of the ego-dissolution inventory (EDI)," *Frontiers in human neuroscience* 10 (2016): 269.

[28] I've taken the term "psychedelic unselfing" from the following paper: Juuso Kähönen, "Psychedelic unselfing: Self-transcendence and change of values in psychedelic experiences," *Frontiers in Psychology* 14 (2023): 1104627.

[29] For a discussion on psychedelic value changes, see, for example, Kähönen, "Psychedelic unselfing."

[30] Albert Hofmann, *LSD my problem child (4th edition): Reflections on sacred drugs, mysticism and science* (MAPS, 2017).

[31] For a recent discussion on the risks, see Bridget Huber, "What do we know about the risks of psychedelics?" accessed July 1, 2024, https://michaelpollan.com/psychedelics-risk-today/.

[32] For a recent overview on the science-based benefits of volunteering, see "Volunteering, health and wellbeing," Volunteer Scotland, accessed July 3, 2024, https://www.volunteerscotland.net/research-evaluation/research-publications/volunteering-health-wellbeing.

[33] Netta Weinstein, Andrew K. Przybylski, and Richard M. Ryan, "Can nature make us more caring? Effects of immersion in nature on intrinsic aspirations and generosity," *Personality and social psychology bulletin* 35, no. 10 (2009): 1315-1329.

[34] Weinstein et al., "Can nature make us more caring?"

[35] See, for example, Yannick Joye, Jan Willem Bolderdijk, Massimo AF Köster, and Paul K. Piff, "A diminishment of desire: Exposure to nature relative to urban environments dampens materialism," *Urban Forestry & Urban Greening* 54 (2020): 126783.

[36] John J. Ratey, *Go wild: Free your body and mind from the afflictions of civilization* (New York: Little, Brown and Company, 2014).

[37] See chapter 9 in Hari, *Lost connections*; Tim Kasser, "About me," accessed July 3, 2024, https://www.timkasser.org/about-me.

[38] For recent reviews, see Dusica Lecic-Tosevski, "Is urban living good for mental health?" *Current opinion in psychiatry* 32, no. 3 (2019): 204-209.; Mazda Adli and Jonas Schöndorf, "Macht uns die Stadt krank? Wirkung von Stadtstress auf Emotionen, Verhalten und psychische Gesundheit," *Bundesgesundheitsblatt-Gesundheitsforschung-Gesundheitsschutz* 63 (2020): 979-968.

[39] Joye et al., "A diminishment of desire."

[40] Lecic-Tosevski, "Is urban living good for mental health?"; Adli and Schöndorf, "Macht uns die Stadt krank?"